At the Center of the Frame

Hollywood 1936—Evelyn Venable and Claire Trevor assist Master Dickie Walters in learning his dialogue for 20th Century–Fox's *Star for a Night*. (The Evelyn Venable Mohr Collection.)

At the Center of the Frame

Leading Ladies of the Twenties and Thirties

WILLIAM M. DREW

Lanham • New York • Oxford

VESTAL PRESS, Inc.

Published in the United States of America
by Vestal Press, Inc.
4720 Boston Way
Lanham, Maryland 20706

Library of Congress Cataloging-in-Publication Data

Drew, William M.
At the center of the frame : leading ladies of the twenties and thirties / William M. Drew
p. cm.
Includes bibliographical references and filmographies.
ISBN 1-879511-42-8 (alk. paper) — 1-879511-44-4 (paper : alk. paper).
1. Motion picture actors and actresses—United States Biography.
I. Title.
PN1992.2.D74 1999
791.43'028'0820973—dc21 99-32498
CIP

∞™ The paper used in this publication meets the minimum requirements of American National Standard for Information Sciences—Permanence of Paper for Printed Library Materials, ANSI/NISO Z39.48–1992.
Manufactured in the United States of America.

To the one who kindled my passion
for the films of the twenties and thirties

Contents

Acknowledgments

While working on this book, I have received assistance from numerous individuals and organizations. I wish to express my thanks and appreciation for their invaluable contributions, which helped make this project possible.

Kevin Brownlow from the beginning offered ideas and encouragement. He also reviewed the manuscript and lent stills from his personal collection. Amy Glover was tireless in her research for photographs at the Museum of Modern Art Stills Department. Daniel W. Morrissey played a vital role in the research. Lynn Weber, Alyssa Theodore, and the staff of Vestal Press deserve special thanks for their work in editing and designing the book. Bob Cosenza and the staff of the Kobal Collection were generous in loaning stills from their remarkable photo archive.

Also providing valuable research for stills were Ned Comstock, curator of the University of Southern California Archives of Performing Arts; Maxine Fleckner Ducey and the staff of the Wisconsin Center for Film and Theater Research; Terry Geeksin of the Museum of Modern Art Stills Department; Kristine L. Krueger of the National Film Information Service of the Academy of Motion Picture Arts and Sciences; Rolf D. Lehner of the Luis Trenker-Zentral-Archiv-Kitzbuhel, Tyrolia; the staff of the Will Rogers Memorial Commission, Claremore, Oklahoma; Gayla Raoul of Film Favorites; Claire Brandt of Eddie Brandt's Saturday Matinee; Larry Edmunds Bookshop, Inc.; Jerry Ohlinger's Movie Materials Store.

I owe a special debt of thanks to those who graciously provided stills from their personal collections: Jamie Brotherton, Dorothy Lee Calderini, Steven Hill, David Jaffe, Cole Johnson, Billie Dove Kenaston, Jim Knuttel, Paul Melzer, Annabella Power, Fay Wray Rothenberg, Edward Watz, Doretta Whalen, and Rosalia Woodson. (All stills not credited in the text are from the author's collection.)

For their input and support in the development of this project, I am deeply grateful to the following: Bambi Ballard, Margaret Bauer, George Baxt, Jeffrey L. Carrier, Eve Golden, Grace L. Houghton, Margarita Lorenz, Randal Malone, George Shelps, Linda Snyder, Maurice Terenzio, Anne Werner and Boyd Willat as well as my friends, John and Betty. Many thanks, too, to Douglas Fairbanks, Jr., Roddy McDowall, and Robert Wise for providing insights into their work with several of the actresses.

Introduction

There are two contrasting histories of film. One, too often, is standardized and predictable in its opinions and choices, Procrustean in its attempt to force the current of the cinema's heritage into a pattern that is conformist and male-dominated. It ranges from the simplicities of a commercial television broadcast reducing the entire history of American film to a few clips of several past Academy Award winners to weighty tomes larded with jargon and politically correct ideas that solemnly "explain" and minimize the achievements of major artists. Whether deriving from the briefest of clips or the densest of theoretical prose, it does not seek to expand appreciation for the film art. Rather, it attempts to leave things as they are with film history being defined by privileged commercial and political elites. So whether the cinematic past is layered over with a patronizing nostalgia, painted in scarlet with lurid allegations presented as facts, or exorcised in tendentious jeremiads as the sinister tool of an oppressive ruling class, the common effect is to distance a later generation from any sense of identification with, or participation in, a living film history.

But there is still another history of the cinema, one that is written in the films themselves and in the hearts and memories of those who shaped that history. This is the real history of the motion picture, one that is vast and mysterious with visions and perceptions elusive to the conformists of profit and theory, with innumerable undiscovered treasures hidden from view in uncharted seas, a universe of unknown films and artists, a storehouse of memories not yet tapped. Beyond the ennui-inducing lists of names and dates, beyond the conventional opinions and theories lies this realm, often contradictory, sometimes disturbing, many times rewarding—but nonetheless relevant to our present understanding of an art that seeks, above all, to interpret the human experience.

As might be expected from a conformist presentation, women have repeatedly been ignored. The early women filmmakers including the brilliant Lois Weber—one of the most significant figures in the birth of Hollywood—were almost forgotten in its pages. The contribution of the American cinema's legion of women screenwriters and their role in shaping the perceptions and values of the culture has yet to be fully explored. And even the actresses who became some of the best-known women in the world have in later years either suffered from neglect or been, in some cases, subjected to condemnation and outright ridicule.

By comparison, male actors, like male writers and directors, have on the whole, fared much better. The consequences of this preference for males is all too obvious in the sexual imbalance that colors our understanding of film history even though it was women who so often prepared the way for both male and female performers in the cinema. I write these lines exactly one hundred years after the first projection of motion pictures in New York City on April 23, 1896. On that historic date, the hit of Edison's Vitascope presentation at Koster & Bial's Music Hall was the life-size appearance of a young woman named Annabelle dancing on the screen. Described by film historian Terry Ramsaye as "the first celebrity of the motion pictures,"[1] the dancer thrilled the crowd who "went wild and cheered" her.[2] Prior to this, audiences had been transfixed by movement itself as in Eadweard Muybridge's galloping horses or the Lumières' *Arrival of a Train*. Now they had discovered the magic of talent on the screen through the grace and individuality of a woman. And within a decade and a half, the development of individual talent in narrative films would lead to the star system pioneered by Florence Lawrence and Mary Pickford.

Despite their pivotal role in formulating the language of performance in the cinema, women silent stars in later years have received far less attention than their male counterparts. For example, there have been numerous centennial tributes to Chaplin, Lloyd and Keaton but none for Mabel Normand, the great female silent comedian whose mastery of pantomime and characterization provided the precedent for these later male comics. Books and celebrations abound for male silent stars from Lon Chaney to Tom Mix but not female stars such as Bebe Daniels and Norma and Constance Talmadge, although they were among the most popular box-office attractions of the 1920s. The silent serial queens Pearl White, Ruth Roland and Helen Holmes who rivalled, indeed, anticipated such men as Douglas Fairbanks in action films are also overlooked.

In the sound era, it is not the imbalance by writers that is problematic but the interpretation. In recent years, biographers have reflected the prevailing bias casting ambitious female stars who remained at the top in the industry in a more negative light than equally ambitious and popular male stars. Joan Crawford, Bette Davis and Barbara Stanwyck are among those who have been posthumously vivisected in numerous books and articles. Relying heavily on rumor and speculation and without taking into account the obstacles these gifted actresses faced in confronting, then triumphing over, a male hierarchy, writers have sought to "expose" their private lives as completely at odds with their public persona. On the other hand, Humphrey Bogart, John Wayne and James Cagney, who pursued their careers with equal zeal, have remained American icons. Biographers, on the whole, have treated them with a basic respect and affection. Such contrasting images convey the traditional message that ambition, regarded as a positive attribute in a man, is a trait that defies a woman's very nature.

To this point, feminists have not erupted in outrage at this pattern of neglect and misrepresentation. In truth, while there are perceptive and sensitive feminist critics such as Molly Haskell and Jeanine Basinger, too many doctrinaire feminist writers on the cinema have promoted a version of history in which women are always the victims of an oppressive patriarchy. However, such a limited view does not acknowledge an historic time and place when women were able to express themselves in the mass medium of film. That a male director could appreciate and absorb a woman's point of view as he worked with actresses and female writers or that, in the collaborative environment of the cinema, women could have the opportunity to project their feelings into their roles seems to have eluded the more strident critics. Whereas the sexist derides any assertion of feminine equality as against nature, the ultrafeminist too often dismisses any evidence of women freeing themselves from their Victorian bonds as against history when their view of history is one of virtually unrelieved exploitation and victimization. Thus, the common effect of both the sexist and the doctrinaire feminist is to produce a climate that dismisses women's contribution to the shaping of film art.

As is so often the case with social issues, the subject of women in film has rarely been viewed in the context of cultural history. For most of the theatre's existence, women were barred from representing themselves on the stage. Indeed, the innovation of actresses in live drama in place of female impersonators, far from being a marginal footnote in cultural history, was in itself an advance for women's rights. While the cinema was obviously never an ideal realm of sexual equality any more than the stage in modern times, there were far more opportunities for women than the standard histories suggest. But critics and historians have too often disregarded films and filmmakers that, in one way or another, furthered the cause of women's rights. Lois Weber was, like D. W. Griffith and Cecil B. DeMille, a force to be reckoned with in early Hollywood. Yet in her last years in the 1930s, she was passed over by the pioneering archivists and historians of film alike. In traditional cinematic historiography, Griffith's *Way Down East* with Lillian Gish as a woman who suffers, then rebels against a sexist double standard was routinely described as a "quaint," even absurd melodrama, whereas a film about injustices suffered by men such as Fritz Lang's *Fury* was taken seriously by critics. And while there are heroic images of women that parallel the struggle for equal rights, Dorothy Dalton's brilliant lawyer in *The Weaker Sex* (1916) and Agnes Ayres's daredevil racing car driver in *Racing Hearts* (1923), just two long-forgotten examples from a host of others, were ultimately too out-of-the-ordinary for a "history" which relegated such images to obscurity. So the sexism came, not when these films were being created for the mass audience and contributing to the empowerment of women, but during the selection process in which history became an outlet for a male backlash.

The present volume is a collective biography of ten prominent film actresses of the 1920s and 1930s. Their careers best exemplify the dynamics of change in the film industry from the peak of the silent era through the introduction of the talkies to the subsequent perfection of sound films in the 1930s. Containing the actresses' reminiscences, they relate their experience in those extraordinary years with clarity and detail. A sequel to my earlier *Speaking of Silents: First Ladies of the Screen,* which includes the recollections of ten major actresses of the silent era, the new book is even more varied in its grouping. Some of these actresses had film careers that have spanned the better part of this century, while others were in films for only a few years. Some ranked among the top international box-office attractions of the era, with their names alone selling the film, while others remained leading ladies throughout their careers, prominently cast in important films but sharing the spotlight. Some are still widely known to the public, while others are all but forgotten. Some thoroughly enjoyed their years in films as a fulfilling experience; others became dissatisfied with the course their careers took. Yet all had not only beauty but talent—the ability to project their "personhood" before the camera illuminating the films in which they appeared.

This book also endeavors to serve as a counterbalance to a largely male view of the cinema's history by presenting it as it was lived and shaped by these women. Far from being habitually dictated to by autocratic male authority figures, they were able to draw on their own thoughts, feelings and experiences in creating their roles, and their relationship with outstanding directors was a partnership, a shared enterprise producing works of art. In their association with studio heads, they, like their male counterparts and contemporaries, often collided head-on with an assembly-line approach to film-making that they found stultifying. Yet despite all the inevitable heartbreaks and frustrations, they have, for the most part, expressed a sense of fulfillment in these interviews. That they have been so long neglected by the "established" critics and histories is the shame of the current approaches to cinema studies. That they live so fully on the screen and in these remembrances is their lasting triumph as women and as artists.

Left to right, Matthew Betz, Cesare Gravina, Fay Wray, Dale Fuller and Hughie Mack in *The Wedding March.* (Fay Wray Collection, USC.)

1927—SILENT GLORY

By 1927, the cinema had long since evolved from a store-front novelty to a major art and industry. Central to that development were the directors—titans who had fashioned the cosmos of the silent screen. Whether it was Cecil B. DeMille transporting the audience to antiquity to witness the life of Christ in *The King of Kings;* William Wellman soaring into the clouds to recreate the thrills and terrors of aerial warfare in *Wings;* Sergei Eisenstein empathizing with Russia's surging revolutionary masses in *Potemkin;* Robert Flaherty capturing the vanishing paradise of the South Seas in *Moana;* Fritz Lang envisioning mankind's destiny in a city of the future in *Metropolis;* D. W. Griffith combining the fantastic and the realistic in *The Sorrows of Satan;* or Buster Keaton blending comedy with an epic depiction of the Civil War in *The General*—there seemed to be no limit to the director's power to move freely in space and time in the universal language of images.

The directors had been granted their authority by producers, impressed with their proven records as money-makers. They were able to choose their stories and their technicians, develop their scripts, supervise the editing of the film and its subsequent release and exploitation, even contribute ideas to the musical score. But it was in their choice of actors and actresses that the directors exercised their greatest power as, with the use of the close-up, they could establish an immediate emotional contact between the performer and the audience. This mystic partnership between the director, the camera and the player, even more than the use of spectacle, was at the heart of the new silent language and created a galaxy of stars with worldwide popularity.

The model the filmmakers of the twenties sought to emulate was D. W. Griffith, who had developed an intense artistic relationship with his players, particularly the actresses. Mary Pickford, Blanche Sweet, Mae Marsh, Lillian and Dorothy Gish, Carol Dempster—all had emerged as stars under his guidance. *Broken Blossoms, Way Down East* and *Orphans of the Storm* with Lillian Gish are examples of the dramatic heights that could be attained when, without the constraints of a large studio system, a symbiosis existed between the director and the performer.

With the precedent of Griffith and Gish before them, Lois Weber and Erich von Stroheim in America and Abel Gance in France—artists who controlled all aspects of their productions in the mid-twenties—were sensitive in their choice of actresses who could best incarnate their visions on celluloid. For her realistic studies of women in contemporary American society, Lois Weber, the dominant woman director in Hollywood since the teens, cast Billie Dove in the principal feminine roles of *The Marriage Clause* (1926) and *Sensation Seekers* (1927). Erich von Stroheim, the most uncompromising and controversial director in Hollywood, selected Fay Wray for the heroine of his powerfully naturalistic *The Wedding March* (1926–28), contrasting her innocence with the corruption and decadence of Hapsburg Vienna. And Abel Gance, for his extraordinarily innovative *Napoléon* (1925–27), a romantic historical epic of Bonaparte and the French Revolution, chose a newcomer he renamed Annabella to project a feminine image of gentleness and devotion counterbalancing the hero's martial exploits, Josephine's worldliness and the revolutionary leaders' fierce fanaticism.

The course of the actresses' careers would be dramatically affected by their work with these directors. Billie Dove, already a prominent leading lady when she worked with Weber, became one of the great stars of the silent screen and managed a smooth transition to talkies; Fay Wray, with a few years' experience in comedy shorts and westerns, emerged from her association with von Stroheim a major silent cinema actress who found continuing success in sound films; Annabella, making her film debut with Gance, went on to a career as one of the brightest international stars of the 1930s.

The directors' careers, however, would take a far different turn. Within the space of a year, Weber, von Stroheim and Gance, like Griffith and Keaton, found themselves increasingly at odds with the studio system. By the late twenties, production costs were soaring, encouraging mergers. Also, faced with added competition from radio and spurred on by the success of Warner Brothers' Vitaphone releases, the film industry was gearing up for the change-over to sound.

In this climate, Weber found her opportunities diminishing in the new Hollywood after the commercial failure of her last silent film, *The Angel of Broadway,* released in the fall of 1927. Soon, she would disappear from filmmaking altogether.[1] As for von Stroheim and Gance, their tendency to push the medium to its limits through their attention to detail, shooting reels and reels of film for lengthy, elaborate works, was an anathema to an industry bent on economizing by streamlining production.

In von Stroheim's case, Paramount took over the distribution and editing of *The Wedding March* in 1927, delaying its release for over a year. The film was divided into two parts with the second, retitled *The Honeymoon,* shown only in Europe. In the United States, coming out at a time when the public was fascinated by the new talkies, it failed at the box-office. After its disappointing returns, producers interfered with von Stroheim's subsequent projects, forcing him to return to acting, his original profession.[2]

Even though he never set foot in Hollywood, Gance faced similar difficulties with a major American company, Metro-Goldwyn-Mayer, which had contracted to distribute *Napoléon* internationally. After its triumphant Paris premiere in 1927, Gance's masterpiece was shown by MGM in various mangled and mutilated versions in England and France in 1928. Finally, after many months of delay, it reached the United States in early 1929 in a 72-minute version without its revolutionary three-screen climax. It was a dismal failure with

Billie Dove and Huntley Gordon on board a yacht are caught in a storm at sea in *Sensation Seekers.* (Billie Dove Collection, Courtesy of Paul Melzer.)

As Chakatouny watches from the left, Annabella is caught in the storm of the French Revolution in *Napoléon*. (Courtesy of Kevin Brownlow.)

critics and public alike. MGM's handling of the film would cast its shadow over Gance's career in France in the early thirties as he was shunted into minor commercial projects that offered him little chance to display his genius.[3]

But even as these pioneering cinematic visionaries vanished from the scene, those talents they had molded continued to grace the screen, their images on film reflecting the beneficent influences of the directors who had guided them across the threshold of success. Transformed by their work with Weber, von Stroheim and Gance, Billie Dove, Fay Wray and Annabella became screen goddesses whose legendary fame survived even their years of retirement from films. And during the centennial of the cinema, these women, still vibrant, provided a vital link to the enduring glory of the silent era when their incandescence had first lit up the screen.

Billie Dove

Dubbed "the American Beauty" from the title of one of her films, Billie Dove at her peak in the late 1920s ranked with Colleen Moore and Clara Bow as among the most popular actresses in the cinema. Indeed, for a time she surpassed Pickford, Swanson and Garbo at the box office. She was renowned for her physical perfection, her complexion so flawless that she was a natural choice for some of the earliest films in Technicolor. Her sensitive mouth and large, expressive hazel eyes communicated emotion with an electricity that made her a worldwide symbol of glamour and romance. In sharp contrast to her friend and contemporary at First National, Colleen Moore, who was thin and flat-chested and projected a comedy style that deemphasized glamour, Billie was full-bosomed and played romantic roles, always elegantly costumed, in the genre popularly known as the "woman's film."

Born Bertha Bohny, soon renamed Lillian Bohny, on May 14, 1903 in New York City, Billie was the daughter of middle-class Swiss immigrants. As a child, she was sweet, imaginative and, by her own acknowledgment, naive—the product of a somewhat Victorian upbringing where even receiving a letter from a boyfriend who signed it "with love" overstepped the bounds of propriety. Nevertheless, despite the emotional asceticism of her childhood, her longing for excitement was fed by the early motion pictures and she determined at a tender age that she would have a career in films. In 1916 she appeared on stage in the cast of *Peter Rabbit in Dreamland* at New York's Century Theatre. At fourteen, she became one of the army of extra and bit players working at the film studios in Fort Lee, New Jersey, the American cinema's first capital before the aftermath of World War I once and for all established Hollywood as the center of American filmmaking.

It was, however, her appearance on the stage in *The Ziegfeld Follies of 1919* that first brought her fame. In those years, to be one of Flo Ziegfeld's "glorified American girls" was the height of glamour. His theatre was alive with the music of Victor Herbert, Irving Berlin and Jerome Kern and the comedic antics of Bert Williams, W. C. Fields, Eddie Cantor, Will Rogers and Fannie Brice. And the *Follies* became the gateway for many of the silent screen's loveliest stars—Olive Thomas, Mae Murray, Marion Davies, Dorothy Mackaill, Lilyan Tashman, Jacqueline Logan, Nita Naldi, Louise Brooks. None would prove more popular than Billie Dove, the living embodiment of Berlin's perennial "A Pretty Girl Is Like a Melody," fortuitously first heard in the edition of the *Follies* that introduced Billie.

On the strength of her work with Ziegfeld, it was not long before she was given leads in films made in the New York area, first shorts and then features. (One of them, the Constance Talmadge vehicle, *Polly of the Follies,* in which Billie had the second lead, was the first of several films capitalizing on her work as a showgirl in the *Follies.*) In 1922, she was brought out to Hollywood on a year's contract to Metro and soon garnered feminine leads in a variety of films. In her second film produced in Hollywood, *All the Brothers Were Valiant,* the first screen version of Ben Ames Williams's whaling story, she worked with Irvin Willat, a prominent director of action pictures, whom she married in 1923.

For four years, Billie played leads for all of the major studios in Hollywood, proving herself a hard-working, capable actress with an ideal "movie star" name that was immediately recognizable to

With Walter McGrail in *American Beauty.*

the public. Two of her films were shot in two-color Technicolor, the 1924 western, *Wanderer of the Wasteland,* and Douglas Fairbanks's 1926 classic adventure, *The Black Pirate.* Fairbanks, who was always seeking to expand the frontiers of film art, had a solid hit with *The Black Pirate,* the most successful use of Technicolor up to that time. As a princess rescued by Doug from captivity on a pirate ship, Billie's soft, voluptuous femininity complemented her leading man's energetic virility.

Billie also appeared with Douglas Fairbanks, Jr., in two Paramount silents. His recollections of Billie were

> all very pleasant. I was only about fourteen years old the first time I met her in the film *The Air Mail* and I was as smitten as any male of *any* age would be. She was not only lovely to look at but perfectly charming to work with. However, there was an added obstacle to my expressing myself: The director, Irvin Willat, was her husband!
>
> The following year, we worked together again—this time I played her brother in a western called *Wild Horse Mesa.* Her romantic leading man was Jack Holt.[1]

In 1930, the younger Fairbanks worked for a third time with Billie, but now in a sound film as her romantic lead in *One Night at Susie's,* produced by First National.

Despite her exposure in prestige productions such as *The Black Pirate,* Billie still needed a director who could bring out her full potential as an actress. That director turned out to be Lois Weber, the preeminent woman director of the silent era. In 1926, she chose Billie for *The Marriage Clause,* which she scripted and directed for Universal. In

With Warner Baxter and Douglas Fairbanks, Jr. in *The Air Mail.* (Courtesy of Kevin Brownlow.)

the film, Billie plays an actress who suffers a nearly fatal breakdown but is saved by the love of a theatrical director. Weber found Billie an ideal interpreter for her vision, a quietly realistic style that avoided melodramatic villains and sensational plot motifs and concentrated on the minutiae of daily life and behavior. In so many films, Billie had been primarily decorative, a beautiful image to be sought and won by heroic leading men like John Gilbert, Tom Mix and Doug Fairbanks, but with little chance to develop her own persona. But now under Weber's sensitive, intuitive direction, Billie blossomed as an actress. Ivan St. Johns wrote in *Photoplay* in 1927: "Having seen her performance in *The Marriage Clause,* the whole industry stood up on its hind legs and woofed. The 'sleeping beauty' had awakened. Galatea had come to life."[2]

So effective was the combination that the two quickly reteamed for *Sensation Seekers,* another film produced for Universal. Billie appears as an emancipated young woman of the Jazz Age in a narrative that enabled Weber to comment on the new morality and social hypocrisy. Mordaunt Hall of *The New York Times* was impressed with both Weber and Billie. Of Weber's direction, he described her presentation as "so natural that many other directors would do well to study Miss Weber's style" and went on to praise her "vivid conception" of the characters and her ability to picture the details of "everyday life." Concerning the leading lady, he wrote that "Billie Dove actually submerges her own personality in the character."[3] The two films

With Douglas Fairbanks, Sr. in *The Black Pirate.*

with Weber, as Myrtle Gebhart noted in a contemporary profile of Billie, proved to be "the turning point in her career. She played interesting, womanly characters in both films, and the sympathetic understanding of the woman director, Lois Weber, made her feel more at home, at ease, in her work than ever before."[4]

Companies that had ignored her as only "a pretty lead" now suddenly "started bartering for her services."[5] Indeed, before *Sensation Seekers* was released, Billie signed a contract with First National where the studio created star vehicles for her. Now she was central to the plot, her name was above the title and she was box-office dynamite. She received critical recognition for such films as *The Night Watch* directed by Alexander Korda in 1928. Billie, in the role of Yvonne, a French naval commander's wife caught up in a shipboard romantic intrigue during World War I, demonstrated once again that she was an actress of "rare ability,"[6] performing with "considerable charm and intelligence."[7]

Now a star in the full sense, Billie's personal life was played up in the movie magazines. Her marriage to Irvin Willat was good copy in 1927 with writers rapturing over the happy couple and describing Billie as an "ideal wife and homemaker."[8] Before Weber, it was, in fact, Willat who had championed her career and "whose faith in her gave her more confidence."[9] Yet in the wake of Billie's increasing celebrity, the two grew apart and soon separated.

Widely regarded as the most beautiful woman in the world, "the Dove" had legions of admirers. Legendary jazz-blues singer Billie Holiday took her first name in honor of her favorite actress. One of the film star's more persistent devotees was the maverick heir to a family fortune who had begun dabbling in movies, a young man by the name of Howard Hughes. At the time they first met, he was starting to make a name for himself in Hollywood, producing a succession of remarkable films including his pet project, *Hell's Angels.* When the World War I aviation epic was completed in 1930 after three years in production, its lavish premiere shared top billing with the Billie Dove–Howard Hughes romance that was the talk of Hollywood. Several times they seemed on the verge of marrying, but eventually, their relationship, for reasons she would refuse to disclose, came to an end.

In the meantime, Billie's career continued unabated even as the coming of sound created a cinematic revolution. A later myth has it that she could not cope with the new medium but, in truth, her voice had a silken quality and recorded well. She played leads in eleven talkies from 1929 to 1932 in a variety of roles that confirmed her versatility as an actress. Still the romantic heroine in her early sound films for First National, she showed she could act with the same restraint and subtlety she had in silents.

It took Howard Hughes, however, to bring out her talents as a comedienne when he cast her in a madcap role in *Cock of the Air,* a screwball World War I romance written by Robert E. Sherwood and Charles Lederer. Billie plunged with gusto into the part of Lilli, a French actress who gets into a series of slapstick confrontations while leading an ardent would-be seducer, an American aviator (Chester Morris), on a merry chase. The climax has Billie lying on a bed encased nude in a suit of armor as Morris "comes after her with a can opener." The film's bawdy humor outraged the officials of the Hays Office, who regarded it as "obscene and immoral in title, theme and portrayal."[10] They wrangled with Hughes for months over changes they requested. Finally, after extensive cuts, the film went into release in early 1932 and "stirred up many a hearty laugh" from audiences. Billie had done "extremely well" in her startling transition as an actress.[11] But the battle with the censors had taken its toll and when the even stricter Production Code went into effect two years later, *Cock of the Air* was banned outright.[12]

Powerful forces would also affect the outcome of Billie's next film, *Blondie of the Follies,* an original written for the screen by the celebrated scenarist, Frances Marion. In yet another challenging role, Billie plays a gutsy showgirl competing with Marion Davies for the love of playboy Robert Montgomery. This time, it was William Randolph Hearst who weighed in when he feared that Billie was outshining his Marion. He intervened to change the concept of Billie's character, making her more of a heavy and depriving her of a dramatic closing scene. Though Hearst's input did not diminish her part significantly and she gave an excellent performance, it would be Billie's last film. Unlike so many of her silent era contemporaries, she did not fade into the obscurity of Poverty Row pictures or bit parts. She was still in the limelight, her name featured in the main title in 1932. Her retirement, she said, was not due to career disappointments but because she wanted to have a family.

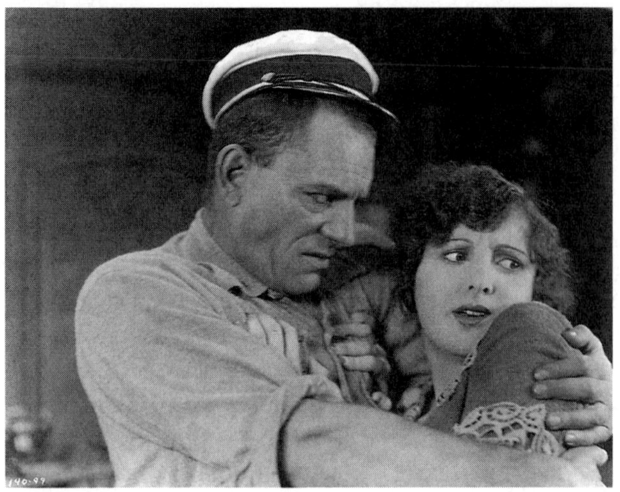

With Lon Chaney in *All the Brothers Were Valiant.* (The Kobal Collection.)

She married Bob Kenaston, a rancher and real estate investor, in 1933. They soon had a son and later, when she found out she could not have more children, they adopted a daughter. Within a year after their marriage, they moved to Pacific Palisades and lived there for many years. (They also maintained a winter home near Palm Springs.) Among their friends and neighbors in Pacific Palisades were Eddie Albert and Margo who, in fact, bought one of the Kenastons' three lots from them and lived next door.

After thirty-seven years, the Kenastons' marriage fell apart, a victim of Bob's drinking. They divorced and not long after, Billie remarried, this time architect John Miller, a younger man whose companionship she enjoyed because he made her laugh, as she put it. The marriage, however, was short-lived and Billie reclaimed the name of Kenaston after her second husband's death.

When I interviewed her at different intervals from the spring of 1993 to the summer of 1995, Billie was living in her Rancho Mirage home at the Thunderbird Country Club, a residence she had shared with Bob Kenaston. There, surrounded by memorabilia and in the company of Timmy, her beloved white poodle, Billie, the last of the silent movie queens, wrote poetry and answered stacks of fan mail from around the world. She was active in the society of her community as well, and among her intimate friends in Rancho Mirage were other Hollywood greats Ruby Keeler, Ginger Rogers and Alice Faye. Her contemporary, the brilliant comedienne Laura La Plante, was also a close friend and neighbor for many years; in 1985, the two traveled to New York together to appear with Lillian Gish and Leatrice Joy in a silent film tribute in *The Night of 100 Stars,* a TV special benefiting the Actor's Fund.

Projecting a radiance coupled with an air of coquettishness, Billie in the 1990s had retained the sweetness and charm that made audiences fall in love with her. Now that her hair was completely white, her eyes dominated her features even more. With the demeanor of a woman conscious she is a lady, she nevertheless lacked pretense and was disarmingly informal, laughing easily. She had a beauty that belied her age and continued to possess the transcendent quality that established her as a lasting legend and one of the cinema's true deities.

I was born in New York City where my father, Charles Bohny, was a hotel manager. My parents were both born in Switzerland but from different parts. They didn't meet over there. They met in New York and years later after my father died, we found in his desk a very formal invitation to their engagement party. My parents took me to Europe twice when I was a child. The first time was when I was a still a baby and the other time was after my brother was born. I was older than my brother by two years. Language is no barrier to a child at all. They just pick it up right away and my brother and I got along just beautifully when we were in Europe. So I spoke Swiss before I spoke English. We were in the German part of Switzerland first and then when we got to the French part, I couldn't understand the children at all. There was one boy who was German and German is close enough to Swiss that he would be the translator. We'd play in this haystack and it meant nothing at all. But after I got back home to New York, I was used to being outside so my mother would let us go out and play in the streets. Of course, there were no cars where we were in New York in those days—just apartment houses. The children were speaking a different language, English, and I didn't understand English. Then one day, I came upstairs, my mother asked me a question and I answered her in English. I wasn't going to be left out of the children's games because I couldn't speak their language so everything was English from that time on.

A studio portrait of Billie with her mother Bertha Bohny and her brother Charles. (Billie Dove Collection, Courtesy of Paul Melzer.)

My father was a linguist. My mother was not. She was a housewife and she learned to speak English she said from me. But I don't know how she learned to read and write English. Mother had something very charming about her speech. You wouldn't call it an accent at all. It was not guttural like German and it wasn't squeaky like French. It was just her own charming way of speaking. She would ask for a "cup coffee" instead of a "cup of coffee" but that was her only trace of an accent.

My parents' religion was Lutheran and many of our friends also went to the church. I played on the girls' basketball team and things like that at the church. When I was playing with the kids, they gave me the nickname "Billie" so I've always been Billie. The "Dove" came later when I was doing extra work in pictures. But in grammar school, the children called me Lillian. I was a good student, an A student. History was different but I crammed just before examination so I'd make it all right. But if you asked me the same questions the next week,

I couldn't answer them. It was date-event, date-event, very dull, and today the books are absolutely wonderful. I've seen my grandson's and they're just great about wars and everything.

When I was in school, I think we had about thirty in the classroom at that time. There were two desks with one seat big enough for two to sit on. I had a very nice little black girl who was with me. Our teacher was very austere and very wonderful. One day, she said, "Billie Bohny, please come up to my desk." Well, I didn't know what to do. Everybody was looking at me—twenty-nine pairs of eyes. I could feel my face getting redder and I thought, "Oh, my God, what have I done?" because I was a good student. Finally, I got up and I kept my eyes down and looked at the floor. The desk was elevated at the front of the room. She wore her hair back very prim and her collar up to her chin. She had a bosom but you'd never know it because I think she plastered herself down or something. She was really modest, very stern and a very good teacher. Finally, I looked up at her and she was straight on me with a card in her hand. She didn't smile or anything. I took the card in my hand, I glanced at it and it said, "Billie Bohny, an excellent girl, fine arithmetic, fine grammar," with the teacher's name and the date. I put the card in my pocket and, of course, everybody wanted the recess to come. But that was my precious thing and when recess came, I wouldn't show that to anybody. I kept it and I have xeroxed copies of it. I just loved so much for her to do that—that she appreciated me as a good student. She never did that for anybody else and then she did that again to me.

Billie with her father Charles Bohny and her brother. (Billie Dove Collection, Courtesy of Paul Melzer.)

We were out of the theatrical district but we had movie houses. We didn't even live anywhere near where the theatrical people were. We were five miles away from Times Square. It could have been a thousand miles away it was that different. But my family and I went to the movies. Every Wednesday night, we went to an open-air theatre. There were just chairs out there. We didn't go in a car—nobody had cars then. I've often wondered what they did in the rain—whether we just sat with our umbrellas or whether they called it off. I have no recollection at all. But every Wednesday night, we saw a serial called *The Black Box.* I remember that I guessed who did it and it was not the butler. I also saw *The Birth of a Nation* and sent a fan letter to a boy who was in the picture. I remember standing up on a trunk and writing him. Of course, I didn't get an answer.

After I graduated from grammar school, I went to Eastern Gains Business School for a while when I was fourteen. At that time, I had a beautiful friendship with an elderly lady. She was the mother-in-law of my mother's sister. Aunt Alice was so different from my mother. She was very happy and glorious and always having a good time. She would smoke a cigarette or take a drink or anything she liked. Her name was Anna when she met this chap who was adopted by wealthy people. Now they didn't like the name of Anna so they changed it to Alice when she married their son. Aunt Alice and her husband were living a full life—sort of crazy and wonderful. But her mother-in-law was living alone. She had gray hair and she was slight. She was near the Eastern Gains school. I hadn't been there too long but every day I would come into her place and we would have tea together. She had a great big room that she rented. It had everything in it but the johnnie. I don't know how the money situation was but the room that she had was tremendous and she had it by herself since her husband had died. We became the best of friends. She would wait for me and have the tea all ready and she'd bake something. Her education was just beautiful and I would ask her questions of what was so-and-so and what I didn't understand. I'd say, "Tell me about this. What did they mean when they did this?" And any subject, no matter what it was about, whether it was history, whether it was conversation, anything at all, she was always willing to answer me. And the friendship of a grandmother and a young child is beautiful.

I had a boyfriend who was older than I when I was going to Eastern Gains. He had graduated from high school and had a job and we had enough money. Maybe we'd hold hands or maybe we wouldn't. We were still kids. We'd take the subway and he had balcony seats for Helen Hayes's show or Katharine Cornell's. We never saw a musical comedy but we saw those shows.

I just had to walk out of the business school when I started in show business. I had always liked the movies period. All of the girls wanted to be in the movies. I didn't *want* to be. I knew I was *going* to be. I didn't know when or how and it never bothered me. I just knew that I was going to be. I'm not psychic but there have been instances in my life when I have been absolutely so sure of something and this was one of them. Now there was a woman in the apartment house where we lived who was an extra in pictures. She knew that I was definite about being in pictures so she gave my mother addresses where to register me as an extra. They would call me and then I could work that way, you see.

That's how I met the director, George Archainbaud, when he made a test of me at the studio in Fort Lee, New Jersey. They gave me a dressing room and said, "Make up," and I did. Then pretty soon, there was a knock at the door and I said, "Come in."

George Archainbaud's assistant, Phil Masi, came in, took one look at me and said, "My God, what have you done to yourself?"

I said, "Well, you told me to make up."

"Oh, not that way." So he took his hand, put it in Abolene, a cold cream in a can that was greasy but very good, smeared it all over my face and took all of it off. I was putting the make-up on like at Ziegfeld's and, of course, you don't do that. On the stage, you have to over make-up so they can see you in the back row and in pictures, it was light they applied. But no one told me that so he said, "I'll make you up," and he did. That's the way we came to know each other. They were to use me in a picture for three days to see how I photographed. I was to play a nurse and then they found out that the nurses all had to wear masks. I told George Archainbaud he wouldn't be able to tell about me if I had to wear a mask. So they let me be the nurse wheeling the patients into the operating room. They asked me if I wanted a five-year contract. They were fine if you were making a big salary but with my small one, I figured that if they thought I was worthwhile taking a chance on, in five years I could be somebody but I'd still be getting a small salary.

George Archainbaud and Kitty, his girlfriend whom he later married, became good friends of mine. George's assistant, Phil Masi, was also his best friend and I fell in love with Phil as much as you can at that age. We used to go together. Later on, when I became a star out here, George and Kitty had a little bad luck. He'd gotten into a mess, money was down low and he called me to ask if he could borrow six hundred dollars. I had money then so I just sent him a check for that amount. Later, he returned it and said, "Well, you certainly know who your friends are."

I was an extra in a Mabel Normand picture they did at Fort Lee. I remember I was there one day and there were a lot of people in front of a house. The director told me that all these men were marching home from the war. He pointed out one man and said, "Now, look, that man over there is your brother. When you see him walking along, you run down these steps and you just jump up upon him and kiss him you're so happy to see him. He's just come home from the war." I couldn't wait for the picture to come out and surprise all of my friends. Fortunately, I didn't tell any of them that I was in it. I told them it was supposed to be a very good picture. We all went to see it. I was waiting for that scene and he'd cut me off at the knees. So thank heavens, I hadn't told them.

Besides my work as an extra, I also modelled for artists in New York. I posed for this one picture that was an advertisement for Mulcified Cocoanut Oil. I was in a bathing suit that was up to my neck. You didn't see any bare skin at all so I wasn't a bathing beauty. I was sitting on the grass and there was a pond there. We all had long hair, you know. I had my head thrown forward and my hair went way over my face but away from it so you could see it. It was a colored picture. The artist had painted my hair four times its real width. It was curly and he had painted it red.

Mr. Ziegfeld saw that picture in a magazine, a paper or something and he had one of his men call me. We lived in a four-story house. It was a walk-up and we were on the third floor. We had one telephone down on the main floor, the manager was in the back and he would hear it ring. But the telephone didn't ring often for anybody. But this one time it did so he called Mrs. Bohny, she answered and he said, "There's a call here for Miss Billie Dove."

I was upstairs so I came down and answered and a man's voice asked, "Are you Miss Billie Dove?"

I said, "Yes."

And he said, "Well, Mr. Florenz Ziegfeld wants to see you at three o'clock tomorrow at his office."

I said, "Well, what does Mr. Florenz Ziegfeld want to see me for?" I didn't want to go on the stage. I wanted to be in the movies and frankly, I don't know whether I even knew his name or not. I told this man—oh, I thought of every reason why I didn't want to go see Mr. Ziegfeld and I kept on telling him all about this. But then I thought maybe that's the way to get into pictures. I was so eager to get in because I was just doing little day-work once in a while. Finally, I said, "Well, I'll be there. Where is his office?" I didn't even think of the theatre so he told me it was in the theatre and where it was.

I went down there, they called me in and as they did, Mr. Ziegfeld got up from his chair and walked around the desk. I didn't know whether he was going to accost me or what but he took a look at me, turned around and went back to his chair. He was surprised, I guess. He didn't think I was going to be so young and maybe he forgot that he had seen the picture. All the other girls were dressed beautifully. We didn't have much money and my mother was not a seamstress but she always had me clean and pressed. She put together a very plain dress with little white cuffs and a collar. I was courteous and he took it for granted that I wanted to be in the show. He didn't even ask me. He just said, "Well, now, you go two doors to your right. You'll find a door there saying 'Ned Wayburn.' You go in there and he will be there with a little rod in his hand. There'll be girls walking in a circle and they will be learning how to do the Ziegfeld walk. So you just join them."

I did as I was told—I went down there—but I thought it was kind of funny. If that's what he wanted, though, all right. I went into the circle and Mr. Wayburn would say to different girls, "Your feet are too far apart. Put your head up higher. Put your shoulders back more." This went on for three days and I thought, "Well, this is ridiculous." So I just left. But I was courteous. I sent Mr. Ziegfeld a note of resignation and then I wasn't even in the show. He had a man call me up and have me come down again. He wanted to see me. Then I came in and he said, "Well, what's the matter?"

I said, "Mr. Ziegfeld, I don't want to be a chorus girl."

He said, "Oh, we'll take care of that. You go on back to where you were with the other girls and forget it. We'll take care of it."

It was not the beginning of the new show, *The Ziegfeld Follies of 1919*. In the very beginning when they'd started to put it together, Eddie Cantor and a few of the biggies went out on strike and some of the girls went with them, too. Mr. Ziegfeld was not taking those girls back so we were there to take their places. But I didn't want to be a chorus girl and I didn't want to be on the stage. I still wanted to be in pictures. Well, they had this round circle made of metal and it had a little piece of wood at the bottom you could sit on. I had on a Ziegfeld costume they had made for me and I sat on the little piece of wood. A couple of men pulled ropes and they pulled me to the top of the stage while a leading man sang to me. I just sat up there smiling at him and I smiled at the audience. I made the program. Mr. Ziegfeld did what he said. He had me listed as "The Girl in the Hoop, Miss Billie Dove" and that is how I happened to start in the *Ziegfeld Follies.*

Then he had me in a tableau. You know how in the Pageant of the Masters in Laguna Beach they

Billie as "The Girl in the Hoop" in *The Ziegfeld Follies of 1919.* (Billie Dove Collection, Courtesy of Paul Melzer.)

dress people all in white stuff to be replicas of real statues. They put them in the position that the real statue is in and you have to stay that way all the time the curtain is up. Well, he didn't copy statues—he copied pictures. I was in one of those with the other girls. I was supposed to do what the girl in the picture was doing and we had chiffon dresses on but you couldn't see through them—there was no nudity at all. Then he gave me a costume of my own. I had a black velvet drop, I was barefooted and bare to my knees, and I had a pair of raggedy shorts on, kind of corduroy and old-looking. There were two men who did the music. One of them tore off his shirt, tore off the sleeves to the elbows and then ragged them up a bit. He said, "Here, put this on." So I did and I had my own hair not combed, just hanging down in the back. Then as far as the audience was concerned—oh, I could hear them. I'm turned to you sideways, the backdrop is behind me and I'm with my back hand to you. I have an apple in my hand, it's above my head, my head is up just about to take a bite of the apple and they open up the curtains. That's what you see and I'm alone there. He gave me that, you see. Then I did the numbers with the other girls but I didn't feel like a chorus girl so I stayed with the show.

I was one of the six special girls in the *Follies.* Ziegfeld made me a special girl and the other five were a little bit taller than me. I did not do any professional dancing although I was a good ballroom dancer. But I did not high-kick, I did not tap. Little girls who were like the Rockettes would do all the hard dancing in the *Follies* and they got thirty-five dollars a week. We got fifty dollars a week and we dressed in the costumes that Ziegfeld saved for us and did the Ziegfeld walk. We talked on stage, too. Whenever Eddie Cantor or any of the other principals spoke to us, we answered—whichever one he was speaking to.

The first night the show was on, all the cars came with the boys and the high hats for their girlfriends in the *Follies.* They had chauffeurs and everything else. And I had somebody meet me, too—my mother came down to pick me up. Can you imagine that? The mother of a Ziegfeld girl coming down to pick her up! I was a kid and she came to the stage door just to see that I got home all right. I wanted to drop through the floor and when we got out, I said, "Mother, I know how to get home. All I do is walk up the corner, turn left and get on the express subway." I told her where I got off. Then we walked a block and a half and there was the house. She never came there again after the first night.

When I started working in the *Follies,* I was very naive. Growing up, I knew nothing about sex,

Billie recreated her Follies background in a number of films including her final one, *Blondie of the Follies.* (The Kobal Collection.)

nothing at all. We had a very normal life at home. But my parents brought us up so that they just didn't show their love for one another in front of the children. They didn't put their arms around one another, they didn't kiss one another—nothing at all. Everything was at night in their bedroom with the door closed. This is a strange thing to tell you but it went to this length that when I developed into a woman, I thought I was dying. They hadn't even told me that. I think probably that was the way they were in that country. They are in certain countries. I don't know if their religion had anything to do with it or not but they never told me anything. Now when I was put in a dressing room with three other girls at Ziegfeld's, I was just being very quiet and I was learning about sex and boyfriends and that sort of thing from them. The girls understood perfectly well by the way I listened and some questions I asked that I didn't know anything. When they introduced me to guys, they'd always say, "Lay off." And the men understood and they did. After all the things I'd heard the other girls say, I told them, "I decided I'm going to be a virgin when I marry." And I was—I was still a virgin when I married.

I was not flat-chested but I didn't bobble when I ran or anything. I never wore a bra—it wasn't necessary—and I couldn't imagine why women wore them. I thought that a bosom was part of you just the way your knees are or your toes until I was in the dressing room with the girls. We'd be changing clothes and I noticed that their bosoms kind of dropped a little bit. One time one gal said to me, "You don't have a bra on, do you?" And I thought, "Oh, my God, I didn't think she could see through this dress." It never occurred to me that breasts had anything to do with sex.

Besides appearing in the *Follies,* I worked in *Sally* with Marilyn Miller for Ziegfeld and *The Midnight Frolic* on the Roof for him. Ziegfeld had called me in one time and asked me if I wanted to go on the

An early portrait Billie inscribed to her father. (Billie Dove Collection, Courtesy of Paul Melzer.)

Roof. I said yes because that meant more money. That was like a nightclub and you worked from eight in the morning to eleven at night at the show down below and then you worked from twelve midnight to two in the morning up there. So I was working very hard all the time and getting more money.

I remember a lot of the beautiful girls who were in the *Follies* like Jessie Reed, a very lovely, stately, red-headed girl. And Dorothy Mackaill who later was under contract to First National when I was there. She was very young, too, and she'd come over from England. I don't know whether she worked on the Roof or in the *Follies* but that's when I first knew her. I started my autograph book at that time, too. It's really valuable to a collector. So many of the people aren't with us anymore—Cecil B. DeMille, William Randolph Hearst, Louis B. Mayer, Mary Pickford, Lupe Velez, Thelma Todd, all of whom I met later in Hollywood. And autographs from those who starred in the *Follies* when I was there—Eddie Cantor and Fannie Brice who was darling. She wrote in my autograph book, "Always your Jewish friend, Fannie Brice."

When you were with Mr. Ziegfeld, you weren't supposed to work in a picture one day because if you did and he knew it, you were fired. One night, one of the three girls in the dressing room came to work and she looked just dreadful. She was so worried about something and we didn't know what it was. Finally, we asked her and she said, "Well, all right, I'll tell you. Nobody knows about it because Ziegfeld musn't find out but I am signed up with a movie company. I called them up this morning to find out if they could use me as an extra and they said no, they didn't need me that day. So there's another company that I'm also affiliated with. I called them and they said yes, they could use me. So that was fine. However, later on in the daytime, the first company called back and said, 'Yes, we do need you. Our plans are changed.' " She hurried up and called the second company. They had told her where to be but they had closed for the day. Then she had two appointments at two studios that she was supposed to go to and she was terribly upset. Suddenly, she stopped and said, "Billie, you have worked in pictures as an extra, haven't you?"

I said, "Yes."

She said, "Well, would you do one for me?"

I said, "Sure."

Oh, she was so relieved! She told me what to do and where to be. She said, "It doesn't make any difference just as long as you show up because you're background like a tree." She was a very nice girl but she had been cheating. She had signed with two studios as an extra to get some more money and nobody knew about it. We didn't even know about it and it was so sad because she didn't know what to do. Then she said she thought of me. So that was an opportunity for me. I wouldn't put it on her but I always levelled with Mr. Ziegfeld.

I went out to the studio and did her part as an extra for a day. She had said, "Now when you finish, here is the address. You go there and you get your check for your day's work."

I said, "Okay."

As I was going up the steps, Johnny Hines who was a comedian at the time and his manager were coming down. They took a look at me, turned around and followed me up the steps. I went into the inner office to pick up my check and they asked somebody in the other office who I was. They said, "She's a Ziegfeld girl." So they accosted me when I came out and said, "Would you like to take a test for the leading lady of Johnny Hines's present picture?"

I said, "Yes, I would."

The next day, I went to a place. I think it was a theatre because it was very, very dark and that's probably why we were on a stage. They had little lights when they were filming. All they wanted to see was how I photographed. A day or so later, they called me up and said, "We'd like to see you again. Would you come by so we can check something?"

I said, "Of course."

So I went by and they acted so silly. One of them got up really high—he was looking down at me. The other one was down low looking up at me. Pretty soon, they looked straight at my face and then they looked at me from the side. I thought they were crazy. Then we got all finished and one said to the other, "Well, I think it's because we used only one light." I had photographed cross-eyed. Imagine a Ziegfeld girl being cross-eyed! But they gave me the part and I didn't photograph cross-eyed. So that's how I started as a leading lady in a one-reel comedy that would be shown in movie houses with the long feature and the newsreel.

Mr. Ziegfeld was one of the kindest men I think I've ever known. He was just such a gentleman always. We didn't have a father-daughter relationship but that's the closest it would come to because I was unsophisticated. I heard people call him "Ziggy" but I never did. In fact, I still call him "Mr. Ziegfeld." I don't believe we ever shook hands when I was in the *Follies*. He was always behind a desk and I would be standing up in front of him.

As I said before, he didn't approve of anybody working for him going into pictures. Though I loved the *Follies*, I wanted to be in pictures so I would send in a letter of resignation to him. I had good manners and every gal wouldn't have been like that. Then I'd be called into the office and he would say, "Well, what's the matter?" Then I would tell him and he'd say, "Well, we can fix that." He never said no to me. I thought he was getting a kick out of it and that it struck him as funny. I thought that he would go home to his wife, Billie Burke, and tell her, "Oh, that young gal with the plain dress came in again and she had sent in a note of resignation." But I didn't know anything about Mr. Ziegfeld's home life, about his family and whether he had any children or not. I never asked him and we never discussed it. Our association was strictly professional. And I didn't know whether he had any girlfriends. That was none of my business.

After I left the *Follies*, I almost got a job in a picture in New York that was to star Lillian Gish. I was so thrilled because she was a wonderful lady and everybody thought I had it. There were so many girls trying to get into pictures—poor girls with brown hair and the same amount with blonde. Two girls would be chosen to play sisters in the picture and for some reason or other, they had to be opposites. One had to be a short blonde and the other had to be tall and dark-haired. So they placed them all up and down the line and they kept getting back to me. Finally, they had nobody but me so I played the taller, dark-haired girl with every single one of the blonde girls. Then we went to dinner and one girl said, "Well, this is ridiculous. Why should we go to dinner when you know you have the part?" Well, I knew it, too—you couldn't help but know it.

We came back—and I didn't have the part. They couldn't find a blonde girl to do the other part. I swear that was their reason. So somebody else got the job and I just went home and cried myself to sleep. I thought, "Oh, that was my chance, my one chance in this world to work with Lillian Gish and I just didn't make it." But that taught me a lesson. The Gish picture never finished. They ran out of

With Doris Kenyon in *Get-Rich-Quick Wallingford*. (The Kobal Collection.)

money and nobody got paid. And that gave me the biggest philosophy I've had in my life—never depend on anything unless you're actually doing it. Otherwise, you're letting yourself in for a disappointment.

I finally got *Get-Rich-Quick Wallingford.* That was in New York with Doris Kenyon, Milton Sills and Norman Kerry. Kerry played my beau and he was Sills's best friend in the picture. I don't remember anything else about it at all. It was just a regular picture. It wasn't bad and I think it must have been a nice picture.

Norma Shearer and I started about the same time. She was cross-eyed and bow-legged, too. More power to her for being able to do what she did. She was signed with an agent, Eddie Small, who I think was the most wonderful guy. I didn't have an agent so I signed with him, too. Then I got a picture on my own and I never heard from them after that. They never took any part of my salary which was very nice of them. They probably just threw the contract away because I was getting things on my own. I was popular at that time. Norma Shearer made one or two pictures, I believe, for Christy Cabanne at Robertson-Cole in New York. They were paying her fifty dollars a week and I think they wanted her for another one. But she wanted a raise which would make it seventy-five dollars a week and they wouldn't give it to her. They got Billie Dove at fifty.

I did two pictures that Cabanne directed for Robertson-Cole—*At the Stage Door* and *Beyond the Rainbow*. At that time, they didn't have stars. You were just playing in the picture. You had to buy your own clothes, you used your own make-up and did your own hair. Clara Bow played in her first picture in *Beyond the Rainbow*. She was not well-dressed. She looked as though she'd just come off the streets from playing tag or something like that. Nobody would ever think that she'd become the "It" Girl but she did. She was just a very nice little thing, a happy person as I remember, always smiling. We got along beautifully.

At that time there was a press agent in New York, Nils T. Granlund. He was the best there was—they always got him. They were opening a theatre in Boston and they wanted a Ziegfeld girl. All she had to do was walk across the stage and not say anything at all but just do the Ziegfeld walk. I did that in Boston and a man came up to me and said, "We have a theatre that is running one of your pictures." (It was one of my Robertson-Cole pictures.)

With Huntly Gordon in *Beyond the Rainbow.*

"We're playing that next week. Would you care to come here and make a personal appearance?"

I said, "Sure," never thinking they could ever get in touch with me—I was that stupid. I mean, why was I there in the first place? Naturally, all they had to do was call Nils Granlund.

The next week came and I got a call in the morning from Nils. He said, "Billie, there's a man on the other phone and he's calling me from Boston. He said you told him that you would make a personal appearance with the picture that they are showing starting tomorrow. It's running for a week and you said you'd appear with it."

I said, "Oh, my God, I couldn't do that."

He said, "What do you mean you couldn't do that?"

I said, "Nils, I'd be scared to death."

He said, "Now wait a minute. Do you want to get along in pictures?"

I said, "All right, you've got me. What do I do?"

He said, "Meet me at the Astor at twelve o'clock for lunch. I'll try to get reservations for you and your mother tonight to go to Boston."

I told Mother. She got my things all ready and then I went down to the Astor to have lunch with him. He said, "All right. Now tell me about the picture they're showing." So I told him about the different scenes and he'd say, "No, forget that one." Then I'd tell him about another scene. "Yes, use that and in your own words. Use that one, use this, use that and don't use this." He gave me something to say at the end. It was really very catchy, very good. Then he said, "Oh, I couldn't make a reservation tonight on the train for you and your mother so I've made one in the parlor car and you go tomorrow. Tonight, I'm giving a party in my flat. You come there. I want to hear you."

So I came to the party at his flat. He took me into a bedroom where there were a couple of beds. He put me against one wall, he was against the other one and he said, "Okay, go ahead now." Then I went through the whole thing and I memorized when he told me to come in and when I said anything. After I finished, he said, "Okay, you're on, go ahead."

I left then and the next morning, Mother and I got on the train. All I did was look out of the window and she said, "Billie, aren't you going to practice?"

I said, "Oh, Mother, I'm afraid I'd forget it." I was really scared.

Billie was photographed in this car in Georgia during her personal appearance tour of the South in early 1922. (Billie Dove Collection, Courtesy of Paul Melzer.)

We got there where there was an automobile waiting for us and they said, "We're sorry but you can't go to the hotel yet because your picture is playing now. By the time we get there, it'll be over and you have to go on."

So we had to go right to the theatre from the train and when we got there, there was a tiny mirror just as big as your head, I guess, out on the side. I tore off my hat and combed my hair and then I put make-up on so I could be seen in the back row. I knew how to do that because of having been in the *Follies.* Then they shoved me on when the picture was over and a great big light came on—so bright that I could not see the first row at all. I started talking and I said, "Well, you know, when I was standing outside waiting to come on, I was so nervous my knees were just rattling. But after your wonderful ovation, I feel right at home. I'm not a bit nervous." I didn't even hear the ovation I was so nervous and with the light on, I could not see anyone in the theatre. It was quiet when I started and I went through different scenes. No sound so okay, I'm talking to an empty theatre. It's afternoon—who should be there? Billie Dove above the marquee and nobody knows Billie Dove—how could they? They must have used publicity or something.

I went on to say, "And then if you remember the snow scene and oh, it snowed so hard. It got higher and higher and higher. Finally, I lost my way and I fainted. Then Huntly Gordon came in." I crouched down and I put my two arms down like that, cradling as if you were going to pick somebody up. And when I was down there, I looked up at the so-called audience that wasn't there. I said, "I like that part of it," and I had a big smile on my face. All of a sudden, I heard this roar through the theatre. It was packed and that was the first I knew that there were people in the house. It was the biggest success and when I came to the end that he gave me, it was a honey—really. You couldn't resist it. You had to like me. They gave me the biggest ovation and it was just great.

Then the people with the theatre said, "We forgot to tell you that we have two theatres here. Your picture is running at the other one now and we have to go. You can't go to the hotel yet. When we get to the theatre, it'll be time for you to go on." I had done it once already and it was a success so it wasn't quite so hard the second time. Finally, I got to the hotel.

For a whole week, I played the two theatres in the daytime and then I'd play them at nighttime. I would have a short dress on in the day and a long dress at night. Pretty soon, I was invited to the men's club as a guest. I would get up and speak and I got used to that. The week I was there, I got flowers, publicity, everything. I got five pound boxes of candy that I didn't know what the heck to do with so I sent them to my friends. It was a big, big success which is hard to believe. Who would expect a young girl to get up and speak like that? Then they had me in Rhode Island the next week and they booked me up all over the North. I couldn't imagine that I was such a success and surprisingly so but at the very last minute, they cancelled the North and had me come back to New York. They said,

Hollywood, 1922: Billie standing by her first car, a black Buick. (Billie Dove Collection, Courtesy of Paul Melzer.)

Billie standing in front of her first house in Hollywood in 1922. (Billie Dove Collection, Courtesy of Paul Melzer.)

"Well, we've changed our minds. We're sending you to California on a year's contract to Metro." When they said "Metro," it might have been shoelaces—I didn't know it was a studio.

Joe Engel, the head of Metro, was a lovely man and we were such good friends. He's the one who cancelled my Northern tour and signed me up to come out here. On the way to California, they sent me to the South and I went to Memphis, Tennessee, Birmingham, Alabama and New Orleans for a week apiece instead of the North. While I was out on tour there, Joe Engel sent me a wire saying, "It's lonesome without you. Say hello to Mumsie." But I thought it was all kidding.

When Mother and I arrived here, he met us and said to me, "Well, now, Billie, I knew that you didn't know anything about California. I have a two-story house with a housekeeper and I have an extra room upstairs. You and your mother are most welcome to stay there till you know where you want to live. I have a man and he will take you around and show you the studio, show you Hollywood, Beverly Hills and all around." So the man took us around and we would find out where we wanted to be and everything. He showed me a car, too—a black Buick with a soft top. A young guy had bought it and he couldn't afford to make payments on it anymore. He didn't want to sell it for what it cost him to begin with. He just wanted somebody to take over the payments. Then this man of Joe's taught me how to drive. That was wonderful for me. I had my first car and now I knew how to drive.

I had just learned to drive when Nick the Greek called me up. He was a gambler whom I'd met in New York. We were never alone or anything like that but he was a gentleman and he respected me. When he stopped in Los Angeles, he telephoned, said he was there, did I have the evening free and would I care to come down and have dinner with him at a restaurant? I said, "I'd love to," and I drove downtown in the Buick with the soft top that I never put down. There wasn't much traffic then and I turned in the middle of the street but I didn't turn far enough and I hit the curb. So I had to back up and I had to sit there and think, "Now, what do I do first? Okay, first, I turn on the motor, then I have to put the stick in the one, two, three or four, then I have to put it in reverse." I figured that out—I caught on quickly. So I had a lovely dinner with Nick the Greek and then I drove home.

Mother was tired one night and she went to bed. Joe Engel and I were watching the fire. He never touched me but he had his hand behind me on the back of the divan. He said, "Billie, I can't ask you to marry me because I promised my mother while she was alive that I would only marry a Jewish girl." I had no idea he was in love with me—none. I'd thought it was all in fun so I couldn't say anything.

On location for her first West Coast production, *Youth to Youth*, with director Emile Chautard to Billie's right. (Billie Dove Collection, Courtesy of Paul Melzer.)

Billie, her chaperone Mercedes seated next to her, listens to a radio on board the whaling boat during the filming of *All the Brothers Were Valiant.* (Billie Dove Collection, Courtesy of Paul Melzer.)

I was not like the other gals who all had boyfriends, chauffeured cars and everything else. But I had fun and I was invited to all their parties. We all had chaperones in those days and my mother used to be mine. But she was taken ill and then we had another. There were a couple of gals that she liked very much, one of them between her age and mine. Her name was Mercedes and she was a friend of both of us. Later, we had a gal from the *Follies.* I think her parents must have died or something and Mother liked her so much and she loved my mother. Anytime you had a vacation or went on location, you always had a companion or a chaperone—that was the general thing.

Hollywood was a very nice little town then. It wasn't at all the way it is now with nothing but shops all over the place. We stayed with Joe until such time as Mother and I found a little house in Hollywood where we wanted to live. So we rented it and both of us moved in there. But my father stayed back East and so did my brother who was going to military school.

Joe gave us a little time—it wasn't too long but it wasn't right away—before I made my first picture for Metro, *Youth to Youth.* Cullen Landis was the leading man and it was directed by Emile Chautard who was George Archainbaud's foster father.

I made a second picture for Metro, *All the Brothers Were Valiant* with Lon Chaney who was very nice. Irvin Willat was the director. I made several pictures for him but I think he was a man's director—very definitely for men. He did westerns and boat pictures. And in *All the Brothers Were Valiant,* we were supposed to be in the middle of the ocean on a whaling boat. I had my companion, Mercedes, with me and we had to meet the other people down below in the hotel at four o'clock in the morning and then we'd go down to the boat. They had two boats in the picture. One caught the

A snapshot pose with co-stars Lon Chaney and Malcolm McGregor during the filming of *All the Brothers Were Valiant.* (Billie Dove Collection, Courtesy of Paul Melzer.)

Smiling for the camera on board ship during production of *All the Brothers Were Valiant.* (Billie Dove Collection, Courtesy of Paul Melzer.)

whales but ours didn't. My God, we smelled enough as if we had—it was terrible. I don't know how they make perfume out of that odor. I remember we went up to the San Francisco Bay for that picture. Mercedes and I were the only two women on the boat and that's why Irvin took advantage of us. The whaling boat joined us and we had to go way out past civilization and all the way, Irvin kept saying to me, "Marry me, marry me, marry me, marry me," a million times. We were on location for a whole month and all the way back it was "Marry me, marry me, marry me" until finally I said "yes" just to stop him. But I liked him—I liked everybody.

I was still unmarried when I went to Fox to make my next picture, *Madness of Youth.* Jack Gilbert was my leading man and we got along beautifully, just fine. He was an awfully nice person, great to work with, lots of fun and very handsome. A funny story about it—it's so ridiculous really—is that he was married to Leatrice Joy. They had a quarrel and during the making of the picture, he asked me to marry him. I said, "Sure," not kidding exactly but, of course, I wouldn't have married him. I wouldn't have married any actor, as a matter of fact, no matter how much I liked them. If I saw somebody coming up powdering his nose and putting lipstick on, I changed my mind awfully fast. We were good friends and everything but there was nothing serious about it at all. He just said, "Will you marry me?" and I said, "Sure," with no intention of marrying him. But he took it seriously. Then Leatrice and he made up and he sent his friend, Paul Bern, over to see me to explain the situation and it wasn't necessary at all.

Irvin Willat was a little odd character in certain ways and before I married him, he said, "I think it might be a good idea for us to see a doctor to make sure that we're okay to get married." Well, I didn't know anybody except Joe Engel's doctor who saw my mother. His name was Kahn and I went to him.

Later on, I ran into Joe and he looked at me and said, "Billie, I saw Dr. Kahn yesterday and he told me that you were a virgin."

I said, "But, Joe, I told you that I was." Well, he looked so perplexed. Some awful person had told him that I wasn't. Isn't that a lousy thing to do? Dr. Kahn was surprised, too, because Joe and I were such good friends. But that's all we were. Doctors are not supposed to discuss their patients but Joe and Dr. Kahn were very good friends.

Irvin and I were married in 1923 in the pastor's house. We were fine but it was not the sort of love that you have in marriage, you know. It wasn't that kind. We lived in a nice two-story house in Hollywood. Before we were married, he had given me a thousand dollars to furnish it. Money was that low then that you could furnish a house for that amount. The upstairs bedroom in our house went from the front to the back and right into my dressing room. Then I was surprised—he had a colored window in parts and he had Shakespeare's "Good night, good night, a thousand times good night" put in there. His son Boyd and I are good friends—his family and I. Boyd told me when we met, "Dad never got over you." He said that I just lived in that

With John Gilbert in *Madness of Youth.*

house with them afterward years later and that I was part of the family. He's managing that old house and they use it for an office now. They still have my bedroom and everything. I think it's so funny.

After my year's contract with Metro was finished, I worked for everybody that asked me to and I worked all the time. I remember I did a picture with Edward Everett Horton and he gave me some lovely earrings and antiques—they were just darling. He was so sweet—he always gave presents to his leading ladies.

I was out in the desert all the time because I made so many westerns. That way, they didn't have to put up sets. They just used the mountains and the sand. I worked with Tom Mix, Hoot Gibson and Jack Holt and whenever one western was finished, they'd say, "Where is Billie Dove?" and the next day, I'd be in another one with Tom Mix. It didn't make any difference to me. I was in motion pictures and I loved it.

When I was making a picture with Tom Mix, I just missed a train in one scene so he came along with his horse, took one arm and pulled me up. Then we were galloping trying to catch the train and I was supposed to put my hand out and get on the back of the train. Off of the parlor car, there was a little opening in the back that had wrought-iron around it. Of course, they had a double for

The wedding photo of Billie and Irvin Willat. (Courtesy of Boyd Willat.)

me, a stunt man or woman—I don't know which. And they had a camera inside the car where I was supposed to get on. They would do that part later but with the camera farther away. Then my double would get on. But all the time Tom had me on the side, I was slipping down just being held by one arm while he was galloping his horse. As we came to the train—I don't know why I would do this but it was a lot easier to me to get on the train than have Tom galloping and I'd probably have to fall off the horse. So I just put out my hand and got on the train. The cameraman said, "Well, I'll be damned," and I could hear him sigh. The stunt man or woman was there all ready to go and they had nothing to do because I did it. Usually, for things like that, they had stunt people. It was taken for granted that we would go right up to the train, then, of course, they would cut, the cameras would film the double and they would get a close-up of me later getting on the train. But that wasn't necessary because it was easier for me to get on than to hang on the horse. But then I'm strong. I'm not bulging with muscles or anything like that but, for instance, inside the calves of my legs are just as hard as they can be. I've walked a lot. My father walked a lot and I take after him.

Another time on a Tom Mix picture, I had a horse run away with me. We were working on a Sunday night and I had my mother out there. It was in a place that was all enclosed by a black wrought-iron fence with two exits. Tom said, "Come on, let's take a couple of snapshots for publicity." So I got on Buster, a beautiful horse that doubled for Tom's horse, Tony. We didn't bother changing the stirrups or anything else that didn't fit me—they were actually too long. We got up on these steps and the photographer went to work. But when I was on Buster, the horse just felt at ease to run so he ran out of one of these gates. Here I was flying with this horse and he wouldn't listen to me at all. I'd pull the reins but he wouldn't stop.

One man who was a rider for Tom was very brave. He was on the truck with all the lights outside and he got in the middle of the road trying to stop the horse. I waved very hard with one hand for him to get out of the way. The horse would have killed him we were going so fast. We were going across a main street and we couldn't see whether cars were coming because there were trees on either side and that worried me. My cap fell off, my curls came down and I had to clutch with my knees because I couldn't touch the stirrups. And I pulled on that horse and he paid no attention to me at all. We got there and thank God, there were no cars. As long as we crossed that street, we were all right. Then we kept going until Buster just ran out of breath. We found out later that he hadn't been exercised.

Of course, everybody else just dropped everything, left my mother there and got in the cars. The cameraman was on the running board with his camera. He was going to get me whether I was down or not. Tom was on his horse and they were all running after me but they couldn't catch us because Buster could outrun Tony. By the time they got to me, we were going in a circle and my horse was foaming at the mouth he had run so hard. I was still clutching him with my knees. Tom said, "Now get off and get back on again or else you'll never get on a horse again. You'll be too scared." So I got off and got back on and Buster reared me up in the air which wasn't fair. Then I got off and I stayed off. I thought, "The hell with it! I don't think I want to get on a horse again." But later I thought that I musn't be scared and I did go riding many times after.

Tom Mix was a darling. We were very good friends. He had those extravagant costumes but I didn't ask him why he always wore white gloves. He and his wife took a few of us, Leatrice Joy and I've forgotten who the other girls were, on his boat. We took a ride overnight, I think, because when Leatrice was up and awake, she saw me sleeping and I remember she said something about it.

I did several pictures that were from stories by Zane Grey. One of them was *Wanderer of the Wasteland* which Irvin directed for Paramount. Jack Holt was my leading man. It was one of the first Technicolor features and Irvin was going back East because the film would have to be developed there. He wanted me to go back with him so I did. I was along in case he needed me. If they wanted to take a close-up of me to put in the film or any retakes, I would be handy. While I was there, I learned to cut films. I took the remnants of the film, the outtakes, learned how to splice them together and made my own little film.

Then on our way home, we went across the Gulf of Mexico and we got on the train to go up to Mex-

Lunch break on location with Tom Mix and his company. (The Kobal Collection.)

ico City to visit Mr. Jenkins, a wealthy American living there who owned twenty-six theatres—all the film theatres in Mexico. On the way, there was a stop—I can't think of the name of the little town but it was just charming. The women were washing their clothes in the nice clean water running down the gutter. The whole little town was so clean and everything that Irvin and I decided to stay overnight and take the train the next day.

When we got into Mexico City and checked into the hotel, we called the Jenkins family and they said, "Where are you?" We told them and they said, "What? You're staying with us." Well, we hadn't realized they'd invited us to actually stay with them. But they came right down, took our packages and things and moved them into their house. They had a big piece of property outside of Mexico City where they had a tile tennis court and where they were also making a river so that it would be like Xochimilco with the little boats. Before we got there, Mr. Jenkins had been parked in a car with his daughter when somebody ran into them with another car and marred his face—not much but he didn't smile as much on one side as the other. He was so conscious of it that his wife could not get him to go out. She was so glad that we came because he happened to be a fan of mine and he was so pleased we were there that he gave a party for me. He didn't give it at his home. He had a special house for parties. They were awfully nice to us.

With Zane Grey, a visitor to the location of *Wild Horse Mesa*. (Billie Dove Collection, Courtesy of Paul Melzer.)

They took us around to places like Guadalajara, for instance. And they kept us there in Mexico a whole month before we returned to California.

I met Zane Grey when I was on location in Arizona for another of his stories, *Wild Horse Mesa,* which George B. Seitz directed for Paramount. We had to go to Flagstaff on the train and then go for miles and miles, hours and hours and hours to get to this Indian reservation. They had three bedrooms there and the rest of the cast slept in tents. We ate under a great big tent, too. Zane Grey came and stayed a whole week with us and we got to be very good friends. As a matter of fact, he bought a ring for me from the finger of an Indian woman—it was silver and turquoise. Whenever I wasn't working, we'd get on horseback and we would ride around and watch the wild horses. We had some pictures taken of us and in this one picture, we're looking at

Billie in back of car, director George B. Seitz on camera platform filming a scene for *Wild Horse Mesa*. (Billie Dove Collection, Courtesy of Paul Melzer.)

each other and talking dressed in western clothes. That's when I'd cut my hair—we all had long hair before, you know. Then in another picture, I'm sitting on a horse with a mallet as though I were going to play polo and he's just looking at me.

When he left, he stopped at a hotel and wrote me a letter. He said, "If I didn't write this now, I never would." He wrote me a beautiful letter and said that I was so much like his favorite character. I had asked him whether he ever let anybody read anything of his before it was published. He said, "No," but he gave me something of his to read which I did and he said, "Don't forget." I never heard from him again—it was just that week that he was there.

I've met other famous writers over the years. Scott Fitzgerald and his wife, Zelda, came to my house one time when I was married to Irvin to see a picture we were showing. They were late so they came indoors on their hands and knees and just sat on the floor so they wouldn't bother us

The screenwriter Charlie Lederer, who was Marion Davies's nephew, introduced me to many of the leading writers of the day. Alexander Woollcott was supposed to be sarcastic but he couldn't have been nicer to me. And Dorothy Parker and I liked each other right away when I was taken to her house. She gave me the sixth copy of her new book. Her dog had chewed it which I thought was funny. She inscribed it, "To Billie Dove—God loves her, I do, too, Dorothy Parker."

Many years later, I met the humorist S. J. Perelman who came out to interview me. I was married to Bob Kenaston at that time and he was awfully nice in the interview about us. He had a cocktail

Billie on horseback for a scene in *Wild Horse Mesa*. (Billie Dove Collection, Courtesy of Paul Melzer.)

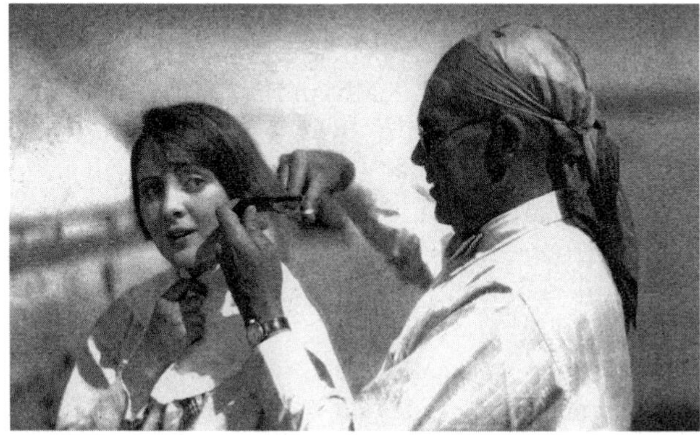

Make-up man Archie Stout on location cutting Billie's hair for her role in *Wild Horse Mesa*. (Billie Dove Collection, Courtesy of Paul Melzer.)

with us. Because he was such a witty writer, I didn't know what he'd be like. But he couldn't have written a nicer article.

Douglas Fairbanks, Jr. and I were in several pictures together. Irvin directed us in *The Air Mail* which we did in Nevada in 1925. This little town where we were was completely deserted. Nobody was living there anymore because the town went broke. We each had houses that we had to board up with paper, wood and everything so that the wind wouldn't get through. Young Doug was still just a kid. I have some stills of the two of us dancing together in what was really a wasteland. I worked with him later, too, and he was always quite a charming man.

I also worked with his father in the Technicolor feature, *The Black Pirate*. Douglas Fairbanks, Sr. had advertised extensively that he wanted a leading lady who was not professional. She had to have no experience at all. I was making a lumbering picture, *The Ancient Highway,* for Paramount. I was again Jack Holt's leading lady. We were up in Washington state when I received a telephone call from Doug Fairbanks, Sr. He said, "Billie, are you finishing that picture?"

I said, "I haven't the vaguest idea."

He said, "Well, when you know it's going to be finished, I want you to call me because I want you for my leading lady in *The Black Pirate*." Doug must have seen *Wanderer of the Wasteland* and liked the way I photographed in Technicolor. That's the only way I can figure out why he should suddenly want me instead of a non-professional.

As soon as I knew I was going to be finished, I called him. When I got there, they had the clothes ready, they had a wig ready and everything else and I started working right away. I didn't have many scenes with him. I had a very small part—all I did was stand around and look scared. But it was a good picture, really good. The color in it was so beautiful. They did it all in sepia and every scene was a work of art.

Doug was very, very nice, just straightforward and a gentleman. He was very brave, too, and I think he did the scene where he slashed the masts with a knife and went down the sails. He did that himself if I'm not mistaken. He had a friend of his who was a fan of mine and they'd come over to my house—not every day but often after we'd been filming. They'd bring over a liqueur. I wish I'd have kept the recipe. It was called "something delight"—I've forgotten. And we'd have this liqueur together.

Mary Pickford wouldn't permit Doug to kiss any of his leading ladies in a picture so I wondered how they would be able to end it without our doing that. But when I went to see the picture, I found out. In the scene where I was supposed to kiss him, she doubled for me in a long-shot. She put on my wig and clothes but the camera was so far away that you couldn't tell if it was me or not.

After *The Black Pirate* was released in 1926, I went to Universal to make *The Marriage Clause* directed by Lois Weber. I'd never heard of her before but she was the best director I ever had. She was very down-to-earth and very understanding. If I'd had anything to say about it, I would have had her direct all my pictures. I had a lot of men directors that I liked, too, but she understood women. It was so easy to work with her—she was so gentle and a lovely lady. I called her "Miss Weber" although I never thought of her as being older. Everybody adored her and to everybody she was very much a lady. Her husband was with her a lot on the set. They called him "captain." I don't know what he was captain of but they got along very nicely and seemed devoted to each other.

I gave a good performance in *The Marriage Clause* and I had a very dramatic scene at the end of the picture. I was an actress on the stage in love with my director, Francis X. Bushman, but he had left because he couldn't compete with the producer, Warner Oland, who had inserted a clause in my contract forbidding me from marrying. In this scene, I was dying and in a coma. I was so much in

With Douglas Fairbanks, Sr. in *The Black Pirate*.

love with Bushman that I had become ill. I always tried to be what the character called for—I believed in realism. I didn't want to look glamourous and I would not want my hair to look good. I wanted to look ill so Lois Weber let me take off all my make-up, pencil deep circles under my eyes and have my hair straggling around. They used the first take because it was so good—perfect. It was a very long scene but well-played by both of us. Bushman was trying to make a comeback in pictures at the time and he should have because he was great. But he never quite made it again. He comes rushing over when he hears I'm ill. He calls out for the things he needs to direct me like a megaphone. Then he stands up there as though he were putting me through the scene, like he was saying, "Lights! Action!" and he was the director pulling me through the coma. So very slowly, I start to come to. He gets me back to life and the last thing I'm in his arms.

I received a letter about my work in *The Marriage Clause* from Hope Loring after it was released. We didn't know each other because she wrote "My dear Miss Dove." She had a very big position in the industry. She was a very well-known scenario writer. She said that she just had to write me and that everything, my timing, my characterization—she mentioned everything and said it was just perfect. She said if she were a critical writer of pictures and performances and were writing about my performance, there was just one word that she would use and that was "flawless." She was that taken with my performance in that picture. She said that Lois Weber was certainly lucky to get me to play the part. Well, I thought that I was lucky to get Lois Weber. It was a beautiful letter—I just cherish it.

A frame enlargement from *The Marriage Clause.* (Courtesy of Doretta Whalen.)

Soon after, I worked for Lois Weber in another picture, *Sensation Seekers.* It was an entirely different kind of part—a flapper role. I don't remember anything else about it except I didn't know how to smoke and didn't want to. They all laughed at me and had to teach me to smoke—in fact, they had to light the cigarette for me. There was one scene where I was sitting up on top of the back seat of a large open car waving my hand like Lindbergh and smoking at the same time. Unfortunately, I got hooked on smoking for some years. But I thought it was a stupid habit and I soon gave it up.

I don't know what happened to Lois Weber after I made those pictures for her. I'm sorry I lost track of her. There was a time that was very bad for the motion picture industry and I think Lois Weber stopped directing because most women directors weren't asked to come back and some of the men weren't, either.

I was still freelancing at the time I did *The Marriage Clause.* In that same year of 1926, I was in *Kid Boots* with Eddie Cantor and Clara Bow which was made by Paramount. And I made a picture with Bert Lytell for Harry Cohn at Columbia, *The Lone Wolf Returns.* It was the first picture that Columbia could get into a big house—not because of me but probably because of Bert.

I never had an agent or manager, ever—I just did everything myself. After practically every picture I made, I had an offer of a five-year contract but I would turn it down because I didn't think I was making enough money. I wasn't making much but I would just up my salary a little bit in the next picture for the next company. Finally after I made *The Marriage Clause*, I had an offer from every studio in the business so then I had to make up my mind. The first would have been MGM but, after all, Norma Shearer and I would play the same kind of parts. She became Thalberg's wife and, of course, she would get the better pictures. Greta Garbo was there, too, but I don't count her. We all loved her and we couldn't beat her. Joan Crawford was also at MGM. She would make some pictures that required dancing but she also played the same parts that I did. So I had to put MGM out and I put everybody out until I came to First National. There

Billie signing her 1928 First National contract with studio head John McCormick and M. C. Levee. (Courtesy of Cole Johnson.)

they had Colleen Moore who was a comedienne. And Dorothy Mackaill—we weren't exactly alike. And the Orchid Lady, Corinne Griffith—we didn't play the same parts, either. So I chose First National and I stayed with them for four years.

When I signed a contract with First National, I became a star. I had a five-year contract with them. Most of the gals had those but there was a catch to it. It was for forty weeks a year and when you didn't work, you didn't get paid. I was in New York on a little vacation when I met the man who was the head of First National then. I've forgotten his name—he wasn't there very long. I told him, "Look, I know that I'm making money for you. I love to work and I'll work as many hours as you want me to. But I would like a fifty-two week a year contract."

He said, "Well, see me when we get back to Hollywood."

And when we got back here, I went right up to his private office at the studio and said, "Okay, I'm here about that contract." He turned around, got my contract out, tore it up and gave me a fifty-two week a year contract. So they thought I was good, didn't they?

Shortly after I had made some pictures for First National, I had had some time free. That's when I wanted to go back to New York for that little vacation and say hello to my friends and everything—after all, I was born there. Then I thought, "Oh, I think I'll go up and see Mr. Ziegfeld and say hello to him." I went up—I might have shaken hands with him—and said, "Hello."

He told me that they were just starting a new *Ziegfeld Follies* and he said, "We're going to Atlantic City for the tryout. Would you care to come and see how it's done?"

I said, "Why, I'd love to. I think it would be perfectly wonderful."

I had a gal friend there for a companion and we went to Atlantic City—probably on the train. I remember we sat up in the theatre's balcony and watched what they were doing on the stage. It was very interesting—I had never seen how a show started. Then Mr. Ziegfeld came and sat down in the next seat to me. This was after he and Marilyn Miller had had such an awful quarrel—I didn't know anything about that then. So it was a big surprise to me when he said, "We have decided to make you the star of this *Follies.*"

Well, I didn't want to be the star of the *Follies.* It would have been ridiculous because I'm not a singer and I'm not a professional dancer. I was in

With Gilbert Roland in *The Love Mart.*

motion pictures where I wanted to be and fortunately, I was able to tell him the truth. I said, "Oh, I'm so sorry, Mr. Ziegfeld, but I am under contract, I am starring and I can't make any other commitments." I thanked him very much. He was very proud that I had made the grade. As a matter of fact, when I first came out here, he had given me two letters of introduction, one to Jesse Lasky who was the head of Paramount and one to Mr. Brulatour whom I had never met before—he was the head of everything. Well, I never gave them the letters, I never went to them—in fact, I still have the letters. Mr. Ziegfeld mentioned when I saw him this time that they hadn't written him anything about the letters and that they hadn't received them. I explained why I didn't go to see them. But it was very kind of him to write them.

I was starred in a series of pictures at First National including *An Affair of the Follies* and *American Beauty.* It was always a pleasure working out there but I don't really remember any of the stories. After all, if you make more than fifty pictures, you can't remember all of them. You just finish one, you make another one. I do recall *The Love Mart* directed by George Fitzmaurice was a very pleasant picture to work in. That's the one where they thought I was a mulatto and they were going to sell me to work for people. Later on, I found out that I wasn't a mulatto at all. Gilbert Roland was my leading man and I remember his picking me up and carrying me across the cobblestones because they were wet.

I'd never forgotten the wonderful lesson I'd learned when I didn't get the part in the Lillian Gish picture. One time after I'd signed up with First National, I thought I was going to play in a goody directed by Alexander Korda, *The Private Life of Helen of Troy.* It was just the part for me and absolutely everybody raved about it. They all said I was it. But they looked at me and they kept saying, "Well, you never seem to be smiling about this."

I said, "Look, I haven't been assigned to the part yet. My philosophy is to wait till I'm actually doing something and then you'll see smiles out on me if I happen to get the part." Well, I didn't get it. He had his wife, Maria Corda, do it. I wasn't disappointed—that didn't make any difference to me. So that's a good bit of philosophy to follow. Then Korda used me for four pictures after that because his wife didn't make it in Hollywood.

With Paul Lukas in *The Night Watch.*

When we were filming, we'd have a little orchestra of about three pieces on the set that would just play anything. You'd rehearse and you'd have to learn the whole script. Although the pictures were silent, you'd have to know exactly what the script told you to say because there were lip-readers in the audience. You couldn't fake it—I mean you couldn't play a love scene and then joke on the side. But I was very earnest and working all the time. I went to the rushes every day. That was the thing everybody did to see the work you did the day before and to find out how you were doing and how you were connecting one day with the other.

In those days, I had my picture on the cover of every motion picture magazine. Clara Bow had the most fan-mail of everybody in Hollywood, I was second, and then one summer, I beat her. I have a letter the Burbank postmaster gave me and it says I received in one month inclusive thirty-seven thousand, three hundred and twenty letters—that's more than a thousand letters a day. I don't think they were writing to the president very much in those days so Clara and I probably had more mail than anybody in the world.

I never thought I was particularly prettier than anybody else. But the story went around that if you asked any man you ran into who was the most beautiful girl in the world, he'd say "Billie Dove." I thought, "Well, the publicity man put that out." But I finally heard it so often and in such different places that I started to wonder about it way later. When I was younger—I'll put it that way—I was pretty but I never thought that I was better-looking than any other girl I worked with. That never occurred to me.

With Antonio Moreno in *Adoration.*

Women began copying my hairdos. I had first cut it straight around like Colleen Moore in her pictures. Then I fooled around with it and put it behind my ears. And then I went to the beauty shop and said, "I want a shingle." But they didn't know what I was talking about so I finally had to go to a barber and say to him, "Would you mind cutting the back of my hair like you cut a man's, only not that short?" And that was how I got my shingle. Mary Astor was the very first actress who copied me—the exact hairdo but I had it first. And I got a letter from a hairdresser who was a fan. He wanted to thank me for cutting my hair because, as he said, "You brought me more people who wanted a Billie Dove haircut. However, there were a couple of women who were disappointed when I finished with them. They said, 'Well, we don't look like Billie Dove.' "

After I became a star, I couldn't shop anymore because I was surrounded so much by people. I'd go to a tailor, to his home where he lived with his wife and their child, a boy. I hated to shop anyway and he had a figure of me. When I'd order a very simple, long dress, I'd get six of them made in different colors—very plain but of beautiful fabrics. And the shoe man knew my size. I'd call him up, tell him what I needed and he'd come out with a whole bunch of shoes in boxes.

At the First National studio in Burbank, I had a suite with a kitchen, a walk-in closet, a sitting room and a dressing room. Dick Barthelmess had the suite next to mine. We were near the tennis court. We didn't have any hours at the studio. You had to do a certain day's work and if you didn't finish by six o'clock, you stopped working and you had to go to the cafeteria for dinner. Then we'd work from seven until twelve o'clock at night—we had to finish that day's work. Then, of course, I had to go take a shower, take my make-up off and everything, drive home and get up at five o'clock in the morning to go all the way back to the studio.

With her 1928 Cadillac town car in front of her dressing room at First National. (Billie Dove Collection, Courtesy of Paul Melzer.)

One night, we had stopped working at twelve o'clock as we often did. It was probably my gal's day off since I was alone. I was driving home in the closed car that I had then when a man in another car began following me. Nobody else was on the road this night. The two of us were coming down from the hill and he was trying to push me into the mountainside. But I kept driving faster and faster so he wouldn't catch me. I was a good driver and I could drive as fast as he could or faster. Finally, we got to civilization and I got down on Hollywood Boulevard in front of the Pantages Theatre. That was on my side of the street and I stopped there. But he parked there, too. I saw him getting out of his car so I got back in mine and started it up. He followed me in his car and I just drove like crazy. I parked my car by the police station and that was a smart thing to do. Oh, brother, he didn't want any of that. I don't know where he went but he didn't come my way again.

In those years, I loved to work so I didn't want days off or anything. But I was getting only a couple of hours' sleep so very often, I'd just stay overnight at the studio. Near my dressing room, I had a bed and my companion-maid, Mary Fitzpatrick, would sleep on a couch in the sitting room. I finally moved out to the Valley to be closer to the studio. I took a big house there and it was perfectly wonderful. I had very good help and—oh, I hate to talk money but I paid twelve hundred dollars a month for it. Finally, my time was up and I wanted it for something like another nine months or another year. The owners came to look at it and they gasped and said, "Oh, my God!" They had never seen it that way before—it was so clean and so neat. Instead of charging me twelve hundred dollars, they gave it to me for nine hundred. They made the suggestion—I didn't. Later, when I gave it up, Adrian, who was married to Janet Gaynor, bought it. They lived in it for a

In her new Lincoln coupe. (Billie Dove Collection, Courtesy of Paul Melzer.)

while and then they sold it. It was so big that the new owners divided it and made it into two houses.

After I'd been with First National for a while, I bought two Cadillacs. I had custom-made a Cadillac limousine in a beautiful shade of light blue on the outside and gray on the inside. The chauffeur drove in the open part and I was inside with a telephone in which I spoke to him. Everybody admired the car so much. Carl Laemmle, Jr. admired it too much. He had it copied and then every place that he'd go, people would say to me, "Oh, you were with so-and-so last night, weren't you?" It wasn't me at all. It was Carl Laemmle, Jr. Then on the chauffeur's day off, I had a Cadillac convertible for me to drive. That was a fine car, too.

I have a great love for dogs and when I was at First National, I had Beau, a black poodle who was smart and wonderful. When I'd get in the limousine to go to the studio, he'd sneak in the car, too. And he was right there with me when I'd get out to go to my dressing room. He'd go under my dressing table like he was sound asleep—ha, ha, ha! He wouldn't hear us calling him at all until the chauffeur gave up and left. Then he'd open his eyes and walk around the room. He was able to stay with me the whole day. He lived to be seventeen and a half. He was blind and deaf then but I could have my house full of people, he would go around smelling them and finally, he would end up at my feet where I was sitting.

All of us actresses, the ones who were starting out, had a club. We had our little meetings at somebody's house and we brought our sewing and our needlepoint. Nobody drank anything or smoked in those days. Sometimes the actresses' boyfriends would come in later about ten-thirty or so and the hostess had a buffet with a little cold something to eat on the table. Mary Pickford was our honorary president. She never came to the meetings but she invited us up to her place one time. I didn't know her really well but she was darling.

The parties at Pickfair were lovely. I still have a telegram in which Doug and Mary invited me to a party for Lord and Lady Mountbatten. I don't remember if I went but I've never forgotten their party for Prince George of England. George Landy was the head of publicity at First National but I was getting so much mail that a girl in the publicity department who called herself my secretary was handling it. If somebody well-known would want a picture of me, she'd come over with the picture, the ink, and the pen, I'd autograph it and she would take it. One day, my so-called secretary came on the set with a letter from Mary Pickford and Douglas Fairbanks's secretary inviting me to a party at Pickfair for Prince George. It was to be a cozy supper ten o'clock at night and the letter said that the only request he made was that Billie Dove be there. When I met him, he asked me whether I knew the people there. Of course I did—they were all motion picture people. He didn't bring an ingenue. He said, "Well, can't we get away and go on the town?" I told him I was sorry but I was with an escort. Irvin was my escort but I didn't dare tell the prince that he was my husband. I guess people entertained Prince George after that. I'm not sure but there were a few of us who had our pictures taken together. They said that we entertained him. Well, I didn't entertain him. But I danced with him a lot that night and he was very charming.

Marion Davies was a very good friend of mine. I can't imagine Marion without a smile on her face all the time. She never looked unhappy to me, never, and it was a pleasure to go to the ranch. I spent an awful lot of time up there at San Simeon. They would call you and find out whether you were working over the weekend.

Naturally, you would go because it was fun up there. You had a choice of two trains depending upon when you had finished working. If you had only one hour, you would take what was left there

Billie with three of her dogs. (Billie Dove Collection, Courtesy of Paul Melzer.)

at Glendale. If there were two women in your party, you had a compartment on the train, if two men, you had a compartment, and if you were married, you had a drawing room. Then you got off, I think, about twelve o'clock at San Luis Obispo and it took about two hours to get up to the Castle. There was a line of limos and Mr. Hearst never bought the limos—he always rented them. You got into one of those. There was two to a limo and no baggage. The baggage had to go separately and then we went to the bottom of the hill. You'd look up and see this beautiful castle—it was gorgeous. There was a fence all around the bottom of the mountain and then a road going up, of course. But you'd have to go fifteen miles an hour because there were animals. The animals that got along together were in the first partition. Then the driver would get out. First of all, he checked in with the man at the gate as to who you were and whether you were invited. Then you came to the first fence. The driver would get out, open it up, run the car through, get out again and close it. Then there would be that next partition with the other animals that would get along together. But now if one of the animals decided to just lie down in the middle of the road, you could do nothing to that animal. You couldn't honk the horn, you couldn't do anything. You had to wait until he decided to get up. Mr. Hearst would not allow you to touch the animals. Then you got up to the top side and there they had the ostriches. When you went out to ride, you kept away from them because they didn't like the horses.

When I stayed at San Simeon, I had Cardinal Richelieu's room in one of the guest-cottages and we had a double bed in there. I didn't like sleeping in the Castle, though, and I didn't have to except once. I never could go to their other place, Wyntoon. Every time Marion and Mr. Hearst asked me to, they'd say, "Are you working this weekend?" And I'd have to say I was which was terrible. I can't remember if Irvin ever went with me to San Simeon but he went to one party at Marion's house on the beach in Santa Monica. He couldn't swim and Hearst was showing him how which I thought was amazing.

I was there when the statues at the Castle were draped with women's underwear. The men who thought they were funny got the women's garments, the bras and the little things below, and they were waiting for him to come and laugh. They were all hiding and finally, Mr. Hearst came home. He looked around at his statuary and just stared at them and never said a word. He just walked right by them. Oh, brother, when he got out of sight, everybody just ran and took the things off as fast as they could. It was so funny all the boys who were there thought he'd laugh at it but he didn't. He did not think it was funny at all.

Bebe Daniels was another good friend of mine. I spent part of my life down there at her house on the beach in Santa Monica. She was a great gal, absolutely wonderful, she and her mother Phyllis who was there all the time. We knew each other so well that one time they stopped at my house in Hollywood. Bebe said she had this very bad cold and could they stay at my house that night instead of going to their beach house. I said, "Of course," and showed them the room where they were to stay—we were that friendly.

With Marion Davies in a publicity photo for their film, *Blondie of the Follies.* (The Kobal Collection.)

Bebe was in love with Jack Pickford and her studio stopped that. She didn't tell me about it but she then announced her engagement to Charlie Paddock, the runner who was known as the fastest human on earth. He was a very good friend of mine and, of course, so was Bebe. Anyway, she wasn't really engaged to Charlie Paddock although he didn't know how she felt. It was really a tough position that I was in because I knew she was in love with Jack Pickford but I couldn't tell that to Charlie and I wouldn't do that to Bebe. But that was the case. The studio made her get off of her relationship with Jack Pickford—she had to do it. I didn't know him or anything about him. I don't know what he was taking—drugs, I think—but he was doing something that he shouldn't be doing. Later, of course, Bebe married Ben Lyon who was one of my leading men. They were very happy and they did a wonderful job working together in England, I understand.

Joan Crawford and I were friends, too—I think maybe before she even changed her name from Lucille Le Sueur. She was very much in love with a boy of the Heinz family and they threatened to disinherit him if he married her. She used to come over and cry on my shoulder. She really did care about him and that made her very unhappy. We saw each other periodically over the years. When I was married to Bob Kenaston, we went to a party and she asked us to come by her house and have a liqueur on the way home so we did. That's when she owned practically a whole block. Then we saw her again in Hawaii. Of course, by that time she was quite the lady and very much a star. But when we'd get her alone, she'd break down and talk the way we usually talked. I always gave her credit

With Ben Lyon in *The Tender Hour.*

because for what she started out with to become as big as she became, why, I thought she did really a great job of it.

Ruth Roland and I were friends for years. In fact, I was one of her bridesmaids when she married Ben Bard. I was still seeing her after I'd married Bob and left pictures. We were living on Amalfi Drive in Pacific Palisades and one day when I wasn't in, Ruth drove up to my house in her car. She came by herself to see me. It was quite a walk to get to my door. She opened her car door, got out and walked part of the way but then went back. She couldn't make up her mind whether to go to my door so she went back and forth to her car several times. She told me later, why, that's silly that she did this. Finally, she decided she'd go all the way up the walk. My police dog, Boy, whom Bob and I kept as a watch dog was lying on the porch in front of my door. He was getting suspicious when he saw Ruth going back and forth and when she came up to the house, he jumped up and nicked her on the arm but he didn't really bite her. He didn't draw blood and no mark was left on her arm. When she told me about this afterwards, she asked me, "Are you insured?" I said I was so she sued me. She wouldn't have sued if I hadn't been insured so she got the money from my insurance and we settled out of court. She was a nice gal and we were still friends. But the papers exaggerated the story and the hard part for me was that, due to the publicity, we had to send the dog out to a ranch. That almost broke my heart because I love dogs.

I met Greta Garbo on several occasions and she was just as natural as she could be. I saw her one time I think at Bebe's house. And I remember meeting her when there was a party at the Biltmore. All of the picture people who were there respected her privacy. It was when we were leaving the party and waiting outside for our cars to be brought around that she said to me in a low voice, "My name is Garbo." And I responded in a similar tone of voice, "My name is Dove."

The last time I saw her was during the war. My husband was stationed with the army at Newport Beach and we had bought a new boat, the darndest, funniest thing—almost like a rowboat. It had just one seat in the front and one seat in the back. Of course, we all had docks at Newport and anybody could run this little thing—even the kids could run it. The people who ran the opera up in San Francisco, a darling, wonderful couple—he was a commissioned officer—called up and said

With Rudolph Valentino in a 1925 publicity photo. (Courtesy of Billie Dove Kenaston.)

they had Greta Garbo over there with Valentina, the designer. They wanted to know if we'd come over there and take them around the harbor. We couldn't go out on the ocean, of course. So we went over and picked them up. Garbo and I sat in the back and talked. And we showed them all the houses and all the things around there near the harbor. She was so natural and just darling with no make-up—I mean, just a grand gal. I wouldn't call her naive but she was completely unself-conscious.

I met Rudolph Valentino when we had our picture taken and they used that for publicity. I had the magazine *Screenland* under my arm and I was supposed to be interviewed by them. But they gave me a column for publicity's sake because I liked to write. So I interviewed him for *Screenland* and then they put that picture of us in with my interview in the magazine. I never worked with Valentino in a picture but I remember he was just a perfect gentleman.

Another publicity story that appeared in a lot of magazines was that I had a particular interest in brain surgery. But that was just one thing that happened. I think my mother was ill and I was dressed in white for the hospital. Somebody went out there and mistook me for a nurse. I was interested in medicine and I still am. They had me go in to see one operation and it was a brain thing but I didn't stay long. Make nothing of that at all—it doesn't count. They exaggerated it for the magazines.

I'd mentioned that my father didn't come with us when I signed with Metro. In fact, my parents had legally separated before I got into show business. They never quarreled in front of me or my brother and all of a sudden, they were in court. But they never divorced—it was an amicable separation. My father and I often had dinner together. He knew that I loved pictures but he didn't know that I had worked in films or even that I was in the *Follies.* He didn't believe in women getting into show business. He'd say to me, "If you ever get into a crowd of theatrical people, get out as fast as you can. They're bad!" He feared it would change me. But one evening after we'd had dinner, I took him to the New Amsterdam Theatre to see the pictures of the *Follies* stars on the easels in the lobby. There were Eddie Cantor, Fannie Brice, W. C. Fields, Will Rogers and at the end there was a picture of me. I wonder what was going through his mind when he saw his daughter's picture with this odd name he'd never heard before—"Billie Dove." I told him how it had happened and when he realized I hadn't changed, he never again said I shouldn't be in show business. He loved me and he was so proud of me. He put a lot of time into keeping a beautiful scrapbook of my career.

My brother Charles came out to California after he got out of military school and he became a motion picture cameraman—a very good one. He lived with my mother for a while in a house on Fountain Avenue. All of his friends came there—boys like Arthur Lake and Rex Bell—and every one of them was successful in films. Then Charles married a girl who became like a sister to me. I had gotten a bungalow in the foothills and I told them they could live in it. And they moved there for a while.

My mother and I had always stopped to say hello to my father when we were in New York. He'd meet us at the train even if it was a five-minute stop for us. When my brother and his wife found

With John Gilbert at a party. (Courtesy of Billie Dove Kenaston.)

another place to live, I wrote my father, "What are your chances for coming out here? Bring your toothbrush and your comb. That's all you have to worry about. The house is all furnished and ready for occupancy."

He wrote back, "My dream come true." So he moved out to the bungalow in California. I remember he got a Tin Lizzie as they called them and took such good care of it. He did my bookwork and kept track of my income tax, for instance. He and my mother continued to have amicable relations and would often see each other. His birthday was on September 13 and my mother's on September 15 so I would have a joint celebration for them on September 14.

I had had an amicable separation of my own from Irvin when I realized that something was missing from our marriage. Of course, when he'd had to leave to go on location or something, I'd pack his bag and put in a note saying "I love you." I remember we had only two arguments. He never had a sip of coffee. The help would serve him Sanka and serve me coffee. Once they made a mistake. They gave him the coffee and gave me the Sanka. He got madder than hell and blamed it on me. Another time was when he caught me smoking in the bedroom. I don't know how it happened but I found myself on the floor. But we never had any big fight. Still, it wasn't a passionate love affair. So we had a sensible agreement to separate and I went to live with my mother in the house on Fountain Avenue.

Meantime, I continued to star in pictures. When sound came in, First National merged with Warner Brothers and they took a very long, long voice test of me. I had two years to go on my contract but they were optional. One year they could keep me or they could let me go. When I finished the test, instead of doing that, they tore up my contract and gave me a straight two-year contract. I thought that was great since they didn't have to do that. But I think they must have liked me for talkies.

Careers with Antonio Moreno was the first talking picture I did. We were just about to make that when talking pictures came in so we had one scene talking, the next scene silent, the next scene talking, the next one silent. No one ever remarked on it or paid any attention to it. We never thought talking pictures would last, you know.

With Noah Beery in *Careers.*

I remember we did a scene with sound where I was talking through my tears. Noah Beery was the heavy in *Careers.* He was a wonderful actor and very nice to work with. In this scene, he was seated at a desk and I was pleading for my husband. I think that probably Beery was after me. The worse it got for me, the more he'd smile. The director rehearsed us and then said, "Here you start to cry." I said "yes" but I didn't cry in the rehearsal. Always you have different cameras all over the place. There were cameras on the topside, there were cameras on Beery, there were cameras on me, there was a camera on both of us, there was a camera on the whole stage and then they'd break them up when they were filming. So we started the scene and we were supposed to go through a certain part of it. Well, we came to the part where I was pleading and he was laughing and everything. I don't even know that I got on my hands and knees—I'm not sure—but all of a sudden, tears got into my eyes and then I pled and pled and pled. They started to drop down my face, I pleaded more and more and tears just kept rolling down. This went on and the director didn't stop when he was supposed to. It was supposedly very long for a motion picture—either five or ten minutes without a break. And I was crying that whole time, really sobbing, saying my lines through the tears and no stop. I ended up at the other side of the stage, we finished and everybody broke into applause—all the grips and the people behind the camera, the people that were up with the lights topside, everybody on this was clapping. I'll never forget that scene as long as I live. But the director didn't even look at us. I don't know whether he was touched by the scene or why he never looked at us at all. He got up on the other side of his chair and said, "Print it." Then he walked out of the stage and closed the door. We didn't have a second take or anything.

At that time, there was an indivisible line between the stars and the public. All the professional people stayed together so they could let their hair down and have some fun instead of having people come up and say, "Could you sign this for Aunt Susie? She's crazy about you," and then you're on again. So always the people in pictures would go someplace where we could be together. There was a Mayfair Club that was very nice, the Ritz-Carlton in New York and the Biltmore here in Hollywood. I was at a party at the Biltmore one evening when Marion Davies brought a man across the floor over to the table to me and she said, "Billie, Howard Hughes asked to meet you." But he was deadpan and looked at me stiff-faced like a statue. I don't know whether he spoke even. I tried to make polite conversation and there was nothing, nothing. He was absolutely blah. He didn't smile. He just kept looking at me and I thought, "Good God! Is this the guy they're talking about who's making a famous picture, *Hell's Angels,* and is the heir to eighty-four million dollars? Is this the one they're all talking about?" I was glad when he left the table.

After that, knowing him later, I'm sure he had me cased because every time I went out someplace where there was music and dancing, the door would open at some part of the evening and in came Howard. He'd stand there, look all around the room at the tables and find the spot where I was sitting. No matter how many people or how few, he'd come over to that table, draw up a chair, sit down and spend the rest of the evening with me. Brother, he knew every place that I was. Then I got to know him and found out that he was brilliant, that he was charming and had a lovely sense of humor. We laughed together and then we fell in love. That's how it happened. He was very much in love with me, very, very, very much and I was in love with him.

Howard and I went together for three and a half years and ours was a very simple life. It wasn't a seething affair—it was really ordinary but lovely and peaceful. My mother and I lived together not too far from Howard's house—I'd say a mile. We would go to Marion Davies's and Hearst's place but he didn't care for a lot of parties or anything. The things that we did together were very simple—not the crazy things that you read about now. I didn't know that Howard Hughes at all.

Howard had chartered a fifty-foot boat and the captain went with it. When we went sailing on weekends, I would always take with me one of three people—my mother, my best girlfriend or my companion-maid. When Howard and I weren't both working, we'd go on Saturday morning and we'd come back on Monday morning. We would take a little dinghy and go ashore on Catalina where we would eat at these little places there. We had a couple of little horses there, Maggie and Jimmy, and we'd just ride up the island and look over the other side. We enjoyed it very much but we wanted to go in the mornings when it was calm and not return at all in the afternoon because it was stormy.

One time, one of us had to work on Monday so we had to go home on Sunday afternoon. We got aboard and the three of us were talking when all of a sudden, a storm came up. The waves were getting as high as the boat and it was just awful. I was scared inside but I didn't want them to know it. I didn't want to say anything so I just stood up and said, "I think I'll go up and say hello to the captain for a while." Just as I went out, a big wave came up and it was higher than the boat. It tipped the boat over sideways just like when a sailboat goes down

With Walter Pidgeon in *Her Private Life.*

and it knocked me down and started to slide me off the boat. Nobody—not even Howard wherever he was—could possibly have saved me. But the captain happened to see me sliding off. He left his wheel for a second, grabbed me by the ankle, pulled me back into the boat and got back to the wheel. Then I think I got up and went to wherever Howard was and sat down. Now I never told Howard about it but there was no way possible that he could not have seen me because the boats all had glass around them. But he never said a word and I didn't, either.

The next weekend, Howard said to me, "Billie, I want you to meet some friends of mine." Now he never introduced me to any of his friends because he was so possessive and I'd never met any of them. So we got into the boat and went over to Catalina. Finally, we came to this big boat that was about two hundred feet long where he said he wanted me to meet these people. The captain was there with his crew, they let down this little ladder and we got on board. And oh, it was so beautiful, that whole rear end of the boat. It was big, big, big. You could barbecue there, you could dance there, you could get sun, you could fish, you could do anything. There were white cushions that were water-proof all the way around—it was just wonderful. Then we went into this salon and it was gorgeous, too, just beautiful. It had a piano and a phonograph and it was lovely just being in there.

The captain said, "Well, by the way, wouldn't you like to see the rest of the boat?"

And we said, "Yes, we'd just love to see it." He took us in and we saw the rest—the galley with the men working and the dining room with brass all the way around it. The whole thing was just exquisite. Then we went back to the salon and the people hadn't arrived. Nobody said anything about it because that would be rude. We just waited and finally Howard looked at me and said, "Well, what do you think of it?"

I said, "Oh, Howard, it's the most beautiful thing I ever saw."

And he said, "Okay, it's yours." That's the way he bought the boat. It was called the *Hilda* but we didn't like the name. I was making a picture called *The Painted Angel* at the time and my name in it was Rodeo. I think I was supposed to be a young Texas Guinan in it. So we always called the boat *Rodeo*.

This swimsuit photo appears on a German card of the late 1920s.

I was with Howard when his picture, *Hell's Angels,* had a big opening in Hollywood. There was a post-premiere party for him. I didn't invite the press or anything else which I probably should have but I was thinking just about giving him a party and, after all, I didn't know what they did out here. I was the hostess. I had the orchestra leader, Gus Arnheim, for the night and we took over the Montmartre. There were a hundred and twenty-five people there and the party was a success. At the Montmartre, they had these great big louvers and big leather-back booths—several people would fall into them. Being hostess, I went from booth to booth and just said "How do you do" and this and that with everybody else.

I had invited Mr. Ziegfeld and his wife, Billie Burke, to come to the party. We didn't have much time to talk but that was the last time I saw Mr. Ziegfeld and the first time I met Billie Burke. She was very charming. I met her again at a party after Mr. Ziegfeld's death. I know that if we talked about him, I would have said, "I'm so sorry to hear about Mr. Ziegfeld." We were talking very amiably and she said, "You know, I must tell you. You are the only girl in the world who I have ever been jealous of in my life." But she was very, very nice and when she told me that, it was in a very kindly way. She would not have said that to me if she had thought there was anything going on between Mr. Ziegfeld and me. There wasn't anything, of course, and I think she probably realized that then.

I haven't checked my years but I've always been under the impression that Howard was divorced when we met because I don't remember his getting a divorce when we were going together. I heard this woman he had married seemed to be bitter towards me and I always felt so kindly towards her. I thought that Howard did the same thing that I had done. He had gotten married too young. His father and mother died when he was young and he married the daughter of their best friends. I always had heard that she was such a lovely girl and I was so sorry that I had missed meeting her—I always said that. I heard she was in love with him but they had just married too young.

Irvin wouldn't give me a divorce. That story about the money is true. Howard gave him three hundred and twenty-five thousand dollars to let me divorce him and that's a hell of a lot of money, especially in those days. I begged Howard not to but there was nothing I could do once he gave the money to Irvin. I felt like I'd been bought and sold. I lost all my respect for Irvin. In fact, I tore his name out of my scrapbooks. But Howard and I were still very much in love and I told him, "I'll go to Las Vegas for six weeks and establish residence there."

He said, "What, you go to Las Vegas? Without me?"

I said, "Well, yes. Then I'm free to divorce him."

He thought about it for a while and then later on, he came to me and said, "Billie, get Mary. Tell her to buy you a dress, very plain and long, something that a farmer's wife would wear, and get some horn-rimmed glasses and some little thing for the top of your head." I didn't question him so I told Mary, my companion, and she got them.

The day came and I put those clothes on. I had no make-up at all, no lip rouge but horn-rimmed glasses, my hair pulled back straight, a little something on my head, a very plain dress and ordinary shoes—nothing fancy. We were going on a train and I carried a small valise. We usually drove in his car—of course, he had a medium-priced car. As you know, he never carried any money, not even change, and he made that known. If he wanted to telephone, he'd send you down for the change and everybody knew that. This time, he went in my car. I had a chauffeur and Howard came and picked me up. He had plain glasses on and this little floppy hat and ordinary clothes. You wouldn't

With Jack Holt in a lobby card for *Wanderer of the Wasteland.* (Courtesy of Jim Knuttel.)

take him for Howard Hughes and you wouldn't take me for an actress, believe me. We went within walking distance to the train, my chauffeur let us out and we told him what time to meet us there and what day. Then Howard and I went our own ways until after we'd gotten on the train. Of course, nobody would recognize us—we looked entirely different. Then when we were together again on board the train, Howard told me, "We're going to Nevada but you're not going to Las Vegas." What I got out of it was that we were going to get off at this tiny little station. Nobody else got on or off but we did and you could see nothing around. I don't know the name of this place or anything else.

Then we got into a car and were driven quite away out into the desert. Finally, we came to this farmhouse. There was another building or something next to it that they had for my residence. Why I don't know because Howard couldn't fly his plane there to come to see me—there was nothing but sand—and I couldn't leave because I was supposed to stay in Nevada. Of course, the person who told Howard about this place had never seen it. The building where I was to stay was a funny-looking thing, not half as large as your kitchen probably. I think maybe it was built to store food for the winter and then they abandoned it. I don't know—I never asked any questions of the farmer and his wife with whom we were staying. But the building was nothing but concrete. It had a place for a door but no door, it had a place on two sides for windows but no window.

We told the farmer and his wife that we were brother and sister. I've forgotten the names that we used but we had entirely different names. They were all prepared for what I don't know but we were to stay there. Howard had his room and I had mine. Now I'd never done any housework—I was always so busy working—but I would watch this woman, the farmer's wife. She was very busy putting up jellies, bread, vegetables and things like that and the man was busy outside doing work on the farm. I stayed with her, she would wash the dishes and I would dry them. Then we went to bed. I watched her and in the morning, tried to do exactly as she did. I went into Howard's room and fixed his bed and I hadn't made a bed in my life. Then I fixed mine up.

We worked as farmers for a couple of days before we went home. We didn't stay because it didn't work out the way we wanted. We did it all wrong and it would be another year before I got my final decree. But while I was there, I worked with the woman as a farmer's helper. The farmer and his wife were very lovely, very charming and hard-working. They never asked about what I was to buy or anything and I worked like I'd been used to doing these things all my life. Then Howard went outside with the men. I didn't see him until he would come in later on in the afternoon. We would go take a walk and that was all the time we'd spend together.

When it was time for us to go, they came to pick us up in the car. We left on the train where we sat together. But when we got off, we parted company. He went to one side and I went to the other. When you get off, there's a ramp coming from the train to the outside. We were walking up there and all of a sudden, we heard this racket and I almost passed out. Howard did, too. There were hundreds of people there just looking down at the train, waiting and almost cheering. And here we were trying to be so very careful. Finally, we got out and walked separately to where my car was waiting. We asked my chauffeur, "For heaven's sakes, what are all those hundreds of people doing there?"

And he said, "Well, the train that came in after you was carrying the president of the United States." Herbert Hoover it was then. I met him, incidentally, when I was in Washington, D.C. I was invited to visit the White House and I think the president was pleased to see someone who didn't want anything from him.

Howard was hard of hearing. I was never conscious of it but I always modulated my voice to a level he could hear. We went to Europe together to do something about his hearing. I took my companion-maid and we had a suite and he had a room. We went to London first and then around Europe. We received unfortunate news in Czechoslovakia where the best doctor in the world for ears was supposed to be. But we learned Howard's were incurable. It was something that was malformed and hereditary—his uncle Rupert Hughes had it, too—and they could do nothing about it.

As for the pictures I was making, I thought some were good but some of them I didn't like. I look

With Matt Moore and Chester Morris in *Cock of the Air.*

at those now and I know I wouldn't think they're wonderful. However, I suppose people thought otherwise in those days. I never said anything about the pictures at the time. They told me what to do and I made the picture period. I did one where Basil Rathbone played the violin, *A Notorious Affair,* and I thought that was a terrible picture. Basil was very nice, though, and so was Montague Love who played my father in it. I had known Monty in New York. There wasn't anybody I worked with that I didn't like.

I took singing lessons at this time like a lot of stars were doing then. Evidently I was doing all right because the teacher asked me if I wanted to have Howard come to listen to one of my lessons. So I had him come. But then a couple of lessons later, I finally asked her, "When are you going to lower my voice?"

She looked absolutely astonished and said, "Lower your voice! You are a natural soprano." That's supposedly really something but I couldn't stand sopranos then. They seemed to be screeching to me. So I never sang again.

After I left First National in 1931, Howard produced two of my pictures for United Artists. That was a crazy thing. He bought my contract and I didn't know it so I can't tell you whether he did just those two with me or some back before that. But it hadn't made any difference to me so what the heck? The first picture I did for Howard, *The Age for Love,* was no good—that was namby-pamby. Lois Wilson was in it. She was a wonderful girl and a friend of mine. We used to lunch together.

Then I made *Cock of the Air* and that was a good picture before they cut eighteen hundred feet out of it. It was a comedy and I didn't make comedies as a rule but this was very good. I was in France during the war and then I was taken out of France and put in Italy because I was disturbing the French army with my whims. I get spanked in it and the whole works. I squirt this bottled water or something into Chester Morris's face and it was really funny. I think "Milly"—Lewis Milestone—directed most of it. I recall George Cukor was called in to do just one scene where Chester and I were supposed to be talking and making no sense. Howard was very pleased with it before it was cut. We were splitting up at that time but he wired me about *Cock of the Air:* "You were great in it. I didn't know you could do it." Then Will Hays came into the picture and cut eighteen hundred feet out of it. Eighteen hundred feet! That's a lot of footage and it wasn't as good then. I don't know why they cut it. Maybe it was because my dresses were too low and there was cleavage or because Chester Morris was chasing me all through the picture and I would keep saying, "Later, later, later." But whichever it was, after they cut it, it didn't make any sense. One minute I'd be in France, one minute I'd be in Italy, and you wouldn't know where I was or why.

Howard, as the other girls have said, was very possessive. Oh, heavens, he wouldn't let me out of his sight. I was in love with him and I was the one who told him to go. But both of us still carried torches for one another. People have been so interested in knowing why we split up and I think it's none of their damn business. As Ol' Blue Eyes, Frank Sinatra, would say, "I did it my way." Well, I did this my way and it's my business why we broke up and nobody else's. It had nothing to do with any man or nothing to do with any woman—nothing at all. It was something personal but nothing important. It was really such a tiny thing that you wouldn't believe it if I told you.

After we had finished our romance, then all of a sudden, Howard turned into a womanizer and he was not like that at all when we were going together for three and a half years. Way later, I read in one of these tabloid magazines—I can't think of her name, but she was going with him and she said, "I hate it when he mentions his lovers." She said, "He must have been particularly interested in Billie Dove because there isn't one day goes by that he doesn't at least mention her name once." And at this point, here I was married with children.

Howard and I were very friendly when we ran into each other after we broke up but we didn't discuss ourselves at all. One time when we were both in New York, we had a lovely lunch in my hotel suite. Another time, we were at San Simeon and he asked me whether I'd like to fly back with him. I thanked him and said no. I thought I'd better go back on the train with the people that I came with. I'm glad I did because he had to make a forced landing in somebody's backyard on a ranch or something. And when he was in the hospital years later after that terrible plane accident, I called up the next morning to find out how he was. He was so touched that he sent me a telegram thanking me for my concern.

I never flew with Howard because I was scared to death of planes. But after we broke up, I took up flying. I didn't give a damn then. I went ahead and said, "Oh, the hell with it." I took flying lessons from the guy who flew his planes because he was a wonderful flier. He tested all of Howard's planes before Howard even bought them. So he was the one who taught me to fly. I didn't solo, though. I had finished my upper work, my figure eights and everything in an open Fairchild and the instructor was in front of me. We had sticks. Then we'd finish the tap work and I was on landings and take-offs. So we'd come down—he'd have his hand on the stick and I'd have my hand on my stick. If he wiggled his stick, it meant that he wanted to take over and that I wouldn't go touch mine—I'd just leave it alone.

Well, we were coming down one time doing the same thing over and over again and we crossed some fields. As we were taking off on the other side, I speeded up again and we went bang into what I thought was a hole. I thought, "Well, this is a crazy thing to have a hole on a strip like this" but I thought nothing more of it. Then I did the figure eights and whatever the heck I wanted to do he let me do. But as we were coming down, he wiggled his stick so I let mine go. Then as we came down, he stopped the plane which was unusual. Usually, we'd go right across. I'd go slowly and then give it the gas and speed up when I was taking off. But he landed the plane way out there on one side. Then he turned around to me and said, "We have a flat." We hadn't gotten into a hole—we had had a flat tire but he didn't tell me when we were in the air. We had to walk back to the hangar and that was quite a way. All the other aviators laughed at us—you know, walking back from an airplane ride. So I thought, "Well, I'll fix you."

The next time I went out, I had a pair of roller skates and I was just tossing them around. They thought it was a terribly funny gag that I should carry roller skates so this time I wouldn't have to walk home. They thought it was so funny that it got to the studio and, my God, I was in the middle of a picture. And did they stop me but fast!

My brother was taking flying lessons, too, and we vied. We had a bet on to see who would solo first. Well, of course, he made it and I didn't. I've flown as a passenger only a few times in my life. Once I went to New York and back several years ago and I've flown to the Hawaiian islands twice. But I don't like planes. I would have a cocktail before I went and the hell with it.

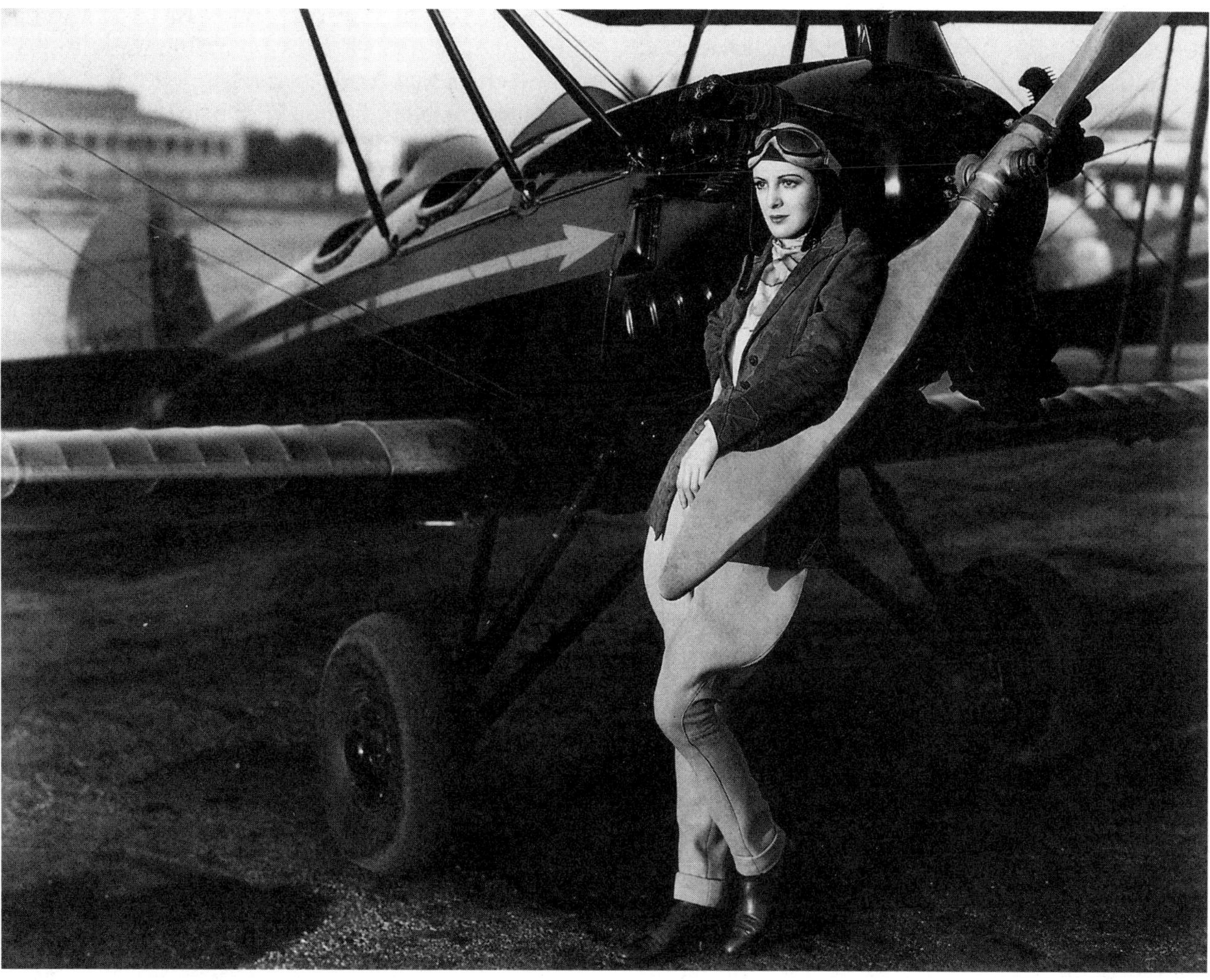

Billie when she was taking flying lessons ready for a hop in a speedy Fairchild 21 at the Metropolitan Airport near Hollywood. (Courtesy of Jim Knuttel.)

Jimmy Walker, the mayor of New York, was a friend of mine and I saw a lot of him whenever I went back there. He had been going with Betty Compton. He and his wife were Catholic and Betty saw that nothing would come of it so they broke up for a time. Howard and I had broken up, too, by this time. So Jimmy would pick me up on Mondays always at the Palace—they had a new show every week. We'd have a motorcycle escort in front of the car. We were very friendly and we did hold hands but there was nothing serious about it at all. We just liked each other and had lots of laughs and everything. When we were down in the aisle of the Palace, everybody would stand up and applaud. He was so popular—a great guy, wonderful guy. They tried to make something of it but then they realized that we didn't mind going together because there was nothing to it that way. They had quite a few pictures of us in the papers. He wanted me down at City Hall for a charity or something and he was holding a banner at one end and I was holding it at the other. I was his date for New Year's Eve and we took my mother, too—I mean, that's how we were. So he doesn't come into my life at all except as a very, very good friend.

I don't think I was unattractive but during my years in pictures, I was never accosted for a casting couch, you know. They respected me and I was always good friends with everybody. It was great and I had a lot of fun. But I met George Raft when I was still in pictures and many years later, he lied about me in a book written about him. I had read part of it in one of these tabloid papers and it said that Raft and I were going to go up to a room when somebody came and told him that Howard was in the hotel and so he didn't go up—one of those crazy things they write. Well, that made me mad—it certainly never happened. After this book came out, I was having lunch in a restaurant and Raft was there with a couple of his men. I got up, went over there and gave him hell in front of his men. Their mouths were agape really. I said, "What is this thing you're saying about me—that we were going to go to a room? Why do you tell such lies?" Oh, he couldn't say a word, believe me. He was just trying to bring my name into it but it wasn't true at all.

After Howard and I broke up, I started dating again. When I was taking flying lessons, a girlfriend of mine had asked me if I would like to go to the pier at Santa Monica with her and whether it was all right if she could have her boyfriend, Jack Kenaston, come over. I said yes but because Jack was not available at the time, his brother Bob came instead. Bob was very handsome and we began dating frequently. He was one of six brothers who inherited a small trust from his grandfather.

Not long after I met them, Bob and Jack took a trip around the world. Their grandfather had wanted them to travel. They had just returned to California but they had never been to New York. They asked me to go with them and have a lot of fun. I needed a vacation and I wanted to show them New York so I said, "If I have time to go with you, I will."

I made arrangements and I was about to leave for New York. My trunk had been put on the train and everything else when somebody called me and said Harry Cohn wanted me for a picture. We had already worked together so I didn't have to take a test or anything—he knew my work. I told the man on the telephone, "I'm terribly sorry but I'm leaving for New York tonight."

Well, in ten minutes, Cohn called back and said, "What's this I hear about your going back to New York tonight?"

I said, "Yes, Harry, I am."

He said, "Is that more important to you than making my picture?"

I said, "I'm awfully sorry but it is." And it was as important to me. I had a wonderful time with Bob and Jack in New York even though it was the time of the great bank failure. The management of the hotel gave me fifty dollars a day which I repaid later. The telephone operators and the other people in the hotel liked me so much that they later sent me a telegram saying they'd like me to consider the hotel my second home whenever I was back East. After a week in New York, the Kenaston boys and I got on board a boat that sailed through the Panama Canal Zone and ended up at San Francisco. I remember Dixie Lee Crosby and Sue Carol were among the other passengers on the ship.

Louella Parsons either liked you or she didn't. She liked me and she loved Howard. Howard had nothing to do with it but in 1932, she gave me a big birthday party at her house and it was filled with all studio people—upstairs, downstairs, outside, a beautiful, beautiful party. Edmund Goulding, the director, was there and he came up to me and said, "Billie, I've got the most wonderful part for you. It's just great."

He was raving about this part that would be perfect for me and I said, "Well, tell me about it. What is it?"

He said, "It's about you, Marion Davies and Robert Montgomery."

I said, "The three of us in the same picture?"

He said, "Yes."

I said, "Oh, no. Look, we're stars in our own right." That was the time when they did not have all-star casts as a rule and I wouldn't make a picture with two other stars. I wouldn't even read the script. But he kept trying, saying "It's wonderful," and I was not interested.

Later on at the party, Irving Thalberg came over to me. He was a quiet, darling little man—very, very sweet and everybody loved him. He had a script in his hand and he said, "Hi, Billie. Would you do me a favor?"

I said, "Well, if I can, I sure will."

He said, "Would you read this?"

I said, "Yes, of course, I will." I just took it and that night I read it. The next morning, I called him on the phone and said, "You've got your little lead. When do you want me to start?" It was the most wonderful part and I thought, "Oh, they were right when they said it's just for me and I'll be great

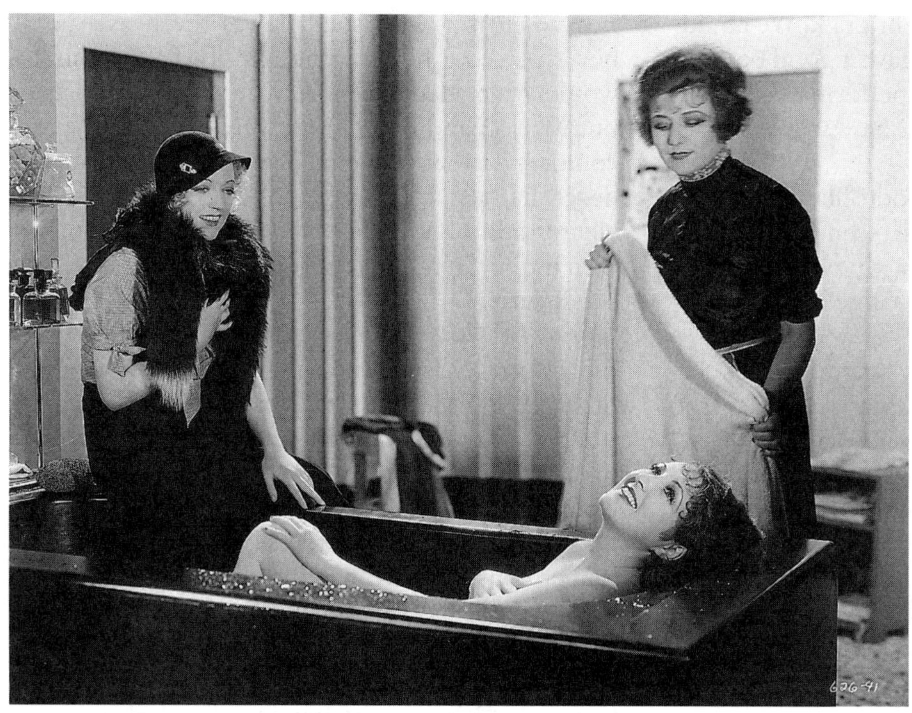

With Marion Davies in *Blondie of the Follies.* (The Kobal Collection.)

in it." I couldn't turn it down so I told him, "Yes, I'm delighted. I'll do it."

So I made *Blondie of the Follies* for MGM. Goulding was the director and he was really fine. In the story, Marion and I were sisters living in a tenement. I was the extrovert and she was the introvert. She was perfectly happy there but I wanted to get up and go and do something for myself. The part was just great, just wonderful—I was making everything run but she was playing a nothing. Her part was just terrible. Why they would give her such a sappy part, I don't know because she was a wonderful comedienne and a wonderful gal. In the picture, I couldn't get her to leave but pretty soon, I did. I came back all dressed up in fur and had a guy with me. He was keeping me evidently and everything else. I loved my sister but she only came with me when I came to get her. I said, "You're coming with me and I'm not taking 'no' for an answer. You're getting out of this tenement and you're going to make something of yourself." We took her along. I was in a show and I got her in the theatre, too. Then during one of the scenes, there was a chorus line with one girl, then two girls, then three girls, then four and by the time you get to those ten or so, it goes all the way around, comes back to that tenth girl, then the eleventh girl comes around, then the twelfth, then the thirteenth. Pretty soon, you have a long line not parallel to the audience. Now I am the last one with the exception of Marion who is the one girl left. She is supposed to come all the way around the chorus line and then take my hand. Well, my hand is ready, she comes up, misses it and falls into the orchestra. I am just beside myself. Here I loved her, I had gotten her into this and she has fallen and probably crippled herself.

We had made the whole thing with the exception of the last scene when she's in the hospital and I realize she's fallen in love with my guy so I give him to her. I would do anything for her and that even helps my part—it's just great. Now we're going to run the picture. It's all done except for that last part in the hospital. The cameraman is there, all the other players, the place is filled with people who are interested in the picture, and Hearst is there. We see it and when the end of the picture comes, nobody says a word—we just can't. Finally, it comes. Here is rotund Mr. Hearst, a wonderful guy. He's been my host up at San Simeon so many, many times and every time I went up there, he always acted as though I were doing him a favor by coming. He always spoke very quietly and out of his mouth comes, "Well, it's a good Billie Dove picture." This was why we couldn't talk. We could see it—it was my picture and I gave a good performance. I gave a damn good performance in it. Goulding couldn't say anything he was so embarrassed and so was Thalberg.

When Hearst said it was a good Billie Dove picture, we didn't make that last scene then. We stopped working for ten days with everybody on salary. They got writers in to change some of the scenes Marion and I had together and then they added some others. We had several weeks of reshooting. In the scene where Marion misses my hand completely, they took hands of two other people for inserts—I didn't even know about this until I saw the picture later—and they showed what was supposed to be my hand throwing her into the orchestra. It wasn't a mistake and it made a very bad heavy out of me. Of course, it just about broke my heart because I was really good in the picture. Anyone who was there can tell you that.

With Bob Kenaston. (Billie Dove Collection, Courtesy of Paul Melzer.)

But when it was finished, I was the heavy and I never played a heavy in my life. In fact, I think I would have sued when they changed the picture but Marion and Mr. Hearst were my friends and I couldn't do that to them. Thalberg said this would never happen again with an MGM picture but what I didn't know was that Hearst was putting his own money in it. I had thought MGM was the sole producer.

Blondie of the Follies turned out to be my last picture. Bob Kenaston and I fell in love and when we married in 1933, I retired from the screen. I was still in my twenties and I wanted to live as other people lived. I wanted a family and in those days, if you married that was all right but if you had a baby, then you were out of pictures because you were no longer considered romantic. Although I was terribly disappointed when they changed *Blondie of the Follies,* my leaving pictures had nothing to do with that at all. I had worked since I was a kid and I thought, "It's time at my age that I should get married and have a family." I wanted four children. I had two, a boy and a girl. It just doesn't exactly work out the way you planned. But Bob and I had years of happiness while we were raising the children. Bob's father had died before I met him but I became very close to his mother. She was a saint and she became a very good friend of my own mother, too.

John Ford had directed me in a picture called *The Fighting Heart* and my husband and I had dinner with him one time. They'd put up a playhouse for his children and we copied it. We made it look like our house—three rooms had miniature tile and the kitchen had running water and electricity with an electric stove. The governess had a wire with two plugs so that the children couldn't use the stove unless she was with them. Then it had a beam ceiling in the living room—everything was miniature—and the little bedroom where my daughter Gail could put the doll to sleep. They could put their toys back in the closet of that little room.

Each year, we had a different type of boat. We had a speedboat first—just a darling boat—and one of the studios called and asked if they could use it in a picture. This was during the war and my husband was with the army in the daytime at Newport Beach and not able to run the boat. The studio said they would pay us a hundred dollars a day so we said, "Sure, go ahead and take it." Some guy ran it into the rocks so they said they would pay to have it fixed. Well, you can't take a boat that's been busted at the bottom and try to run it so we just let it go. Then we got a bigger one, closed in at the front part and open at the back. When Bob had a hernia—in those days they put you to bed for three weeks—his brother came down on his furlough. He tried to run the boat into our dock and the tide was coming against us. The boat was so big he had an awful time and I figured that I wouldn't be able to run it, either. So we sold that and bought a little boat that was easy to run, the one we took Garbo around in.

Since my childhood, I'd been an avid reader. In New York when I went to the library, they would give me three books when I wanted them. Usually, you'd take out two but they got them back so fast, they automatically let me have three. Years later when we were living on Amalfi Drive in Pacific Palisades and the children were in preschool, I went to UCLA. I had so many things I wanted to take up but I took a course in creative writing from a wonderful teacher. When I was a child, I would write about corny things like Tarzan—really childish. Poetry always interested me—meter and rhyme were never a problem to me, ever. I take no credit for that. Rupert Brooke was my favorite poet. He was twenty-seven when he died in the war. All good writers say God-awful things you wouldn't believe it—just terrible. Rupert Brooke would write something like "And when I see you looking with adoring eyes at the stupid fool you've given your love to." Then he'd go on talking about the scars of someone you love and at the end, he said, "And you'll be dirty, too"—things like that, really sarcastic. Then you turn the page and read the most beautiful thing you've ever read in your life.

When I was taking this course at UCLA, we had poetry one week and, of course, that was nice for me. I was supposed to write a poem for the next week's homework. So I took one of Rupert Brooke's poems that was so beautiful. He had written that when he died, he would leave, not special things of his to people, but material things like wet roofs where the rain has just hit, you know—lovely things that he saw around him. Each one was different and separated by a semi-colon. So I just did one on that and then at the bottom, I wrote, "With apologies to Rupert Brooke," because I didn't use any of his words or anything but I used the semi-colon thing—I took the idea from him. When I presented that to the teacher, she read it to the class and at the end, she said, "You don't have to apologize to Rupert Brooke or anyone." She was a wonderful teacher, wonderful to work with.

So I began writing. I wrote something with my tongue in my cheek about cocktail parties sort of making fun of them and I sent it in to *The Saturday Evening Post.* Then another one I did was just the opposite. I was doing exactly what Rupert Brooke did because I loved him. I was published as Billie Dove Kenaston.

Later on, I was contesting and that was a different world entirely—another part of my life that was absolutely wonderful. I won over a hundred prizes—not all first prizes. But the one that was the most amusing was when I won first prize from Proctor and Gamble's for writing advertising for them in a contest. I did it under the name of Lillian Kenaston. The prize was to be a part in a movie and a trip, too, to Hawaii which Bob and I took. They were filming a picture there called *Diamond Head* and I was to be an extra in it. But they sent a paper in which you had to describe who was going to do it and all about that person. I wanted my son to write them about me and when they found out I was Billie Dove, they were very impressed. They took photographs and motion picture footage of me at the studio just to make it legitimate but the footage never actually appeared in the film.

I never returned to motion pictures although I had loved my work and it wasn't difficult at all for me, not hard at all. I never thought much about my being an actress. I wasn't trying to be the most wonderful actress in the world or anything. I didn't get bad notices. I don't think I was worthwhile enough to get notices. I was glad to get a job and glad to be in motion pictures and, as you know, I never had a representative or agent. I had more talent than I showed and I had more talent than I realized how to take hold of myself. But towards the end, I knew. I said, "Oh, I've just gotten hold of something." That's when that last picture was changed and I was made a heavy which was really too bad because I gave a damn good performance in it—I know I did. But then is when I wanted to quit because I wanted to have a family.

A portrait from her years at First National. The Kobal Collection.

A portrait from the late 1920s.

When you're up there on that film, you are that person completely all the time. You think the way that person thinks, you do what that person does and you're not acting. You're actually living it. And, of course, when you finish with her, you have to forget about her because you've gone on to the next one and now you're a different person. Then you want to be that person, you see.

I think the whole thing was misnamed. They should not have been called silent pictures because we talked when we made the film and the audience was silent watching it. So just the reverse is my thought—they should have been called talking pictures with silent audiences.

All these years, I've kept writing. I am a believer that it is not how many years you have lived that makes your age. I think it's what you have up in your brain and what you have here in your heart. Your world is made up of that—what you have absorbed in the time that you've lived, how much of it you use, how much good you've done and how much you have learned. This is my way of living.

Fay Wray

Among the passengers disembarking from the train at the Los Angeles station on a summer day in 1922 was a beautiful dark-haired, blue-eyed teenager. Accompanied by a young man, a family friend, she had come from Utah to escape the harsh winters and recover her health, never realizing that this journey would lead her to a career that one day would make her name known throughout the world.

Fay Wray was born on September 15, 1907, in Alberta, Canada. Years later, a fountain in Cardston, the town nearest her birthplace, would be named in her honor. When she was three, Fay and her family moved first to Arizona and then to Utah where she spent most of her childhood. One of six children, she knew hard times as the family struggled to survive after her parents separated. Fay, who had been in frail health since the great influenza epidemic of World War I in which she lost her cherished older sister, followed her guiding star to Hollywood when she was fourteen.

Like many actresses of the silent era, her first roles were in comedy shorts. Eventually, she played leads for Hal Roach's company, the studio which, along with Mack Sennett's, had done the most to bring about the golden age of silent screen comedy. However, unlike her idol, Mabel Normand, whom she had found "absolutely a delight to watch on the screen," she did not have the opportunity to play the clown in these shorts. Soon, she graduated to leads in western features at Universal, continuing to learn her craft as she awaited the opportunity to demonstrate her talent in a major role.

That opportunity came when Erich von Stroheim chose Fay for the feminine lead in his masterpiece, *The Wedding March,* which began filming in 1926. Von Stroheim said of his new find at the time:

> As soon as I had seen Fay Wray and spoken with her for a few minutes, I knew I had found the right girl. I didn't even take a test of her. Why? Because I select my players from a feeling that comes to me when I am with them, a certain sympathy you might call it, or a vibration that exists between us that convinces me they are right. I could not work with a girl who did not have a spiritual quality. . . . Fay has spirituality . . . but she also has that very real sex appeal that takes hold of the hearts of men.[1]

In *The Wedding March,* Fay plays Mitzi, a Viennese girl of the bourgeois class who becomes romantically involved with an Austrian prince portrayed by von Stroheim. Despite their great love, the Prince is forced by his parents to wed the crippled daughter of a wealthy manufacturer while Mitzi is married off to a vicious, lustful but prosperous butcher. As Mitzi, Fay conveys emotions ranging from tenderness and sweetness in her scenes with the Prince to rage and abhorrence when she is confronted by Schani. The contrast between Mitzi and the animalistic butcher Schani is an early manifestation of the "Beauty and the Beast" theme that would, in very different contexts, reecho in Fay's later work. For all the film's tragic denouement, the love scenes between the Prince and Mitzi serve to affirm love and the human spirit in the face of the world's corrupting materialism. *The Wedding March* would remain Fay's personal favorite and her role the one in which she felt she most fully expressed herself.

In 1927, while the film was still in production, Harry Carr, co-author of the script with von Stro-

A candid of Fay on the set of *The Wedding March* trying to get dry after being drenched during the rain scene. (Courtesy of Fay Wray Rothenberg.)

heim, introduced Fay to the public in an article for *Motion Picture Magazine:*

> This new von Stroheim discovery proves . . . to have brains—a lot. She is, in fact, one of the most remarkable personalities I have ever known in the movies. Miss Wray makes me think a lot of Lillian Gish. She has the same patient tolerance—the same understanding heart—the same level, fearless intelligence; and a gentle distinction and dignity. By the time von Stroheim finishes her training, little Miss Wray will probably be a great actress; in any case she is sure to be a fine woman.[2]

The Wedding March, however, would not be the first major production featuring Fay released to the public. When Paramount took over the distribution of von Stroheim's film, they also inherited her contract. The studio launched her as a new star in *The Legion of the Condemned,* William Wellman's notable 1928 follow-up to *Wings* with Fay as a World War I French spy caught up in a tempestuous love affair with aviator Gary Cooper. Paramount next cast her as the feminine lead opposite Emil Jannings in director Mauritz Stiller's last film, *The Street of Sin,* before finally releasing *The Wedding March* in the fall of 1928.

Although Fay felt the coming of sound destroyed a unique art, she successfully survived the change-over and appeared in a variety of talkies for Paramount. She thought some of her roles like the gangster's moll in Josef von Sternberg's *Thunderbolt* (1929) were not suited to her. Others she saw as giving her more range to develop character, such as *The Texan* (1930) in which, according to Mordaunt Hall of *The New York Times,* she "has never been more captivating than she is as Consuelo," the Hispanic heroine.[3]

Her work at Paramount had led to her marriage to John Monk Saunders in 1928. He was a talented screenwriter, a young man of great promise with impressive achievements to his credit and seemingly an even brighter future. His screenplays included the classic aviation epics *Wings* and *The Dawn Patrol.* One of the few times he ventured into the theatre was with the 1931 play, *Nikki.* Saunders modelled the title role on his wife. While the play closed after only six weeks, a drama critic for *The New York Times* wrote that "her quiet impersonation (of Nikki) in her Broadway debut is almost a lone gesture towards saving the evening."[4]

Fay and Saunders became part of the Hollywood set of the late twenties and early thirties. They lived in a Spanish-style home that King and Florence Vidor had built, complete with tennis courts, on Selma Avenue in Hollywood. They entertained frequently, their friends in the film colony coming for tennis and tea. They were a popular twosome, hobnobbing with Tinseltown's elite.

But Fay was never so caught up in the social whirl that her work was affected. Indeed, within a three-year period after her contract with Paramount ran out, she was the leading lady in twenty-five features—more than some prominent actresses made in their entire careers—and worked for every major studio in Hollywood. She kept up a hectic pace, relying solely on her natural energy and en-

"Dan - Dan - you're not going to ----"

With Richard Arlen in *The Conquering Horde.*

thusiasm. While she did not strive for the lavish lifestyle of many actresses of the era, she said she felt like a true star when she asked the director to let her stop work at six.

One of the twenty-five films she did in that period assured her place as a screen icon and made her a figure in folklore and myth. *King Kong,* among the half-dozen most famous films ever produced, was an original conception for the screen. This 20th century version of "Beauty and the Beast" was created by co-directors Merian C. Cooper and Ernest B. Schoedsack with the assistance of special effects wizard Willis O'Brien who made a remarkably innovative use of stop-motion animation and

With Lionel Atwill in *The Mystery of the Wax Museum.*

rear projection. Although it inspired sequels, a remake and many imitations, the original *King Kong* remains unique and unequaled. Unlike so many of the others, the 1933 film imparts a kind of humanity in its strange, poignant tale of the giant, dark ape's love for the five foot-three Fay (who wore a blonde wig to contrast with Kong). A creature of both terror and pathos, Kong tries to protect the fragile Fay from dangers both real and imagined. Succeeding generations have embraced the film. Most people today immediately recognize its legendary climax with Fay and Kong atop the Empire State Building and the ape plunging to his death when he is shot down by aviators. Even before its release, its reputation in the industry as a "chiller" led to Fay being cast in the horror films, *The Most Dangerous Game, Doctor X, The Mystery of the Wax Museum* and *The Vampire Bat. King Kong* has been the subject of countless essays with varying interpretations of its symbolism. As for Fay, she would be kept busy in later years writing about it and making personal appearances in connection with its numerous revivals and commemorations.

Although *King Kong,* like its title character, has towered over most of her career, Fay showed she was capable of playing everything from an assertive woman lawyer in *Ann Carver's Profession* to an artist's model of the Italian Renaissance in *The Affairs of Cellini* and the mysterious, seductive title role of *Woman in the Dark.* And in still another variant on the "Beauty and the Beast" theme, in the sweeping epic, *Viva Villa!,* she is an elegant lady of the Mexican aristocracy whose initial attraction to Pancho Villa, portrayed by Wallace Beery as a heroic, idealistic yet brutish revolutionary leader, turns to revulsion in the end.

In the later thirties, her personal life took precedence over her film career. Although she had hoped the birth of their daughter might bring them closer together, the problems in her marriage to John Monk Saunders proved insurmountable and led to a painful divorce in 1938. The following year, while working in a stock company back East, she met and soon became romantically involved with noted playwright Clifford Odets. In 1940, Fay heard the shocking news that Saunders had committed suicide, a tragedy that could have overwhelmed her except for her strength of character and deep-seated faith in the spiritual. By 1942, she had embarked on a new life when she married screenwriter Robert Riskin, a relationship that brought her years of happiness and two more children.

In the 1950s, when Riskin became ill, she was forced to return to acting after a decade of retirement, appearing in many films and television shows. Among the pictures she did were *The Cobweb* (1955) directed by Vincente Minnelli for MGM and a tough crime story for Warners, *Hell on Frisco Bay* (1956), with Edward G. Robinson. She remembered Robinson as "a delight to work with, totally professional, who became a different person when playing the role of a gangster who was mean to me." Her television work in the fifties included *The Pride of the Family,* a series costarring Natalie Wood whom she adored, appearances on the *Perry Mason* show and a number of roles in live drama like *Playhouse 90.*

Fay withdrew from acting in the sixties, subsequently marrying Dr. Sandy Rothenberg who had been Robert Riskin's neurosurgeon throughout the long, difficult years of his illness. Not content to just retire, however, and feeling she must do something creative, she turned to writing, concentrating on plays and stories. In 1989, she published an autobiography, *On the Other Hand.* An outstanding movie memoir, it is an honest, sensitive, unsensationalized account of the joys and sorrows in her life—and the triumphs and setbacks in her career.[5]

Although widowed in the early 1990s, Fay had scarcely withdrawn from the world at the time I interviewed her in December, 1994. She divided her time between her apartments in Century City and Manhattan and, energetic as ever in her late eighties, she was still driving, enjoyed going to the theatre, visiting with her children and friends and making personal appearances at screenings of her films. She had continued to write and was working on autobiographical stories she called *Thinking It Over.* Her conversation showed the same gift for observation and sensitivity to detail that was evident in her writing. She had a knack for encapsulating in a few words the essence of a person or a happening, as in her recollections of the great songwriters she knew: she was "mystically in tune" with George Gershwin when she danced with him at a party; Jerome Kern was "elegant in white spats"; Irving Berlin was "a very gentle, nice person, almost preoccupied with the music in his head so that there was not much dialogue with him."

Equally rooted in her character were a strong liberalism and a mystical, non-dogmatic faith. She believed in reincarnation, appropriate for a woman of such resilience, and was a devoted reader of Whitman and Emerson. She maintained that external conditions should not invade the spirit, that knowing oneself and thinking positively can help an individual deal with problems while dark, angry thoughts only make one ill. Spirited but gentle, buoyant but thoughtful, she had attained screen immortality through her skill as an actress in a career that linked the silent and sound eras with the age of television.

My father's family arrived here from England. I'm not prepared to give you the date but my father was certainly born in England. There are various productions of genealogy that one gets. My sister did things like that and I've never kept them very carefully or paid a lot of attention but my father's parents were English and perhaps some Welsh because he had a beautiful singing voice and I've always thought maybe that's where it came from. My father was a child when he came here—I think around ten or twelve, something like that. He was in Utah or Idaho is my impression.

My mother's family were Scotch, Irish, English—certainly Anglo-Saxon. We were given the impression by my mother that we were related to Chief Justice John Marshall but I think that was fallacious. It had never been established and I never followed it to find out whether it was true. There was certainly a Marshall from Virginia in the background but whether that was Justice Marshall I'm not at all certain. My mother's father was an interesting man. He had been born in Missouri and I believe his parents died from some kind of an influenza—they probably didn't call it that then. So he was orphaned when he was very young, around twelve, and he was apprenticed to a saddle-maker in Missouri. Then when he got to be about sixteen or seventeen, he went off to be in the service in the Mexican War. After that, he became enormously interested in the idea of going to California and joined with a company that was going there. He became ill on the way having injured himself when he put his pistol into his holster. It went off and wounded him severely. The company had to take care of him and make a special stretcher for him on the back of a horse. When they got to Salt Lake City, instead of going through to the California Gold Rush, they left him there. That turned out to be a great joy to him because he met a beautiful young lady who was a Mormon and that changed his life. He married her and many years later, he wrote a book about his time called *Forty Years Among the Indians.* He liked the Indians very much.

My parents met in Salt Lake City, fell in love and ran off to Canada after my mother had had an unhappy first marriage. I was born in Alberta and I do have several memories of Canada. My father had built an extraordinarily wonderful house in a rather remote area and I remember the playground that he

A 1928 Paramount publicity photo with Fay costumed as Kiki, the title role of a popular play of the era. (Courtesy of Fay Wray Rothenberg.)

built for us. I remember his setting up the teeter-totter. I remember sitting in my sister Vaida's lap in the swing and the color of the coat she was wearing. I remember being on the verandah looking out over the meadow in front of the house and being on a sled that was being pulled on an iced lake. There was a crack in the ice, my oldest brother Vivien was holding me and we went down into the icy water. I remember his brown shoes sticking up but these are fragmentary memories, you know. Even in Canada, I had a desire apparently to be before an audience because we had at one point been in a Sunday school situation. I have a little memory of it, not much, but my mother told me that when the minister finished his little sermon, I held up my hand and asked if I could come up. Of course, I had a piece to say, too, and did and embarrassed her quite a bit because she had taught me little recitations. She had found that I learned very quickly and she enjoyed teaching me little verses. She had taught me "What are little girls made of" but that was not appropriate, especially for a Sunday school.

I believe I was around three and a half when we moved to the United States. We went to Arizona where my father bought land and attempted to be a farmer. But he didn't have the same talent for that that he'd had for all the things that he did in Canada and he didn't prosper. Things just went poorly for him and anyway, it was a depression time, I think. Then we went to Salt Lake City where my father got a job as a night watchman at a mill.

I liked school very much. Everything was inspiring about school—I just loved it, I really did. I don't know the date but I think I learned to read around the age of five. It just suddenly came to me. I remember a book I was reading called *Fred and His Sled*. Oh, my, suddenly I just saw those words and it was just a revelation. It was so beautiful to be able to read and be transported to some other place in the world through words. I don't think my mother had the time to supervise my education. There was too much to deal with—looking after children, you know. There was no help in the house. Women had to do so much—my goodness, the baking, the laundry, the ironing, the tending to the children. She did inspire you, though, with a great appetite for culture. She had a brother in Arizona who was Speaker of the House but most of her family were educators. I remember she had a great book of poems. I think that book was about six inches thick—huge like a dictionary.

I don't remember what the first film I saw was but I remember the effects of it. This was when we were living in Salt Lake City. There was this small theatre and this wonderful beam of light was coming from the rear of the theatre over the heads of the audience. The things were moving on the screen and I didn't know really what it was but everybody seemed so happy and I just thought that was so great. Everybody had this feeling of happiness really from in essence a light that was pouring through over the heads of everyone. A cousin of mine, a gentleman who was much, much older, asked me if I thought I would like to be up on that screen sometime. Now I think I had to be about six years old and I said, "Yes, because people are so happy at what they're seeing." I didn't know exactly what it was, just motion, but that was a very strong impression.

I didn't see any more films than that in Salt Lake City but very soon we were in a tiny town in Utah called Lark where my father found work in a copper mill. Just about the only thing you could do really was to go to films and I think it cost five cents. There was a building that had what was called a saloon. I guess it wasn't entirely Prohibition at that time but that's beside the point because my father never had anything to drink and so there was no sense of drinking in our life at all. But half of that building was a saloon and half was a movie theatre with a player piano. The theatre seated maybe four hundred people. I remember seeing films with Mary Pickford, Wallace Reid, the Farnum Brothers, Bill and Dustin, and I believe Charlie Chaplin and Harold Lloyd. And there was a film called *The Eyes of the World*—I remember that title.

I now had five siblings—three brothers and two sisters. But when I was nine, my parents parted and strangely enough, it didn't seem so terrible because we had small quarters—a very small house to live in—and when there was dissension between the parents, it just wasn't very wonderful, you know. We left that town then soon after that separation and went back to Salt Lake City without my father. Pretty soon, all the children were working at something. My mother stayed in the house to keep it in good order for us. It never occurred to her that she

With Melvyn Douglas in *Woman in the Dark.*

should go back to work, I'm sure. But my oldest sister, Vaida, was old enough to work in an office, the next oldest, Willow, was old enough to work in a photographer's studio tinting photographs, and I even worked in a store—not too successfully. But I did get a job filling envelopes for a newspaper—*The Salt Lake Telegram,* I guess—when I was twelve. They were having a contest to see who could sell the most subscriptions and whoever sold the most could get a screen test. Oh my goodness, that's the way it was. It had nothing to do with merit. I was very industrious about going from house to house which was a perfectly safe thing to do in those times. And I sold a lot of subscriptions to the newspaper and I won the right to have a screen test. It is laughable now but that test was shown on the screen in Salt Lake City and I had the pleasure of seeing myself for a few moments—probably not even a full moment. The man who was running this contest had a camera and went up to the University of Utah and had some people wearing uniforms. This was a period piece and I was supposed to be the leader of this group of soldiers. We just rode toward the camera, then we stopped and that was all that was ever filmed of that. Then he went off to do the same thing in another town, I guess, to operate as a promoter for newspapers. I never heard of him again.

Not long after that, the nationwide influenza epidemic of 1918 hit and we were all ill. My mother had a cousin who was a doctor. He sent a nurse to the house to look after all of us. Everyone was in a bed or cot. My older sister Vaida was just seventeen and very, very beautiful—a very talented girl. Tragically, one night she got so seriously ill that they had to take her to the hospital and I never saw her again. I was ill it seemed to me for a long time after—actually for two winters. Now I wonder if it wasn't just the tragedy of losing her in my life because I admired her so much. We had a pleasant little house. It was nice—it was a bungalow with a very civilized look to it. Then after Vaida who had been working and bringing some income into the house passed away, we had to move to an even smaller place. There again, I was ill the next year, I had to miss some school and I had to go to summer school to catch up.

My mother felt that I shouldn't go through another winter in Salt Lake so she let me go to California with the understanding that a cousin of hers would soon arrive there and look after me. So I went off with a young man who was an art teacher, William Mortenson, and a friend of my second sister, Willow. This seemed kind of an odd thing for a mother to do—to let a little girl of fourteen go off under the supervision of a male teacher. But he

With Gene Raymond in *Ann Carver's Profession.*

just was a very intelligent and artistic human being who was very strict with me and supervised me. I soon was staying with friends of a girl I had met in the newspaper office in Salt Lake City. She had also worked for the paper to try to get subscriptions. She and her family went to Los Angeles and I was in touch with her soon and went to stay with them.

Hollywood was very like a big village at this time. In fact, this young teacher with whom I'd ridden on the train got me some extra work through people that he met in a little studio called the Century Comedy Studio. I think I had an extra job and then the next thing very soon, they gave me a little bit to do. But there was no question of giving up school for this. It was just in the summertime. My mother then arrived in California and we moved into a living situation together. One day, she and I were walking along in front of the Century Studio and some of the executives if they can be called that who were running this studio came out. They were the Stern Brothers. I suppose they recognized me as someone who had worked there because they stopped and said, "Would you like to have a lead in a little comedy that we're going to be doing soon?" Naturally, one said, "Yes, of course." I think the film was called *Gasoline Love* but I don't know what it was about. I know that there was a comedian, kind of a big fat fellow, and there was no story line that I was aware of at all. I thought I was going to be a comedian. In the first scene that they took, I thought I could make faces and be funny but they told me no, I just had to look pretty and not do any of that stuff.

I next worked in a short comedy with an actor named Robert Gordon at the Fox Studio on Western Avenue. He was a friend of William Mortenson's. They had known each other before so that was an introduction that I guess made it possible for me to do a lead with him. Again, there was not much consciousness of a story line, just being in scenes, you know. Fox was not really a big studio then, I don't think. I made a test to get that thing with Robert Gordon and I remember the man told me afterwards, "I just liked your spirit. You had a kind of a fighting spirit in the test." Again, that wasn't serious or like the beginning of a career or anything. It was just an interlude that was between school. The school was the important thing.

After these short comedies, I played the lead in an independent feature, *The Coast Patrol.* I'd like to see that again. A pretty nice little man, Bud Barsky, produced it but that was a little rough on him because I had to be out in a boat all day one day. The sun just burned me in such a way that the next morning my face was twice its size and it was partly because of wearing make-up. I guess the combination of the sun and the make-up did something chemically to my features. I remember Spottiswoode Aitken played in it and he was kind of a wonderfully dignified old gentleman. I doubt that there were any interiors—you know, that's expensive stuff. Mostly, *The Coast Patrol* as the title can sort of tell you it was an outdoor movie.

In the meantime, I had been acting in high school plays and it was wonderful to do that. I went to Hollywood High where there was a very good teacher, Arthur Kachel. He liked to perform *Disraeli* for us and he directed the Tarkington play, *Seventeen.* He was an inspiring teacher. There was a fire burning in him to be an actor. He would have liked to have been an actor and he *was* one when he taught us. I guess the thing that actually propelled me to go to Hal Roach was the fact that when this teacher took the role of Pontius Pilate in *The Passion Play,* the summer play that used to be presented every year in the hills of Hollywood, he took about six of us students up there to be extras. That was about three girls and three boys. I was sixteen and I suddenly realized that it was possible to work on something with real continuity. We were there every night and I thought, "Gee, if I could get a job in a studio, I could work every day." Certainly, my family needed that help.

I had heard about a man named Richard Jones who had been at the Mack Sennett studio and was now head of production at the Hal Roach studio. (Coincidentally, my mother's maiden name was Jones.) I thought, "If I went to the studio, asked for an appointment and talked to him about how I'd like to work, maybe something could come of it." It didn't occur to me that this was unusual for anyone but it was certainly unusual to be given appointments. I don't think I even sat down when I went in his office. I just remember standing there and telling him that I'd like to work. He had a great deal of charm—that is, he always just seemed to twinkle. He said in a very amused manner, "Well, I think maybe we could give you a six months' contract." And so they did. He was married to a young lady named Irene who absolutely adored him. She subsequently became the best designer in California. She was very distinguished and did beautiful clothes but at a fairly young age, she committed suicide. Richard Jones died young, too. I saw him only a few times after I got the contract. I did not know Hal Roach well, either, but there was a sense of a family feeling there at that studio and he was sort of the father, you know. He was the symbol of that because he gave you presents at Christmastime and it was the most attractive atmosphere.

When I went to work for Hal Roach, I got a Model T Ford. My mother had to borrow the money to get that car—I think it cost six hundred dollars. My oldest brother, Vivien, taught me how to drive it carefully and always be careful at intersections. We lived at that point on Fairfax Avenue near Fountain in Hollywood and so I had to drive to Culver City where the studio was. That was a bumpy road. You got on to Robertson Boulevard, I think, in order to get to Culver City, however far that is—I don't know in miles.

A 1925 publicity photo from the Hal Roach studio. (Courtesy of Fay Wray Rothenberg.)

I don't remember how I met Janet Gaynor to tell you the truth but certainly she was under contract to Roach in the same way that I was. She did not have a car then and I would go and pick her up. She lived in a modest little house on Selma Avenue. She was a darling girl. She had such personality and was just fun to know. You went to the studio every day because you were under contract and your presence might be needed. In fact, there is just a pencil on paper of my schedule. They showed it to me at the University of Southern California and I apparently was placed in maybe five pictures a week, a little bit here, a little bit there, really for extra work, you know. So I earned the sixty dollars a week that I got for sure. But that was really being in the movies.

I also played leads opposite the comedians at the Roach studio. I worked with Charley Chase. I think the film was directed by Leo McCarey but I don't remember the title. I hardly knew that pictures really had titles then. Charley Chase had that funny style that you probably remember. I dare say I never even talked to him because there was no personal relationship with anyone that you ever worked with at that time. I was in a film with Stan Laurel before he got tied up with Oliver Hardy. He just had that kind of wistful little lost style. There was one I did with Glenn Tryon and there's a still of me with a pile of furniture. It probably was a gag about moving a lot of furniture. I don't know how that really developed but I noticed in that still that I had a kind of sense of comedy because my attitude was rather fitting for that situation. But it didn't seem to me that anything I did in those comedies was slapstick. I was just a leading lady and a foil, playing pretty much straight because the men were the comedians. I learned early on that I was not to be a comedian.

There were no scripts for the Roach comedies. They were just in somebody's head, I think. There would be an outline of the action only if the immediate scene was being photographed. They didn't play music on the set. There was no music in the Hal Roach studio at all.

There was a lot of nice open space there at the studio. I'm not able to just describe it to you but there was a building that was for the actors. My dressing room was up on the second level and I could look from that down over the whole lot and it had just a pleasant, calm atmosphere from that view. It was not a clownish studio at all. There was a place for cars to be parked and I think I parked my Ford on the lot. It all seemed kind of open. You did have to go through a gate to be checked in but it was nothing forbidding or big. It was a pretty small studio but we did most of our filming there. I don't recall going on location when I was at Roach. For exteriors, they built sets that simulated streets with small houses and shops. The interiors were on open stages.

I had met Paul Kohner who was the casting director at Universal. I don't remember how I met him but after I'd finished my six months at Roach, I got a contract at Universal and I got more money. Now I got seventy-five dollars a week. The same thing happened with Janet Gaynor. She went to Universal at the same time I did which was kind of an interesting coincidence. So we could continue this business of me driving over the hill in the other direction and taking her to the studio. I know we even shared a dressing room at Universal for a while. But my goodness, it wasn't long before she was gone out of that studio to do something absolutely wonderful at Fox, *Sunrise* directed by F. W. Murnau. I didn't see that until about two years ago. They had a special showing at UCLA and symphonic music had been written for it. It was

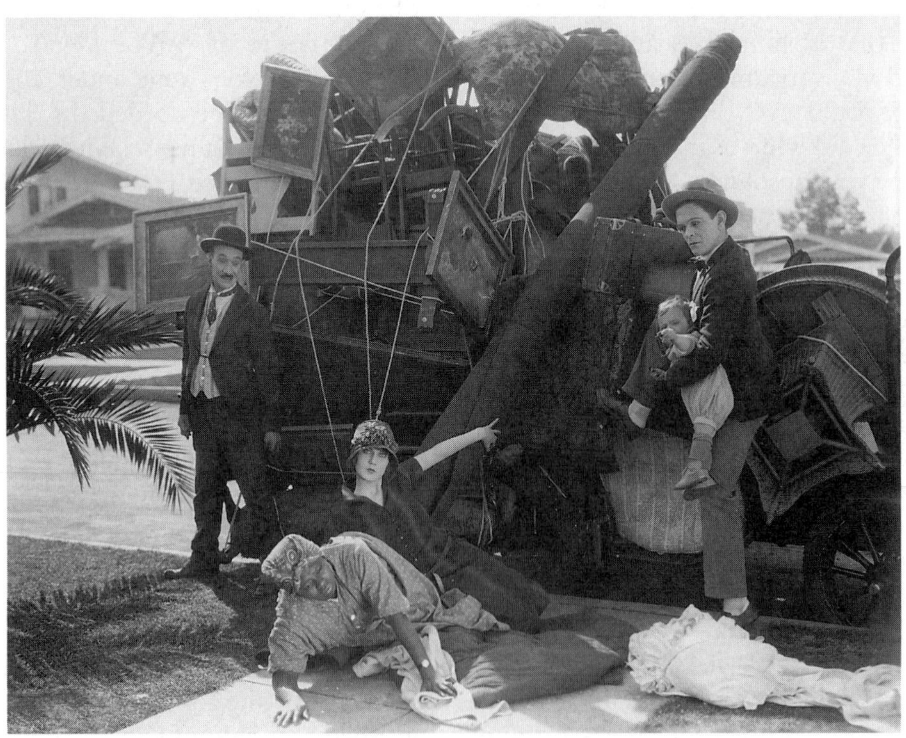

A scene from a 1925 Hal Roach comedy directed by Leo McCarey with Jimmy Finlayson at left and Glenn Tyron at right. (Courtesy of Fay Wray Rothenberg.)

played live in front of the screen and the whole effect was marvelous. It had a power, that film did.

I'd been going to see films throughout the twenties and I think I was aware of the strength of the European talent at that time. I had seen *The Cabinet of Dr. Caligari* and that was such an impressive film. Of course, I'd seen many of the outstanding American films, too, like King Vidor's *The Big Parade*. Oh, that was so wonderful, so beautiful, such a powerful film.

The films I did at Universal in 1926 were much more casual than that. It was more like the Roach studio. The exception here, though, was that at Universal you were very conscious of the network of relatives who belonged to Carl Laemmle so it was like a large family. And if they were not relatives, they were related by coincidence of having been in the same town in Germany at some point.

All the films I did at Universal were westerns. The directors had scripts but not the cast. I don't remember holding a script in my hand at Universal. We didn't have rehearsals, either. Mostly these movies that I did were maybe two, three or four-reelers. They were done on location, very rarely in the studio. You had to be up very early to get the benefit of the sun. It was very awful. The reflectors they used to light the scene could just—well, it was very, very difficult to keep your eyes open sometimes. But it *was* kind of wonderful. It was like going on a very poor picnic with horses and cowboys. I mean the food was not good—not that I was any kind of gourmet at that time but it was just a cold cheese sandwich and an apple that you could have. But that didn't matter. It was fun to be out in the air and fun to watch all the cowboys at work with the horses. It was a good feeling.

I did some stunts in these pictures. There was one circumstance when the horse that I was on was supposed to run away and I was supposed to have gotten my head hanging down with my back curved over the saddle. I didn't mind doing it. It didn't seem so terrible to me to do but some of the men on the set—I mean the crew—shook their heads like they were signalling to me, "Don't do that." But I did it.

I worked with all of Universal's western stars at that time—Hoot Gibson, Art Acord, Edmund Cobb, Jack Hoxie. Hoot Gibson was a very placid person. He was just photogenic, I guess. He didn't seem to have a strong personality at all. Now that was the first time that I ever knew music to be played on a set. We did do a more distant location and my mother sent my sister Willow with me as a chaperone since we were actually going out of town. We went to some place out in the Sierras—it could have been Lone Pine. They had a group of Hawaiian guitars or ukuleles playing and it was very pleasant to hear that. I guess Hoot Gibson had wanted that.

Eddie Cobb was a really nice, shy, sweet guy. He was just apologetic almost about everything. He was so gentle and his wife was a very nice lady. She was on the set a great deal. But he made me feel that he just adored me. He was what we used to call a "pebble-pusher"—an actor who's so shy that he can't speak without kind of kicking the ground. That was the style that Eddie Cobb had. I believe he and his wife came to our house on one or two occasions. My mother liked them and so we had them over. Jack Hoxie, though, was not a person that you could get to know or even want to. He seemed remote and was just a big, good-looking guy without any particular individual style. I never really had any conversations with Art Acord, either. He was a rather quiet fellow and it was my impression that he drank because he smelled of alcohol.

One of the pictures I did with Art Acord was *Lazy Lightning*. William Wyler directed that and there was not the slightest doubt that he had a strength. He was related to Carl Laemmle. His mother was on the set a good deal and I learned little bits of German to say to her. She used to bring presents to me—little antiques. They were interested in antiques. It was such a friendly, friendly time. William Wyler was a very intense director. We were doing a scene where I guess the little boy who was supposed to be my brother was ill and I was sitting by the bed. There was candlelight, it was a very serious situation, and I felt that Willy Wyler was in touch with deep drama.

The Universal studio was in the country and it spread across miles of hills and ravines. I remember my dressing room was in a long, long building. I never was in contact with the big stars at Universal like Reginald Denny and Laura La Plante. That was like a different level entirely at the studio. I mean those were big features and we were just doing small things. The only thing that happened there

With Art Acord in *Hearts and Spurs*. (Courtesy of Fay Wray Rothenberg.)

that was rather extraordinary was that in 1926 both Janet and I were nominated to be Wampas Baby Stars. The collection of ladies in that year was extraordinary—Mary Astor, Mary Brian, Dolores Costello, Joan Crawford, Dolores Del Rio. We went to the Ambassador Hotel one evening. The studio made an evening dress for me which I wouldn't have had otherwise. We were presented at the Ambassador and photographs were taken but there was never anything more than that.

In 1926, I was still living with my mother and my three brothers on Fairfax and Fountain in a very modest, simple one-story bungalow with an orange grove in the little backyard. By that time, though, I had elevated my vehicle. I had gotten a Hudson sedan. It was secondhand but it wasn't just a little old thing, you know. It had some strength to it. I don't know what happened to the Ford. I guess it got turned in on the Hudson probably.

I had at some time earlier met Edna Schley, an agent for writers, in a social way. One day at Universal, I was on the lot not working and she saw me and approached me. This was kind of in an open area between buildings or something and she came directly to me and told me about the film that Erich von Stroheim was going to be making, *The Wedding March*. She said she thought that it would be a wonderful role for me and would I like to go to his studio? Well, he represented at that time the greatest talent in Hollywood. As a director, he just was the tops and I had admired him and admired his work. So although I was under contract to Universal, it never occurred to me for one tiny second that I couldn't just go off and see him.

Mrs. Schley said she'd take me to his studio. This was a very small studio on North Broadway next to a zoo—the Selig studio. We were shown into the office of Emil Offerman, the man who was running the studio, and he immediately said to me, "Oh, you wouldn't do for this role, not at all, because you're too tall in the first place. Von Stroheim is short. He's going to play the lead and he would need someone shorter than he. And also you are a brunette and he wants a blonde for this part." So my mind raced as fast as it could to see how I could get the part. I knew when I set forth to go to that studio that that part would be mine. Now that's what's interesting about people who have the essence of excitement about something in their souls. It just was there for me. I believed it so that when he rejected me, I was thinking, "What can I do? What can I do?" Well, I could come back tomorrow with flat heels and not wearing these high heels. And I'd do something with my hair. I had it all piled up that day because I wanted to look like a leading lady but it made me look too tall. So when I asked him if I could come back the next day because I might look a little different to him—something like that—he said, "Well, all right."

I told Mrs. Schley what I could do and I did rearrange my appearance, put on flat shoes and let my hair hang down. That was a different look, I guess. Anyhow, when we went in the next day, Mr. Offerman said he would let me go on in to see von Stroheim. He led us to von Stroheim's office and I was so surprised at the quality of that man. I had visualized him like most people do—being someone in a uniform with a dictatorial style. But it was summertime and very hot so that he was wearing white clothes. The top that he was wearing was like a BVD to compensate for the heat that was everywhere and he had on white, beautiful shorts. But that was a gentle-looking person—that was not a fierce military man. And against that white, his skin was the color of—oh, just a tawny, tawny tan but velvety-looking so that it was not as though he had been out in the sun to get that effect. That was just the way von Stroheim was made when he first entered this world, you know. But he was so sensitive

A portrait from *The Wedding March.* (Courtesy of Fay Wray Rothenberg.)

and so searching. His eyes were just searching my face. He began to tell the story of his film. Mrs. Schley sat at one end of his desk and I sat directly across from him. There was no thought of handing me a script to read but he was just telling the story and oh, I was so excited. A sweet tension came over me about the whole thing he was telling and he was observing my reaction, I think. But suddenly, he came around and stood in front of the chair where I was, he held out his hand and I stood up to reach his hand and I just couldn't because he said at that moment, "Well, good-bye, Mitzi." And it was as though he were saying, "This is for you. You are Mitzi." And I just put my face in my hands and cried. So then he was excited and he said to Mrs. Schley, "Oh, I can work with her." Then he said, "Let's go see Mr. Offerman," and they just left me.

The contract had to be worked out because Mr. Offerman told me that I had to get out of my contract with Universal because they could not take me on as a leading lady and pay Universal for me. They would want to have me free of Universal. Mr. Offerman said, "I don't know. You may have to lie or something to get out of your contract." But when I left there, I thought, "This is too important to do anything except tell the truth. That's the only thing that I must do." And I made an appointment with Paul Kohner, the casting director I knew who was a friend of von Stroheim's, too. I went to see him and I told him the absolute truth about this and he was sensitive enough to know that this was a great opportunity for me and that he was the one who would have to lie for me. I never thought about it that way before but that's really sort of what happened. He took me to see Mr. Laemmle in his office and explained that they weren't really doing very much with me and perhaps it'd be just as well to let me go. It was like a rejection scene and Laemmle was ready to agree with whatever this fellow said. So they did just let me go.

We didn't do much rehearsing on the film and I never saw the script. Von Stroheim would just tell me what the scene was about. Of course, he had the script and that was his—he was writing it. There was only one time when I saw a couple of lines in it because there had to be some dialogue used and he let me see that. The dialogue was very important in *The Wedding March* even though it was silent and if you learned a few lines of dialogue, you didn't really change it because you had absolute respect for it.

I didn't see the rushes, either. You didn't get invited into those things almost ever. At the beginning, they did a sort of test of me and I did see that. I was just absolutely startled at the difference between the photography in a western and the photography in a beautiful, big production. I looked lovely. I didn't look just like a girl with too much lipstick on or too much make-up and the contrasty look that developed with those early films. This was soft and lovely and it was almost like I had a halo the lighting was so beautiful. I don't think von Stroheim was present when they took that. This was just a photographic thing.

When von Stroheim directed me, he just explained the scene that we were going to do and then we did it together. Just automatically, things had an easy and a natural flow. In fact, the first scene that we did together, he was tired because it was almost daylight and he had been working all

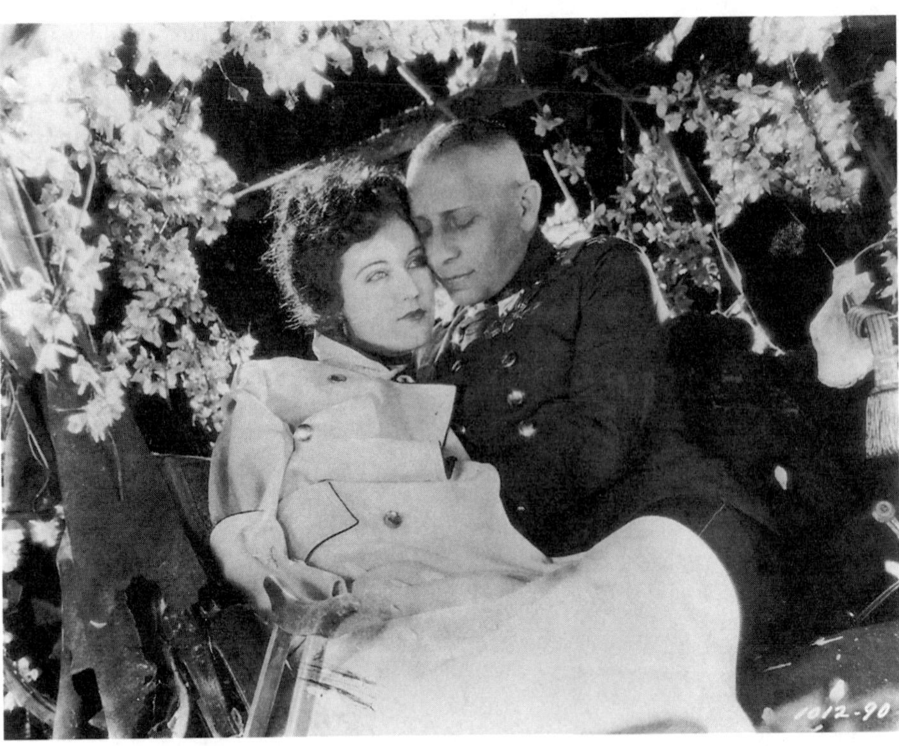

With Erich von Stroheim in *The Wedding March.* (Courtesy of Kevin Brownlow.)

night. I had been playing a harp in a scene in the wine garden and had worked a long time before to learn to simulate playing it in the film. Then they were ready for me to do the scene with him and he couldn't remember his line. And I threw him a line that made it easy for him to go on. He couldn't believe it—you know, that I could do that. But it was because I was so thrilled and so happy to be in this and felt that with the quality of the scene and everything, there was no reason to stop, just to keep going. Those were some beautiful scenes, really lovely, between von Stroheim and me in the wine garden with the apple blossoms. He had thousands of those apple blossoms handmade of wax and the effect was totally believable. For music, there was a small portable organ and a violin. That was going in between scenes and I suppose even during the scene because it was not a sound film so it was just a stimulus for charm—a wonderful, charming feeling. That first scene was photographed just before the dawn came up and naturally, I'd been up all night. But I just felt good as I was going home in my Hudson early in the morning. I drove with my right hand on the steering wheel and my left hand holding my forehead. I just felt like I had to hold my head—I was so tired—but at the same time I was so happy because it was just a beautiful feeling to be in that film.

This romantic mood, complete with music on the set, continued during the filming of our love scenes when we were in the broken-down fairy coach at night in the orchard amidst all the apple blossoms. And there was one rather humorous moment in the scene when I put on his coat. But the last of the scenes in the orchard was just eerie when I envisioned the Iron Man, an alarming omen of tragedy, a foreboding that was implicit in the story.

The scene where I had first met von Stroheim in front of the cathedral was sweet and enchanting. He was on his horse right beside me and he was watching me. I was smelling violets and he indicated I should take a violet and put it in his boot which was a good receptacle for flowers. So I did that when I was sure I wasn't being watched. That was an example of his imagination and was a good way to show two people connecting without words.

In the scene where I'm in the hospital bed after I've injured my ankle and he presents me with a box of chocolates during his visit, he gave me a charming bit of direction. He told me I should put the string of the box around my neck and save it like a poor girl who saves every little scrap.

Von Stroheim was highly appreciated by those of us working in the film. Even the extras all felt there was an air of excitement about working with him. He was so meticulous and he was so detailed that every moment had an implicit urgency about it. There was nothing loose or clownish or anything about working with him. Some of the scenes like the ones in the butcher shop were so awful but so realistic that there was no sense of acting. I didn't even think about acting—I just was being.

A number of the people in the cast had worked with von Stroheim before. He liked these people and he wanted them with him. It was like a stock company and I guess Matthew Betz and I were probably the only interlopers. Cesare Gravina, who played my father, was kind of a gentle little soul. Dale Fuller, who played my mother, I thought was unrealistic to look at and I felt she overacted. I thought so even afterwards when I saw the picture. I think that von Stroheim and I had some sense of realism going between us and the others were broader. But he didn't seem to mind that. He liked the broad, broad style.

Hughie Mack played the butcher's father and oh, my gosh, the size of him would stand out anywhere. ZaSu Pitts seemed a little detached from everything but then that was her role. She was a rather pathetic, lost creature and so it was appropriate for her. But I had the feeling that she had worked with von Stroheim enough to perhaps not even like him a lot. Matthew Betz played Schani, the butcher who pursues me and he was pretty detestable in that role. I didn't talk to him much. I didn't want to have anything to do with that creature. His wife was on the set all the time and I guess he was a perfectly fine fellow in real life. But I really didn't want to spend any time with him because he threatened and was somebody in the film that I didn't like so I was not going to break through. I think von Stroheim liked the brutality of those scenes.

The only man on the film that I spent time with and talked to was Harry Carr who co-authored the script with von Stroheim. I didn't even talk a lot with von Stroheim but I did have some nice discussions with Harry Carr. He was the top film critic with *The Los Angeles Times.* He stood in back of the camera and the first solo scene that I did without von Stroheim he was watching. He had a way of wiggling his nose—it was like a nervous tick. But it was increased nervousness—it ticked very hard as though he were pleased with me, you know. We got to be friends. I went to his house and visited with him and his wife. He took me subsequently to meet Lillian Gish where she lived down at the beach. I was happy to meet her because I had admired her so much in films like D. W. Griffith's *Orphans of the Storm.* I remember she was brushing her long blonde hair as we talked. Harry Carr was crazy about her and he was crazy about Ramon Novarro, too. He wrote a beautiful piece about me for one of the movie magazines and I just was charmed by it. So he was a nice man.

Hal Mohr was the cameraman on *The Wedding March* and he was very good. A good cameraman like that doesn't need to be supervised by the director because he knows the scene. He had a wonderful personality and great admiration for von Stroheim. But there was a confrontation between them. I wasn't present but Hal Mohr told me about it later. It was summer and very hot with no air conditioning. Von Stroheim was complaining about a cyst on the back of his neck that was showing up in the picture and Hal Mohr said, "I'm a cameraman, not a plastic surgeon." So he left the production after that.

The Wedding March was funded by a very nice Irish gentleman named Patrick Powers and von Stroheim and he were together, I think, on the basis of their mutual Catholicism as much as anything. But I think it worried Mr. Powers a lot how much money was being spent by von Stroheim. He, too, became my friend and we had a long friendship. He had a gorgeous house up in Flintridge and invited me and my mother to dinner. He was like my sponsor.

The studio, as I mentioned, was very small. It was in an area where a big general hospital is now but in those days, it had the feel of the country. We sometimes heard the lions in the zoo next to us but we were making a silent film so it didn't bother us. My dressing room was in a little, medium-sized cottage. They put a harp in the room so I could practice for my scenes in the picture.

Although it wasn't really an open set, we had visitors. I remember Paul Whiteman visited the set and I was pleased to meet him because he had enjoyed such success with his music. And Douglas

Fairbanks, Jr. also came on the set. He wanted to talk to von Stroheim about doing a film version of Rostand's play, *L'Aiglon,* in which Doug would play the lead. They never made it but I got to know Doug in later years and he's always been a very caring man.

The sets for *The Wedding March* were remarkable. The replica of St. Stephens Cathedral was wonderful. The set was built on kind of a big open area much as it was in Vienna. Of course, the height was not there but it was sufficiently large. The facade was very impressive. The wine garden where Mitzi, my role, lived with her parents was set in an orchard with apple blossoms as you know. It was quite extensive and realistic-looking because not only was it the orchard but it was the place where people sat at tables to have food and drink. Then it continued in a kind of a circuitous way. There was a tunnel that you could walk through—a narrow tunnel just to take you to the butcher shop. Nothing was photographed in that tunnel, I don't think ever, but it just was the shape of a real place. Where we were in the wine garden was a country inn that was like on the edge of Vienna, I guess. The street scene with all the shops was back in the big part of Vienna where they had the big parade in front of St. Stephens Cathedral.

With Erich von Stroheim in *The Wedding March.*

Von Stroheim's own house was a little one-story bungalow on Oxford Street near Beverly Boulevard. I think I went there twice—the first time to try a wardrobe on and then I went subsequently at Christmastime. Of course, I met his wife Valerie and their little son Joseph. Valerie was a very large, handsome woman like a Juno. Von Stroheim, though, was certainly not what you would call a handsome man and there were people who thought he was rather ugly. I never saw him as ugly. He certainly wore his uniform with style. There are many people who have said over the years that they thought he was born in Brooklyn and that his background in Austria was all a legend, a myth that he made up about himself. I don't believe that for a minute. It's impossible for anyone to behave with the meticulous style that he did as a military man who hadn't lived it.

We went up to the mountains for some location scenes and oh, he was so nice. Listen, when people say he was "the man you love to hate"—my, he was so good to my mother. She went in out of the sunlight, didn't see the step in the restaurant where we stopped and twisted her ankle—I guess sprained it very, very badly. He just got a pail of hot water, he sat down in front of her and he bathed that foot. He couldn't have been kinder.

He was not a gloomy man. He had a sense of humor and I remember seeing him laugh although the man who played the violin was our court clown. As a person, von Stroheim had a lot of warmth. He had the temperament of an artist, I think, if he had temperament. Oh, he could shout and be angry if the horses and the soldiers in those big parade scenes weren't doing what he wanted. He could tell them off but that was just the urgency of wanting to get things right because Pat Powers got really concerned it was running too long as every von Stroheim film always did, I think. I guess he didn't have unlimited funds to keep feeding into it so he contrived very shrewdly to make a deal with Paramount to get them to take it over. It was going to be that kind of a release. Once they took it over, then they were not going to stand for any continuing stretching out of time and schedule. I think we probably did some filming at the Paramount studio after they took over the responsibility for *The Wedding March.* I do know that we had one big interior set at the Paramount studio that represented a mountain. But they could see that there was so much film already that they probably had enough for a feature so they just stopped production on it.

It wasn't released for over a year. That might have been partly because sound was coming in and they wanted to add sound effects and music. Color, too, was affecting the release of it, I believe, so, as you know, they did one color scene and I think one big bell-ringing scene with sound. As I recall, it got wonderful, wonderful appreciation when it was shown. I cannot say how it was received in Europe. I read only the reviews here and they said absolutely wonderful things about it. I think the only disturbing element was that it was just a little bit too much on the edge of changes in the world of filmmaking.

I do have strong feelings about what happened to von Stroheim. In the first place, if I could have done one or two more films with him, it would have meant so much to me because we did have an absolutely almost magic understanding of one another. It was intuitive on my part. I was not a trained actress but I did have a quality that I could respond to his style. He loved working with me and we could have done other things. It would have been very, very nice but he just loved to keep shooting. He could never be quite satisfied so he had so much material there. And then they put Josef von Sternberg in the cutting-room to cut Erich von Stroheim's film. This must have been devastating to him. But I did not continue to see him personally or his wife. It just was like a severing, you know.

Years later in the early forties, I met him in New York when he was in *Arsenic and Old Lace* on the stage. A lady who was working in that knew me. I'd been doing, I think, a radio show with her and she said that he would like to see me. Of course, I was delighted to go backstage and see him. Then later, we met at Willy Wyler's house in California. It was a big evening party. He was having too much to drink and he was very emotional about how tragic it was that he had left Hollywood for France. He should have stayed in Hollywood, he said, but then that was just an emotion of the moment probably because he was well-appreciated in France.

I didn't see him or correspond with him in later years when he was back in France. Then sometime much, much later after I last saw him and he had passed away, a man who was a professor in France came to see me. This was touching almost beyond belief. He came with a man who was with the Academy of Motion Picture Arts and Sciences and they had a meeting with me at my house. The professor didn't speak very much English and I didn't speak very much French. I assumed that he was there because he was going to be writing about Erich von Stroheim. Then at the end of this interview, I asked, "Are you writing about him?"

And he said, "No, he just asked me to come and see you." Before von Stroheim had died, he said to this man, "If you ever go to the United States, I would like you just to go and see her." Now, wasn't that touching?

I think von Stroheim's career as a director came to an end because he took too much time, he ran far over schedule, he spent too much money. It's similar in a way to Orson Welles's difficulties because Orson certainly didn't cater to limitations. I guess the way I expressed it in my book is about the way I feel. I said that the way von Stroheim treated time was like any artist should treat time. He just ignored it.

We had been filming *The Wedding March* for nearly a full year and I did not make any other films during that time. As I said, we did some filming at the Paramount studio toward the latter part of it after they took over the whole situation. I think my contract with Mr. Powers was part of that arrangement. I got a wonderful salary for *The Wedding March*—five hundred dollars a week. Considering I'd been getting seventy-five from Universal, that was a big, wonderful jump. My salary continued on the same basis when I got a five-year contract with Paramount.

Of course, the Paramount studio on Marathon Avenue was very large. There was a wonderful sense of space about it all. I think most people are familiar with that archway—the gate that allows cars to go through. I'd drive through it and park near my dressing room. Adjacent to that big gate, there was a series of office buildings that represented the administrative part of the business. That was to the left of the archway. To the right of the gate, there was an area that was for the wardrobe and the designing people and all the costuming. Directly in back of the administration buildings, there seemed to be a nice sense of space before any other buildings came into view. There was a long row of small buildings, just one-story buildings that were dressing rooms. I had one of those very nice dressing rooms with two rooms—a sitting room in the front and then in the rear, the dressing room itself.

We had make-up people at Paramount. At Roach, I had done my own make-up and I didn't use any make-up at all when I was in *The Wedding March.* Von Stroheim didn't wear make-up, either. But we were doing big productions at Paramount and you felt you would have been robbing people of jobs if we had done the make-up ourselves. Then when I did *Captain Thunder,* an early talkie on loan-out to Warner Brothers, I had one very good make-up man from Germany who showed me how to do my own make-up in a way that was suitable for me. After that, I did my own make-up myself.

There was no social activity of any kind within the Paramount studio that I remember at all. I was just doing what I was supposed to be doing. I saw the producer B. P. Schulberg from time to time when a picture was coming along or another was being developed. But Jesse Lasky was one of the executives with whom I had the most relations socially. After I was married to John Monk Saunders, I went frequently to see Jesse Lasky and his wife Bessie. My husband already knew their family very, very well. The Laskys had a wonderful house on the beach in Santa Monica and every weekend, they had guests at their soirees for swimming, Ping-Pong, dancing and so on. I would not say that influenced Jesse Lasky to apply himself to supervising my career with any special concern or interest. He would have been interested but it was the immediate producers of whatever film I was doing who reported back to the executives of which Mr. Lasky was one.

The Legion of the Condemned was the first picture I made for them. It was a story of World War I aviators written by John Monk Saunders. I met him in that film since he was on the set a good deal and having met him, I got to know him more during that picture. Of course, he had already written

With Gary Cooper in *The Legion of the Condemned.*

Wings which had been produced at Paramount. That was the first great aviation story and it was a tremendous success so it was followed with *The Legion of the Condemned.* The same director, William Wellman, did them both. I think my role was one who remained on the ground. I didn't have to go in the air but I did go up in an airplane while that film was being made. And I appreciated the opportunity to get up in an open plane with only a seat belt on and the wonderful feeling of actually flying—it was great.

I liked William Wellman very much. He had a lot of energy and enthusiasm and while he was never as sensitive a director as Erich von Stroheim, he had something burning in his system that was very appealing as a director. He would praise his actors which was stimulating. We had a written script and whatever it was, we just did it as it was supposed to be done. I think they tried to adhere to the story line. I don't think it was off the cuff at all—unlike Universal where the director gave us a general idea of the film and we did each scene as it came along. At Paramount, the flavor of the scene came to life after it was set down on paper, of course, but I don't think they changed it markedly.

Gary Cooper was my leading man in *The Legion of the Condemned.* He was so quiet and an extraordinarily unexpressive individual. But what he had was the most wonderful face and the slightest little change of expression just registered so wonderfully in the camera. He really had a beautiful face. I don't mean feminine beauty but strength, a lovely

With Mauritz Stiller and Emil Jannings during the production of *The Street of Sin*. (The Museum of Modern Art.)

shape, great eyelashes and really unusual lines—not lines *in* his face but lines *of* his face.

My next film for Paramount was *The Street of Sin* with Emil Jannings and directed by Mauritz Stiller. It was set in Soho in London and I had a leading role as a Salvation Army girl. Stiller was Swedish and he had trouble with the language expressing himself. I felt that he was a very sad individual and he was trying to work with apparently a broken heart over Garbo whom he'd discovered. He did not finish that picture and I know he went back to Sweden. It was completed by Lothar Mendes, a director who was under contract to the studio and who worked on various films as an auxiliary director. *The Street of Sin* was Josef von Sternberg's story but just because he became a well-known director, there are those who think that if he had anything to do with it, it meant that he directed it. That's not so. I can remember Stiller's style. He'd say my name like it was all one sound—you know, "FayWray." He'd say, "Don't go before you don't start, FayWray." So that was not thrilling direction. Anyhow, he seemed to be very, very sad and you couldn't converse with him. At least, I didn't know any language but English and Emil Jannings didn't really care about learning English. But it was a silent film so that was all right.

I thought Jannings had a quality of being larger than life and I had admired him very much in films I'd seen before. He wanted everything for himself, though. He was a very selfish person, I believe, and perhaps there was nothing wrong with that. He was the star. But for instance, I had a death scene. Especially in silent films, I guess that was an important element of a role because it was dramatic and it created a good deal of caring and sympathy from the audience. He got that changed so that *he* had a death scene instead of me having one. So that was the first time I recognized that the power of a star was quite strong and it was a little dismaying. But I never was a person who felt that anything was ever done against me. If he wanted that death scene, then he got it but he didn't get it away from me particularly. I never felt those competitive angles at any time.

Olga Baklanova, the Russian actress, was also in *The Street of Sin*. I have no particular memory of doing any scene with her but I do recall she was a very vibrant lady with a very dramatic quality about her. She had the brightest blue eyes I ever saw.

After that, I worked again with Gary Cooper in *The First Kiss* directed by Rowland V. Lee. Because I was so well-appreciated in *The Wedding March* and Gary was so well-appreciated in one scene in *Wings*, he became a focus of possible stardom and so did I. Right away, there was the idea that Gary and I would make a good team and we were advertised as "Paramount's Glorious Young Lovers." Oh, my goodness! Do you see what a commodity that seemed to make of you? I found that very unfortunate and also Gary Cooper was an actor who was a "pebble-pusher." I was rather shy and retiring, too. That was my nature and so we were not a good complement one for the other. He needed a fiery lady like a Lupe Velez and I needed a stronger male vis-à-vis my style so it was just not the right chemistry, I don't think. I always thought of Gary as being a nice, big, gangly kind of brotherly person. I never saw any great romantic quality in him and I imagine—I don't know, he never told me how he felt about me.

We filmed part of *The First Kiss* on location at St. Michaels in Maryland. Oh, it was beautiful to see the way that the grass grew right down to the sea. That was startlingly beautiful to me. There were no wide beaches or anything like we had in California. Everything was lush and green right to the edge of the water. That is my memory and I may have it wrong but this was Chesapeake Bay and St. Michaels was a very small town that was near the bay. It had a kind of an

With Gary Cooper in *The First Kiss.* (Courtesy of Fay Wray Rothenberg.)

easy charm. We lived in a big kind of country hotel, a vacation-type hotel, and it was humid. We didn't go into New York at all. We just stayed in St. Michaels where it was filmed.

This was the first time I had gone back East and my mother had come, too, to be my chaperone at such a distant place. I think John had proposed to me before we had ever left so that there was a strong bond between us. But he came to St. Michaels and talked to my mother. When he told her about wanting us to be married, she said, "Yes, of course," because she admired him very, very much. He was a very attractive, intelligent and extraordinary young man. So we were married there in June of 1928.

John Monk Saunders was a contract writer at Paramount when I was also under contract to them. He was a fine screenwriter and a good craftsman. He certainly had done and continued to do some fine films, mostly connected with aviation because no one else seemed to have the flair that he had for that, having done *Wings* and then *The Legion of the Condemned.* Later, he did *The Dawn Patrol* and he had a great appetite for the romance of aviation, especially in films. Now as a literary writer, I don't think that he really did nearly so well because he came to consider himself part of the so-called in quotes "Lost Generation" and Scott Fitzgerald and Hemingway had already taken quite good care of that. So by the time he wrote a novel that had all those elements of "Lost Generation" behavior, it was almost like—well, not a good copy. Personally, I think he was very narcissistic. He had a great gentility. I think he was very vulnerable to the way ladies adored him and I think he rather believed in being responsive to that kind of attention. I think he wanted not to be that way but to have a true direction of his affections. But he just would fall into temporary relationships even after we were married, you know, and that was very hard to understand, hard for me to deal with that. And the other thing that was against his nature or that he accepted as being okay rather, was to drink more than he should. At that time, there was still Prohibition so whatever people were interested in drinking, whatever they did get to drink was pretty lousy stuff, I think. Physically, it was just devastating. I wouldn't know too much about the extent of drinking in Hollywood then but if he's an example, I would say that he did get caught up in that style.

I don't know what influence he had on my acting career. He wrote a leading lady role I did in one picture at Warner Brothers, *The Finger Points,* but that was not particularly for me. He did use a lot of

With John Monk Saunders. (Fay Wray Collection, USC.)

my personal style and expression and character and quality in a novel he wrote called *Single Lady*. Then it was made into a film, *The Last Flight*, and that might well have been an appropriate part for me because a lot of it was my style. But Helen Chandler did that instead with Richard Barthelmess. Then it became a musical in New York and I did do that.

In the twenties, the contemporary behavior of the time influenced my husband and to that degree, it was an influence on me. But I never thought about the popular attitude or cared. I had much more of an old-fashioned character and quality and I was not a flapper or a dancing girl. I was always looking for intellectual relationships and not for the popular.

I worked in *The Four Feathers* after I did *The First Kiss*. Merian C. Cooper had been making pictures far, far away in distant places and then he decided along with Ernest B. Schoedsack, his partner, to be involved in this film, *The Four Feathers*, which had been an English novel by A. E. W. Mason. John Saunders as a journalist in New York before he came into the film business had had a certain literary attorney and Merian Cooper had the same one. Whether they met in New York, I don't know. I think they also knew George Putnam who was the publisher and so they had at the very least a kind of mutual respect for their own backgrounds and the way that they were connected to each other. So when Merian came into the studio, they became friends again and I think it was because of that that Merian gave me strong consideration for a role in *The Four Feathers*. That was a very, very nice experience for me to know him and to know someone of his particular quality who was not just a routine kind of thinker. He was a visionary and had had his wonderful background of travel. He and Schoedsack had done a marvelous documentary called *Grass* that I admired. That was a silent film made in what was then known as Persia or Iran today. And *Chang* was another film they did that was very exciting, made in Siam or Thailand. So Merian was a pretty special individual. He had such a gallant respect for—well, I don't know for every woman he ever met but he certainly had for me. He would send orchids to my dressing room and made me feel like he really had enormous good feeling for me. And that never disappeared, I want you to know, as long as I knew him.

But the part I did in *The Four Feathers* was kind of a routine role for me. I think we went down the coast to perhaps it was Laguna or La Jolla for maybe one exterior. Most of what I did were interiors done at the studio and directed not by Merian Cooper who was the producer but by Schoedsack. And then this same Lothar Mendes who did some of the work on *The Street of Sin* did some of the directing on *The Four Feathers*, too. It didn't feel like a very solid picture to me and I think also at that time, I was not feeling very happy at home so there was a certain atmosphere of—there was no joy about any of it for me except my good regard for Merian Cooper. But I do remember one most amusing thing that happened when we were making *The Four Feathers*. Schoedsack was directing and we had a dolly shot that was on rails. We were walking with the camera going backwards—I guess this was Dick Arlen and myself. Something bothered Schoedsack about it and he said, "Cut, cut, cut!" No one paid any attention. We just kept going because the thing was rolling so we walked with it. And when it came to a stop, Schoedsack said, "Hot dog, that was a good scene!"

The Four Feathers was the first time I worked with Richard Arlen. I did a lot of films with him but I never got to know him away from the studio. As you know, I just had an appetite for intellectual company and I always wanted to exchange with people who were like that. Arlen was a kind of a happy-go-lucky guy who liked golf and there was nothing to discuss with him. He was an admirable person, he was fine, but there was no conversational intrigue there for me.

By this time, sound was coming in and it seemed to be something that gave people concern. My feeling about sound was that it was an interruption in a beautiful art form because silent films had meant so much to me always. The industry had grown strong based on that and I thought that sound was diminishing and I still think so to a great degree. I'd like to see someone make a film that's almost entirely silent because there's a beauty and a power and a joy in that kind of filmmaking. However, there it was. The sound was there and everything suddenly seemed to be small in terms of the expanse. The view of things was reduced—as much as anything because of the mechanics that went on. Other people have told you this, I'm sure. The microphones were pushed in your face or hanging from the ceiling and everybody had to be concerned and watchful of that or watch out for mike shadows. Have you ever heard that Hitchcock had a whole list of names of people? Mike Shadow was one of his. I think that the people who came from the theatre at this time apparently had and perhaps should have had a particular advantage because, like Ruth Chatterton, they had been great in the theatre and they could handle all the dialogue in the world with the greatest of ease.

However, when I took my voice test, that was just easy to do. I think that Roy Pomeroy, the sound technician, had the respect of John Saunders and they talked about me doing a test. So Roy Pomeroy was happy to have me come to the sound stage or wherever it was they were working and do a test to see if my voice registered all right. I recited "Father William" from *Alice in Wonderland*—that was the choice of John Monk Saunders. He thought that would be nice for me to do. Roy Pomeroy was very, very sweet and very nice. I read that most people thought he was a real horror but I didn't. I couldn't tell that at all. I thought he was a real gentle, nice person. You know, the recording equipment then seemed to emphasize the higher tones so looking back at it, I think that there was a kind of light and tinny tone to the sound itself. I was not particularly thrilled with the way I sounded but everybody else sounded much the same way except the men, of course, and I guess the women who came from the theatre.

The Four Feathers was said to have sound but it was silent and there was sound added, I believe. My first talkie was *Thunderbolt* directed by Josef von Sternberg. I think he was not too happy because he had a great talent for composition and photographic strength and at that time, the cameras were wrapped and housed in a lot of stuff that made them very cumbersome. They were no longer just a wonderful lens that you knew was there. There was this contraption sort of thing and the protection of the whole metallic part of it so that it would not interfere with the sound. It seemed to be bulky and unattractive and there's something about a lens for someone who's been in films. There's an intimate relationship with the actor or actress and if you get used to that and then have it suddenly all bundled up and taken away in a sense, that's kind of dismaying. Also, more than once I was asked at Paramount to do roles that I had no business doing. And the role I had in *Thunderbolt* was a gangster's moll. I was supposed to play that and I had

With George Bancroft in *Thunderbolt*.

nothing to base that on in my own life, no appetite for it, and I felt strange. My hair was cut. I had beautiful, long, curly hair and there was a certain pride to me in having that and to have it just cut off short, bobbed, then I felt decapitated.

I'm sure von Sternberg was experimenting with the new medium of sound when he made the film. He was an imaginative man and he was an artist. I didn't feel any of the closeness or the warmth of the man but I'm sure it was there. I never had the impression that he did a lot of retakes. He seemed a little distant from that. That wouldn't mean he wouldn't make a good film because he had the talent.

George Bancroft was my leading man in *Thunderbolt* and I have to laugh because he was attended to with such utter devotion by his wife. She told this story or he did and it was told without humor. He slept with his mouth open. When it was time to wake him up, she got a nice slice of ripe peach to put in his mouth so that he could just chonk on it and that woke him. That's how carefully she attended to his persona. Now, have you ever heard of anything more kind than that?

A lot of these circumstances at Paramount were kind of alien to me. The quality that I had expected to find in making films just seemed not to be there. It seemed to be commercial. They just put certain personalities in because they were paying them a weekly salary and did not take much consideration about the individuals or the particular talent of the individuals. They just shook them together and saw how they came out. For instance, in 1929, I did a musical, *Pointed Heels,* in which I was supposed to be a chorus girl. A chorus girl? Well! You had one little tap dance lesson and then you danced. That was not native to me, either, that kind of thing. However, I did have the opportunity to work with William Powell and he was really a wonderful person. He really paid attention. He was not preoccupied with William Powell. He was interested in the story and in relationships of the other actors to it and that then certainly included me. I really had great appreciation for that. I don't know whether it was in that picture—it probably was—but I had to play a drunk scene. I had never done such a thing and he helped me. He was like a teacher for me. I thanked him very much because I appreciated him a lot.

With Hal Skelly and William Powell in *Behind the Make-Up*. (Courtesy of Cole Johnson.)

Bill Powell and I also worked together in *Behind the Make-up*. Hal Skelly was my leading man and he came from the theatre. I had at least a character in that. I was always hoping to get something that wasn't just a pretty girl—that wasn't decorative or something. But this was a waitress. I forget what motivated her in particular but she was a character and so I liked that. Dorothy Arzner directed the dialogue and we sort of counted on her more than the credited director, Robert Milton. He was a theatre director but he was not a very good film director, I didn't think, unlike another theatre director I worked with at this time, George Abbott. I think George Abbott was pretty comfortable directing films. As long as he could go dancing in the evening, he got along fine. He just loved to dance. He directed me in *The Sea God* and we were at Catalina for the locations.

I also did several westerns at Paramount in 1930—*The Border Legion, The Texan* and *The Conquering Horde*. But the only one of these that I remember or care particularly about is *The Texan* with Gary Cooper. That was an interesting role because again, I could play a character. At least, I could play a Spanish girl. John Cromwell was the director of that but the man who helped me with my dialogue or dialect was Jack Wagner who was a wonderful person. People like that sometimes had more relationship, or at least I remember them more strongly than the director because when they worked on the dialogue, you related to them. They

With Richard Barthelmess in *The Finger Points.*

were somehow more supportive to you than the director could have been. We were on location but we never went that far away. There were plenty of places to go in California. That's one of the great things about California. I liked *The Texan* the best of these westerns because I just thought it had some charm. I liked working with Gary in that because I was a better foil for him being a Spanish girl than I was as an American girl.

Pretty soon, the business was in trouble. The stock market had crashed in 1929 and things really began to go downhill. So Paramount began loaning out people to other studios. Again, you were a commodity. I was loaned to Fox for *Not Exactly Gentlemen.* I remember that we went into the far, far desert for it and at Christmastime, too. Nobody got home for Christmas. I was required to ride a thoroughbred. There was a race across a desert for what reason I don't know—maybe to get land or something. You know, these were not strong roles or strong stories. A lot of them were just good entertainment. Anyhow, it was interesting to get on a horse that really, really, really went. Oh, that was nice because those horses were so smooth. They just absolutely flew and it seemed as though they would never stop. But then I knew they would because the cowboys could also go fast and catch them.

The leading man, Victor McLaglen, was a remote person. He had his own world. He was tall and he lived up there in that world. But he had political ideas, I guess—at least I heard—and because of them, he wouldn't have been anyone who would have interested me.

Just after that, I worked at Warner Brothers opposite Richard Barthelmess in *The Finger Points* which was written by John Monk Saunders. Richard Barthelmess had a great quality and he and his wife Jessica were good social friends of mine and of John Saunders. We spent many, many hours at their house and they at ours. I thought that Dick was so real, so sincere as an actor. He was not arrogant at all. He was almost shy and he wanted so much to do right and do well that he was just almost like a beginner sometimes. And that was fascinating.

Paramount next loaned me to Columbia for *Dirigible.* Frank Capra directed that just before he began his long association with Robert Riskin. He was a fine director but I think that, like von Sternberg with *Thunderbolt,* he was overwhelmed by technical matters when he made *Dirigible.* It was a large-budget adventure film about polar exploration but,

Frank Capra directing Fay and Jack Holt in *Dirigible.* (Fay Wray Collection, USC.)

of course, I wasn't in the big ice scenes. I played a home person. Jack Holt, the leading man, was incredible to me in that my oldest sister, Vaida, whom I adored, had had a crush on him on the screen. So I had great respect for him since he had meant something in her life. But he just was a fine-looking human being. He didn't have much to say. He seemed like a kindly soul who just did his job and he was not a personality that you could discuss anything with. At least, I wouldn't have known what to discuss with him. But he was an impressive-looking person who stood straight and tall.

Back at Paramount, I did *The Lawyer's Secret* with Clive Brook and Jean Arthur. I loved working with Clive Brook. He was a proper fellow, very decent, very gentlemanly, very British and just charming socially. His wife, too, was very, very nice. I never got to know Jean Arthur well. I had good friends, the Swerlings. I think Jo Swerling was a writer on *Dirigible.* They had a house at the beach in Malibu and Flo Swerling loved to entertain. We often had evenings there and at least on one occasion, Jean Arthur was there and had a wonderful time. It was fun—she sat on the piano and sang. But I think she was supposed to be very shy. I guess she always was.

The Unholy Garden with Ronald Colman was again a loan—this time to Sam Goldwyn. George Fitzmaurice who directed was a routine, pleasant director who had no particular dynamics, I didn't think. But Ronald Colman just seemed like my forever friend. He was not garrulous but he sort of let you know in a tacit way that he had good regard for you and I respected him very much. He was really—it seems like a cliche to say that he was such a gentleman but he was.

One evening when I was making *The Unholy Garden,* the police stopped me for driving too fast on my way to the studio for some filming at night. But that was fun. Oh, that's a beautiful thing to remember! I had had a glass of champagne with John Monk Saunders—we had dinner at home—and then when I was driving, I was real easy and happy and humming and singing going back to the studio. I made two policemen pull me over and I said to them, "Oh, look, I was so happy, singing and having a good feeling and now look what you've done"—like that, you know.

And they were so nice. They each gave me a card and said, "If you ever need any help or anything, just let us know." Imagine that happening today—imagine! It couldn't. So that's really part of what the Golden Age was all about, I do believe. But when I got to the studio and told Ronald about that, he said, "Well, Fay, you should do that more often. You should have a little champagne more often."

By this time, Paramount had really gotten into deep trouble. Their stock had gone from big numbers down to zero practically and they did have to let people go. They let me go, they let Mary Brian go, they let Jean Arthur go and I really can't remember who else—maybe William Powell. I associate him with that circumstance because he came to dinner at our house—John's and mine—and we tried to be brave about it and say, "Well, isn't it wonderful that we're out from under this big institution?" Then we went out on the lawn and danced around in a circle. Some of that feeling was false probably but I think there was a little bit of truth in it as well.

After that, I did *Nikki,* a musical co-authored by my husband, on Broadway. But it was not successful. I think for one thing nothing was successful in New York then. It still was Depression times. I lived at the Pierre Hotel. I had a five-room suite for thirty dollars a day and they were glad to have me there, glad to have anybody in their hotel. People didn't have money to go to the theatre but also there was something not quite shaped right about that particular play. It was a musical yet there were tragic elements in it. Maybe that was part of it. It had been taken from *Single Lady* so it was very, very much like *The Sun Also Rises.* I did no dancing in it but a little singing. But the idea about this character was that she didn't do anything very well. She was just charming and lovable so it didn't matter a lot whether I had a good voice. I said something in it that I had picked up from Janet Gaynor. She had a little phrase that she used—"on account of," "I can't do that on account of." She never said "because" and it just had a little different tone to it. John was very good at picking up dialogue. He had an ear for the unusual phrase and that was one of them he used for that character.

My leading man was a handsome young actor by the name of Archie Leach. He played a character named Cary Lockwood in the play. He got his new first name from that part and soon changed his name to Cary Grant when he began making films.

With Clive Brook and Jean Arthur in *The Lawyer's Secret.*

He had an outstanding quality and he made me keen about getting to the theatre every night. I never had any stage fright and no concern about anything. I was just happy to be working under those circumstances and sharing evenings with Cary Grant. It was really nice and he was very generous. If I had a scene where the focus was to be on me, he made sure that his back was to the audience so that it all went to me, you know. He was a very dear human being.

When I got back to Hollywood, I saw Merian Cooper about a new film he was planning for RKO. David O. Selznick, who had been with Paramount, was now running the RKO studio. Merian Cooper had been his good friend for quite a period of time. But as a matter of fact, Merian had left Hollywood in anger over *The Four Feathers.* He didn't like what Paramount had done to it—that would include Selznick—and he decided he'd just quit Hollywood so he went away. But then he was influenced by his friend Douglas Burden who had brought back from some far-away place some giant lizards and given them to the Bronx zoo in New York. They did not survive and I think that that was the key to the idea that built up in Cooper's mind about bringing some great animal from a far-distant place into civilization and he would not survive just because of civilization being an opposite, his enemy. So Cooper must have begun at that time to think about that story and begun to realize that Willis O'Brien had developed his work in animation to quite a wonderful degree. O'Brien had made *The Lost World* some years before but I had not seen it. I didn't know anything about all that stuff.

With Ronald Colman in *The Unholy Garden.*

When I saw Merian, he said to me, "You're going to have the tallest, darkest leading man in Hollywood." That quote is absolutely true. I didn't have to search for that line. Because I had just recently been working with Cary Grant and knew that he was coming to California, I wondered how Merian had found out about Cary and sensed that I might have liked him and was accommodating my interest. But how funny that it was just this little drawing he had of a gorilla that he showed me and said I was going to work with him. Then we went for a walk in the studio's back lot where he showed me a little setting with an eighteen-inch model of the gorilla. We were walking a little further when Merian stopped and said, "I think I'll call him Kong," and after a pause, he added, "King Kong!"

Edgar Wallace was credited as co-author of the story of *King Kong* with Merian Cooper. I met him only once. I spent an hour or so at Merian's apartment in Hollywood when Edgar Wallace was there. But he died of pneumonia shortly after that and I never was aware that he really contributed anything that was used. I don't believe even the names of the characters, the story development or the details were in any of the work that he had produced.

The screenplay itself was written by James Ashmore Creelman and Ruth Rose, Ernest Schoedsack's wife. Creelman had been under contract to RKO and I think that *King Kong* was not the only film he did that I was in. I can't remember what the other ones were but I was very much aware of him. Not only that but at a later time, I had been separated from John Monk Saunders and I was living in a very large and attractive apartment building called the Chateau Elysee. A lot of people in Hollywood used that in between circumstances. He was living there, too, and on many occasions I played tennis with him. So that's how I knew him more than as a studio person. He was a little ponderous. He puffed a pipe, he walked slowly and thought a lot about it before he served. "Ponderous" is a good word for him except that you have to be pretty big to be ponderous and he wasn't really big. He didn't have a big frame. I didn't see that he had a sense of humor particularly but his humor might have come out very well on paper or at times when I didn't see him or know him. I don't mean any of this in a derogatory way because he was a perfectly nice guy but a little heavy.

I knew Ruth Rose very, very well and she was a woman of great character. She and Schoedsack had a son who was born with great handicaps. He was very, very bright but I can't remember—it might have been muscular dystrophy that he had, I'm not sure. There are other things children have that are almost impossible to overcome. But she took care of

With Bruce Cabot in *King Kong*.

him so well and she had great integrity. She had been an actress in the theatre for a brief time with William Gillette. I think that what she brought to the script of *King Kong* was invaluable. She brought to it an absolute simplicity. For instance, when they didn't know how they were going to get King Kong from the island to New York, she said something like, "Oh, just put it in lights over the theatre—the greatest show or something." And she erased all the complications and uncertainties just by doing something like that. The dialogue, too, was simple, never hoity-toity in any way, and I think she did a lot for it.

I didn't spend any particular special time with anyone on *King Kong* except Cooper. I just met Willis O'Brien one day when he came on the set. I saw him standing there looking very tall and very silent and he went away. But I spent a lot of time with Cooper and Dorothy Jordan when they got married. He was the nearest thing to the best friend I had while I was in it.

Bruce Cabot and Robert Armstrong, my co-stars in *King Kong,* were people who were just good professional workers. Certainly, Robert Armstrong I would have to say that about. Bruce Cabot, though, they had to go find sometimes. He wasn't always ready to work and he was not so responsible as he really should have been, I think. But certainly Robert Armstrong was first-class as an actor and he did a wonderful job in that film. I had lunch with him and his wife a couple of times afterwards.

We worked on the set of the back lot at the Culver City studio with that big wall that had been used for *The King of Kings.* Then we worked at Long Beach for the scenes when we came on the shore of the island. I'm pretty sure we worked down at Long Beach on the boat as well. The scene in the theatre was filmed at the Shrine Auditorium. Of course, the set for the Empire State Building was replicated at the studio because I never was in New York for locations.

It was never stated how tall Kong was but in my own mind I made him about forty feet high and that was helpful to my own imagination. For the scenes where I was in Kong's big hand, we worked on a stage. This large hand had a big steel bar through it and was operated by the men. There was a lever that pulled this up into the air but before they pulled it up, they put these flexible fingers of the hand around my waist and secured them as tightly as they could. Then they lifted it up to be in good range of a camera so that it would match with some background that they had there, I guess. I didn't even pay any attention to what the background was at the time but I would do my best to look as though I were trying to get away from him. In fact, I was trying to hang on because every move I made caused the fingers to open a little more and very often I was concerned that I would fall through onto the stage floor. It would have been maybe six feet or something but that would be a big thud to come down through those fingers, you know. So I would call out, "Let me down!" And they would do that. Then they would tighten those fingers up again and up we'd go but it just seemed funny to me. In fact, I heard Johnny Carson say one night, "She always seemed to be trying to get away from him. Suppose she did up there by the top of the Empire State Building. She would have fallen all the way down." So it just was an illusion that was necessary for the film.

With Kong. (Courtesy of Fay Wray Rothenberg.)

I didn't work with the miniatures. They had a little tiny figure, I think about three inches long, and when I'd go to the rushes to see these things, sometimes I'd think that that must be the little wooden doll they had put in the small creature's hand, the miniature Kong's hand. I was satisfied that that was it and then when the little doll began to move, I knew that it was me. So that just fascinated me but never enough that I wanted to find out the technical way they did it. It was more fun and had much more pleasure for me to believe that it was true than to analyze it, you know.

The first scenes that I did for *Kong* were a new thing that they were using at that time or perhaps it was used for *the* first time involving rear projection of the animated creatures. Cooper filmed me in a tree alongside a big screen on which was projected the battle between Kong and a tyrannosaurus. That was very difficult for me because the filming went on for an entire day and a night. Of course, I was very tired when we finished early in the morning. Cooper told everyone afterwards that he'd just worked me for twenty-two hours. But I was young and strong so I came through.

I wasn't worn out from all the screaming I did in the film. When a woman who's an opera singer sings an aria, is she exhausted? You don't expect that so it's a similar thing. I mean you're just using your voice in a different way. I did think there was too much screaming for my taste but later I realized there had to be extra screaming that I did because that was what really animated and made alive the little doll. But it wouldn't have been appropriate to scream during the climax on the Empire State Building because she was not being touched by him. He had put her in a safe situation, he thought, and she was just trying to press her body against the wall till someone could come and get her, I think. When he took me there, he was trying to protect me or keep me from things that he instinctively thought were wrong.

I think the contrast between reality and fantasy is what carries the story and the construction of this film is extraordinary. It builds a suspense as well as any film that you can tell me about. And there must be a dozen different theories about the film. Kong has been analyzed as a tragic hero. The environmental aspect would be easy to do since they take him away from his natural habitat. One woman wrote me a letter and said she knew now that she had to go into volunteer nursing. That's what she learned from that film. And I remember there was a wonderful little sign, "Kong died for your sins."

There were some scenes that the censors cut out when it was later reissued. I think there was a scene when Kong crushed a man into the ground—they took that out. I think when he bit a man in half—they took that out, too. And there was the scene with me and my clothing. Of course, he never was peeling off my clothing. That was just an illusion caused by the fact that I had cut my own dress and that made it possible for them to tie wires on to the pieces so that each little wire pulled off little sections of the skirt. I knew what was going to happen and it just seemed like he was peeling off the clothes but he was never doing more than that.

Still, in the long run, I think Kong was a sympathetic character, absolutely. As a matter of fact, just in this last month, there's a piece I wrote about *Kong* in a magazine called *Premiere* expressing a lot of the things we're talking about now. But mostly, I think it's a warmer thing than I've ever done before and has more of my feeling about Kong. It was so horrible when he was killed at the end. That creature was up on top of that building and he didn't have a chance to get away. And both Schoedsack and Cooper decided to be the aviators who went after him. Did you know that? So they contributed to his death.

Cooper and Schoedsack were totally different personalities. I think they complemented each other by their mutual interest in exploring different parts of the world and that really held them together. I think that neither one was a very good director. They were just good strong personalities and they certainly worked together effectively. I think that Cooper had a stronger sense of what movies were about and had a lot of good ideas. He had really big ideas and he was so enthusiastic. If he'd tell you anything about what he was going to do, it came out like a kid with great joy. Whenever he'd see me, he'd beat his chest like Kong. Schoedsack was not as expressive or he was a more controlled person, let's say. He and his wife, Ruth Rose, continued to be my friends. I would visit them in later years at their home because they didn't go out much after Schoedsack lost his sight. But even when he was losing his sight, he applied himself to carving and making things and having a wonderful sound system.

As for their direction of films, I know that where *Kong* was concerned, Cooper seemed to handle the special effects things. Now, for instance, the rear projection sequence that I told you about as well as the scenes with me and Kong's big hand where they used the lever, he did all that. Schoedsack was never on the set for those scenes. Then Schoedsack did the scenes with me, Bruce Cabot

Watching the duel between Kong and a pterodactyl.

In the giant hand during the climax set in New York. (Courtesy of Fay Wray Rothenberg.)

and Robert Armstrong. And he did all the crowd scenes with the people in the city and the scenes with Noble Johnson and the natives. I don't know why they divided it that way. I never asked about it. But they allowed me total freedom in developing my character. That was the one time I think I had no direction whatsoever in a role. Only one time did Cooper call out to me and say, "Scream, Fay, scream for your life!" during that twenty-two hour stretch at the beginning. Now I swear to you it was just really lovely to know that whatever I did, they thought was wonderful and that was it—no discussion about what I would do or wouldn't do. For instance, if you remember, there's a scene on the boat when she's getting a screen test. I just thought about in advance what I would do for that. There was one take and that was it—only one take of that scene. So I had absolute control over everything I would do. They never felt any need to tell me what to do. After all, this was a role that was pretty obviously what it was and I liked it because I thought the elements in the whole thing were strong and I enjoyed having that freedom to do it any way I wanted.

I saw *King Kong* at Grauman's Chinese Theatre the first time that it was shown in Hollywood in 1933. The audience gave it a very positive reception and the next day, the reviews were wonderful. I understand that the film saved RKO. They were in a really, really serious situation and it was an immediate hit and went on to make a great deal of money for them.

We worked on *Kong* for over a year and I did four other pictures while I was filming *Kong*. I guess it was because of *Kong*'s reputation that I worked in other scary pictures but I never did like some of the films I did that were supposed to be horror films. I never thought of *King Kong* as a horror film. A science fantasy, yes, but it never occurred to me to think of it as a horror film. But one of the films I did in 1932, *The Most Dangerous Game,* had an interesting story because it was the reverse of what normally would be done with a theme. Instead of man hunting animals, man was hunting man and that was an interesting concept. Schoedsack directed it for RKO while we were doing *Kong* and we were running for our lives in the same jungle set used in *Kong*. I was very taken with the style of the English actor, Leslie Banks, who played the villain. He gave a fascinating performance. Joel McCrea was my leading man and he was a dear person, he really was. A lovely, lovely human being and it was nice to work with him. *The*

With Joel McCrea in *The Most Dangerous Game*. (Courtesy of Fay Wray Rothenberg.)

Most Dangerous Game had a lot of suspense, I suppose. I'm not sure if I ever saw the whole picture. I might have seen it on one occasion. I never saw many of the films that I did. I would say maybe sixty per cent I didn't see at all. I was busy and though I don't have any analysis of that, maybe I wasn't obviously interested in seeing them. It was exceptional to see them in the studio projection room when they were completed. Sometimes they had a first showing and you'd go to those obviously. But somehow—I can't really explain it—I just didn't run to see myself on the screen. That's the truth.

I went to Warner Brothers for two horror films, *Doctor X* and *The Mystery of the Wax Museum*. Both were with Lionel Atwill and were directed by Michael Curtiz. They were also both in Technicolor and because they had to use so much light, it was very, very hot and uncomfortable and really on account of that quite difficult. Lionel Atwill was very proper, very. He'd come from the theatre and he had a wonderful profile and was very conscious of it in a positive way, I think. He had a charming wife who had previously been married to General MacArthur.

Michael Curtiz was very efficient. He certainly had the whole concept of the films he did in mind. But he was very impersonal. He was almost mechanical. He didn't have an iota of charm or warmth about him. I don't remember that he had trouble with the language. He expressed himself sufficiently well, I think, to run the company. But I don't think he had any compassion for the people who were working in the films. I remember on one occasion, he looked in the camera and said to someone in the scene, "Move over a little further. A little further. Now go home." It was a dismissing kind of unpleasant style he had so I wasn't keen about him as a person although I knew that he was an able director.

In 1933, besides the films I was doing for other studios, I got a contract with Columbia for four pictures a year. Unlike RKO, which seemed to me a grown-up studio already, Columbia seemed to be kind of pushed in together to accommodate the buildings that were more than the land could handle. For example, the dressing rooms were kind of upstairs over the administration offices. But it had a heart even though you were supposed not to like Harry Cohn because it was said nobody did. But I think he had a winning kind of way because he was so enthusiastic and he cared a lot about making films. I think he had a good instinct for drawing good talent into his orbit and I think he appreciated them. Even if they resented him, they knew that they had his okay to do all that they could.

One of the pictures I did for Columbia was *Ann Carver's Profession* and the best thing about that film was that it was written by a good writer, Robert Riskin. I didn't meet him then but I recognized a quality of work that was superior to the other scripts I'd been doing at Columbia. He had a true gift for dialogue and characterization. They go together—you can't separate them. The leading man, Gene Raymond, was very good, very nice to work with. The director, Edward Buzzell, was very good, too. He had a nice quality, gentle and enthusiastic at the same time. It was a pleasant experience. I really enjoyed that film. I played a professional person, a lawyer, in it. I really don't know how well I did it to tell you the truth. I guess it was all right. I know that I liked it and I know there were some lovely scenes in it that had nothing to do with the courtroom perhaps but still, it just was a superior piece of writing.

With Glenda Farrell in *The Mystery of the Wax Museum*. (Courtesy of Fay Wray Rothenberg.)

We went to Catalina for another Columbia film I did, *Below the Sea,* and we were out on a boat quite a bit. Ralph Bellamy was the leading man and Al Rogell was the director. Rogell wanted some seagulls in the background for a love scene between Ralph and me. He had the property man sprinkle crumbs on the railing of the boat to attract the seagulls. Well, the seagulls came, ate the crumbs and flew off before we could finish the scene. They did the same thing on the second take. Finally, Rogell shouted, "Send the seagulls through one at a time!" I think some people have thought Rogell was just teasing but I was there and I know that it was kind of a ridiculous moment for Al Rogell. He must have later tried to give it a different aspect but it was true that he just was angry. He was not fooling or trying to do anything tricky with the property man. So it was kind of a wonderfully absurd moment but nobody was going to take advantage of Al Rogell and say, "Aren't you foolish?" or anything like that. It just passed—the words went out on the waves and the ocean. But it was such an unusual and a crazy kind of thing that it got a lot of currency. It was told and retold over the years.

I worked for every one of the big studios in Hollywood at this time. For example, at Paramount in 1933, I had the role of a bad girl in *One Sunday Afternoon* with Gary Cooper. That was such a relief to get something with a character like that. I enjoyed that very much. It wasn't just a pretty girl, you know. I had the opportunity to do something different.

For Darryl Zanuck's newly-formed 20th Century which was then releasing through United Artists, I played in *The Bowery* with Wallace Beery, Jackie Cooper and George Raft. Wallace Beery was just

With Gary Cooper in *One Sunday Afternoon.* (Courtesy of Cole Johnson.)

Wallace Beery in a wonderful way. I never talked with him very much. I think he savored his own quality and character and his style of performing so that it seemed to me everything that he did was always Wallace Beery. If it fit the character, fine, but it had to be that way. I don't think he could have transformed himself in any way. But little Jackie Cooper—oh, he was so beguiling. He just had that great, wonderful, lovable pouting lower lip and was very, very winning. George Raft was a very contained individual. We'd had to do a scene where he hit me and he hated so bitterly to have to do that that it had to be take after take until we got it right and then he apologized to me very urgently. The director, Raoul Walsh, had an air of certainty about him. Whatever he did, he did it with an ease and a very good style and I admired him.

At Fox, I worked with Spencer Tracy in *Shanghai Madness.* Now he was the most true actor. There was an actor without any pretensions about him. He was certain of himself, he was certain of his scenes, he was certain of his dialogue, he was real. He just had something special that most actors do not have. It was an ease, a reality that was just beautiful. And it wasn't a great role that he had and it wasn't a great role that I had. I wore no make-up in the film because it was summertime and I had a little tan. He didn't wear any make-up, either, and I just felt that it was appropriate for me to be as undecorated as possible, you know. I thought that was a good feeling and we had a great cameraman, Lee Garmes, as well.

I went to MGM for *Viva Villa!* I was asked to do it. David Selznick called me and said they would like to do a test and I said I didn't want to do a test. That just seemed inappropriate but he said, "It'd have to be very, very bad for you not to do this part."

And I said, "Oh, well, all right." He was someone I'd had a good feeling for so it was okay for me to do that. As a producer, David Selznick had taste. He had indifference to cost. He thought bigger than most producers would because he really didn't have anyone hovering over him. He was ultimate so he had the power to do what he wanted and he wanted things to be good so that was nice. I didn't see him come on the set, though, when we were filming. Producers at his level didn't spend a lot of time on the set. They were not "hands-on" like that. They looked at their rushes and they were either satisfied or not and had a conference, I think, with the director. But I don't think there's any doubt how hard-working Selznick was. As a mat-

With Wallace Beery in *Viva Villa!*

ter of fact, I knew him well enough personally to be aware that he would work through the night. He was very, very genial, really a nice guy. I used to play Ping-Pong with him at their house—David's and his wife Irene's—and he was always very pleasant. He wasn't heavy in manner. He had an eager quality about him like the next thing he was going to do was going to be better than the last thing. He was like a big kid but enthusiastic about whatever he was doing, I think.

Jack Conway, who directed *Viva Villa!*, was a good director. He didn't set the world on fire but I think he was a very good craftsman. Wallace Beery played Pancho Villa and, as I said before, I think he just put on a different hat when playing the role. Leo Carrillo who portrayed his sidekick I remember as kind of a jolly fellow. Joseph Schildkraut played the villain but, of course, there was nothing sinister about him in real life.

I thought I had a nice role and I liked the way I was able to look really almost like a Latin although my eyes being blue photographed rather light. That didn't seem to be as it should be but that was no deficit, I don't think. I had a very personal role involving conflict. The strongest scene, I think, was where there was a beating of this girl I played. I didn't analyze the film. I didn't study the structure of it or the politics of it. I played my role and that was it. But I guess anything about Mexico was really interesting to me because of my grandfather who had loved Mexico and Mexican people and spent quite a little time there. He translated *The Book of Mormon* into Spanish so he had a certain culture that came from that experience. And I was very simpatico with the Mexican people, too.

Mostly, I just worked in the studio. I think I was in a scene outside in *Viva Villa!* that would have been done as usual in the San Fernando Valley. I think the film was beautifully photographed. For one thing, James Wong Howe was a great cameraman. I have not seen the whole film, perhaps ever. I've seen fragments. But it was an elegant-looking film certainly. I thought that it had stature, that it was a picture of worthy quality. Anything that's historical takes on added glory when it's made into a film—more than in any other kind of picture.

I was also doing films for Universal. *The Countess of Monte Cristo* was a comedy with Paul Lukas and Patsy Kelly. I liked Paul Lukas. He just had a beautiful quality, very sensitive and I'm amazed he was in that movie. I didn't think it was that good. Patsy Kelly was fun. She had a good comic style and she was robust in her approach to everything.

Another film I made at Universal was *Madame Spy*. It was a nice film directed by Karl Freund. He had been an outstanding cameraman and he was also a good director. He was one of the few directors I remember with great pleasure. Nils Asther, the leading man, was one of the handsomest men you could look at. He was just elegant-looking but he was fairly remote. I think he was not comfortable with English because he was Swedish. But he looked so good on the screen and he was charming.

With Fredric March in *The Affairs of Cellini.*

Not long after that, I worked in *The Affairs of Cellini* with Fredric March and Constance Bennett for the 20th Century company. That was—fun is not the word but it had a little more stature than some of the other pictures I did. Gregory La Cava directed. He liked to think a lot about the scene and review it in his own mind and just see how he could change it. There were lots of waits in between because of that and maybe it was good but it's the way he wanted to work and the way he did work.

Fredric March had a real sparkle and he was a handsome guy. I knew him and his wife, Florence Eldridge, and enjoyed their company. It was pleasant to work with Fredric March. But I think in that picture, the one who gave me the most fun to work with was Frank Morgan. Oh, he was so funny! He had a stumbling style that he developed so that it was as though he didn't know what he was going to say next. Louis Calhern, who was also in it, had a kind of elegance and a certain resentment when Constance Bennett wanted to leave the set before anyone else did. So he just said something to the effect that the order of things was a little bit sticky for him.

In the summer of 1934, I was in *Woman in the Dark* with Ralph Bellamy and Melvyn Douglas. That was made in New York and I'm not aware of any other films I made there. I really don't know why that was done back East. I think it was less expensive. They didn't often film on the East Coast in the thirties. Usually, these things are done for economic reasons and one has to accept that. There were no scenes on the street, I don't think. It was all done in the Biograph studio in uptown New York. I liked the film. I can't tell you too much about the details of it but it was quite a good role.

I'd done several other films with Ralph Bellamy. He was a warm, gentle and unpretentious person and I think whatever he did, he did very, very well. He just was likable. I'd worked with Melvyn Douglas before in a horror film, *The Vampire Bat*. He had a certain elegance. He was very quiet, very controlled, very professional. I use that word a lot but it does mean something. And working with him, I think the quality he had was one of a kind of remoteness that was very compelling. There was a quality of high intelligence about whatever he did that I think was quite appealing. Not only to work with but as an actor, I'm sure the audience felt that about him, too. I knew his wife, Helen Gahagan, as well. The first and the most important reason

With Ralph Bellamy, Roscoe Ates, and Nell O'Day in *Woman in the Dark*. (Courtesy of Fay Wray Rothenberg.)

was that she was a friend of Merian Cooper for whom she did the film, *She*. She would sometimes be at the Coopers' house for dinner and that's when I would meet her because we had a pretty strong social relationship with the Coopers.

When I got back to Hollywood from New York, I was in a comedy at RKO with Joel McCrea and Miriam Hopkins, *The Richest Girl in the World*. William A. Seiter directed and I thought he was wonderful because he had such high good spirits. He laughed a great deal and I enjoyed him. Miriam Hopkins was good, too. I learned something working with her that I never did forget. I think very often if an actor or actress is told they've done something wrong in a scene, they can kind of curl up. But I just loved the way she responded to Mr. Seiter when he brought something to her attention. She said, "Oh, thank you, thank you." And I wasn't aware that she even meant it—maybe she did—but I just thought that was wonderful. It opens up a different aspect of a relationship between a director and an actor that for me, anyway, was great.

The Richest Girl in the World had a good script by Norman Krasna. He had been really a protégé of Robert Riskin. In fact, he said that most of what he knew about writing scripts, he learned from Robert Riskin who was a towering talent.

My last films in 1934 were made for Columbia, *White Lies* with Walter Connolly and Victor Jory and *Mills of the Gods* with May Robson and again Victor Jory. I'd worked with Walter Connolly in two earlier films. He was a brilliant character actor and a very gentle, easy-going, sweet man with a strength of style and quality of intelligence in his performances. May Robson was a very strong actress and very real. She had a real quality of the theatre in back of her and a sweet arrogance. Victor Jory was quite fascinating to work with. He had kind of an electric quality that really lighted up the scenes, I felt. He was a little on the tough side because he fit it. I think he was born up in the Yukon and he used to get into fights. He had to learn not to do that. He was just a very open-hearted and very gifted actor, I thought, and I enjoyed that.

It was at this time that the various guilds were being formed. I remember it had been about a year or so earlier when the Screen Actors Guild had its beginning at the home of Freddie March and his wife. They invited maybe about six people to come one evening to listen to what Robert Montgomery

An early '30s costume party at Pickfair: left to right, Douglas Fairbanks, Jr., Mrs. Johnny Mack Brown, Joel McCrea, John Monk Saunders kissing Countess Dorothy di Frasso, Mary Pickford with her arm around her cousin, Sonny Chalif, Fay, Mary Brian, Richard Dix, Johnny Mack Brown, David Rose. (Fay Wray Collection, USC.)

had to say about starting an actor's guild and it was a lot to digest for me. I didn't get the whole slant on it but I was interested in being present and nothing more than just listening developed that night. But soon there was a meeting that I went to at the Writers Guild. That was the night of the great earthquake in 1933, I think. So it then began to take shape that night as a fact that there would be a Screen Actors Guild and I was certainly a founder-member.

I'd been doing so many films, just one after another. About once a month, I started work on another one—not ever on the same day, though. That would be a little bit too much. I don't think I could have done that. One had to make preparations for wardrobe and such things. In fact, I'm aware of a strange situation about the timing for me. It seemed about every fourth Friday I was going to a studio to get costumed for another movie and that was really awful, terrible. But don't forget that a lot of people were not working, it was a difficult time and so I guess whoever was my agent at the time was delighted with me because at least I was busy. It was not good judgment, though. Also, I think there was a system whereby on Saturday night, they could work very late like into three o'clock in the morning because you wouldn't be coming back under the Guild's rules until Monday. So you had a space of time and they took advantage of that by asking you to work late and there was no rule against it. In fact, it was a regular thing. As time went by, they changed those things but that's the way it was then.

That sort of thing certainly would cut into social life but then it should. I mean work is first, social life is second and has to be. John and I often did have our friends over at our lovely house on Selma Avenue. In the summer, we rented beach houses. At Christmastime for shopping, I had a driver to take me here and there. But mostly, I continued to drive myself. I drove a Packard at the time. I had a more modest approach to life than others. I never wore a lot of sequins or beads or that kind of thing. I preferred simple, classic clothes without a lot of jewelry. Extravagance never was an attitude of mine, I don't think, not at all, because I was interested more in books and in good conversation and maybe playing Ping-Pong—I was skilled at that.

I did get to know many of the stars like Mary Pickford, Gloria Swanson and Dolores Del Rio. I recall Mary as being a happy creature, a content person of great charm and with very good taste who gave wonderful costume parties. I greatly admired Gloria. She was an elegant and attractive lady and very much a star in her behavior. Dolores and I were like sisters. She was a great beauty who had

Fay inside her Selma Avenue home in Hollywood. (Courtesy of Fay Wray Rothenberg.)

an almost mysterious quality. She was attentive to her beauty but her religion meant a lot to her and she was serious about her work. I remember she wanted to study acting in New York.

I knew Charlie Chaplin in those days, too. I would meet him at Douglas Fairbanks's beach house and also when he was visiting his friend, Lord Bernstein. Chaplin was very charming and very voluble. He liked to talk and tell anecdotes. I didn't see him in later years but I thought it was tragic the way he left the country. Chaplin felt he was a citizen of the world and the way he was treated was pretty rough.

I left Hollywood with John in late 1934 and went to England to make films mostly, I think, because I really wanted to break this chain of pictures like *The Vampire Bat.* I don't know—that must have come along about 1933 but I associated that with the reason I wanted to get away. It was not a good picture and to put Melvyn Douglas and all those people in it! But people needed work.

So I did two films for British Gaumont. The British Gaumont studio was outside the city. It wasn't a big institutional-looking place. It was small-

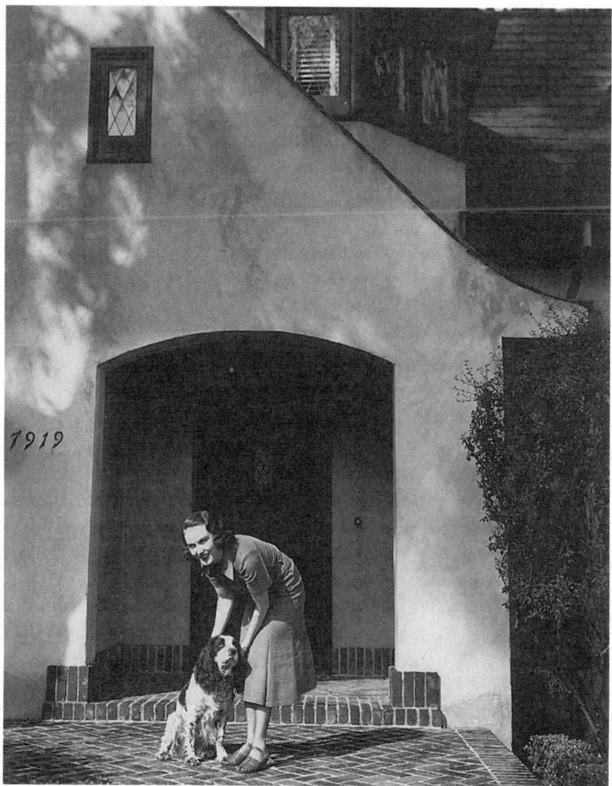

Fay at the entrance to her Selma Avenue home. (Courtesy of Fay Wray Rothenberg.)

ish—maybe a couple of sound stages and I don't think more than that. The first thing I did there, I think, was *Bulldog Jack* with Jack Hulbert in the lead and Ralph Richardson in support. Jack Hulbert was unrelated to life as a person, it seemed to me. He was an image and he was very popular as that image—that big, long jaw. He was funny to the English people. I couldn't think of him as an individual but rather as a comic and that was the beginning and end. Ralph Richardson was a wonderful person, easy to talk to, very thoughtful, very accomplished and he cared about his role. Even though it was not a topflight picture, he gave everything to it just the same. He didn't toss anything off, ever.

Then I was in *The Clairvoyant* with Claude Rains. I knew him well during the making of that film. He was an excellent actor, too. He applied himself and thought through the role and had good control. You had to give him a lot of respect. I certainly did.

After that, I did two other films in England with Jack Buchanan for another organization because they asked me to. Jack Buchanan was a dancer who had been with *Charlot's Revue* and was very, very popular in England. He was not a serious actor. He just had enormous grace and style and everything was contrived to provide him to express that. So neither of these films had any depth to them. *Come Out of the Pantry* was one and *When Knights Were Bold* was the other one. In one of them at least, he was able to do a sand dance where they put sand on the floor and the dancer makes a wonderful little scraping sound while tap-dancing.

Before I went to England, I had had a contract for three films at Columbia and I had at the same time a contract with RKO for three films. I would not have deserted any contract situation that I had going so when I came back to Hollywood in 1935, I got a new contract with Columbia and made four films exclusively for them until 1937. I was developing a child when I made *They Met in a Taxi* with Chester Morris. He was a very good actor who had been in the theatre. I loved films and I loved film actors but I must admit that there are times when you recognize a kind of style and quality about someone who'd been in the theatre that serves them well overall. And later I was in *It Happened in Hollywood* with Richard Dix. He was as handsome as we all know him to be and very impersonal but in a pleasant way, you know.

I made fewer films in the late thirties because my

With Claude Rains in *The Clairvoyant.* (Courtesy of Steven Hill.)

daughter was born in 1936 and that made quite a difference. But I did do summer stock and that's when I got to know Sinclair Lewis. That was a very interesting experience. I had met him socially in Hollywood before and he was performing in Cohasset, Massachusetts in a dramatization of his novel, *It Can't Happen Here,* at the same time I was doing a play there. He was doing a leading part, he was falling crazy in love with the theatre and I think he felt that he could be a very, very great actor. Well, he couldn't. He just was a wonderful, wonderful writer but he had nothing to work with as an actor. He didn't know it and that was really just too bad. But then he was personally very interesting, wonderful to listen to when he had the people from the theatre come to his place in the afternoon or after the performance.

My next job was in the theatre up in Saratoga, New York. Lewis had an idea about a play that he wanted to develop and he really just followed me there in order to augment that idea that he had in his mind. He talked to me about it and I made my contribution, my comments about it. Then when I went back to California, he wrote to me and I wrote to him and commented on what was developing. I had my suggestions so it really was a collaboration by mail, there's no question about that. But it was stimulating to relate to him. He was so fast-thinking, that man. He just had a beautiful mind. Our collaboration became a play, *Angela Is Twenty-Two,* which Universal made into a musical film called *This Is the Life* in the forties. I never saw it, though, but I think it was rather a lame little thing that was adjusted to accommodate different kinds of people.

I returned to pictures and continued to make some until 1942. I liked doing *Adam Had Four Sons* with Warner Baxter and Ingrid Bergman. Warner was nice to work with and I thought Ingrid had a wonderfully simple style that was very real. Again, it was almost like Spencer Tracy with no sense of performing. As a matter of fact, I think I had only a few scenes with her but I really felt a good thing about working with her.

About the same time, I worked with Jean Hersholt in *Melody for Three.* He was a very true, simple actor and gentle in his style. In real life, he was a most kindly, noble person, the most humanitarian man I ever met. He put up his own money to buy the Motion Picture Home.

By then, my life had changed so markedly. I had separated from John Monk Saunders and there had been a very difficult divorcing situation. I think obviously because of that, I wanted to be away from California and to continue in New York if possible. That seemed to be a better milieu at the time.

It was while I was in New York that I attended the premiere of Orson Welles's *Citizen Kane* in 1941. I think the first time I met Orson was at a party where he was dancing with my close friend, Dolores Del Rio. He was quite radiant. He was happy and in love with her. There was an ebullience about him that was shining. He was just a

With Ingrid Bergman in *Adam Had Four Sons.*

shining personality. They invited me to come to New York for the opening of *Citizen Kane.* I let my little girl, Susan, go with her wonderful nurse and stay with her family in Charlottesville, Virginia, while I went to see *Citizen Kane.* It was very quiet sitting watching that. My escort at that time was Clifford Odets and he was terribly impressed. We were all impressed but there was no big fanfare like when people stand up and cheer. It wasn't as exuberant perhaps as one might imagine. But it was wonderfully, beautifully impressive.

I did a few plays back East as well as a ridiculous radio series. I did that in order to stay in New York and that wasn't a great thing to do. It wasn't a soap opera. It was designed around a girl who had a pet shop and so the parakeet had quite a lot to say. There was a man named George Putnam who was the announcer for that. He subsequently became very strong as a radio announcer in California.

I was working in the theatre in New York in a play called *Golden Wings* when Pearl Harbor happened. We listened to Mr. Roosevelt—the audience and the cast. We had opened the play that night and the play closed that night. I think it was over in one night really because of this shocking thing that had happened and the world had changed.

I had been seeing Robert Riskin for some time. The first time we had spoken was about my getting the part of Maria in *Lost Horizon* which Bob Riskin was scripting for Frank Capra. He was on the tennis court when we met. I was interested in the role because it was not an ordinary one but rather that of a girl who reverts to her true age when she leaves Shangri-La. The part went to Margo instead and I never asked if he'd spoken to Frank about me. We next met at Dick and Jessica Barthelmess's Christmas party in 1939 and then we began seeing a lot of each other.

After completing *Meet John Doe* with Frank Capra in 1941, Bob was in England working with Edward R. Murrow before we got into the war. He had been in the Navy in the First World War and after Pearl Harbor, he wanted to do what he could for his country. He was ready to leave Hollywood and go to work for the Office of War Information. He established a really strong organization that was called the Overseas Motion Picture Bureau and they made a lot of wonderful propaganda films. He brought people from Hollywood who were very gifted to work on them. So he was coming to New York then and that was when he wanted us to be married. I was ready to do that and we were married in August of 1942.

With Robert Riskin in the early 1940s. (Courtesy of Fay Wray Rothenberg.)

He was overseas during much of the war and I was living in New York. But by the end of the war, we were back in Hollywood and he resumed writing films. I had stopped working, however, because I was busy raising our family—my older daughter, Susan, and my two children I had with Bob, our son Bobby and our daughter Vicki.

In the late forties and early fifties, the McCarthy time came to Hollywood and it was horrifying. Oh, my, how tragic it was! It's unbelievable. I mean Gary Cooper went to testify against actors. But I don't think I had any intimate association with people who were blacklisted. It's interesting that Robert Riskin was a liberal but he never had a finger pointed at him. It was somehow like he was outside of that. He was respected but, of course, he would never have been a conspirator of any kind.

As for myself, I was not a highly political person or if I was, I kept it largely to myself. I think that I had been brought up by my mother as a little Republican. But then I was married to John Monk Saunders who was a Democrat and he was really shocked that I would consider voting for a Republican. But the first person I voted for was Franklin Roosevelt in 1936. Because of having been born in Canada, I had not been a citizen and so just prior to that election, I had to apply for my citizenship. And in 1944, I gave a speech at a New York rally for President Roosevelt's reelection.

It came to be necessary to return to acting when my husband became ill in the early fifties. So much of our funds were taken with long periods of illness and so I began working in pictures again as well as television. For instance, I was in a film with Joan Crawford, *Queen Bee,* and she was dandy. She made you feel almost that she was Miss Motion Pictures and that she was in charge of the whole industry when she said, "We are so glad to have you back in films." She wrote me a note to tell me that. I didn't know her very deeply at all but she expressed a good regard for me and that was nice.

We still needed money after my husband passed away in 1955 so I continued acting into the sixties. I did a few TV things—one I remember was with Ralph Bellamy when he had a series at MGM. But when the assassination of JFK took place, somehow that just changed my attitude. I thought if I could get by without working, it would be better. It was a strange phenomenon. My younger daughter, Vicki, was away in school at Stephens College and we talked long over the telephone about this event. Of course, I'm not the only one whose life was changed by that happening. She went to school in Europe and when she wanted me to come and see her, then I went and I just thought it was more important to relate to my kids than it was to work. I'd done a few TV shows when I had to get up at four-thirty in the morning to go to work and it was no longer any special joy. It was tough to try to manage everything, you know.

With Edward G. Robinson in *Hell on Frisco Bay.* (Courtesy of Fay Wray Rothenberg.)

Much later, in 1980, I had a part in a TV film, *Gideon's Trumpet* with Henry Fonda, and that was really what you might call nepotism because my daughter Vicki had married the man who wrote that, David Rintels. She wanted me to do this role and at first I said, "Oh, no, no, no."

But she put her head down and said, "I think it would be wonderful," so that's all she had to say. I would do it if she wanted it.

I hadn't known Henry Fonda before but he was a rich experience. He was so concentrated in his role. I just had great respect for him and I think we shared a mutual warmth that I will not forget. He gave me a drawing that he'd made. He was very gifted at drawing. I think it's a litho of a drawing that he'd done—a page in *The Grapes of Wrath* and he emphasized a paragraph in the center of the page by laying a magnifying glass over that. He drew that so it just looks wonderful. He did all that fine lettering to enlarge that and it is a very, very nice piece of work.

Looking back over my career, I would have loved to have had more roles of more unusual character and depth and I often thought that was too bad. However, it's a strange thing. I think I have at least one film that people have cared enough about to make them feel good. I think it's a strange, strange kind of magic that *King Kong* has. People who see it—their lives have changed because of it and they have so told me. I mean professors as well as youngsters have been very much affected by it and if I'm a part of that at all and it continues to have a life, it's kind of nice.

I feel silents were easier to make because that was the original form but I don't think that the sound film was a negative for me. However, I think—you know, this is speculation—if I could have gone on and done a few more films with Erich von Stroheim, my career would have taken a different quality and character. Now, for instance, Ernst Lubitsch I would have loved to work with and he told Irene Selznick he would have loved to have worked with me. But, you know, circumstances, situations, the economy, personal life, whatever—things just took a different shape than what I would have

A portrait from the 1930s.

liked. I think when I was first married, I was really concerned that my energy and my drive and my vision of myself might be interrupted—and it was. It just was interrupted but that is how it was and it's not to be found disturbing.

I keep going because I think essentially I am more of a spiritual person than I am a materialistic person and that gives me a lot more strength than I would have otherwise. I feel good, I feel wonderful, I love life, I love people. I have a lot of precious people in my life. I love to make people joyful. That's a good motor to have and I've still got it.

(The Kobal Collection.)

Annabella

A 1932 booklet on a rising young film actress published in Paris proclaimed that "The talent of Annabella, the distinction, the sensitivity and the intelligence of her face finally brings us a French star of 'international class.' "[1] Indeed, no one on the screen more fully incarnated the joie de vivre, the insouciant gaiety and vitality of France in those years than the beautiful Annabella whose birth in Paris on July 14, 1909, coincided with her country's national holiday.

She had been born Suzanne Georgette Charpentier to a cultured, well-to-do and close-knit French family. Growing up with her parents and two brothers in a large country house outside Paris, she had an idyllic childhood. Her father was a magazine publisher and, from an early age, she imbibed the literate atmosphere of her parents and their friends. Her father had also developed the scouting movement in France, instilling in her a love for outdoor activities. Under these influences, she grew into a dreamy child who cherished books and moments of solitude yet was a gregarious tomboy who swam, hiked and played tennis.

She was crazy about the movies, too, so much so that she would sell her children's books to buy fan magazines. That love of films led to her being suggested for a part in *Napoléon,* an extraordinary new epic film being planned by Abel Gance, the greatest French director of the silent era. His vast project, which began filming in 1925, was replete with revolutionary techniques that defied cinematic conventions—rapid montage, the handheld camera and a huge three-screen process utilizing the expanded canvas for both far-flung panoramas and parallel images.

In order to give life to the era of the 1790s, Gance blended historical figures with fictional characters. Particularly significant was the part played by Annabella, Violine, a wistfully romantic girl whose mystical love of Bonaparte from afar was intended to represent the heart of the people. The 1932 booklet on Annabella commented on her role in the film: "For the first time, the delicate sensitivity of the ordinary people of France . . . came through on the screen."[2] Yet although Annabella had a leading part in the definitive six-hour version which Gance had intended to be shown over several days as a series, her role was diminished or eliminated when the film was cut to satisfy the commercial interests of the exhibitors and distributors.

Despite this, *Napoléon* commenced her career and she went on to make two more silent films, *Maldone* (1927) and *Trois jeunes filles nues* (1928). But with the arrival of sound she became more prominent with each successive role until, in 1931, she had the opportunity to work with René Clair, another visionary director. Clair, who was light and satiric in his approach, genially ruling over his kingdom of the imagination at the Epinay studio, had become France's preeminent director in the early sound era. When Annabella played the leading feminine role in his classic musical farce, *Le Million,* the film's international success made her an immediate star.

Soon, directors were clamoring for France's most popular young actress—and not only in her own country. Two of her greatest films were directed by Paul Fejös, *Marie, Légende Hongroise* (1932), filmed in his native Hungary, and *Sonnenstrahl* (1933), which he made in Austria. In *Marie,* she plays a Hungarian peasant who is seduced by a well-to-do bourgeois and is then persecuted by her fellow

As Violine in *Napoléon*. (Courtesy of Kevin Brownlow.)

villagers for giving birth to a child out of wedlock. In *Sonnenstrahl,* a film about ordinary people with scenes shot on location in Vienna, she, together with her boyfriend, struggles to survive amidst the poverty and unemployment of the thirties.

Her second film with Clair, *Quatorze Juillet* (1933), brought her continued critical acclaim. A French reviewer of the time commented: "As in *Le Million,* Clair finds in Annabella the ideal interpreter. She brings to the character of the Parisian working-girl a freshness, a rightness of tone rarely encountered in French cinema."[3] When the Museum of Modern Art revived the film in 1981, Catherine Ann Surowiec wrote in the program notes that "Annabella's radiant and poignant performance as the gamine flowerseller is the core of the film. The rightness and honesty of her playing is remarkable. . . . she is both childlike and playful, womanly and tender, plucky and independent, and, above all, romantically wistful."[4]

Although her performance in *Quatorze Juillet* enhanced her reputation as a symbol of France on the screen, her string of triumphs included some decidedly non-Gallic roles such as the Japanese woman in *La Bataille* (1934) and the North African girl in

With George Rigaud in *Quatorze Juillet*. (The Kobal Collection.)

La Bandera (1935). Her recognition in Europe peaked with her portrayal of the wife of a captured World War I naval commander in Marcel l'Herbier's *Veille d'Armes,* a role which earned her the best actress award at the 1936 Venice Film Festival.

Her English-language films made for 20th Century–Fox in England and the United States introduced American audiences to a European actress very different from other Continental actresses who had come to Hollywood. Such stars as Pola Negri, Greta Garbo and Marlene Dietrich had played sirens, sometimes long-suffering, often remote and with a touch of mystery that seemed worlds removed from most American-born actresses. Annabella, however, even when cast in an aristocratic role, maintained a kind of democratic demeanor that bridged the gap between the Old World and the New. While skilled in high drama, she had a lightness of touch unusual for a European actress appearing in English-language films. In *Wings of the Morning,* she is a Spanish princess of gypsy descent who disguises herself as a boy and winds up romancing Henry Fonda. In *Dinner at the Ritz,* she is a resourceful heroine who dons a series of disguises in order to track down her father's murderer. And in *The Baroness and the Butler,* a sparkling comedy which brought her to Hollywood, her noblewoman is a match for William Powell's suave butler.

With Henry Fonda in *Wings of the Morning.* (Courtesy of Annabella Power.)

During the making of her next film, *Suez* in 1938, Annabella met and fell in love with her leading man, Tyrone Power. For the third time, her work with an actor had led to romance. Early in her career, she was involved with an actor who became the father of her only child, a daughter whom Annabella nicknamed Doode; she was christened Annie and in later years renamed Anne after Annabella's friend and sister-in-law, Anne Power Hardenbergh.

Annabella had met her first husband, actor Jean Murat, during the filming of *Paris-Méditerranée* and the two reigned as the glamour couple in French film circles of the thirties. But it was her second marriage to Hollywood's dashing, handsome matinee idol, Tyrone Power, that would become legendary. Hollywood had not seen such an international romance since the days of Greta Garbo and John Gilbert, Vilma Banky and Rod LaRocque in the twenties. Their wedding and European honeymoon in 1939 were publicized throughout the world. The two settled in a beautiful home in Brentwood and Annabella went about the business of decorating it, demonstrating exceptional talent. The Powers, among the most prominent figures in Hollywood society, had a list of friends that read like a fan magazine—Clark Gable, Humphrey Bogart, Myrna Loy, Bette Davis, Joan Crawford, Fredric March, Laurence Olivier, Vivien Leigh, Alice Faye, Jack Benny, Orson Welles, Frances Farmer, Howard Hughes to name a few. For three years, Annabella and Tyrone were extremely happy, a blissfulness clouded only by the fact that they could not have children. However, Annabella's daughter was close to her new stepfather who legally adopted her. (Throughout the thirties, she had been living with her mother in France and Jean Murat had also been a loving father to her.)

World War II changed the golden couple's lives dramatically. Tyrone joined the Marines and Annabella, who had supported the French resistance movement, now helped in the war effort by selling bonds and entertaining American troops overseas. Her own family was caught up in the war in France with her adored younger brother, Pierre, captured by the Germans; he died in a POW camp. When Tyrone and Annabella were reunited after the war, things were never the same. In later years, she would maintain that their wartime separation contributed to their breakup. There is little doubt, however, that Tyrone's affairs with other actresses including Judy Garland and Lana Turner added to the strain.

In recent years, some writers have insisted that Tyrone was bisexual, an allegation Annabella laughingly dismissed. To those who would paint Tyrone, in her words, as "the king of the homosexuals," she had this to say: "Unfortunately, I think his life shows that he was a little too much on the *other* side." Despite their divorce in 1948, his two subsequent marriages and her later romantic involvements with several prominent men, they remained friends. Indeed, she was godmother to Romina, Tyrone's daughter by Linda Christian, and to Tyrone, Jr., his son by his third wife. There were times he asked her to remarry him but she refused, in part because she could no longer have children and in part because her pride would not let her. In retrospect, she believed that had they remarried, he might not have led a life of dissipation and died so young. In truth, she had never ceased to love him and after his death in 1958, she reclaimed his name.

As far as her career was concerned, Annabella had continued to work throughout the forties although Darryl Zanuck, who opposed her marriage to his star, Tyrone, and may have had designs on her himself, saw to it that her opportunities in Hollywood were limited to *Bridal Suite,* a 1939 MGM production, and a few war films for Fox. She had more choice roles on Broadway in those years, including the 1944 hit, *Jacobowsky and the Colonel,* and the 1946 production of Jean-Paul Sartre's *No Exit* in which she had an atypical role as a villainous lesbian.

After her return to Europe, she made several more films in France and Spain including *Le Dernier Amour* (1949) in which she worked with a new actress by the name of Jeanne Moreau who would later become her friend. But aside from an appearance as Empress Zita in *Elizabeth* for French TV in 1982, Annabella made no more films after 1950. With her daughter now grown and married to the actor Oskar Werner, she was on her own and in her early forties. She might have continued her career for many years but, as she said, she craved a less public life; perhaps, too, she felt she had achieved her ambitions during her quarter of a century in cinema. Her life had been bound up with the heroic prewar years of Gance, Clair, Fejos and L'Herbier in Europe and with Tyrone in the now-vanishing Golden Age of Hollywood. The post-war cinema by comparison had lost much of the color, romance and pioneering spirit that had so attracted her. Whatever the reason, she found her own Shangri-La, a sheep farm she called Contramundo, with a large two-story house in the south of France in the heart of the Basque country. When not on the farm, she resided in various apartments in and around Paris, all the while working on her social concerns including alleviating the plight of prisoners in France.

At the time I interviewed her in the summer of 1992, she was as active as ever, entertaining friends at her country house in the grand European manner, taking part in local religious festivities, still driving her car and finding time for a swim in the

With her daughter Anne in the late 1930s. (Courtesy of Annabella Power.)

Atlantic Ocean. A small, rare American flag in a frame, a large crucifix, and several paintings by her close friend, Anne Power Hardenbergh, highlighted the living room in her apartment in Neuilly where she spent part of the year. Her strongest tie was to her daughter, with the two frequently exchanging visits, Annabella traveling to the United States to stay with Anne in her home in New Hampshire and Anne making the trip to France each year to spend time with her mother.

Of medium height, slim, with blonde hair and brown eyes, Annabella was stunning-looking and in her eighties could pass for a woman much younger. She spoke rapidly in excellent English but with a strong, charming French accent. An enduring romantic, she had not lost her enthusiasm for life, a quality Abel Gance considered essential and one which she possessed in great abundance. She had a sense of humor and an appetite for adventure and, like a wide-eyed kid, could still marvel at an experience like riding the Chunnel when it opened in 1994. A cultivated, well-read woman whose companions included some of the most eminent writers of the century, a lady who had survived the terrible sorrows of the war, Annabella had an indomitable spirit that carried her to success as a great actress and fabled star and served her well in life.

I was born in Paris during a visit of my mother to her brother on Quatorze Juillet, the Fourteenth of July, and they didn't expect me that day. I was born about a week ahead of time. They had beautiful clothes ready for me at home but then I was born not in my mother's house but her brother's and not when I was expected. I was rolled up in a towel—that was my beginning being elegant.

My father's name was Charpentier. He served in the First World War. He didn't like to be in the mud and what they called the *tranchées.* But he was in the army and dressed up as a zouave because he was very young at the end of the war. He enlisted because he was very brave—he was wonderful. As a child during the war, I lived with my mother in Paris and in the country. I remember that during the last year or two of the war, my father wrote to my mother every day so they were a wonderful couple.

My father had a little money and after the war, he directed a magazine called *Journal des Voyages,* a travel magazine he published. When I went to his office in Paris, I saw beautiful things coming from Spain and beautiful things coming from China because he sent a lot of writers all over the place. So even when I was a child going with my mother and my brother to visit him in his office on the Rue Montmartre, he already gave me a taste of traveling. I was so anxious to see the whole world when I was a kid. When we were playing on the beach, we saw a plane passing by and they told me where they were going and so on. Before beginning to be an actress, I thought of becoming a stewardess and that I would travel all around the world.

My father not only directed the *Journal des Voyages* but also introduced "scoutism" in France because when he was young, he met Baden-Powell, the founder of the Boy Scouts. I had an older brother who was not very healthy and didn't care too much about being a scout and another brother

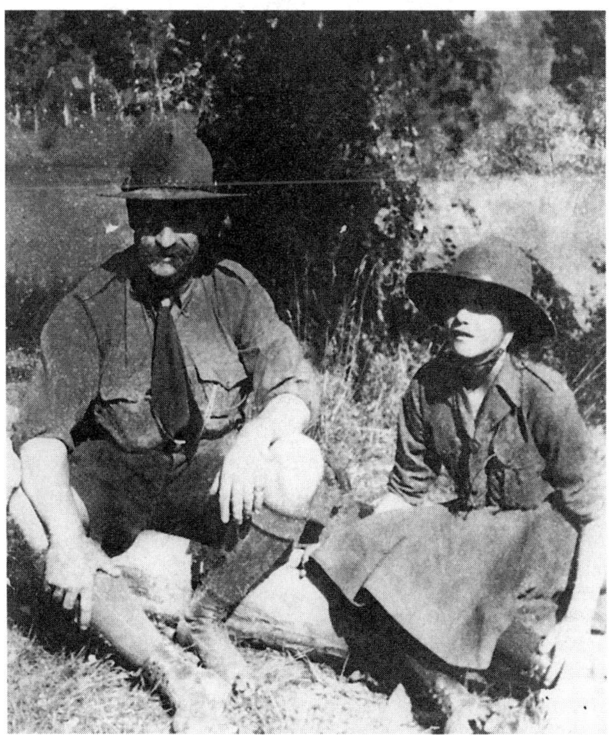

With her father Paul Charpentier circa 1919. (Courtesy of Annabella Power.)

who was too young. So my father was taking me around to all the scout meetings because it was fashionable for a girl to be with the scouts and so I was a girl scout. When I was in the American army during the last war playing for the troops, it was a life very dull and the other actors were complaining a little bit that it was not comfortable but as I had been a scout when I was a little girl, I thought it was perfectly normal and I could sleep on the floor.

My father was also a writer and a poet. I have a volume of his poems which I keep with me always. My mother was very artistic, too, very musical. Her brother was married to Germaine Dermoz who was the sister of the great painter, Jacques Dermoz. Germaine Dermoz herself was an actress at the Comédie Française. So the atmosphere was a very artistic and literary one but there was no one in the family in films before me.

I was very happy then. A lot of people are sad about their youth but being a child—for me, it was a dream. We were in the country not very far from Paris. We lived near the river La Marne in a very nice house with a garden and I began to love animals and gardening. The river Marne is not a river you can go swimming in now. Like all the rivers in the world, it is spoiled. But at that time, it was wonderful. My father would put a rope around my waist and he'd throw me in the water. That's why they called me *loutre* or *otter, une loutre joyeuse* because I was always in a good mood and I adored to go swimming.

I went to a little school where two old ladies who were kind of dumb were the teachers. I stayed a few months and then they put me in *l'école communale* for everybody. I always worked very well when I was crazy about my teacher and I had a wonderful teacher about history and another one about literature. Because of that, those are the two things I like the best. Don't ask me about mathematics because for me to add two and two, I'm not gifted.

As a child, I was fascinated by the movies. Maybe I was ten years old when I saw Lillian Gish in D. W. Griffith's *Broken Blossoms* and I thought she was wonderful. Coming back home from the movie, I remember getting up on a chair looking at myself in the mirror above the fireplace trying with my fingers to make my mouth smile as she did when she was very sad. So moving the faith I had, I thought I would like to do the same thing and be an actress like she was. I didn't go a lot to movies since we were living in the country but I remember I did see films with Chaplin in those days, too, and he was like a god. Years later in Hollywood, I met him at a dinner. There were about twelve of us. He was standing against the fireplace and he began to tell stories—it was marvelous, fascinating. But the one who had made the big impression on me was Lillian Gish in *Broken Blossoms.* Some years ago, I saw her when she made a grand appearance in North Hampton, New Hampshire where my daughter has a house. She was very pleasant, very intelligent and I think she was a wonderful person.

So after I saw *Broken Blossoms,* I was crazy about the movies. At the end of the garden, we had a chicken house with no chickens in it so I made it into a studio—a make-believe studio on the wall. I was the director, the writer, the actor and everything. I adored it just playing by myself. My cousins and brothers weren't allowed to enter.

I was crazy to read, too. When I was twelve, I began with *Les Trois Mousquetaires* and afterwards, I went on to the Russian literature—Dostoyevsky and Pushkin, Gogol and Tolstoy. I knew everything when I was fifteen. I like it better than the French literature. I don't know why although, of course, I love Victor Hugo.

One day, a girlfriend of mine said, "Listen, I am working in a *maison de couture* where they make dresses and gloves and they're looking for a little girl to start wearing dresses for the children ten years old, fifteen years old. Why don't you come? Maybe you can get a job."

So I went there. I didn't take my mother and father. The man at the shop made me walk in this dress and said, "Okay, you can come and work tomorrow. What's your name?"

And you know what I answered? "Natasha Rostov," because at that time I was reading *Guerre et paix*—you know, *War and Peace.* I thought it was like real life and when they asked me what was my name, I gave the name of Tolstoy's heroine. So I always lived more with a dream.

In those days, I didn't know anything about movie people or their lives. Don't forget, I was in a family where the theatre was not that important even though my mother's sister-in-law was an actress. My father was directing a magazine so he liked writers. My mother liked to play music and

SON PREMIER RÔLE: VIOLAINE DE "NAPOLÉON"

chacune est, à quelque degré, « un être qui a perdu son moi ».

Une telle constatation ne présente rien, au reste, qui puisse étonner. Elle souligne seulement quelques-uns des aspects essentiels du dernier venu des arts. Il n'est personne, sans doute, pour contester que le cinéma ne soit la forme la plus moderne de la magie. Comme la magie, il permet d'évoquer des ombres, de les animer, au point de croire à leur présence. Comme la magie, il se meut dans un univers étranger aux lois de l'espace et du temps. Comme la magie, enfin, il nous dispense les nécessaires enchantements.

— Pourtant — disent ici ceux qui ont besoin d'illusion mais n'aiment pas à en convenir — pourtant les entités que nous aimons sont des êtres réels et non des fantômes. Ils sont nés en un coin de terre, ils ont eu une enfance, ils se meuvent dans un entourage vivant. Le fait qu'ils possèdent un état civil, qu'ils ont une biographie, contredit vos affirmations. —

A quoi il faut bien répondre, que leur état civil réel n'a souvent rien à voir avec le nom sous lequel l'écran les a popularisés et que leur vie personnelle ne suit pas nécessairement le même cours que leur carrière d'artiste.

C'est ainsi que naissait à Paris, le 14 juillet 1909, dans cette atmosphère étonnante de fête nationale qu'avec quelques lampions, des couples qui tournoient et des violons qu'on râcle, M. René Clair nous a rendue merveilleusement sensible, c'est ainsi que naissait, voilà

4

These photos of Annabella as Violine and one of the first scenes filmed of her in *Napoléon* appeared in a 1936 French magazine, *Annabella: Sa Vie, Ses Films,* especially devoted to her. (Courtesy of Annabella Power.)

she played the piano beautifully. We had in the family a surgeon so I didn't know the world of actors at all. Lots of young people then didn't take my sensitive side very seriously. But ever since I had seen Lillian Gish, I wanted to be an actress.

One evening, my father went to a dinner at the home of the great painter, M. Jacques Dermoz, and he talked with him. My father was very close to him and he had many friends. One of them was a writer called t'Serstevens. My father was showing them photographs, not only because he loved his children but because he loved to see how he was taking pictures. He made them small, he made them big, he made them in color. It was his hobby—he was crazy about taking pictures. Next door to my "movie studio," my father would take pictures. When I was a child, there were two sentences that I didn't care too much about. My father would say, "Come on, little children, Daddy is going to take pictures of you." And my mother would say, "Come on, Suzanne, I want you to take a piano lesson."

M. t'Serstevens looked at all the pictures and he looked at the one of the little girl that I was then and said, "She's not bad, that little girl there. Would you mind if I take her to Abel Gance because M. Gance is looking for a young girl to be dreaming about Bonaparte in his new film, *Napoléon*?"

My father came back and said to me, "You know what? I've made a date for you." So one day, M. t'Serstevens took me to M. Abel Gance and all because of a picture that my father had taken when I was a kid. That's funny. Life is wonderful.

Gance took me on for a part in *Napoléon* and it was during this film that my name was changed. If they called me by my name, Charpentier, I thought it was like a soldier. My mother and father always spoke of me as Suzanne and my mother also called me Zette. But I'd just read a poem by Poe called "Annabel Lee" and I started calling myself that. When I met M. Gance, he told me my name would be only one word, Annabella. So Annabel Lee became Annabella in films—that was Gance's idea. My idea was from the poem and to be sure that people I didn't like or didn't know would not call me "my darling Zette" like my mother did.

I was a little scared the first time I went in the studio because I didn't know any actors. And they were big actors—very well-known then. Everyone was making a lot of noise talking very loudly and knowing each other. But they never talked to me and I felt quite lost. They were dressed up like in the French Revolution so I thought it really was Marat and Robespierre who had come back to life. They scared me to death when I saw Marat in the bath—oh, I was running away! Everybody was roaring in the crowd scenes and I didn't like the Revolution at all. When a little girl has seen the Musée Grévin with Louis XVI and Marie Antoinette, you are a royalist like everyone. Now I'm for "liberté."

But I was fascinated by M. Gance. It was very funny because everybody thought that Gance was crazy, putting the camera on a bicycle, on a boat, on props, anyplace. They'd say, "It's amazing. He's going to have three screens!" But I thought those people who said Gance was crazy were not too bright themselves.

I thought it would have been quite normal of Gance to put the camera on the ceiling or ask us to walk on the ceiling and put six cameras together but then I always believed in fairy tales. So already I had a great admiration for Gance. I found him to be kindness itself and he had a tremendous personality. We would say now his presence was commanding. Not that he was bossy and would shout but he was so intelligent that everybody would just do what he wanted. His imagination was so beautiful. For me, still a little girl, he was a magician with all of his screens and images and pictures. And he could put into words what he wanted to see on the screen. I could see it myself from the way he talked. I would have done anything for him.

I always called him M. Gance. Even when much, much later I would write to him, I would always say "M. Gance." You can see from his pictures that he was a handsome man but to me, he was almost like—not a grandfather, of course, but like somebody not quite real. He was such a great figure and I felt like such a dopey little girl but not because of M. Gance. He always treated me as a lady. He would always call me "Mademoiselle Annabella" and he would make jokes to me sometimes to get me to relax—the kind of jokes that you make with a child but he was not talking down to me. He had that kind of mind like Hans Christian Andersen or Saint-Exupéry. So M. Gance and I used to talk together like children but it was not baby talk. We were talking the way that children imagine and without the problems that adults have.

Gance already had in the back of his mind, which I didn't know, for me to be the girl who was going to be the most important—for whom Bonaparte will become a god. But at first I was asked to go to Corsica to play a little sister of Bonaparte. That was the first journey I'd ever made. Everyone was very kind and wonderful. We all walked because I think the Corsicans had been seeing the people who were supposed to be hiding in the film. The Corsicans got on well with everyone of us. It was all very beautiful and I remember the "parfum," the scent of Corsica was wonderful. I wasn't at all surprised to see M. Gance put a camera on a horse. People said, "Have you seen what he's daring to do now?"

Lunching during the Corsican location shooting of *Napoléon*. Left to right: Eugénie Buffet, Felix Gugliemi, Yvette Dieudonné, Simone Surdieux, Albert Dieudonné, Abel Gance, Emile Pierre, Annabella, Margeurite Gance, Rauzena, Morlas. (Courtesy of Kevin Brownlow.)

And I said, "Gance can do anything."

At that time, I thought that for the role of Violine, the little girl who adored Napoleon, he had already engaged a young English girl. Everyone joked about it and said it was annoying that an English girl would play the part of a French girl who admired Bonaparte. On Corsica, M. Gance made a few tests of me for the part of Napoleon's kid sister. I remember I saw the tests afterwards but Gance said, "No, you are not going to have that part. You can go back to Paris."

I thought, "Oh, I'm not good enough." In fact, I thought I must have been awful. But when they came back from Corsica, somebody else did the tiny little part of Bonaparte's sister because he thought I was too good for such a small part. And he came to me and gave me the bigger part of Violine when I was a little older. I remember I wore a beautiful dress like Marie Antoinette in the picture.

For me, *Napoléon* wasn't a silent film but a film to music because M. Gance always had a man playing a violin wonderfully in back of the camera. That was to get you in the mood for a romantic scene or a dramatic one. It was like when I was a child and my mother was playing the piano all the time. She won second prize at the Conservatoire—a big distinction, you know. I had always played in the house with music in the background giving life to my games. So when M. Gance used a violin, I thought I was in a fairy tale and "working" for Gance was living a dream again. I didn't talk about it. I didn't think about business or success. I just loved my part and I thought it was wonderful to admire someone who made marvelous things like Bonaparte did.

As I've said, Gance was always *sympathique*. Of the actors, Albert Dieudonné who played Bonaparte was an angel for me. He was the one who was really nice to me. It's one of my very best memories. But sadly, I think it ruined his career playing such a great role as Napoleon. That's what I've heard. He took himself seriously and you musn't take yourself too seriously in this business as far as your success is concerned. Although M. Dieudonné was kind to me, all the others like Gina Manès who played Josephine—they called me *la gosse, le môme*—a kid in French, you know. When I went up to a group, they'd say, "Oh, here's that kid again. No joking." They didn't know me—I was nothing. Even when I was sixteen, I looked fourteen. They thought I was completely idiotic. So I went away and kept to myself. But I did like some of the Russian actors who were in the film. Chakatouny, the man who played Pozzo di Borgo, was very kind. He later became a make-up artist when sound came in because he didn't speak very good French. He did my make-up in *Le Million*. And I adored Nicolas Koline who played Tristan Fleuri. He was also very nice and we worked together again in a film of Marcel L'Herbier's.

I continued to live in the country during the filming of *Napoléon*. I didn't come to the studio all the time. My father and mother brought me from the country by auto. I remember at that time how disappointed I was to hear in the kitchen my mother's little maids very sad because "Valentino was dead." I did not say anything to them but I thought, "What a pity really! If one day I go to that dreamy, wonderful place called Hollywood, I won't be able to meet him."

When *Napoléon* had its premiere at the Paris Opera in 1927, I was very sad because most of my scenes were cut and I was really not in the picture at all. So I didn't see it and I didn't go to the premiere. It was because of my friend Kevin Brownlow's sweet invitation that I finally saw *Napoléon* in London with the wonderful orchestra. I'll never forget my emotion!

Although I had been disappointed when my scenes were cut from the premiere of *Napoléon* at the Opera, I was not surprised. I thought, "Oh, well, I was so stupid, I was so dumb." I was so glad to have had that one chance—it was fun—but I thought that was the end of it. And then—I don't know who it was who had shown some pictures of me from *Napoléon* to a friend of my father's but he had seen them and he said to my father, "She is really very good."

Then Jean Grémillon, the director, saw the pictures, too, but he had also seen *Napoléon* with all my scenes and he said to me, "I want to put you in my picture."

I said, "Do you mean it, do you really mean it?"

He said, "Oh, yes, you were very good in that and you are very good on film." So that's how I got a part in another film. Isn't that a gag?

For this second picture I made, *Maldone,* we shot scenes in the French Alps by the Plateau d'Assi

With Albert Dieudonné, Serge Freddy-Karll and Nicolai Koline in *Napoléon.*

over near Italy but I didn't care very much for the film. Jean Grémillon was very much in love with a beautiful girl and I had a little part. For instance, when we went on location, they were all living in the same hotel, having lunch and dinner together and laughing between themselves. But they put me in a little room in somebody's house in the neighborhood so I wasn't part of their group. Only Charles Dullin, the star of the picture, was very, very nice to me. After we were back in Paris, I went to see M. Dullin at his theatre—he had his own theatre. And I rehearsed something else for him.

It was around this time that I had my daughter. I had met her father when I was working in pictures. He was crazy about me and I was too young to have a child when I began to work. I saw him again after she was born but I thought I was too young to get married. And I wanted a daughter for me alone. You know, I've been asked five times in my life to get married but the first one to whom I said no was the father of my daughter. I was married twice after, first to Jean Murat and then to Tyrone Power.

I continued to work in pictures and I began to adore to work. A few years after I made *Maldone,* I went to play in front of Louis Jouvet, the great, great actor to try to get a job. He said, "Okay, maybe I'll go on the road with the play. Maybe I'll take you with me with my company." Later, he wanted me to come and see him in Paris where he'd take me to play small roles in a picture to be filmed by one of the city gates—something like that.

I was always staying with my family in the country at La Varenne where our house was. So one day going to Paris to see M. Jouvet, I took the train. At Joinville, a gentleman got on the train. It was Henri Fescourt who was a movie director. He was sitting opposite me and he said, "Would you like to be in a picture I'm going to make in London? It's a difficult part but I think you could do it."

"Oh," I said, "my goodness!" Not only was I excited to be asked to do another picture but in London! So I did go to Jouvet but I said, "I'm terribly sorry, M. Jouvet, I cannot go in your company. In the company, I would be the one who opened the door and said, 'Lunch is ready!' " I told him I was going to London to make a picture.

I made just one picture with M. Fescourt but he was very, very nice. For me, the idea of a trip to England was wonderful. But I was just in the studio in Twickenham near London when we made the film, *La Maison de la Flèche*. I never went out because I didn't know a word of English at the time. *La Maison de la Flèche* was in the French language and it was one of my first sound films. But I'd always talked in pictures. I spoke my lines in *Napoléon* and the other films where my voice wasn't heard so sound didn't bother me.

At the beginning of my career, it was not fashionable to look very young like they do nowadays. So they often told me, "Come back in a few years." But the thing was I wanted to work all the time. I didn't care to go to school because in school, they were telling me, "Oh, come back in ten years so you can take it." So any part in films I did because I wanted to work. I wanted to learn, too, but I didn't like any school.

About this time, I played in a film for Gaumont called *Deux fois vingt ans*. It was a story of older people. I had a very little part but I took everything. When they asked me if I was fit to play the part, I said, "Yes, yes."

They said, "Do you know how to drive a car?"

I said, "Oh, yes, I do."

"And do you know how to ride a horse?"

"Oh, yes, of course I do," I said. But that was not true then. So each morning before going to the studio, I was taking lessons to drive a car. I'd go through the Bois de Vincennes in a big Delage while an instructor initiated me in the mysteries of the gears and the pedals. At first I drove very badly. In the scene in the picture when I drove the car, I went right in a tree.

They said, "Oh, what happened?"

And I said, "Oh, I'm sorry. I didn't see it." In the end, though, it worked out all right.

I fell off the horse, too. I was learning to ride in the evening. I was with a very nice woman from La Comédie Française who'd been in some well-known plays. We were playing on the horse only the horse was very clever and he knew somebody who didn't know a goddamn thing was on his back so he threw me off. It was just a little spin for the film but I never said no when I wanted to do a picture. Apart from that, that also worked out well. It was very pretty, too, because we were filming around the Bois d'Arcachon.

One day, I read in a magazine that they were going to make a picture in Berlin, *Le Barcarolle d'Amour*, with a very important German director. He was coming to Paris and they would also make a French version in Berlin with a French director, Henri Roussell. They were looking for the part of a young girl so I went to their office. It was full of girls—four beautiful young actresses who were laughing and had known each other. They left me in the corner—you know, they didn't take very much care of me. I heard two secretaries saying, "Oh, look at the poor actresses, the poor girls. They each think they're going to play that part but M. Roussell is going to Berlin with his own girlfriend to play the part."

So I didn't care for that. I was a little fighter and I asked the secretaries, "Oh, but monsieur le directeur, the German director—is he at the Crillon, the hotel in Paris?"

They said, "No, no, he's in another one." They gave me the name of the hotel and I said, "Oh, excuse me, I have to go."

"Oh, but you can't go," they said. "You have no chance, anyway."

But I left. I took a taxi—I had very little money. I went to the hotel and asked to talk to the German director, Carl Froelich. He was surprised and said, "Yes, I'm staying here in the Montmartre. I'll see you downstairs."

When he got there, I said, "Monsieur, it is not fair. I want to be an actress. Here are all my pictures. I love to work—to be an actress. And the French director wants to take his girlfriend. He doesn't care a bit because like that, he won't have to pay for the train and the hotel. It's not fair, monsieur. I want to play the part, I want to be an actress."

With Charles Boyer in *La Bataille*. (Courtesy of Annabella Power.)

He began to laugh, "That kid—that kid is crazy." Then he said, "Okay, I'm going over there now. I'll take you with me." I arrived with the German director and I got the part. I think it was in that picture I was supposed to be the little sister of somebody. I went to Berlin and they paid me to take the beautiful sleeping car but I took the day train because I wanted to see the country.

Charles Boyer was the leading man in *Le Barcarolle d'Amour* and that was the first picture we made together. I didn't know the trick of movie actors. He was turning very, very slowly during the close-up so little by little he was in front of the camera and I was showing my back. But I didn't realize it. I just thought of the lines I had to say, of the feeling of my heart. And the director laughed and said, "Annabella, be careful. We'll put that mark so M. Boyer doesn't move and you stay so it has to be two profiles but I don't want to see your back." But I was such a kind of kid about those tricks that I hadn't realized it.

I came to know Charles Boyer so well and so long but he was so different off-camera. When he was acting, he was always the professional and by that I mean, he was thinking first of all of himself. He was very French as an actor that way—very different from the American actors. He thought about what was best for his role and yet when I knew him off-camera, he was so warm and—how do you say it—"listening" when we talked. His wonderful wife, Pat Paterson, who was the *témoin,* the witness at our wedding, Tyrone's and mine—she was wonderful for Charles and they were so much in love. They loved to read and to talk about serious things. We talked a lot about philosophy, religion and faith. He was so kind and so good-looking and he knew so many people. Everybody liked him and he spoke English very, very well. So he was a very good friend.

When I first began to be in the movies, I went to Paris one day—I was still living with my family in the country—and I saw a magazine with my face, my picture on the front page. I was so proud I bought that magazine, came back home and then I began to laugh because my father had bought it, my mother had bought it, my two brothers had bought it and the maids had bought it. So the house was full of them. I said, "That's a little too much," but I was very pretentious for forty-eight

With René Lefevre in *Le Million.* (The Kobal Collection.)

hours. Two days after, I learned that it was the producer of the film and the publicity man who paid the magazine to have my picture on the cover. From that very day, I was never touched by publicity. I just laughed and said, "Ha, ha! That's business and they paid for it."

Le Million was directed by René Clair and that was my first big success. I don't remember how René Clair decided to get me. He wanted me. He must have seen something because he wanted me for that part. He was a darling, it was great fun and so many laughs. But René Clair was a strange man. Six months before, when he was writing the script, he stayed at home and worked like a slave to get it ready. He didn't want to see anybody, not even his friends, he didn't answer the telephone. His lovely wife said, "He didn't even talk to me." When he had all the world anxious, he wrote the word END on his script and then the fun and a million gags began. At the studio, it was wonderful, it was happy, it was marvelous—more like a school at the time of recess. The actors, the cameramen, the electricians—everybody had fun and stayed longer to play gags even when the work of the day was over.

M. Clair's studio at Epinay did not really seem like a studio—at least, not the way that you think of a studio and that I came to think of it. It was not at all deluxe or the swanky, fancy setting that you imagine. It was really like a very big garage. Inside, it had the sets and everything that was needed to make the film and so it looked like a little village under a huge tin roof. But there was only one dressing room for the women. The studio was very simple and maybe that was why the people were more simple and it was much more fun filming there.

When I played in *Le Million,* I was still finishing a silly little picture at the Gaumont studio in Paris—nobody would remember it because it was so silly. I had been working all day and I was going in a cab to Epinay which is a suburb of Paris when I began to play for René Clair. So I was making two pictures at the same time but, as I said, I adored to work. I went back and forth between the studios only for about two weeks but we would work long days. I would go to Gaumont sometimes at eight or nine o'clock at night and nobody thought that was unusual or strange.

I played a ballet dancer in the Opera in René Clair's film and you know what I did in *Le Million?* I taught myself—I learned to dance on the top of my foot, I learned myself alone. And after that, they thought I came from the Opera and to tell you the truth, I lied a little bit because I said, "Oh, yes, as a kid, I was dancing in the Opera." But really, when I was alone between scenes, I was practicing. I was not the pretentious one but oh, I was a real worker.

At the end when we all dance and sing together, that was recorded at the time we filmed it. We were all singing and there was no dubbing. But I never thought of the techniques of sound. I thought it was a dream, I thought I was playing like when you're a kid and I didn't know the technical side of movies at all. I just took the sentiment, the feeling. I put my heart in it like if it was real and true.

When we were filming, René Clair did not make changes. He followed the script completely because of all the work preparing the script. He did everything. Making that picture was always delightful even though the working hours were terrible at that time. René Clair sometimes stayed at the studio until eight or nine in the evening. He even slept at the studio sometimes because he loved the atmosphere. He played gags on me because I believed everything. I was starting to become known and one day I was told that there was a telephone call for me from Berlin. They wanted me to go and make a picture with them. I don't know why but they asked for me without an agent—that was very funny. Of course, I was pleased and flattered and I told René Clair who said, "Oh, no, no, you're not free for that amount of time."

Some time later, the people in the office at the studio told me, "There's a man from Berlin waiting for you at the door."

But René Clair said, "No, no, you're filming, no."

So I asked a young man to go and see what the man was like. I was very proud he'd come all the way from Berlin to see me. The young man told me, "Oh, dear, he's got big boots, he's got a big beard, he's covered in scars, he's horrible."

And I said, "He can wait, he can wait!" Do you know what René Clair did? He made me leave by the window and all the people in the studio were in on it. It was an extra that he'd had made up like that.

So I thought I'd get back at him with a gag of my own. Everybody was playing with yo-yos at that time and René Clair was crazy about it. All the time,

René Clair directing Annabella and Aimos in *Quatorze Juillet.* (Courtesy of Annabella Power.)

when the cameraman and people said, "M. Clair, the actors are ready. We are waiting. The lights are ready," he said, "Coming, coming," and he was in a corner like a crazy playing with his yo-yo.

So one day, I said to the cameraman and the electricians, "Let's play a gag." They hid the camera and lights and when René Clair was playing in the corner of the studio, they were shooting him without his own knowledge. We were all laughing and said, "We are going to look at the rushes in the evening and what's he going to say when he sees himself playing with his yo-yo?"

In the middle of the afternoon, a big director from UFA came from Berlin and René Clair said, "Oh, it's wonderful you came from Berlin to Paris. You are going to look at the rushes."

We all looked at each other and I thought, "Oh, my God, what's the big director from UFA going to say when he sees René Clair playing like that? René Clair is going to be mad at the cameraman, the electricians and myself." We didn't know what to do because the film was in the camera and couldn't be cut.

At the end of the afternoon, we went to the movie room to see the rushes of the day and then all of a sudden, there was René Clair in the corner playing with his yo-yo. We were scared to death because we thought he would be furious with us. But when the lights came back on, René Clair stood up and said, "Did you notice, people, I did all the work with the left hand?" And he was very pleased and very proud of that.

As I've said, *Le Million* was a great success for me, first because of René Clair—after all, he is the one who later opened the door of the Académie Française for the movies—and then because the public liked me and thought I was different from the other actresses. Maybe the best quality I had was that I was absolutely sincere, always playing it with my heart. After *Le Million,* I even had an invitation to go to America to make a picture. I did not because I knew a lot of girls who were going, staying months and months and not working. The day I would come to America, I would come as a star, not just a little ingenue. And besides, my family thought I was too young then.

I followed *Le Million* with two pictures I made with Albert Préjean, *Un Soir de Rafle* and *Un Fils d'Amérique.* I enjoyed them very much. Albert Préjean was a wonderful partner, terribly nice, but he fell a little bit in love with me, talked about marriage and so on. He was very, very French, very

With Albert Préjean in *Un Soir de Rafle.* (Courtesy of Annabella Power.)

Parisian, a little like Maurice Chevalier but Chevalier went around the world. Préjean, however—his brain was "Le Grand Boulevard," "Le Casino de Paris." And his family was very limited while my father was very intelligent so I never thought I would marry a man like that. He just wanted Paris and I wanted the world. But he was so dear and so loving. He gave me a bracelet made of jewels. I often wore a heavy, thick bracelet but I would not wear a bracelet like that which was so very valuable and which sparkled so much in the light. It was not an engagement gift really but he had asked me so many times to marry him that I felt the bracelet should belong to someone in his family. That was why I gave it to his son recently. I think that the wonderful thing about these memories I have is that I am able to give things to people who were part of them.

Simone Simon played in *Un Fils d'Amérique*. It was one of her first films. I don't remember the story of that picture and I don't know if we had many scenes together. It was only later that we became friends. She was so good, so laughing, so funny, so beautiful and men were crazy about her. She was also very, very artistic. I think sometimes people looked at her and thought because she was beautiful, "Oh, she is dumb." But she was a very, very good painter. She would copy paintings and she could fool you. Tyrone and I had one of her copied paintings in our home at Saltair and everybody thought that it was an original. She was also a real champion with crossword puzzles in both French and English. I remember she won a contest where there was a clock ticking. It is so sad now that she is blind but we still talk and are friends. We were both working at Fox in the thirties when I met Tyrone. One day, when I was in Paris and she was leaving America, she took a long letter from Tyrone and she brought it to me. So she was the mailman for me.

I liked the next picture I did after the films with Préjean very much. *Paris-Méditerranée* was a wonderful film and very funny. I met my leading man, Jean Murat, for the first time in that film. There was something really funny that happened when we made it. There were two versions, one in French and the other in German with different actors. There was one scene we made on location where I had to come out of a house and get into a car in the street. After we filmed it, they redid the same scene for the German version with Magda Schneider playing my role. At that time, people didn't really know much about how movies were made and two old ladies who had watched the filming said, "Oh, dear, that little girl—they're remaking the scene with another girl. The other little girl" (that was me) "musn't be very good."

Afterwards, the cameraman said, "See how the light has changed. Now we'll have to redo the French version."

So we reshot it with me doing the scene again. Well, the two old dears said, "Ah, well, no. You see we were wrong. The first must have been the best because they're bringing her back."

Jean Murat was very, very attractive, much older than I was and so nice with me. Maybe he had been an enormous success with women because he was very elegant, very smart and so well-dressed. I didn't fall in his arms while on the journey during the picture. But he took me to a bar and when I was shopping, he came with me. He did everything—you know, he was my Pygmalion. I thought he was very nice but I remembered that Préjean was in love with me so I was very cool yet very nice. But when the picture was finished, I was lost because he was like my father and my mother. He took me everywhere and he was very clever. He knew the producers and a year later, he made their big picture called *Mademoiselle Josette, ma femme* or *Miss Josette, My Wife*. The part was for me—he insisted on me for that role. And when I saw Jean

With Jean Murat in 1933. (Courtesy of Annabella Power.)

Murat again when we made the film, I was delighted and I fell in love with him. We played winter sports in the mountains and he played music for me. I was still a kid and I was shy. My mother never got out of her music and my father was very busy so Jean Murat made a woman out of me.

He was always such a gentleman and so protective of me. But, you know, he paid more attention to me in some ways than to the script when we made a film together. He said often that acting was ridiculous for a man but not for a woman. Sometimes he would not even read the script to the end if he was not in the last scenes. I remember for one of our pictures—was it *L'Equipage?*, I'm not sure now—as we went to the premiere, he said to me, "Oh, I wonder how this is going to end." And yet he would memorize his lines and be ready each day. But he really thought that films were a way of showing how beautiful women were and he saw himself as a kind of companion for women. He was not as funny as Rex Harrison, for example—he did not have that kind of humor. But he was very French and very suave. He knew how to treat a woman and he saw himself as an actor in relation to women.

During all this time when I was making films, I had the country house when I was with my family and after that, a little flat in Paris that Jean Murat bought for me before we married. He gave it to me—he was so wonderful. In the beginning of my career, I was taking the train and the cab to go to work. But very soon after I did *Le Million,* my mother made me buy a car. It was a Ford car—in my heart, I was terribly pro-American already. It was very nice and I was going to the studios in Paris in my little Ford—I loved it. Of course, I always drove my cars myself. I never had chauffeurs because I was never pretentious, not even in later years when I had a big Packard car with gray on the outside, red inside and very beautiful. At home, we had a cook and my mother had maids but I didn't have any servants.

I didn't care about money. In fact, I never thought about the contracts or the money. My father did that and then when I was married to Jean Murat, he handled all the money. For me, to add two and two makes three. I could tell you absolutely zero about business but I don't care. I never had an agent in France. I didn't need one because I'd been in so many pictures. I suppose I was different from the other stars. They called me or they called my father or afterwards they called my husband when they wanted me for a film. But they didn't deal directly with me about the business angle. The difference in Hollywood was that the star system was more developed there than in Europe where the director or the author of the script was more important than the actor or actress. It was really only in Hollywood when I was married to Tyrone that I began to understand the contract system. Tyrone never wanted to do the business for me and so I became much smarter about it.

In the title role of *Marie, Légende Hongroise.* (Courtesy of Annabella Power.)

Paul Fejos was one of the directors I liked the most. I made one picture with him in Budapest and one in Vienna. The first one, *Marie, Légende Hongroise,* was based on a Hungarian legend and I did it right after *Paris-Méditerranée.* I'd seen a film that Paul Fejos had made a few years earlier that was marvelous and I was very pleased to meet him.

When I arrived at the hotel in Budapest, I was told, "Oh, yes, there are two other French companies here. That will work out cheaper for M. Osso." Adolphe Osso was the French producer of *Marie* and, as I'd thought, he was having other films made in Hungary. I can't imagine anything close between Osso and Paul Fejos—one was a businessman and the other a poet—but M. Osso is the one who had made me go to Budapest. I'd already read the script and the character I was going to play, Marie, was absolutely adorable. Then I spoke to the concierge and just at that moment, two actors were coming down the stairs saying, "Say, darling, are you coming for a drink? Have you seen so-and-so? Doesn't he look old?"

I said to myself, "My God, are they going to talk films all the time?" I was already little Marie, the Hungarian legend, so I said to the concierge, "Please, monsieur, if you wouldn't mind, I've got something for you. Would you have my luggage brought down, call a taxi and give me the name of a hotel on the other side of the Danube?" So I no longer had anything to do with the film trade. I was the character, not even an actor. I was living the part like if it was a novel or my own life. I've never cared about publicity and all that as I said. I like just to play the part like I like to read a book. I remember once I was in the middle of a chapter in a book when I was riding on the metro and I said to myself, "Why do I want to get back home so quickly? There's no one waiting for me." I was living with the book. And I lived the same way with films. Some people want to have a beautiful part. For me, I didn't care. I wanted to make the part good but I never thought the part was really me. I thought it was a close friend of mine and when I looked at myself on the screen, I was saying, "Oh, she is good in that. Oh, I love her voice." But it was her—it was not exactly me. It was very funny because I was becoming the person of the script.

With Gustav Fröhlich in *Sonnenstrahl*. (Courtesy of Annabella Power.)

We stayed in Budapest while we were making the film and we shot nearby in a little village. Before we began filming, Paul Fejos gave me time so that I could be a tourist and get the feeling of what the country was like. He was the most wonderful director to work with because if you had a moving scene, he had tears in his eyes as he was behind the camera looking at you on the other side. Oh, I adored him! He knew my thoughts about the two parts I did for him and the strange atmosphere. He knew I felt right and he enjoyed very nearly guessing what I should do. There was no advice from him—just sharing each scene. He had authority but he was quiet and he listened to you. That was what was so different about him. He was the director but he was listening to what I felt and somehow, I then could listen to what he felt even though he did not use as many words as René Clair or Anatole Litvak, for example.

The second film I made with Fejos was filmed in Vienna. It was called *Gardez le sourire* or *Sonnenstrahl* in German. My leading man, Gustav Fröhlich, was very nice but we had very little conversation because he didn't speak very much French and I didn't speak very much German. But I thought it was a wonderful part for me. Making it wasn't always fun, though. Fröhlich says in the picture, "There's no work in Vienna," and he is about to drown himself when a sad little girl appears—that's me—and throws herself in the water. Well, that makes him change his mind. He wants to save the little kid because he sees a sign saying, "Every rescue reaches so many more," so he throws himself in the water, too. But what the audience didn't know was the hours spent throwing yourself in the water, getting out of it and throwing yourself in again. But that was a beautiful film, very good.

In between the films with Fejos, I made another picture with René Clair, *Quatorze Juillet*. That was with the blonde girl, Pola Illery. She was very pretty but I didn't get to know her. This time, I had my own dressing room at the studio in Epinay—a poor, sad little dressing room but I must say, it was watered. One day, while I was washing my hands, the sink—the whole thing—fell on the floor and the water overflowed.

I had a great success in *Quatorze Juillet* but I didn't expect it. I still felt much younger than everybody else on the set. And although René Clair had a wonderful sense of humor as always, still, he was Monsieur le directeur, he was a great man and I was just a young girl who, to her surprise, was in another movie for him again. With all of the fireworks, the celebration, the ball and the role I was playing in the movie, I felt that I was just beginning again. So I did not feel like a star and everybody treated me as a pretty but very young girl whom they just had to show what to do.

With Jean Murat and actress Danièle Parole in the garden of their rented Hollywood home in 1934 when they were part of a group of French actors on the West Coast during the production of Annabella's first U.S.-made film, *Caravan*. (Courtesy of Annabella Power.)

In 1934, I made *La Bataille* with Charles Boyer. The story was set in Japan and the make-up artist had to make me look like a Japanese girl. It was rather painful because my hair was pulled in all directions to change the shape of my face a little bit. Then they put my hair up very high under the wig. Oh, my goodness, I had such headaches in the evening. But I loved the part, I loved the dress and the director was very nice. And because I liked to be somebody else, that was fun for me.

After that, I was asked to go to Hollywood to do the French version of *Caravane* or *Caravan* for Fox. So I went to America for the first time. But I didn't speak a word of English at the time and Jean Murat came with me. (I was not yet married to him but he was following me already.) I had the part that Loretta Young had in the English-language version and Charles Boyer, who was in both versions, was again my leading man. *Caravan* was a silly little story but I loved the clothes. I was a princess and I wore these beautiful costumes. In one scene, I wore a dress that was so lovely—a ball gown with white fur on the sleeves. But I was so unhappy because I didn't speak English and everybody else spoke English. They were filming the English version at the same time. There was just nobody to talk to and I was so far away from home. I didn't like the German director of *Caravan*, Erik Charell, very much, either. I know it looks like I was always smiling in the picture but oh, no, I was not happy at all.

Many directors in Hollywood wanted me to stay and make pictures for them. Because I was photogenic, they thought I was gifted and so on. But Jean Murat said, "No, you are going first to learn English and not come back here like an idiot who can't speak English." He was the boss for me but really wonderful. He taught me life. For instance, at the beginning before we were married, if we were supposed to meet in a restaurant, I didn't dare to come in. I would be at the door and say to the man, "Go, please, and tell M. Jean Murat that I'm waiting at the door." And he came to pick me up. I hadn't been brought up as a kid of today. The world has changed now but I don't know. I had a good time, I had a wonderful youth and such a marvelous father and mother. Jean Murat and I were married after we got back from America. And when I married him, he took me to buy a lot of wonderful dresses, the most elegant dresses that were in the store.

It was about this time that I got a villa by sur le Bassin d'Arcachon, north of Bordeaux. It's a big, wonderful place and it was very funny how we found La Pilat. We were on holiday. I was with my mother, my daughter and my younger brother in my car and I was driving. We thought we were going to Brittany but the weather was very bad so we went south. I stopped the car on the way and we were right to La Pilat. It was the most beautiful kind of place I'd seen in my life. It was near a hotel and was just a dream. At that time, I was beginning to make a lot of money because I was becoming a star. I said, "Oh, that's a dream place. How I would love to have a house by the top of an inn!" I called Jean Murat in the evening. He was working in a picture but he came the day after and bought a piece of land near where I bought some land. It was along the sea with a big tennis court. The view was marvelous and I adored it.

My first picture in France after I got back from America was *Les Nuits Moscovites.* That was a great success. Recently, it was played again in France on the television and I had so much mail about it. It's not one of the pictures that I adored but it was very good. Harry Baur, who was in it, was a great, great star. He scared me a little bit but he was very nice. We didn't become friends like that, though. He later did an English version of the picture with Laurence Olivier.

Then I made *Variétés* for a German company. It was filmed in France and I worked like a dog in that because I played in both versions, the French one and the German one. I learned a little bit of German for it. Jean Gabin and Fernand Gravey were in the French version only but I was up on the trapeze for both versions. I was going up to the trapeze and I was holding it like I was jumping but then they had to double me since the actual jump was done by real trapeze artists. But I *was* in the trapeze for hours with Jean Gabin and Fernand Gravey. After that, when they finished the French version, they went out to have a drink, read the paper and walk in the yard. And I had to do it all over again with Hans Albers and another German actor. So I was very tired of that picture.

It was also in that film that I was to work with a bear who was trained for the circus and very good

With Harry Baur in *Les Nuits Moscovites.* (The Kobal Collection.)

with people. I had worked with the bear in rehearsal but the first time it came on the set, it was very different. The bear was frightened by the lights and the noise and it backed up and knocked me down but did not scratch me. But my foot was broken and I was in plaster.

When we were filming *Variétés,* Jean Gabin was telling me he was going to make *La Bandera* with Jean Murat and Julien Duvivier as the director. He said it would be wonderful and he would have the best part as a soldier in Africa with a wonderful dancing girl from Morocco as his partner. He talked to me a lot about it but I was so tired of playing in *Variétés* that I left for a long vacation at my house by the seaside. Two weeks later, I was still with my family on holiday at the seaside when

In *Variétés.* (Courtesy of Annabella Power.)

Gabin sent an assistant from the studio to beg me to come back in a hurry to play the part of the girl. He said, "Please, Jean Gabin wants you back. Please, M. Duvivier would like you to come."

I asked, "Why?"

He said, "Because the girl from Morocco is a good dancer but she's a very bad actress. Please give up your holiday."

I said, "Oh, listen, give me a week to think of it. I'm so tired. When you've played a French version and a German version, it's a little too much. So give me a week."

He said, "Yes, yes, I understand, madame, but I have your tickets for the train. You leave tonight and you work tomorrow morning."

Of course, when I arrived, M. Gabin and M. Duvivier were delighted and they were two darlings with me. The picture was very good and I have a wonderful memory of it. At lunch time, I had a teacher dancing with me after filming in the morning. Like Charles Boyer, Jean Gabin was a wonderful actor. A lot of people thought it was not so pleasant to work with Duvivier. He was supposed to be tough but he was an angel with me when directing *La Bandera.*

The film was done in France at the studio in Joinville. The scenes of the war at the beginning of the picture were made on location in Morocco by another company—another unit. But I didn't go to Morocco. I'm sorry I didn't because years ago when he was prince, the now-king of Morocco was speaking French beautifully when he had conferences in Paris. I heard him twice and I thought he was very intelligent.

In 1935, the same year I did *La Bandera,* I was in *L'Equipage,* directed by Anatole Litvak. Tola was a wonderful friend, very Russian, and when during the war much later he was in the army, I saw a lot of him. He was terribly nice as a friend but I didn't like him very much as a director. My husband, Tyrone, made a picture with him afterwards and he had the same feeling because Anatole Litvak made actors do the same thing six, eight, nine times but he was always using the first take in the film. It was very funny.

Jean Murat was in *L'Equipage* and it was also my first picture with Jean-Pierre Aumont who was one of my favorite leading men. In fact, Jean-Pierre is like a brother to me. Two years ago, we were to-

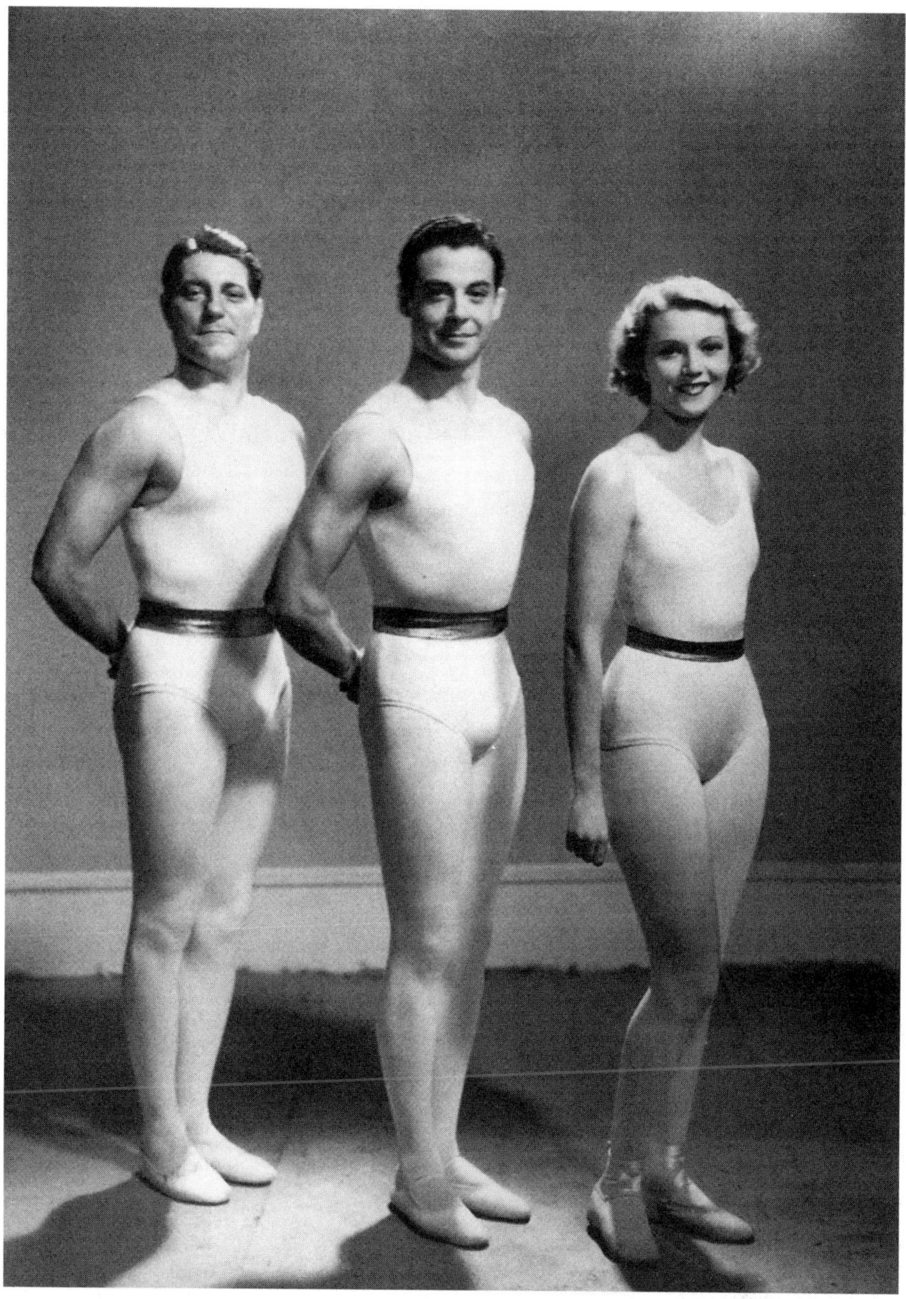

With Jean Gabin and Fernand Gravey in *Variétés.* (Courtesy of Annabella Power.)

gether all the time when we came to Hollywood for a big gala. Sometimes we talk on the phone but he's still working, you know. He plays older men. He's married to a charming girl and he has beautiful kids.

I made two pictures with Marcel L'Herbier, *Veille d'Armes* and later *La Citadelle du Silence.* He was one of the greatest directors. He was kind of cool and dignified but such a wonderful man, very clever and elegant. I really liked him and I felt that we knew what one another was thinking. I suppose I had to have been good with him because I got the Volpi Cup, the award at the film festival in Italy in 1936, for *Veille d'Armes.* It was given to me in Venezia by the Volpi family. I wasn't one to take part in big public fêtes—that was not my own

With Robert Le Vigan in *La Bandera*. (Courtesy of Annabella Power.)

personal taste—but since I was getting a prize, I went to the Venice Film Festival. The Volpi Cup was a beautiful, heavy marble thing. When the war came, the Germans took everything in my parents' home near the Marne and they stole my Volpi Cup. Victor Francen was my partner in *Veille d'Armes*. He was a very good actor but between scenes we had nothing in common. He was much older than I was.

After we made *La Citadelle du Silence,* Marcel L'Herbier wanted to give me a gift—he was such a kind man. He gave me a full set of dishes with little cups, little saucers, tureens and things for the sauce, all the egg-cups and every kind of dish you can imagine. Each piece of white china has a different scene from the movie and the scenes are like cameos in shades of brown or sepia with gold borders—they do not cover the entire plate. When I later was working in California, L'Herbier called me from Europe and asked me to make a third picture with him in Italy. I couldn't come back and I felt sorry as he wanted so much to have me working with him again.

In 1936, I played the title role in *Anne-Marie,* directed by Raymond Bernard. He was terribly nice but I knew him very little. The leading man, Pierre-Richard Wilm, was a very polite gentleman but he liked to be alone in a corner so we never became friends. *Anne-Marie* was a story about flying and Antoine de Saint-Exupéry, the great aviator and writer, wrote the script for me. You know, I was still a little shy and I met him just to say "hello" and so on when he came to visit us during the making of the picture. Years later, when I came to see him in California—that's when we became friends.

I was very lucky during my career and I had a good time. I was just thinking of the humanity of people. The most important thing in life is sincerity. I want to feel that people speak from their hearts. If it is just blah-blah to impress me, there is a wall. I was always very friendly with the directors although as long as I was in France, I didn't call them by their first names. It was always *Monsieur* Clair, for instance, or Monsieur Gance. I was also friendly with the cameramen and with the electricians and machinists. The simple people when they're sincere—I like them. But I was not so much friends with the actors in France. They were always just talking about publicity and the success of the film. Was it going to go around? Will they like the partner or not? For me, I didn't care. As long as I was in France, I loved to be alone to think I was the part like when you're a kid, you think you are a prince or whatever. My real friends were normal people but not the actors who bored me to death with their blah-blah-blah about the movies when they talked about business. But in America, I did begin to love the actors when I arrived there and fell in love with America. I was friends with Douglas Fairbanks, Jr., and Gary Cooper, for example, and they didn't marry big American stars. They married girls from the East so in their houses, you never talked about movies. You talked about art, about travel, about politics. It was a kind of atmosphere I like very much.

When I was living in France in the thirties, my life was my love, my family, the country and to travel. I had not the faintest idea about politics. I think France which is not terribly, terribly big is the most beautiful place in the world because you drive a hundred kilometers and it's *complet fini*—nature, the villages, so many beautiful villages, the churches. It's a different style, you know, so you have everything. You can travel in France forever and always see some old castle and wonderful things. But the French people—I think I feel much closer to the American people than the French people.

At that time when I was a star in France, I was very commercial. I don't like to be pretentious but as an actress, I was like Coca-Cola for a drink. They wanted to have me because it made the picture work.

With Signoret in *Veille d'Armes.* (The Kobal Collection.)

For example, I knew Jacques Feyder and he wanted to have me in a picture but it didn't work out.

Years later, I was invited to the biggest film festival in Cannes and they were going to let me stay ten days. You have beautiful affairs and you have the lunch parties there. I spent one day with Jean Cocteau because he was very intelligent and we went to visit the church where Matisse had done beautiful paintings on the walls—it was wonderful. But I didn't stay ten days. After three days, I left because I was sick to see all the big producers talking about money, money, money and all the beautiful girls ready to fall in their arms willing to do anything to have a part. I didn't care a bit for that so I left.

After I made the second picture with Marcel L'Herbier, we went to London, Jean Murat and "moi"—myself—to find out if a family could take a girl so I could learn English and work in British movies. I looked the young girl that I was and Jean Murat was older than I was. We went to different families but he didn't want to leave me alone so he put me in a family where there were already two girls, one eighteen and the other sixteen. The mother was gone but the father was a doctor of the Duke of York. He was called Professor Varley and they had a beautiful house—a capital place. Jean Murat didn't say he was my husband. He said he was my uncle and he wanted to leave his little niece in a good family. He didn't say I was in movies because they were very old-fashioned. I stayed with them for two months. In the morning, I went to the Berlitz school—it was not a lack of culture at

With Jean Murat. (Courtesy of Annabella Power.)

all, it was just to learn the language. In the afternoon, I went to see British movies. Jean Murat came several times to see me and have dinner at the house where I was staying. I spoke with the girls all the time. The one who was sixteen years old—we had fun with each other. She didn't know I was in the movie business. Sometimes we were taken out to Oxford but with a chaperone. Nobody knew I had been an actress or that I had a child. They thought I was just a kid and that was the best way for me. So I worked like a dog to learn English.

In three months, I was able to accept my part in *Wings of the Morning,* a picture that I made with Henry Fonda in London and around there. It was filmed in Technicolor at 20th Century–Fox's British studio which was an enormous place, beautiful and wonderful. They were able to make two or three pictures together at the same time and I was very lucky because it was during my first stay in London apart from the film I did years before with M. Fescourt. I did some shopping in London and we were going to the zoo but it didn't happen often because we had a lot of work to do, especially me who was playing two parts in the picture.

Wings of the Morning was a great film—a marvelous picture. I loved the director, Harold Schuster. I loved Henry Fonda. The big singer, John McCormack, whom I met sang in the picture. With the Technicolor and the singing, the picture was a dream. That was when I said, "I think I should be paying you to do this for a living. You should not be paying me." I adored to be in England and the weather was divine. We had picnics every day. And Henry Fonda was dancing with me. Each time we didn't work, we were dancing. He was one of my favorite leading men. I was not at all in love with him but I did have a crush on him as a *copain,* a friend. He was so gentle and very, very good-looking. He was so nice to me on camera because I did not know English very well and I really felt relaxed around him. We could have fun together like kids. And I thought he was always thinking first of me in the scenes.

When they gave me the script of the film, I took the habit of studying it like René Clair did. I read it from the first cover until the very end. I knew my part, I knew the part of everybody else, I knew the moves of the camera. I thought I would be perfect. I had learned the script by heart but one day on the set, an electrician said, "Miss Annabella, the light is bad right now. Move on the left." But that was not in the script so I said like an idiot I didn't know what he was talking about. I was just beginning to learn English.

Wings of the Morning is the picture I enjoyed the most doing because I played two parts so I had more fun with that than any other film. I played my great-grandmother, a gypsy, I played myself normal and then I played dressed up like a little boy so I could escape from the war in Spain. I loved dressing as a boy. That was very much in vogue then with lots of actresses. And, of course, lots of actresses dress like boys in Shakespeare, too. They had made a suit for me at the studio but I took the old suit of my

With Henry Fonda and director Harold Schuster during the filming of *Wings of the Morning*. (Courtesy of Annabella Power.)

brother to wear in the film. He was thirteen years old—about my size—and it was an old suit he'd had for two years to go to school in. I had the shape of a boy, I had no make-up on and I had a little beret like the Basque beret on my head. Sometimes when I'd finish my scene, I would go next door to watch the beautiful star Merle Oberon making a movie. One day when I was coming inside and looking, one of the electricians said, "Oh, here's that kid again. What a boy! He's all the time looking at pictures being made. Get the hell out of here." And for me, it was the biggest compliment because they thought I was really a young boy.

Wings of the Morning was the first Technicolor film made in England. It was filmed all around in England and Ireland with races and horses. Of course, for the horse scenes in the picture, they had to have a double for me. We couldn't see the rushes in the evening. They had to send what we did back to America where they began to do everything in Technicolor. At the beginning, they'd go wild. You had a blue hat, a red dress and green shoes. They said, "But your shoe looks good enough." And after when they saw it, they said, "Ah, it's the best." They used to use color like mad. The soft and romantic color of England they couldn't understand.

Henry Fonda and I were best friends forever after, even when I was married to Tyrone and Henry

With David Niven in *Dinner at the Ritz*. (Courtesy of Annabella Power.)

was married to Frances Brokaw whom he met on the set of *Wings of the Morning*. In fact, Henry and Frances helped Tyrone and me pick out Saltair and they helped us buy the house. They lived across the street from us. We used to play tennis together. On Sunday mornings, we used to have these brunches and they came over for that. Their daughter is the very well-known Jane Fonda. I taught her to swim when she was three or four years old. Jane is so sweet. She comes to see me in Paris. It's very important for her that I knew her mother.

My next picture in England was *Under the Red Robe*. The Swedish director, Victor Seastrom, began it but he had problems with his wife and family so he had to go back to Sweden. I never met him. Harold Schuster, who had directed *Wings of the Morning*, did it. I remember I had beautiful dresses in *Under the Red Robe*. The actor I played with, Conrad Veidt, I didn't like at all. I don't like to say anything not nice but nobody liked him too much. Conrad Veidt was madly in love with Conrad Veidt.

My last picture in England was *Dinner at the Ritz* with David Niven and Paul Lukas. That, too, was directed by Harold Schuster. I was not at all friendly with Paul Lukas. We would say, "Hello," "Good morning" and "Good evening." He was kind of a cold person. I suppose he was very polite and very nice but not a friend. But David Niven—ah, I adored David! He was the most gracious of gentlemen and so warm. In a way, he reminded me of Jean Murat. But I also thought David was so funny. You know, I've noticed a few times if you were eight or ten at dinner, little by little, nobody was talking—only David because he was telling so many funny stories.

In my part in the picture we played in together, I had to pretend to be an Indian girl and sometimes I still had a little bit of black on after taking off the make-up. So David said, "Oh, my dear, I have to give you a child." And he gave me one of those British dogs who are white but with a lot of black spots.

I've always worn large bracelets because as a girl, I was so athletic and I loved sports so I always felt that my wrists were perhaps too large and my shoulders too broad. A bracelet I still wear became a kind of trademark and probably the first time I wore it

With her mother, Alice Charpentier, her younger brother Pierre and her daughter Anne in her Bel Air home in 1938. (Courtesy of Annabella Power.)

was when I was filming *Dinner at the Ritz.* It has been with me on many films. There is a dent in it and that happened when it was still very new and I was doing all my own action—swimming and diving—in *Dinner at the Ritz.* In the scene, I had to climb into the water from a ship, but I didn't mind. It was part of being an actress and I loved to do whatever the girl I played was doing. We thought it was quite natural and fun to play scenes in the water as long as we did not have to stay there for a long, long time. I remember there was a scene in *Suez* where I was taking a bath and Allan Dwan, the director, kept getting me out of the water and wrapping me in a robe so that I wouldn't catch cold. But *Dinner at the Ritz* was done much faster and we didn't have so many retakes of the same scene.

I adored everything about England. I thought it was beautiful, everything was wonderful and the country was a dream. My family came from France to visit me. And since England is so close to France, all my French friends came, too, during the weekend. So I rented a beautiful big house with a lovely garden. It was like a fairy tale.

I was getting up around six in the morning to be ready at eight-thirty because the studio was about half an hour from my place or depending on if the picture was on location. But those sorts of details didn't bother me at all. They sent a car from the studio to pick me up. I did drive a little bit in England on the left side and, you know, it was like a forbidden adventure. In one day from the country, I went to London. I drove very, very slowly, my mind all the time being on the left but I didn't care too much for that. Still, it was fun, I tried it and I did it very well.

At the wheel of her Ford convertible with her mother beside her in the driveway of her Bel Air home in 1938. (Courtesy of Annabella Power.)

After I made those three pictures in England, I went to Hollywood to make films for 20th Century–Fox. This time, I fell in love with America from the very first second I was there. I rented several homes in California and I had a secretary of my own. I was still very family-like. I was with my mother, my daughter and my younger brother. Later, my father came, too. Jean Murat also came to visit us. When I arrived at the studio, I had a beautiful dressing room—better than anything I'd had in France. I thought it was like a wonderful gag. I never took myself seriously but I enjoyed everything that was given to me. That's why I never became pretentious and I never became disappointed when I was not the top because I gave it up, you know.

My first picture in Hollywood for 20th Century–Fox was *The Baroness and the Butler.* Walter Lang was the director. I liked that film very much. My partner, William Powell, was wonderful. But he was older than I was and he was sad during the making of our picture so he kept to himself. Jean Harlow, whom he was to marry and who was young and beautiful and full of life—she had just died. When we worked together, he was very correct, very charming, very handsome but he treated me like a much younger girl.

My next picture in Hollywood was *Suez* with Tyrone Power and Loretta Young. It was about Ferdinand de Lesseps and the building of the Suez Canal. I loved Loretta Young. She was beautiful and nice but not a friend. As for Tyrone, all the women were crazy about him but at first when I began to work with him, I was very cool. I'd say, "Mr. Power, I'm delighted" as I was leaving. I never talked with him then. I thought he was very wonderful but I was a little scared to see two or three women just falling apart looking at him. My little brother was always kidding me when I made the picture. He'd say, "Ha, ha, you are going to be with the darling of the world, oh, with Tyrone Power." You know how a brother will kid a sister.

And I said, "Oh, I don't know. I didn't talk to him. He's good-looking and very nice but I'm not—"

With William Powell in *The Baroness and the Butler*. (Courtesy of Annabella Power.)

"Oh, yes, ma cherie," he'd say, "he is the darling of the world." And I was mad at my brother because he was kidding.

Then when we played in *Suez*, there was a big scene when Tyrone sat in a chair and I was on my knees. He was going to build the Suez Canal and he didn't know if it was a good idea or not so I said, "Oh, you should do it. You are going to change the world." And in the middle of the scene, all the lights went off and everything went black. I said, "Oh, something wrong with the electricity?" Although it was dark, I could see that everybody had a very serious face. But I was still very young and like a schoolgirl in class, I had the giggles. I fell on the ground and began to laugh. I said, "Don't be silly. The lights will come back. It's not a big drama. This happens to films in France often. Don't be silly."

All of a sudden, the lights came back on. I was on my knees in front of Tyrone and he told me, "Didn't you know?"

I said, "What?"

"You didn't see it in the make-up room?" he said.

I said, "I'm never in the make-up room. I do my make-up myself in my dressing room."

He told me, "There was a big notice saying there would be five minutes' silence because Mr. so-and-so, a producer, had died."

I thought, "My God, those people were so nice with me. They are going to say that stupid little French frog has no heart at all." I had been laughing like a fool and now I began to cry like an idiot. And all my make-up was falling off. The adorable director, Allan Dwan, said, "Listen, she's too upset. We are going to stop and have luncheon early. Miss Annabella will go in her dressing room and do her make-up again. We'll work after lunch."

Then the electrician came down and said to me, "Oh, listen, kid, don't worry. That man—we didn't care for him so much." He wanted to cheer me up.

So I went to my dressing room and I began to wash my face when somebody knocked at the door. It was M. Tyrone Power's secretary and he said, "Mr. Power and the director are waiting for you in the restaurant."

I said, "Well, I can't. I'm going to take some time to make up." I was only half made-up and since I had a wig, all my hair was bound up underneath it.

He said, "Listen, I would lose my job if I don't bring you back. Come as you are."

So I went back to the restaurant with half of my face made up and still very moved, laughing and

With Tyrone Power in *Suez.*

crying at the same time. Tyrone and Allan Dwan were darling. They even managed to give me a glass of cold port. Nobody was drinking any alcohol. We talked and they were very nice. I had begun to come back to life and Tyrone said, "Have you ever seen a radio broadcast? I'm doing a charity program for the radio downtown today. Have you seen those being done in Hollywood?"

I said, "No."

He said, "Would you like to come with me? We'll have a sandwich after we finish the work and you'll go and see what it is."

I said, "Oh, yes, but I have to call my mother first to tell her that I'm not going back for dinner."

I called my mother and she said, "What do you mean? You're going to have dinner with the wonderful Tyrone Power? You have on your old blue suit and flat shoes."

I said, "Well, Mother, on top of that, I have red eyes and look awful."

So I went with Tyrone. After he finished the work at the radio station, we had a sandwich and he explained to me I don't know what—something about technical things in radio broadcasting. Then he took me back home and from that day, we saw each other every day.

As I've said, I was with my family so I was not alone in the house when Tyrone came there. One time, he came with three musicians and they played during the night under the balcony—it was adorable. The studio was very close to my house. Sometimes when we played in *Suez,* I was not in the scene. I was going later in the afternoon so in the morning, Tyrone passed by in front of my house on his way to work and he put a few flowers on the front door to my car to show me that he came by. It was a dream—it was like a fairy tale.

We had a scene with a big sandstorm in the picture. There was a big golf course not very far from 20th Century–Fox. So they bought the golf course and when we were working inside the studio, they covered it with sand. They went to Santa Monica and took sand to bring it back to the set so that it became like a desert, not a golf course. When we did the scene of the big storm, they had behind the camera a plane with a big wing and we were in the wind. Oh, it was terrible—very, very hot, very tough but it looked very real.

With Jean-Pierre Aumont in *Hotel du Nord.* (Courtesy of Annabella Power.)

With Louis Jouvet in *Hotel du Nord.* (Courtesy of Annabella Power.)

At that time, Tyrone had a very big part in *Marie-Antoinette* opposite Norma Shearer and he was told by Metro-Goldwyn-Mayer that he would, of course, escort her to the premiere. But we had arranged that I would come in and sit next to him. Norma Shearer didn't mind. He was her official escort because of the premiere and the photographers but they were not together. But it was so funny. Tyrone's eyes and mine were bloodshot because of all the sand in them from making *Suez* and we could not even see some of the film. It hurt us sometimes to look at the screen. But when Norma saw us at a party after the movie, she saw that our eyes were red and she said, "Oh, oh, you dears. You were so moved by the film. You are so dear." And Tyrone and I nodded and then we had to get out of there fast because we were laughing so hard inside.

Tyrone and I fell in love and he asked me to marry him. I was still married to Jean Murat but when we had married each other, he told me, "I'm twenty-two years older than you are. Because of that, the day may come when we will not be married any longer. When you want to be free, let me know." So I wrote a long letter telling him that I had fallen in love with Tyrone and he was so kind. He sent me back a telegram saying, "Be happy."

I came back to France in 1938 to divorce Jean and when we divorced, he gave me a beautiful blue ring as a gift. Can you imagine that? A gift for our divorce in memory of all the happiness of our marriage. He was still very much in love and loving but the age difference was so great and the more mature I became, it also seemed the older he became. But this ring I wear all the time in memory of him. We remained very good friends until the end of his life. I am a good friend of his daughter and his grandson who reminds me of him. He is tall and good-looking and very intelligent.

Back in Paris in 1938, I played in a picture directed by Marcel Carné, *Hotel du Nord*. Carné knew all the people he asked to play for him—Arletty, Louis Jouvet and Jean-Pierre Aumont. Of course, the tables were now turned for me in France because, after I had been in England and America, the director was very much in awe of me. He thought coming from California maybe I would be a pretentious star. He had an elegant new dressing room waiting for me—a caravan super deluxe—and everyone treated me as being much older. You know, I was madame. So M. Carné was a little cool at the beginning but I wanted to show him that I was an actress and that I wanted to make the film. When he realized I was just as I am, not playing the "star," we became very close friends. Some years ago, he had a street in his village named "Rue Marcel Carné." A lot of people went to see him—friends and people from the village. But he said to somebody who told it to me a few days ago that he received only two telegrams of felicitation, congratulations and love—from Arletty and myself.

With her trailer during the production of *Hotel du Nord*. (Courtesy of Annabella Power.)

When we were making the picture, Jean-Pierre Aumont and I would play gags all the time. We tried not to ruin the film or wreck a scene but we had known each other so long that I think we were still something like children together. But *Hotel du Nord* is a very tragic film—I attempt suicide at the beginning of it. And so when Jean-Pierre and I would make jokes together, we would do it away from the set because the film was so serious. But it was beautiful filming that sad story on the Canal St. Martin in Paris. People don't know the canals in Paris and that wonderful little hotel—the facade of it, the front part is now a "monument historique." Carné did not simply make up the film. He had his script and it was written for Jean-Pierre and me. But he would shoot lots of scenes and then he really added to it. He kind of made it bigger or changed it as it was going along because Arletty and Louis Jouvet were so good and it just seemed to work so well. Arletty spoke French so different from me with a kind of Parisian accent and there was no one in the world like Louis Jouvet. And so Carné developed the film as it grew. He would shoot lots of film and then he would take some scenes from what he had shot.

Arletty, who has just died, was wonderful—very clever and brave. She was also very Parisian but I'm absolutely the opposite because I made pictures in so many countries around the world. I saw in the newspaper that Marcel Carné went to her funeral. She was always very kind and she said to me a few years ago that her career was owed to me because when we would see the rushes, why, we could see that Arletty's role was getting bigger and bigger and the director was doing that. But I did not object because I thought, "Well, she is a very good actress and so different from me." I thought it was the most natural thing in the world to help her when I could. I would not have wanted to cut her out of the picture because I wouldn't have wanted anybody to have done that to me when I was beginning. So anything I could do to help somebody, I would. Also, I was going back to America, I was in love, my career was very big at that time and I did not worry about another actress.

After I played in *Hotel du Nord,* I got my divorce and I went back to America to marry Tyrone. Darryl Zanuck, the head of 20th Century–Fox, couldn't stand me when I dared to marry Tyrone. I had a big contract with Fox and after *Suez,* in which picture I had a personal success, Mr. Zanuck said I would be the dream star. When I planned to marry Tyrone, he stopped all the proposals for films he'd made to me. But I had had success in pictures and my life was now more important to me than the movies.

Tyrone and I were married in California on April 23, 1939. We had the wedding in the house I was renting on St. Pierre Road in Bel-Air. We could not have a Catholic wedding in a church because I had been divorced from Jean Murat but the presence of God was there. In fact, those were the words which the judge read when he married us: "And in the presence of God whose blessing we now invoke upon this joyful yet sacred service." We made kind of—not exactly an altar but it was in front of my fireplace and it was very beautiful. I wore a dress

With Tyrone Power, Cesar Romero, Sonja Henie, and Henie's mother on a visit to Treasure Island during the 1939 Golden Gate International Exposition in San Francisco. (Courtesy of Annabella Power.)

and a hat in a shade of blue—it was called Nile blue. There had been so much in the newspapers about us and when we went to get the marriage license, there were so many reporters and so many questions. So we wanted the wedding itself not to have too much of that. They took pictures, of course, but it was very small and very private. Pat Paterson Boyer was my matron of honor—we had become good friends by this time. Don Ameche, who had worked with Tyrone in pictures, was his best man. And also Tyrone's mother, Patia, was there and his sister Anne. Afterwards, we got into our car and drove away as soon as we could.

We went to Europe on our honeymoon and in Rome, we received a blessing in an audience with the Pope. Tyrone was the nicest man in the world. The only thing is he was a little weak. When we went to Italy, he wanted the publicity man who came from Fox to go around with us all the time. We went to Pompeii, we went to Naples and the second day I said, "Tyrone, the honeymoon is for two. It's not for three."

And like a child, he said, "Oh, yes, but that man came from Paris just for us."

I said, "What do you mean? He was in the office in Paris. He had two days bothering us in Italy."

Then he said, "Okay, perhaps you're right." They had a big Hispano for us and everything ready for a trip. But Tyrone went to buy a little open Fiat car. We left at four in the morning alone and we didn't go to any place where all the reporters were expecting us. He was delighted but that was my own way, not his. That was the fault of Tyrone but he had no others that I know. He was too, too sweet. We went from Italy to France and I showed him Paris. Then we drove to La Pilat, my house by the sea where my family was. Before our honeymoon, Tyrone asked me to teach him in French all the songs my mother sang for me when I was a little girl. One evening at La Pilat, he knelt down and sang them to "maman." We all cried and laughed at life, joy and love. Tyrone was a dream for me and my family all adored him.

It was on our way back to America that we found out that the war had broken out. That was terrible. My daughter was staying with my parents in France and I thought, "My God! I can't leave her there. And if I could take my brother out of France!" I even had a wild, crazy idea to dress him up as a girl and bring him to America. When I was back in America, I said to Watson Webb, a close friend of mine and Tyrone's, "I'm going to fly back to France."

With Tyrone Power, her mother and her daughter Anne in the Powers' Brentwood home in the 1940s. (Courtesy of Annabella Power.)

Watson was from a big important family. He was a millionaire because his father nearly built the first few trains in America. He was a very close friend of Henry Fonda's, too. He said to me, "You're crazy. Go back to the war?"

I said, "Yes, but if I don't go back to try to help my family, I'll die of shame and if when I'm over there, I cannot come back to see my beloved Tyrone, I'll die of despair." So I went right back to France. I was unable to get my parents and brothers out—they remained there during the war. But I got my daughter out through Lisbon and she joined Tyrone and me in California.

In America, Tyrone and I kept in touch with French people who were in the war. I was very friendly with Antoine de Saint-Exupéry who flew in the war. When he came to California after the fall of France to the Germans, he was not well. He was downtown in Hollywood in the hospital and kind of lonely so I went to visit him in his room. He had a book by his bed, *Les Contes d'Andersen.* I took the book, opened it and there was the story of the Little Mermaid. Then I closed the book and told him the whole story by heart. We became friends through the fairy tale story and he came to our house. Tyrone liked him very much. He was terribly bright and terribly clever doing tricks with cards and things like that. Tyrone wanted him as a teacher but Tyrone was not too much for that.

With Tyrone Power in their Brentwood home. (Courtesy of Annabella Power.)

Saint-Exupéry left for New York. One day, he called from New York and said, "Annabella, do you have a little time? I want to read you something." So I called Tyrone, we both listened to him and it was the first time he told his story of *The Little Prince* in a conversation. He gave me the proofs. I'm one of the few people who has the proofs with his own design and everything the first time his *The Little Prince* had been printed. Saint-Exupéry also gave me a lot of books and so on. He used wonderful words and he adored to fly. For him, it was a religion.

It is not surprising that I have known many of the French authors—people like Camus or Sartre. After all, compared to the United States, France is a small country and the arts are not separated or maybe segregated here. Literature, stage, painting, sculpture, music, dance and film—all of those arts are considered to be very friendly to one another like brothers and sisters and so you get to know people much more easily. But I knew many of the American writers, too. I met Nathanael West several times and I thought him a very quiet man. I was going to say strange but that is not right. He was just quiet and seemed rather sad. I am thinking of that story he wrote, *Miss Lonelyhearts.* I think I really remember his story much more than I remember him personally.

I knew Lillian Hellman. She was very intelligent and we could talk about issues. She really knew and understood things about the war and about politics that other people did not. I liked her very, very much. We all smoked in those days but she smoked more than anybody else. She was lots of fun, too. Of course, they were very different but in some ways, she reminded me of Simone de Beauvoir whom I also knew.

I met William Faulkner but I did not know him the way I knew Ernest Hemingway. You know, I do not like guns and Hemingway was very "macho"—always talking about hunting and drinking all the time with his friends. But he was a very attractive man, too. He liked artists, he liked actors and he loved France. We always liked one another. He had written the part in *For Whom the Bell Tolls* for me. It was when my accent was very clear and he said, "Well, you can play this with an accent and your accent can very easily be Spanish." Gary Cooper, who was such a dream and who lived across the street from me, wanted me to play the role, too. Hemingway showed me the part and we talked about it. We talked it over with Gary, too, but I didn't play the role because I had been blacklisted by Zanuck and the part went to Ingrid Bergman instead.

Tyrone and I had three years of great happiness together until the war came. When he spoke to me, he always called me "My heart, my love, my sweet." He was speaking very good French by then so he called me *mon petit cœur*. He wanted me to know and love America and as soon as he was not working, we took our car and we went all around the Grand Canyon, Yosemite and Sequoia. So I knew America better than a lot of Americans.

We had a lovely home on Saltair in the beautiful suburb of Brentwood, a little closer to the seaside than Bel-Air. We had a lot of servants. We had a cook and a wonderful butler because we had open house on Sundays. We had friends who came and we played a lot of croquet. We played tennis a little bit but I was never a champ because I have a silly heart. Jean Murat had adored to play singles. I could play doubles—otherwise, my heart was beating and beating. I don't know why I'm still around because I have such a busy heart.

We had a very big garden in our home in Brentwood and we had chickens for the eggs, of course. One day, Tyrone saw that in another house they had put the chickens in small little places. So he had one built like that at our home in Brentwood and I felt a little sorry for them. They were like they were in jail. One day, I opened the door of the chicken house and put the chickens outside. They had been cooped up like that for about two months and they could hardly walk for a while. When Tyrone came back from the studio, I said, "It's so unfair."

And he said, "All right, darling. Let's put it down and take all your chickens in the garden the way they like it." That's the way Tyrone acted with me.

Playing ping-pong with Tyrone at their home. (Courtesy of Annabella Power.)

Claudette Colbert was one of our closest friends and she is still a very loyal friend. Some years ago, she came to the hotel when I was in New York to see me even though she was going to act in the theatre. And then after that, she went to a party for me. She was always like that. She worked so hard but she did not look tired at all. She was so much fun. She and her husband and Tyrone and I had so much fun together. I remember once we took a ten-day trip in California by car. We were in a convertible and we would all take turns driving. Claudette's husband was the one who would go in and book rooms for us in the motels because he was the only one that wasn't immediately recognized. And so we laughed for ten days.

Claudette is a wonderful hostess, too. She gives wonderful parties and really treats a guest as though you are the king of kings or, for me, the queen of queens. But you know, she felt awkward when she was with French people because she didn't speak French the way that someone would who had spoken it all her life as her number one language. So she would ask me sometimes, "Is this the way I should say something?" or "Is this the way I should write something?" But she really felt during the war that she was French and it was very hard for her. We have many happy memories of working together for the USO. She is a wonderful actress and I always thought she was not appreciated enough in France. In America, of course, it is different.

As an actor, I think Tyrone was very sincere—a wonderful, beautiful, marvelous actor. All his partners adored him. We acted on the stage together. I had been on the stage once with Jean-Pierre Aumont in a Shakespeare play, *As You Like It.* But it was not a terrific success when we did it in Paris in 1935. I had great success on the stage later in New York and before that, in summer stock with Tyrone. I was a little afraid the first time to be on the stage with my accent so we both would go to rest homes to play *Lilliom* together for a tryout. *Lilliom* was a wonderful play. It was not very far from New York but it was not on Broadway where we did it in summer stock in 1941. We had full capacity because Tyrone was a big star. Our love story had made a big scandal—you know, Mr. Zanuck was so furious. All the newspaper people came from New York and *Lilliom* for two weeks was a terrific success. Then one of the newspapers wrote, "That's a new couple ready for Broadway." Unfortunately for Mr. Zanuck, not only had that French girl married his star but she would make him leave Hollywood for New York. I was told Zanuck said, "Too much is too much."

With Van Johnson, Claudette Colbert and servicemen at the USO in Hollywood during World War II. (Courtesy of Annabella Power.)

The producer of *Lilliom* was Jack Wilson, an American married to Natasha Paley, a daughter of the Grand Duke Paul of the Romanov family of Russia and related on both sides of her family to the last tsar. Although she was a princess, she loved the theatre and worked in several movies before she married Jack Wilson. She also worked for the very wonderful designer, Mainbocher, in New York. I was very close to her because I was playing on the stage in other roles for her husband. Afterwards, when I went in the American army and played in Noel Coward's *Blithe Spirit,* it was because of Jack Wilson. When she came to Paris later, I went to meet her. At that time, you'd still take the boat and arrive by train. I know her nephew, Michel Romanov, too, so I'm terribly close to that family.

Jack Wilson was a very close friend of Noel Coward and after Natasha married him, she became a very strong friend of Noel, too. He would always visit her in New York and she would go to visit him at his home on the island. He wrote the part of Elvira in *Blithe Spirit* for me. He said that with my accent, I could be called Marianne the ghost. I would be the spirit of France and the accent would not be so important because I would not have that many lines. But he wanted me to play that part and he said that he thought the title of the play, *Blithe Spirit,* fit me perfectly. He always said nice things and he was so funny.

I first met Noel when I went to see Natasha in her apartment. Both Natasha and Noel had little white dogs that looked almost like brother and sister. It was forbidden at that time—very *interdit*—to walk with a dog on Park Avenue. They had laws about it and you had to go over to Central Park. Noel always liked to play jokes and he thought it was a great gag because he and Natasha would walk their dogs down Park Avenue and even go right into the middle of the avenue on the grass. Nobody would dare say anything—everybody knew Noel Coward. I remember one day when I was visiting him, he said, "Let's have some fun." And the three of us walked the dogs on Park Avenue.

I came from a very old-fashioned family. When I was living in France in the thirties, we never talked about politics. I'd never been that kind of person. I never heard about what was going on in Germany, never thought about it—just thinking about my parts. I was living my parts and living with my family and my love story. But when the war came, I was making speeches every day on the radio to my own little village in France to try to raise money. It was just before the declaration of war by Mr. Roosevelt. I was ready to do anything and it was very, very fascinating. I'd done all the training for the Red Cross. I was able to drive an ambulance and if the soldiers were wounded, to do the first thing and give them shots. I did all my training when I was playing in Chicago because I thought I would go only in the Red Cross but I found out that they wouldn't send me where I wanted to go. I wanted to go to Europe. I wanted to try and see my mother and my father. So what I did, I cut my day in two. All morning, I was working with the nurses and in the afternoon, I was playing in *Blithe Spirit.*

Tyrone enlisted in the marines as soon as war was declared. I visited him in El Centro, California where he was first stationed. He gave me a mug at that time which I still have—a mug with the insignia of the marines and the name of the base on it. I also went to see him just before he left for the Pacific. I went to see him each time because I was selling war bonds. I had a private plane and it was for the young soldiers who had been wounded—a marine, a flyer, a G.I., you know, any kind. Tyrone gave me a beautiful heart in rubies when we parted. In the summer, I still put it on. People say, "Oh, it's so lovely," and I say, "Yes. When Tyrone left, he said, 'I leave you my heart. Take good care of it.' " And always when I put that heart on—I don't put it on often but when I put that beautiful jewel on, it touches me like if I hear his words. We tried to continue writing to each other all through the war but it was often very slow. For example, in 1944, he was near Japan and I was in Italy.

During the war, I went to the White House and both President and Mrs. Roosevelt were very kind. I was very honored to be there and to meet them. I admired them very much. I was to go to a White House luncheon with other actors and actresses. We were all selling war bonds. Mrs. Roosevelt knew about my work with the Red Cross. It was her birthday so President Roosevelt was giving a luncheon for her where she could meet some of the people that she wanted to. I was asked to come earlier than the others and I was surprised because I did not know that. When I got there and went inside, there was just the president, Mrs. Roosevelt and me. Mrs. Roosevelt told me that she remembered the red dress I wore in the movie with Henry Fonda. We talked about the war, about the fact that I was French and my family was in France and that I had gone back to get my little daughter out so she would not be there during the war. And we talked about how the movies and the theatre were so good to tell people what was happening during the war and how people felt. They said that on the stage, you can see what people think but in a movie, you can see what people both think and feel. They said that they had invited these actors, actresses, writers and directors to the White House today because what we did was very important for people. President Roosevelt was seated behind a desk throughout our meeting. He spoke about my taking a tour of the White House but he did not go with me. It was Mrs. Roosevelt who took me on the tour and showed me their own rooms in the White House before the luncheon.

I remember a funny thing that happened at the luncheon. We were sitting at small tables—maybe thirty people or something like that—and the wife of Errol Flynn, Lili Damita, was there. She, too, was French and it was very funny. She was speaking with a heavy French accent. She did not do that on other days but she did this day. And here I was trying to get rid of my accent. She wore a hat all during the luncheon and she kept a veil on over her

A fashion still from *The Baroness and the Butler*. (Courtesy of Annabella Power.)

eyes and nose. She did not lift it even when she was eating and she was speaking very loudly in this very strong French accent.

In 1943, Fox made me do two pictures as propaganda for the war, *Tonight We Raid Calais* and *Bomber's Moon.* The next year, I was in New York playing *Jacobowsky and the Colonel,* a great success on Broadway which was directed by Elia Kazan. My name in the play was Marianne who was a symbol of France like Uncle Sam is a symbol of America. In the story, I was trying to help a Jewish man and a Polish colonel to escape the Nazis. The theatre was full and we had wonderful notices.

There was something during that play that was the greatest, most moving moment of my life. One day in the middle of a scene, the big iron curtain came down and I said, "Oh, my God, what's happening?" I rushed back and asked, "What is it, a fire?"

They said, "No, no. Annabella, you don't know. Paris has been liberated. We just heard it on the radio. Annabella, you go back to the stage alone. You are going to tell the audience, 'Paris is freed!' " Paris, the symbol of freedom and everything!

They pushed me back on the stage and the curtain went up. I was so moved, so excited because I thought of my family, my friends, the place I was born. The people were surprised to see me. "What's happened? She's alone." Half-laughing, half-crying, I screamed, "Paris is free! Paris has been liberated!" And one thing, my dear, that I will never forget in my life. The whole audience, all Americans, stood up and sang "La Marseillaise!" That was a moment of emotion and everybody felt free.

Let me tell you that there is in life something very moving and strange. I was staying in style at the Hotel Pierre—I had a beautiful apartment there. When I came back to the hotel, I took the lift and a little boy about seventeen was taking me upstairs. He said, "Oh, Miss Annabella, may I ask you a big favor?"

I said, "Yes, yes. What is it? Of course."

"Miss Annabella," he said, "I just heard that Paris has been liberated. May I kiss you?" I thought it was very touching because that boy had never been to Paris. He was a simple little kid—I didn't think he would ever cross the ocean. So the big emotion of the theatre finished with a kiss in the elevator.

Louis Calhern played with me in *Jacobowsky and the Colonel* and he was so kind, so *sympathique* for me at the end of the war and during the liberation of Paris. I would go out and have dinner with him after the show. On stage, his eyes would often twinkle. He would kind of wink and it made it fun to play with him. He was a real gentleman and I liked him very, very much.

I went to Italy in November, 1944 and was there for four months. It was dangerous and fascinating. I was with the Théatre aux armées. It was hard because I was doing two things. I was in the Red Cross in the morning and I was playing *Blithe Spirit* every evening for the boys in the American army—the Fifth Army of General Clark. I had great admiration for the soldiers. The ones playing with me in the company were just actors. But with me—I could go in the hospital every morning and help the wounded soldiers. I always wanted to help them.

Then I was in Paris after the liberation and at last, I saw my family and my French friends again. For a week, we did the play in English for the army, then we went to the north of France and different towns, always doing *Blithe Spirit.* We were supposed to play for General Patton, too, but he went too fast!

Tyrone and I were reunited in America when the war came to an end. He was an angel as ever but unfortunately for me as a woman, he was a man who didn't know how to say "no"—not only in his personal life but in his career, too. After the war, he thought everybody had forgotten about him which was stupid, of course, and he signed a seven-year contract with Mr. Zanuck again. I begged him not to do it but he was afraid nobody would take him for a job.

In 1946, I starred on Broadway in Jean-Paul Sartre's play, *No Exit,* which was directed by John Huston. I was one of the two girls in the play. The other one was a little ex-girlfriend of John Huston's. He loved her very much and she was very nice. The play was a great success with critics but not in the money business because people were still a little scared of M. Sartre and that kind of play. They were a little old-fashioned. John Huston had a great gift to put that girl—I forget her name—to sleep. We were all amazed. He put a handkerchief around his hand and he'd say to her, "You're cold, you're cold, you're very cold." And she was shaking. Then she fell asleep and after that, he said, "And in your heart, you're warm. It's hotter and in

With James Cagney in *13 Rue Madeleine.* (Courtesy of Annabella Power.)

a quarter of an hour, you will wake up." And she did wake up so Mr. Huston had a great gift that I never knew about before.

13 Rue Madeleine, made in 1946, was my last picture in Hollywood. Henry Hathaway directed it and we went to Canada for locations. It was a very nice picture and I liked M. Hathaway. He was a friend and he had made three pictures with Tyrone. We spent a lot of time together later. I took him and Madame Hathaway all around Spain one day. I was a close friend of both of them. James Cagney, the leading man in *13 Rue Madeleine,* was very nice but he was always alone in a corner. He was not blah-blah-blah. He played a good part. He was a wonderful actor, a very dignified partner but not a friend.

In 1948, I divorced Tyrone and I went back to France and made some films. I made two pictures in Spain. I have a friend, Aline de Romanones, the Countess of Quintanella. She's very well-known now—she writes books. When I was not working in the movie I made in Spain, I played golf with her—very badly but I enjoyed it because the place was beautiful. It was on the top of a hill not very far from San Sebastian.

After that, I didn't care so much about movies. I mean, I had wonderful memories but after Hollywood, after traveling all over, what they offered me was not so good and I didn't care to make more pictures. I didn't care for the parts and I wanted to live because I'd been taken so much by working and I wanted to do something. I began visting jails here in France and I became interested in prison reform. After visiting with prisoners three times a week all afternoon, I created a *vestiaire*—a place where they could find normal clothes and where they could look for a job after leaving prison. I had everything from the Secours Catholique waiting for them at my parish.

In the fifties, I also bought a farm in the Pyrenees that I call Contramundo. I'm not young enough now to have a husband or a lover but on the farm, I have dogs, cats and a donkey. And I love gardening. I can go gardening for hours. The farm for me is wonderful. I love animals, I love nature, I love life and I believe in God. That makes me very happy. I'm not afraid of dying because I think I'll experience a lot of wonderful things.

Despite our divorce, Tyrone and I remained close and we continued to see each other in the fifties. In 1958, he and his little wife, Debbie, came to visit me at my farm in the Basque country. I was so happy that Tyrone could see the house at Contramundo because I'd built it mostly with money from the sale of our house on Saltair. In fact, there were things in my house we'd had at Saltair. The three of us wrote a postcard to Watson Webb. (Tyrone, Watson and I had been such close friends that we had always called ourselves TWA.) Debbie asked me if I would be a godmother to the baby she was expecting and I said yes. They said how happy they were and they hoped it would be a boy and he could finally have a son. He invited me to visit him on the set of *Solomon and Sheba* so I went to Madrid to see him. He did not look well and he said to me he was very tired but he thought the film was going to be a good one.

A few days later in Madrid, they were shooting a scene of him fighting when his heart stopped. I was told by his so-nice secretary, Bill Gallagher, what had happened in the middle of the scene. That's how I learned it—by telephone. He was just crying when he told me but I was thanking the world and heaven to have had the grace to have had Tyrone a little while as a guest at the farm. As it was, when both of us were just being alone, it was like coming back to our wonderful past.

So often in that past we had not been alone. At the time I was an actress, if I was going to a restaurant with Tyrone, we had to leave by the kitchen, for instance, because too many people were waiting to see us. But the star system doesn't exist for me anymore and now it doesn't matter. With the

A portrait from the 1930s. (Courtesy of Annabella Power.)

first day I found freedom, I was able to go to a big shop like Saks Fifth Avenue in France. In America, I was still too well-known because I was on the stage and I was in the army. But when I came back home, the first time I was able to go shopping like somebody else, one or two people would recognize me but I was not followed. I thought, "Ah, liberty, liberty!" That's what I didn't want—to become the slave of being well-known.

So I left films but I had made pictures all over the world—in Paris, London, Berlin, Vienna, Budapest, Hollywood. I had a wonderful career. And I think back to the silly, half-dreaming little girl I was, playing and always with the background of my mother playing the piano nearly all day long. I dreamed, I hoped, I knew that one day I would be in *it*—the movies! It is good to be a little crazy, don't you think? And at times, it does work!

Dorothy Lee and chorus in the Technicolor production number, "Dancing the Devil Away," in *The Cuckoos.*

1929—THE SONG-AND-DANCE CRAZE

By a curious irony of film history, Abel Gance's *Napoléon* opened in New York in MGM's mutilated version during the same week of February, 1929, that MGM unveiled its new talking picture, *The Broadway Melody*. *Napoléon* in its original presentation in Europe carried the art of the silent film to its furthest extent yet its influence was not recognized until decades later. By contrast, *The Broadway Melody,* one of the first films to reveal the expressive possibilities of sound, had an immediate impact on filmmakers. True, it was not the work of any individual genius and there was no cinematic imagination in the staging of the musical numbers. But there was a spirit of realism flowing from the dynamic performances of its three leads, silent star Bessie Love, newcomer Anita Page and Broadway veteran Charles King, with the whole production invigorated by the sparkling score of Arthur Freed and Nacio Herb Brown. The result was something new for film audiences, the first of the sound films to be advertised as "All-Talking, All-Singing, All-Dancing."[1]

Until the release of *The Broadway Melody,* the sound film had not advanced much beyond Warner Brothers' breakthrough feature, *The Jazz Singer,* first shown in October, 1927, and an even more popular follow-up, *The Singing Fool,* released the next year and again starring Al Jolson. Both films were excellent showcases for Jolson's remarkable talent but it was obvious that if the sound film was to justify its existence, something far more solid than the exploitation of a single personality, no matter how gifted, would have to come along.

That "something" proved to be *The Broadway Melody.* Instead of the at-times lachrymose assault on audience emotions in the Jolson pictures, the film public was given a vital, sometimes dramatic, often humorous portrayal of the world of show business in the twenties. The result was not pleasing to some. Mordaunt Hall in his review of the film in *The New York Times* did not care for its use of "uncouth" contemporary argot.[2] Other critics of the day, however, were much more appreciative. *Photoplay* stated that "with *The Broadway Melody* the talkies find new speed and freedom. The microphone and its twin camera poke themselves into backstage corners, into dressing rooms, into rich parties and hotel bedrooms. Smart Broadway dialogue . . . is expertly and naturally spoken."[3] The film went on to win an Academy Award for best picture, the second film and first talkie to receive that honor. Its overwhelming popularity not only propelled MGM into the sound era but also inspired a flood of screen musicals over the next two years and influenced French director René Clair in films like *Le Million.*

The early movie musical exemplified the studio system at its best. Standard film historians, however, have too often dismissed this first wave of screen musicals as unimaginative, literal transcriptions of stage productions adding nothing to the cinema except for the works of a few "auteurs" like King Vidor's *Hallelujah!,* Rouben Mamoulian's *Applause* and Ernst Lubitsch's *The Love Parade.* Despite this view, it has become increasingly apparent from archival restorations that the musical fluorescence of 1929–30 was far more creative than these writers had claimed. The Hollywood "dream factories" were particularly well-suited for the collaborative atmosphere needed to produce musicals, bringing together Broadway composers and lyricists, choreographers and performers and combining them with silent veterans to create a special kind of magic on the screen. Unlike the often more leaden-paced dramatic sound films of 1929, the early musicals introduced a fresh realism, advanced cinematic techniques and gave screen comedy another dimension while exposing audiences to the creative effervescence of American popular music of the post-war era.

Filmmakers, encouraged by *The Broadway Melody*'s success, adopted its realistic approach to project the backstage drama in other musicals. Among the best to explore the workaday reality behind the illusion of show business glamour are Paramount's 1929 production, *The Dance of Life,* and Warner Brothers' *Show Girl in Hollywood.* Based on the stage hit, *Burlesque,* and boasting memorable performances by Hal Skelly as a weak-willed comic and Nancy Carroll as his supportive partner, *The Dance of Life* vividly depicts the lower rungs of the theatre that would hopefully lead to Broadway. *Show Girl in Hollywood,* directed by Mervyn LeRoy in 1930, follows the trail from the Great White Way to the new mecca on the West Coast as it traces the contrasting careers of a headstrong new import from the stage (played by Alice White) and a once-great silent star fallen on hard times (Blanche Sweet in a poignant portrayal).

Not only did early musicals often further the cause of cinematic realism, in their more fantastic flights they advanced cinema art. The Marx Brothers' first film, *The Cocoanuts* (1929), introduced the overhead shot of the production number, a departure from the fixed position of *The Broadway Melody* and a technique that was to be copied in many subsequent musicals.[4] A number of these films were wholly or partly shot in two-color Technicolor. Miles Kreuger, the leading historian of the first musical films, points out in his book, *The Movie Musical,* that early color "often adds a charm and a fantasy quality particularly well-suited to musicals."[5] The greatest of the revue films, Universal's all-Technicolor *King of Jazz* (1930), featuring the Paul Whiteman Orchestra, has an array of techniques including startling color effects, miniaturization, animation and superimposition.[6] Another all-color production, *Whoopee!* (1930), starring Eddie Cantor and climaxing the first phase of movie musicals, marked the film debut of choreographer Busby Berkeley who was already employing his signature style of overhead shots of chorus girls arranged in geometric patterns and using unusual camera angles for the closer shots.

The early movie musical also revolutionized the field of screen comedy. Although verbal humor had been a constant in silent films of the twenties in the form of wisecracking subtitles, now it was possible to unite word and image by intermingling comic action with vaudeville repartee. Indeed, Ralph Spence, the dean of humorous silent title-writers, became a major dialoguist for early sound comedies. Added to the films' merriment were numbers that allowed the comedians to use the musical skills they had perfected on the stage. With the new opportunities for song and dance, the movie musical became the vehicle to introduce to the screen the great clowns of Broadway—the Marx Brothers, Joe E. Brown, Eddie Cantor and the team of Bert Wheeler and Robert Woolsey.

None of these talents were more popular than Wheeler and Woolsey, who made their screen debut in *Rio Rita,* a 1929 adaptation of a Broadway hit that established the newly-formed RKO-Radio as a major studio. Like *The Broadway Melody,* its success derived from an excellent score and a splendidly diverse cast that made for an irresistible combination—silent star Bebe Daniels in her talkie debut, tenor John Boles as her leading man, Wheeler and Woolsey from the original Ziegfeld production and newcomer Dorothy Lee as their leading lady. The contrast between the two loosely-linked plots is accentuated by the different styles of singing with Daniels and Boles expertly vocalizing in the operetta tradition and Wheeler, Woolsey and Lee performing in the brasher vein of American musical comedy.[7] Bert, Bob and Dottie brought such vitality to their song-and-dance routines that these numbers became a staple in most of their films. There would be ballads and dances by Bert and Dottie, patter songs by Bert and Bob and mock ballets in which Dottie's athleticism was in full display with all three.

As illustrated by *The Broadway Melody* and *Rio Rita,* the advent of the musical film revived old ca-

Charles King, Anita Page and Bessie Love in *The Broadway Melody.*

reers and fostered new ones. Now, however, rather than a strong individual director, it was the studio system which guided these talents. Bessie Love and Bebe Daniels, among the most prominent silent stars for many years, attained their greatest triumphs in *The Broadway Melody* and *Rio Rita.* These musicals also brought to the fore Anita Page and Dorothy Lee, two newer actresses who had brief but striking successes in the early sound era. Although neither became a solo star in her own right, their popularity unquestionably contributed to the fortunes of their studios in those transitional years. Thus, the work of Anita Page and Dorothy Lee was a testimony to the creativity of the cinematic metamorphosis when the movies not only talked but also sang and danced.

Anita Page

In the silent era, the silver screen was unparalleled in its magnetic appeal to young girls of beauty, talent and determination who were drawn into its orbit. Among them was Anita Page who knew early on that she was destined for a career as a film actress. Born in Flushing, New York, on August 4, 1910, she began her work in films playing bits at Paramount's Astoria, Long Island studio in 1925 and 1926. She made the trek to Hollywood with her mother in late 1927 to further her career in pictures during what proved to be the final period of silents.

She soon got an agent and depended on him for advice, commonplace when negotiating for advantages in an industry now ruled by the contract system. He enabled her to sign with MGM, where she was immediately cast in important roles in their late silent features. But whereas the careers of Billie Dove, Fay Wray and Annabella had been shaped by their directors, Anita developed her talents as an actress under the auspices of the studio system supplanting the reign of the director. Indeed, it was studio executive Louis B. Mayer who insisted on her for the part of Ann in her second MGM film, *Our Dancing Daughters,* over the initial objections of the film's director, Harry Beaumont.

Our Dancing Daughters was the quintessential Jazz Age story which cemented Joan Crawford's status as a star playing Diana, a life-loving, intensely honest flapper. But as her rival, Anita won plaudits in the unusual role of a grasping, materialistic, heavy-drinking girl who wins Joan's beau, wealthy Johnny Mack Brown, by feigning to be a sweet, traditional, "unliberated" girl interested only in a home and family. Joe Franklin wrote in his 1959 book, *Classics of the Silent Screen,* that Anita's performance "was quite the best in the film."[1] Anita managed to bring a touch of pathos to the ruthless golddigger with limited moral education who is the product of an equally materialistic mother. Her sordid life ends in tragedy when she goes on a drunken spree. Anita, who had never had a drink in her life, simulated intoxication by imagining she was dizzy. Intuitively, she was able to get beneath the surface of a character who only pretended to be what Anita was in her own life—an old-fashioned girl. Screenwriter Josephine Lovett must have held strong views about social hypocrisy and the position of women in modern society since Joan Crawford and Anita Page in the roles they portrayed with such sensitivity and conviction overshadowed the other characters in the story.

The on-screen rivalry between Joan and Anita carried over into real life as the actresses' clashing egos created a distance between them that continued in their working relationship in two follow-up films, *Our Modern Maidens* (1929) and *Our Blushing Brides* (1930). Although these films were not sequels, as the titles might suggest, and the characters played by Joan and Anita were friends rather than antagonists, they were intended to capitalize on the earlier film's popularity and the dynamics of the Crawford-Page pairing.

Anita's blonde innocence was also potent chemistry when contrasted with saucy, worldly-wise Bessie Love's portrayal in *The Broadway Melody.* The story casts them as a sister act from vaudeville trying to make it on Broadway. Both are in love with the same man, co-star Charles King. Bessie, who played the older sister, Hank Mahoney, earned an Academy Award nomination for her highly dramatic role in her talkie debut. Although initially

With Conrad Nagel in MGM's all-star musical revue, *The Hollywood Revue of 1929.*

dismayed by her slangy lines, Anita, too, proved she could handle dialogue effectively with her convincing performance as the younger sister, Queenie.

Anita remained with MGM for five years. After her success in *The Broadway Melody,* MGM, the last of the Hollywood studios to make a complete transition to sound, continued to cast her in silents including *The Flying Fleet* with Ramon Novarro, *Our Modern Maidens* with Crawford and Douglas Fairbanks, Jr., and *Speedway* opposite William Haines before featuring her again in sound films in 1930. During her years at the studio, she had the opportunity to work with almost all of their top male stars—Haines, Novarro, John Gilbert, Lon Chaney, Robert Montgomery, Buster Keaton and Clark Gable in his first MGM film, *The Easiest Way* (1931). She also appeared in three of the popular Marie Dressler–Polly Moran comedies—*Caught Short* (1930), *Reducing* (1931) and *Prosperity* (1932).

Despite this exposure, however, Anita became dissatisfied with many of her parts at MGM, feeling that she was increasingly being used for her looks rather than her dramatic ability. She cited her films with Buster Keaton, *Free and Easy* (1930), the comedian's talkie debut, and *The Sidewalks of New York* (1931) as examples in which she felt she was merely adornment. Nevertheless, she continued to give finely-etched dramatic performances—the naive girl who becomes pregnant in *Our Modern Maidens*, the kept woman who commits suicide

Anita and Robert Montgomery watching the shooting of a scene from their film, *The Easiest Way,* director Jack Conway at left by the camera. (The Kobal Collection.)

in *Our Blushing Brides,* the housewife seeking to escape what she regards as an unhappy marriage in *Under Eighteen* (a 1931 loan-out to Warner Brothers), the working-class wife hauled off to jail on a false charge of prostitution in W. S. Van Dyke's realistic *Night Court* (1932).

But when it came to comedy, which she acknowledged was not her forte, and parts requiring physical prowess, she was limited. She led a somewhat sheltered life off-screen; she was one of the few actresses who did not ride a horse or even drive a car except when called upon to do so in her films. This may have explained why she was not compatible with parts reflecting a more liberated woman. However, her last silent film, *Speedway,* casting her as a daredevil who not only drove a roadster but also (in simulated shots) flew a plane, was a decided change of pace.

The advent of sound cut short her evolution into an action heroine. Her Queens accent also affected the type of roles she played. While admirably realistic for her urban heroines, whether slangy and wise-cracking or tenderly fragile, it was less suitable for a leading lady in films with historic or foreign settings. Added to this was MGM's tendency, like other big studios of the time, to view its films and its players as commodities. In fact, Anita was convinced that a new, more lucrative contract negotiated by her agent actually did nothing to further her career although MGM ended up making a profit on her by loaning her out to other companies.

Nevertheless, for a time Anita had a following of fans ranging from Italian dictator Benito Mussolini (who reportedly regarded her as his favorite American actress) to future talk-show host Jack Paar. Another admirer, San Francisco mayor and later California governor James Rolph was her escort at various social functions. But after a spate of films on loan-out from MGM in 1933 and a stage tour that same year in *Billy Rose's Crazy Quilt* (her only work in the theatre), her career suddenly came to a halt when, in 1934, she married songwriter Nacio Herb Brown who had provided the lyrics for *The Broadway Melody.* Their marriage, however, shortly ended in divorce.

Although she appeared in a supporting part in only one more picture, *Hitch Hike to Heaven,*

With Marie Dressler in *Reducing.* (The Museum of Modern Art.)

made for a Poverty Row company in 1936, Anita remained active in Hollywood society for several years, often visiting with her close friends, the Wallace Fords. Indeed, she was in their home the day Martha Ford supposedly talked on the telephone with Thelma Todd shortly before the actress was found in her Lincoln Phaeton parked in her garage, dead of carbon monoxide poisoning.

In 1929, Anita had been the most prominent actress chosen that year as a Wampas Baby Star. But by the mid-1930s, while fellow Wampas 1929 graduates Loretta Young and Jean Arthur were coming into their own as stars, Anita, still in her twenties, seemed no longer interested in pursuing her film career. In 1937, she embarked on a new phase of her life when she married navy pilot Herschel House, the only marriage she, as a devout Roman Catholic, acknowledged as valid. The union was a happy one, producing two daughters. Admiral House served with distinction in World War II and the Houses moved to Washington, D.C., where Anita became a glamourous figure in society and an invited guest, along with her husband, at President Truman's inaugural ball in 1949. In later years, the Houses retired to Coronado, coincidentally, the setting for two naval sagas of the screen in which Anita had appeared, *The Flying Fleet* (1929) and *Navy Blues* (1930).

After Admiral House's death in 1991, Anita moved to the Los Angeles area. She coped with her loss by working on her autobiography and making personal appearances with the encouragement of her close friend, Randal Malone, who became her manager. When I interviewed her in February, 1992, she spoke with incredible rapidity, the words rolling off her tongue, as she recalled in great detail conversations dating from more than sixty years earlier. Ever the performer despite her many years of retirement, Anita could still hold a listener's attention as she dramatized the events in her life with the same skill and emotion she had demonstrated on the screen. Although her performance in *The Broadway Melody* won her a permanent place in the history of movie musicals, she was proudest of her work in silents, a sentiment reflected in the title of her projected autobiography, *Anita Page: The Last Great Silent Star.*

My real name is Anita Pomares which is Spanish. Both my parents were born in this country. My paternal grandfather had come over from Spain and was a consul in El Salvador. My grandmother was definitely Castilian Spanish and very beautiful. But a relative wrote me, "Tradition has it that our lines started in France." Now that is very funny because I have always loved everything French. I like Spanish, too, but I'm really crazy about France.

I was born in Flushing, New York and spent much of my childhood in New York City where my parents, my younger brother and I lived on Riverside Drive. My father became vice-president of Austin and Moore which was an electrical contracting business. He had a very, very important job and met many important people.

I wanted to be an actress from the time I was born, I guess, and I loved the movies. I remember getting into hysterics watching Lillian Gish running around looking for her lover all over France in *La Bohème.* I wasn't crying. I was having hysterics. When it was all over and I went to get up, my foot had fallen asleep and I almost fell on my face. I thought, "Oh, I hope people don't think I've been drinking or something." I was only fifteen, you know. I couldn't get my leg working but I finally got up. That's the way she affected me. Oh, she was marvelous in this thing.

Another actress who made a great impression on me in those years was Madge Bellamy. Oh, I loved her! I remember a scene from one of her pictures where she was sitting on a bench with this young man. It was sort of a dark night and they then cut to a close-up of her and oh, she would melt your heart. I mean, she was so gorgeous. I have a picture of her with a hat on that looks so beautiful and I just love it. But she looked lovely in almost everything. I saw her at a party when I was in pictures—I think it was at Carl Laemmle's big estate—and I said, "Oh, Miss Bellamy, you've been one of my favorites."

And she said, "Well, thank you. You know, some people think we look a little alike." Oh, I was so pleased! I think she said that—I really do. I can't be sure. Maybe I just hoped she did. She did have large eyes like I do and there was something about the cut of the features, the mouth and the smile.

A fashion still from her MGM years.

As I've said, my wanting to be an actress was born in me but I thought I should have two things that I could do in case I failed in one so I took art at Washington Irving High School. I'd heard they had a very fine art class. I was about eleven when I won a prize in a contest for a little pencil sketch of a face that I did.

We used to go to Seacliff on Long Island in the summertime. You know how it is in the East. You work during the winter and then go for a vacation in the summer. That's where we knew the Morrisons and the boy, David Morrison, was a summer beau of mine. His father was a friend of my father's and an artist. He was also Claire Trevor's uncle. Her name was Claire Wemlinger at the time. I met her then and she was a beautiful young blonde child. Anyway, my father took my sketch to Mr. Morrison and asked him, "Do you think she would have a future as an artist?"

And Mr. Morrison said, "Yes, she has life in that drawing." But later my theatrical life started and the interesting part of this is that my daughter is one of the greatest artists. She has inherited the talent for art. She did a beautiful portrait of me.

I think it was fate that got me into pictures—I do believe this. I mean, I'm a Roman Catholic, I believe in God and I just feel that sometimes things are meant to be. My father had been thinking of buying a house in Astoria for some time so my mother went out there and thought she would take a chance on finding a place. If she went to a real estate office, they'd say it was great, of course, but she thought she'd ask somebody who lived there how they liked it. So she just picked at random a door, went up and knocked. This beautiful lady with white hair answered and her name was Mrs. Bronson. Now you see what I mean by fate? There were rows of apartments or houses she could have gone to but she picked the one with Mrs. Bronson. Mrs. Bronson liked my mother terrifically and she said, "Oh, I hope you'll move out here. We love it." She explained that her daughter Betty and Betty's grandmother were out in Hollywood and she was trying to get in films. But the rest of the family was living in Astoria. There were two boys and two girls, one of whom was Betty. So we moved there and we became just so close to the Bronsons. We went to church together and did everything together.

About three months after we moved to Astoria, James M. Barrie picked Betty to play Peter Pan—at least that's the story they gave. I don't think anybody could have done it better than Betty. She had this sort of elfin personality that went along with it and she was fantastic. The Bronsons moved to California as soon as she'd signed a contract. My father was head of a group of the tenants and Mrs. Bronson asked him if he'd watch her house. He said he would. We remained very good friends with the Bronsons and almost every time they'd come East, we'd get together. In fact, one of Betty's brothers was a particular sort of beau of mine for three years. We also got to know Mrs. Bronson's sister and her brother. They used to come down and visit us often. We just all blended and loved each other and that was it.

When Betty came East to make *A Kiss for Cinderella* at Paramount's Astoria studio, she stayed at the Park Hotel in Central Park. They invited us for tea. My mother had on a beautiful brown velvet suit and I was all gussied up so off we went to see them. We had never met Betty but she just took to me and I took to her. We both loved the movies and there was a lot in common. She showed me her pictures and everything. I mentioned to her that I'd been a winner in a beauty contest. She said, "Well, I never was that but I've done very well in the movies. Would you like to try it, Anita?"

Then Mrs. Bronson said, "Betty, you're going to have a lot of people in your big ball scene. Why not pop Anita in those scenes?"

My mother said, "Well, Anita's only fifteen. She's in school and I hesitate to—"

Of course, that didn't get very far. My eyes were popping right out of my head and pouring in her lap practically—"Oh, please, Mother, please."

My mother said, "I don't know whether I like her wandering around the studio alone."

Mrs. Bronson said, "Well, she won't be alone. I'm there always when Betty is there and so is Miss Rachel Smith, her tutor."

Mother couldn't say no so she said, "I'll tell you what. I think she's doing very well in school and I'll check with them." She did and they said yes, I was a very good student and I could have a week off.

That started the whole thing. I got there and I got all done up as a court lady with a wig and everything. I don't know how they could even see me. I'd wanted to wear make-up since I guess I was ten

With Buster Keaton and Trixie Friganza in *Free and Easy.* (Courtesy of Cole Johnson.)

but my mother would never let me do it. So here I was—hooray!—with the puffs and the jar and everything. Mrs. Bronson had to go out for a minute but by the time she came back, I looked like a clown. My eyes were so big and my mouth was pursed up. She laughed and said, "Anita, they want to see your face, not that." So she wiped off everything and, of course, when she did it, I wouldn't dare think of saying no.

A Kiss for Cinderella was quite a big production. Esther Ralston, who had played Mrs. Darling in *Peter Pan,* was Betty's fairy godmother in *A Kiss for Cinderella* and Betty raved about her. She thought she was so beautiful. I wasn't at the studio very long when I noticed a very attractive gentleman. I must admit I was a little bit of a flirt in those days and so for a whole week, he was over there watching me and I was watching him. When Betty's picture was done, he said to me, "I'm an assistant director. Would you like to play a little part in a picture?"

I said, "Would I!"

He said, "Well, it's just a small part but it *is* a part and I can get you right out of the extras."

So I had a little part in *Love 'Em and Leave 'Em* and they left it in, believe it or not. They were the last big studio in the East and I was there about a month. Of course, the weather and everything I suppose made a lot of difference. They could count on sunny skies out here in California so everybody was going West. This young assistant director told me, "I'm so sorry. We're leaving right now." I wasn't the world's most graceful at that time. I guess it was my face that he thought was photogenic. I mean, I had a good body but it was very thin and sort of scrawny yet. So he said, "If you will take dancing lessons and any chance you can get to do pantomime, do it." In those days, instead of just illustrating a story, many times they would have real people illustrate it and they needed people who could get something across in their faces and their body movements. At this time, there were no fifteen-year-olds being pushed as stars. If they were child stars, they left the screen and came back at about seventeen or eighteen as ingenues. Anyway, this man said to me, "I can tell you, in two years, you will knock 'em cold."

That was all I needed to hear. I asked my mother if I could take some acting lessons. I said, "This is what I want to do with my life and I don't want to waste any time." She said all right and I went to this acting school. I didn't like it but there was one thing I loved about it. Martha Graham, the great dancer, was there then and she was marvelous. I think she kind of liked me because I could act. When she said, "Now all pull as though you're Volga boatmen," I pulled so hard it's a wonder I made it. She liked that and felt that was a good interpretation.

Anyway, the long and short of it was I did not like the way they were teaching acting because the man who was head of it insisted that everybody do everything exactly the same and that was not for me. I thought, "No way. You're selling something that's you, not just a copy of somebody else. No, I won't do it this way." The teacher was an older gentleman and he had a wonderful voice. But he kind of liked an older model. He let her teach some of the classes and I liked her but I knew that she didn't know anymore about acting than the man in the moon. At least, that's the way I felt. So I went in and very honestly told the gentleman who ran the school that I really felt I wasn't getting what I wanted. He said, "I'm sorry to hear this because I think you're the only one in this class who's going to make it."

I said, "Well, thank you very much and I appreciate that. I'll remember it." So off I went.

I'd heard of the John Robert Powers Modeling School. He was just starting and he had a nice little upstairs office. It wasn't at all like it is today. The funniest thing happened. Before I could open my mouth to tell him I didn't want to model, I just wanted something for a film, before I could say anything, he said, "You're not the model type. You're for the movies." It shows you how astute he was.

I said, "Yes, that's just what I want. I don't want to be a dress model or anything like that. What I would like, though, is if you have any modeling where you are illustrating pictures, I'd like to do that."

He said, "Well, I'll see what I can do for you." In those days, you just put your picture in, paid them fifty dollars and then they got you work. They took ten percent of it and it was marvelous—no funny business. He was a wonderful man and within three months, I had a terrific job posing for these illustrations. Then he called me and told me a small film studio was starting in New York. They had the lead but they asked him to get a second lead to play the cousin of the girl. He said, "Now in all fairness, I'm sending out eighteen other girls because this job's for them. But I think you're going to get it. They can be on the beach and they'll have their chances to get some work, too."

So I went up to the studio. My mother was chaperoning me but did not go in. She said, "You're the one who has to do it and you have to do it on your own."

I walked in and in about ten or fifteen minutes, I had the job. They said, "Oh, yes, great." We started to work on this comedy, *Beach Nuts,* and within a week, they called me in and said, "We've decided to give you the lead. The lady who's playing the lead can play the second lead."

I was quite surprised. I would never try to take somebody else's job or anything. Since I knew in my heart I had not deliberately done anything like that and since they wanted me to play it, well, then, I'd try and do it. I said I'd love to do it but the funny part of it is that the lead girl, Anne, instead of being angry at me, loved me. We became very good pals and had a very nice time. I think in her heart she knew I hadn't done anything wrong and I think she later told me that.

The picture was never released but the people who made it later came and said they thought they had something nice there. They wanted to take us out to Hollywood—not everybody, of course, but

A scene from *War Nurse*. (Courtesy of Cole Johnson.)

the men who ran the organization, the director, the cameraman, and the two girls, myself and Anne. So we went out to California and the others in the film didn't make it but I was going to make it because I thought I could. I'd had quite a few offers from photographers in New York just to photograph my face. Marland Stone, who was well-known then, was one of them. So I'd had some wonderful pictures taken and one in particular was apparently just the thing that got me in the movies.

In California, we went over to the Bronsons for New Year's dinner and Mrs. Bronson said, "Anita, come in here with me a minute, will you? This is a gentleman who wants to meet you. He's thinking of going into the agency business and he's very struck with your picture."

She'd asked me for a picture and I'd given her *the* one that was so good. I think they were all good but this was a knockout. She had it right on her big table in her big home in Beverly Hills. This man saw it and was very struck with it. He asked me if I would be interested in the movies. I said yes, I certainly would and we talked a bit. But I had been so used to that in New York. The men would tell me I could get in films right away. This man, Mr. Harvey, seemed nice but I didn't think he was that interested in me. He gave me his card and I said, "Thank you."

The next day, my mother said, "Aren't you going to call Mr. Harvey?"

I said, "Well, I don't think he seemed interested."

She said, "Honey, this is a way to get in the movies."

"Well," I said, "I don't know. I don't want to do it." So I didn't call him.

The next day, I got a call from this gentleman and he said, "Where are you?"

"Oh," I said, "you mean you really wanted me to call you?"

He said, "My dear, I don't give my cards out to anyone unless I expect them to call me. Now you be at Paramount tomorrow morning at nine o'clock at the front gate. I'll be there at nine, too. Oh, yes, and bring the picture."

I said, "Oh, well, yes. Thank you very much."

Of course, I was very, very happy about the whole thing. I was there with the picture the next morning and he took me right into the casting office to see the casting director. We talked and then Mr. Harvey said, "Show him the picture."

With Ramon Novarro in *The Flying Fleet.*

When I showed it to him, this man just looked at it and said, "You know, I very rarely ever give a test on a picture but this is so great I'm going to do it. You go down and put on one of Evelyn Brent's dresses and we'll test you." Boom, just like that!

Of course, I wasn't ready for it but it didn't bother me. I thought, "At least, I can tell everybody I took a test and wore Evelyn Brent's clothes even if I never get any further."

After I went down and took the test, my agent, Mr. Harvey, came back and said, "They just said it's great and they're crazy about it but there's something wrong with your upper lip."

I said, "What do you mean, my upper lip?"

He said, "Oh, it's just this baby fuzz."

I told them that and they all agreed and said, "Let's take another test." In two minutes, the baby fuzz was gone. The second test was great and that was it.

I had to wait for a couple of days, however, and I got very nervous. I thought, "Oh, dear, I can't stand this." I said, "Mother, let's go out and ride on the top of a bus. I love them because I can see all over Hollywood."

So we did and talk about the pot boiling! As we were going back to our apartment, I heard the telephone ring. I ran in and somebody on the line asked, "Is this Miss Pomares? This is Mal St. Clair."

I thought, "Oh, brother, this is some of my boyfriends who are kidding me." Mal St. Clair was a great director at Paramount and Betty used to rave about him. I didn't think he would be calling me. So I said, "Oh, this is Mary Pickford."

"What?" he said.

"No," I said, "I made a mistake. I'm Gloria Swanson."

Then he said, "Just a minute," and I heard him talking to this other gentleman whose voice I recognized as my agent's, Mr. Harvey.

I said, "My God, it can't be Mal St. Clair." But sure enough, that's who it was. I said, "I'm so sorry. I thought you were a friend."

Then my agent got on the phone and said, "What are you doing?"

I said, "Is that really Mal St. Clair?"

He said, "Yes, and he wants to test you for a picture."

"Ah!" I said.

"Now look," he said. "You be out at MGM next Tuesday. He's being loaned to Metro to make a picture with Lew Cody and Aileen Pringle and he's looking for a second lead—somebody new and different. So he wants you to come out and make this test at Metro."

I said, "Fine, anytime you're ready."

Anyway, to make a long story longer, I'd gotten myself a good cold having been out, of course, on the top of the sightseeing bus. My hair was drab and my nose was red but like all young people, I figured tomorrow would be perfect and I went out to Metro like I was told. I was to get my clothes there on Tuesday so that I could be tested on Wednesday. I told them my name and asked them where I should go to get my wardrobe. Then this man said to me, "What did you say your name

With William Haines and John Miljan in *Speedway*. (Courtesy of Cole Johnson.)

was?" I told him and he said, "Oh, no, you have to go see Sam Wood."

I said, "Sam Wood? Who's Sam Wood? You've made a mistake. I'm here tomorrow for a test and I have to go down and get my clothes."

"No," he said, "that's all right, darling, but you've got to see Sam Wood right now."

I was very upset. I thought, "Who is Sam Wood? Where is he? I don't even know who he is."

Well, all of a sudden, this man sort of came up like a genie and said, "I'll take you."

The next thing I knew, I was in an office with a gentleman sitting at the desk. He was very, very attractive, very nice, and he took one look at me and said, "Just a minute." And I'm trying to tell everybody that I'm not there for a test. My hair's lank and my nose is swollen but tomorrow I'll be gorgeous.

I kept saying "No, no, no" and Paul Bern, the producer, had been walking me up and down telling me I'd be great in the test and this, that and the other thing. But I said, "I'd rather wait till tomorrow for my test."

The next thing I heard was "Hello, Bill" and then I heard "Haines." I thought, "Oh, my gosh, that can't be Bill Haines." He had been one of my crushes when I was fifteen. Sure enough, it was because Sam Wood said, "Listen, I want you to do this as a personal favor to me." Apparently, Bill Haines had been ready to go riding when he walked in the door. He had on his riding clothes and he looked stunning.

When I heard the name Bill Haines, that did it. I decided that if I never did another thing, if I could just play a scene with Bill Haines, I'd have made it. Anyway, they fixed me up. I don't know how they did it but they put some white grease on the end of my nose. Of course, you couldn't get the swelling all down but that didn't bother me. They did my hair some way with curling irons so that it looked great—clean and everything. Then I took the test with Bill Haines. The next day, I came out all gorgeous, the nose down mostly and the hair done by Sadie Nation who could do what I could dream, and I looked very good in these clothes. They then took the test I had been originally slated for.

I went home and just completely went out of my mind for three days even though I tried not to. I thought, "Now come on, come on. Don't expect anything. Then you won't be disappointed." Finally, I said to my mother, "Let's go out to Metro

With William Haines and Sojin in *Telling the World*. (Courtesy of Cole Johnson.)

and ask them if they don't want to use it, can I buy the test? We'll find out something."

So we did and they said, "No, I'm sorry, we can't do that. It's up in Irving Thalberg's office."

That sounded very good and I didn't push it anymore. I said, "Thank you very much," and left.

I had to wait for another two or three days and then, sure enough, I got a call from Metro and they said they'd like to talk to me. I went out there thinking, "Now don't get your hopes up, don't get your hopes up." I sat down in the waiting room and nothing happened. Now in New York, good gracious, you didn't wait more than five or ten minutes. I thought, "Oh, they can't want you. They wouldn't keep you sitting here for half an hour."

Just as I had decided that, in came a lovely, nice man and he was rubbing his hands. "Well, Miss Pomares," he said, "how would you like to sign with us?" How would I like to sign with them? You know any more funny questions?

I said, "Oh, I'd love to. However, there's one thing I want in the contract and that is that I will be on the screen."

He said, "Oh, yes, you'll either get the lead in Bill Haines's picture or you'll play the other part with Lew Cody."

I told him, "I'm only seventeen so my mother will have to sign the contract."

He said, "That's fine. We don't mind."

When I called her, I was just walking around in the seventh heaven. I said, "Mother, they want to sign me. Will you sign the contract for me?" Well, of course, she would.

Now about a day later, I got another phone call and this time it was the man from Paramount who gave me my first test. He said, "Is it true that you're going to sign with Metro?"

"Oh, yes," I said.

"Oh," he said, "I'm going to get H-E double L for letting you slip through my fingers. Let me ask you something. You know, I did give you your first chance. If we send you a contract and if it's as good as Metro's, will you sign with us?"

Well, that was pretty tough because I loved Metro and I thought it was awfully good for women stars. It was *the* studio, you know. So I went to a very well-known attorney who knew all the studios. I looked at the Paramount contract and, thank goodness, they didn't say anything about putting me right on the screen and the money was less so I could honestly say that was not as good as Metro. My mother had gone down with me to the attorney's and we were going to sign the Metro contract when the gentleman looked at me and said, "Don't sign any of these."

"What?" I said.

"Look," he said, "I will get you a picture so that *you* will be making the deals. You'd have been great in *Gentlemen Prefer Blondes.*" Well, it sounded good but I started to cry. I mean, I had it right in my hand, this Metro thing that I wanted so badly and, you know, you just don't know whether other things are going to work out. Then he said, "Well, don't cry, honey. If that's what you want, fine."

So we signed with Metro and from then on, I kept on going. Within about two weeks, they gave me a lead right away which is something you don't usually get when you've just signed a six-month contract. The reason I'd insisted I wanted to be on the screen is because lots of times girls have been signed up for six months and never gotten a chance to show what they could do.

Metro changed my name when I signed with them because they thought Anita Pomares would be a hard name to pronounce. You know, when you're in the business, you want to be spoken about nicely, of course, but you do want your name to get out there so they know who you are. Many times people will be afraid to mention somebody if they can't say their names right. For years,

With Joan Crawford and Johnny Mack Brown in *Our Dancing Daughters.*

I'd had to say "Po'mares" and then I'd say, "It's actually 'Pomarees' but that will do." That was the reason I was willing for them to change my name but I didn't want them to change Anita. They were going to call me Ann Page and I said no.

My first picture with Metro was *Telling the World* with Bill Haines. I loved working with him—he was so much fun. He'd sing· to me, "Nothing would be sweeter than to be with my Anita in the morning."

I'd crack back, "Now I am not your Anita." And he'd have a smile on his face like a big horseshoe.

The audience liked me from the preview cards. They were very, very keen on me in *Telling the World* but that wasn't as big a picture as my next one, *Our Dancing Daughters* with Joan Crawford. That's where I made my hit. I'm getting a little tired of hearing about *Our Dancing Daughters* and Miss Crawford. She did a good job—I'm not saying she didn't. She gave a very nice stellar performance but I stole the picture. I have all these press clippings that say: "Anita Page steals the picture. All the critics are calling for her to be a star. She brings to this role beauty, humor and magnetic unself-consciousness." Now I have all this. I didn't get an award for it but, of course, the timing wasn't exactly right for that. And unlike Crawford, I didn't stay in pictures for years. The movies were her life, she did become a star and she stayed in films until, I guess, she just couldn't stay anymore.

I was seventeen years old when I did that picture and, unlike the girl I portrayed, I had never had a drink in my life. But I was able to play that part because I was an actress. I threw myself right into it. I knew I wanted that role. As I understand it—now I wasn't a fly on the wall but I heard that the director, Harry Beaumont, went to L. B. Mayer and begged him, "Listen, you can't—this girl's beautiful and she's nice but she's only made one picture. I have to have a consummate actress in this. The whole thing's going to rise or fall on this woman's performance."

Mr. Mayer, who had seen me doing a little acting around about and just liked something, said, "You'd think that she's a Bernhardt." He was a wonderful man—he was always quite satisfied with me—and he insisted. So Harry had to take me. He didn't want to at all—not in the beginning. He was very mean and that's why I love Dorothy

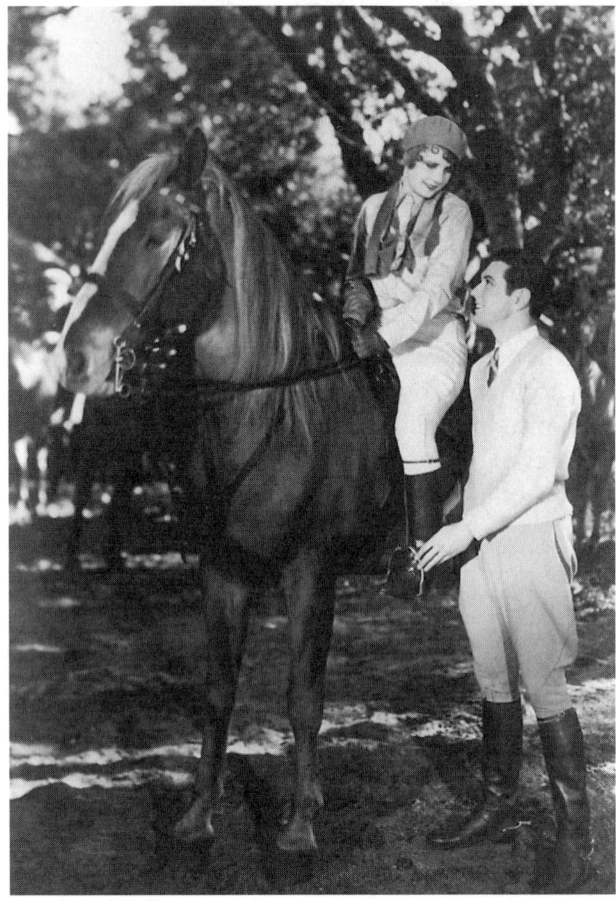

With Johnny Mack Brown in *Our Dancing Daughters.*

Sebastian, who was also in the film, because she saw what he was doing. I think he was hoping that he could scare me out of the role but instead of that, I was doing better all the time.

Dorothy said, "Anita, I've seen the rushes." I didn't even get to see the rushes but she did and she told me, "You are going to be great in this role. Don't worry." And I never forgot her for that.

Finally, when I did all those good scenes at the end, Beaumont said, "Anita, I saw the rushes and they're sensational." He was just so happy that from then on, I could do no wrong.

We filmed part of *Our Dancing Daughters* on location in Carmel. I didn't ride horseback but I knew I had to in those scenes. Right as you see in the picture, I hied myself off and rode a bit. I was scared but I'm the kind who does what I want if I get strong enough and I was strong enough in those days for anything practically. So I rode my little horse and he was all right—he behaved. But that was all. I wasn't a regular horseback rider and I didn't do any other pictures on horses.

A man at the studio—Charlie somebody—said men were asking for me, a lot of cute requests, to make personal appearances because, of course, people didn't know enough about me until they saw this picture. But I wasn't going out when I started at Metro. For instance, Prince Louis Ferdinand came out here and asked the studio if he could take me to the opening of *Show Boat.* I couldn't go unchaperoned because I was only seventeen and they told him, "We'll try but she's not allowed to go out just on a date." My mother and father said no because they were afraid I'd have to be going out here and there all the time and they wanted to be sure I was with the right company. I was pretty smart myself, though. I knew pretty well who I wanted to go with.

After I finished *Our Dancing Daughters,* I played with Lon Chaney in *While the City Sleeps.* I liked him. He was a marvelous actor and I thought he was very helpful. We used to talk about acting and he would tell me what I always felt. He thought that the structure of the face was really the important thing photographically but getting over the emotion was in the eyes.

Speaking of emotion in acting, I've never forgotten seeing Jeanne Eagels in *The Letter* about that time. Oh, God, she was marvelous. She just kept going and going in this scene and I thought, "Oh, my goodness." To me, she's the one who played *The Letter.* Bette Davis, who remade it, was very smart. She didn't try to compete. She underplayed

With Lon Chaney and Carroll Nye in *While the City Sleeps.*

it and she did a very nice job. But Jeanne Eagels was so magnificent. I've heard stories later that she took drugs but I don't care. As an actress, she did the greatest emotional scene in talkies that I have ever seen.

My first talkie was *The Broadway Melody* which won the Academy Award for the best film of 1929. Harry Beaumont directed it and this time, he was very glad to have me. He got along with me very well because he was so pleased with me and, of course, *Our Dancing Daughters* had helped to make him. Now he was very much my friend. One day, I was a little tired. I mean, I'd made about six pictures and I was sitting kind of relaxing. He said, "What's the matter with you, Anita? Are you beginning to believe your fan mail?"

And I said, "Yeah, are you?" By this time, I was cracking right back at him.

He said, "You know, you're magnificent when your back's against the wall." I never forgot that. That has been something that's helped me in my life when things have been tough.

In *The Broadway Melody,* I co-starred with Bessie Love and Charles King. Charles King was a wonderful man. I thought he was a charmer. I wasn't personally interested in him but I mean as an actor and as a human being, I just thought he was so charming. He was married to a relation of the man who was so big on Broadway, George M. Cohan.

I loved Bessie, too. She was just a doll. She was a very good actress and she was great in *The Broadway Melody.* I read years later—and I think it was a very smart thing she did—that she had gone for a twenty-week stint on the stage, probably to learn just what I wanted to—the timing and so on, how to time for a laugh and how to hold. She had learned a lot about the voice. She did that lovely, sad scene with the cold cream and actually did it with the cold cream on her face. As a matter of fact, Bessie was given that marvelous scene. I wasn't there when they did it. From all I can gather, I think Beaumont gave it to her because he wanted her. There were certain scenes in the picture that I think were deliberately thrown to Bessie such as where she looks at me, I'm up on the prow of the love boat on the stage and she's supposed to say, "We ain't never had to get by on our faces before." But if you've seen the picture, you realize that Charlie King says, "Those guys are not going to pay ten bucks to look at your face," after she says, "We ain't never had to get by on our legs before" which kind of takes some of the glamour away from

With Bessie Love and Charles King in *The Broadway Melody.*

it. Most anybody has legs but it was actually my face they were talking about. That's what was written in the script, I'm pretty sure, because I remember reading that. You either have legs or you don't. I mean, that isn't something as important as your face.

I think we just sang the musical numbers as they filmed it. I don't think they dubbed them. If they did, I've forgotten it. Although I didn't do it, I loved "The Wedding of the Painted Doll," the number where the preacher comes down the stairs. Of course, my favorite is "You Were Meant for Me" because that was the one in which Charlie King tells me in so many words that he loves me and that was the crux then—beginning the whole thing of the turning of the movie where Bessie begins to lose him and I get him.

We did some dancing in it although our dancing wasn't the greatest. I had taken some dancing lessons and that had helped. I don't remember going back to anything I learned but it just limbered me so that I was able to do it. Of course, I was older, too. I'd gotten over the graceless years. I think I was about sixteen when I'd begun to mature.

I remember that twice we had trouble with the sound. You see, for me, silents were much greater than talkies because there were so many things you had to worry about in talkies. For instance, we were going to do a scene and everything was fine until we'd start to work. Then we'd hear "swssh," "swssh," "swssh," "swssh," "swssh." Nobody knew what in the world was going on. If you've ever read anything about those days, you may have heard this. Finally, after I don't know how many takes, we found out what was causing it. I had on a taffeta petticoat and when I'd walk, the petticoat would go "swssh," "swssh," "swssh" and that's what was doing it. So we had to change the petticoat.

Then the next thing that happened, I was going to do a scene and we'd hear "tap," "tap," "tap," "tap," "tap." We looked around at everything, did the scene again and still couldn't find out what the "tap," "tap,“ "tap" was. Finally, I realized it was me—it was I, I should say—because I was doing my nails and as soon as I concentrated on that, I'd tap my foot like that, you see. Well, we got rid of that but those were the only two problems with sound that I recall. I did read Cary Grant's side of it. He was telling the troubles that you have in making talkies. He said, "Just to take a cup of tea, you need about ten takes. If the spoon hits the plate, it goes bang when it's not supposed to." Oh. he mentioned so many things I didn't even know about that drove him crazy.

After pictures like *Our Dancing Daughters* and *The Broadway Melody,* I'd hit in a year. I even won a contest in New York. The people wrote in their favorite actress and usually Garbo got it but one week little Annie walked away with it. And there was also a man who wrote for some very fancy magazine. Pare Lorentz was his name. I had a lot of Anita-watchers in those days. I had my own fan club and everything. This friend called me—his name was Mr. O'Malley—and he said, "Anita, have you seen what Pare Lorentz said about you in this magazine?"

I said, "No, what did he say?"

He said, "Well, there's a little blonde in there that's going to knock out the male receiving line."

I said, "Well, what's so big about that?"

He said, "Anita, that was Pare Lorentz! He has never even given Garbo a line."

Of course, that sounded a little different and I said, "Oh, well, that is great, isn't it?" But, you know, this was after all the nice things I'd already had. I was the glamorous girl and this, that and the other. They were copying my eyebrows and everything.

I've forgotten what my salary was when I started with Metro but I wound up with seven-fifty a week. I don't remember all the little goodies in be-

With Bessie Love in *The Broadway Melody.*

tween. But after this success, because of my agent, I made the greatest mistake of my life. My dad had been in New York because he had to tie up his business and take everything with it. He'd just come back here when he got this phone call and I heard him saying, "Oh, really?" and "Do you think so?" and so on and so forth.

Well, the agent had told him, "They promised her that if she clicked, she would get a new contract and she has certainly clicked now. We have to go in and get a new contract." They probably tell that to a lot of people because if they do click, they don't have to do anything about it right away and then later on, they can give them a new contract. That's probably what would have happened to me because Mr. Mayer was very, very fond of me. He was so kind and so was Mr. Thalberg. I was the golden girl that year and I didn't care about the money. I could act—that was what I lived to do. But I was so tired by this time. I'd made about eight pictures. I had an aunt who was almost a millionairess and she could see that I was getting so drained. She said, "Oh, Anita, come on out to Honolulu with me and forget about it."

I said, "I can't do that, Aunt Lillian. This is my life's work right now and I cannot do it."

After all the agent had done for us, we listened to him. He went in to talk to the producers, I think my father had to go in and I guess I had to go in, too. So we had a fight over the money. Mr. Harvey's idea was that if they had to pay me more money, they'd give me better parts. That's for the birds because they didn't need me to live on, you know. It was all wrong. We got this contract all right but I was told later that not a finger was going to be lifted to help me. And I'd been told earlier that I could be made the biggest star at Metro in three pictures with a snap of the finger and I could also dislodge one of the most important stars on their agenda. I won't name her but as it happened, this woman made some more pictures and then never came back. I understand that she expected to.

I was in *Our Modern Maidens* with Joan Crawford when the new contract was signed. Our cameraman, Clyde De Vinna, had filmed *White Shadows in the South Seas* and had won the Academy Award for it. A certain man who I think was interested in Joan's career told him that he wasn't photographing her as well as a pretty blonde in the picture, Josephine Dunn, and myself. Clyde De Vinna said, "I'm sorry but Crawford's just in too fast company." He wouldn't do it and then somebody

With Douglas Fairbanks, Jr. in *Our Modern Maidens.*

else complained about it. But the minute that contract of mine was signed, we got a new cameraman. That's why some parts of *Our Modern Maidens* were so good for me and others weren't. Imagine, the cameraman who was taken off had won the Academy Award the year before and they weren't going to take him off as long as I behaved.

Of course, I was still big box office but what they did was just keep me there. Every once in a while, they'd give me a good part like *War Nurse* or things like *Night Court* but the others were just like the pictures I did with Buster Keaton or the ones I made with Marie Dressler and Polly Moran. They photographed you beautifully but in the picture itself, you had to react all the time or you weren't in the picture. But I did enjoy working with Marie and Polly. They were fun.

Of course, I liked Buster, too. He was a doll. He was so kind to me. He'd have a whole group of us over to his bungalow for lunch. I read the saddest thing—that he died without too much money and he had a fortune in his garage in all these pictures that he'd made. Buster was an original. I mean, who do you know who looks like Buster? I did two pictures with him, *Free and Easy* and *The Sidewalks of New York*. I think he did some flip-ups with me in the second picture but I never did any stunts like Buster did in films.

I did a picture with John Gilbert, *Gentleman's Fate,* in 1931. Many people used to say I was a young Garbo and I wondered if maybe that was one of the reasons he was so nice to me. He asked me to lunch in his bungalow and I'd go. I had no fear because I knew he was a decent, kind man. There was something about him, there was an instinct. He'd tell me how happy John Barrymore and Dolores Costello, his wife, were and we'd chat.

John Gilbert had a scene in the picture we made where I guess he was dying or something and the man just broke down and sobbed with real tears and everything. Now you expect a young woman to be able to do it because little girls are taught it's all right to cry but not little boys. So I asked him, "John, how in the world do you just break down and cry like that? I mean, I think girls can but how do you do it?"

He said, "Well, Anita, if a scene plays true, I can do it every time. Let there be one false note and I can't do it." And I kind of knew what he meant.

With John Gilbert in *Gentleman's Fate*. (The Museum of Modern Art.)

I was the first one who worked with Clark Gable at Metro in a picture called *The Easiest Way*. Of course, he stayed in pictures a long time. He talked about his lovely leading lady, Anita Page. Constance Bennett and Adolphe Menjou were in it, too, and she took the easiest way with either Adolphe or somebody. I was the sweet, honest, good little housewife with big safety pins in my clothes and Gable played a laundryman. He was my husband and we were madly in love according to the story. He used to sit and watch me when I was putting my lipstick and stuff on and he was so nice. He asked me if he could drive me home and I said, "No, I have my own car and driver but thanks just so much."

Then he said if I wasn't around in about six weeks, he'd say, "Where's Anita Page?" My mother usually stayed in the dressing room but he saw her coming down the street, went over and said, "Oh, Mrs. Pomares, it's so nice to see you again. We've missed you" or something like that.

Of course, he was quite the hero at home. My mother said, "Oh, he's so polite, he's so charming" and so on and so forth. And he was—he was very charming. There was never any romance as far as I was concerned but I did like him so much as a person.

I met Carole Lombard at some party years before she married Clark Gable but I didn't know them when they were married. I did hear from a friend of mine who was up in some lovely lake where they were on a vacation. She said they were so happy. Carole would do whatever he wanted, fishing or whatever it was. She'd try and do it, too, right along with him. I think it was one of the saddest things that happened to that poor, dear man when she died in a plane crash.

I made a lot of friends who were in pictures when I worked in Hollywood. I loved Marion Davies. I was invited up to Wyntoon for a weekend and I stayed five months. They wouldn't let me go. She had her old friends around her—I think Connie Talmadge, I'm not sure. Marion had been in the *Follies* and she had friends from there, too. Marion just loved me. She told me, "Anita, you have the most beautiful bone structure I've ever seen."

When she looked at me and said that, I almost fell off the chair. I think I looked particularly well up there. The air agreed with me. I love the mountains. I wouldn't want to live there because I'm too cosmopolitan but it does so much for me.

I knew Thelma Todd, too. She came to me one day and said, "Oh, I've got this man I want you to meet." I don't know—it was somebody that I didn't care to meet at all but I swallowed it because she was so nice about things. She had just married and, of course, she wanted people she liked to have the same kind of happiness.

Although I didn't see her there, she was a close friend of the Fords. Wally and Martha Ford were also very good friends of mine. I made pictures with Wally and Martha was a gorgeous girl. She looked a little like Ann Harding. They'd have parties almost every week and, of course, I used to be out at their place. I was there that day in 1935 when Martha turned around and said, "Oh, that was Toddy. She said she was supposed to be over here but she won't be able to make it." It didn't ring a big bell with me at the time but I remember hearing Martha say that Toddy had called. Later, she said she was sure Toddy was alive at a time when she supposedly already had died because that's when Martha talked to her. Now she would know the cadence of Toddy's voice. She would know if they had a little nickname between the two of them that nobody else knew. Why would Martha get involved in something if she didn't really believe that? So I don't know anything about it. All I know is that Thelma was a lovely girl and it was just a terrible tragedy. She was so kind and so beautiful. There are a lot of theories about what caused her death but I don't think it was suicide. She was too fond of life and had too much going for her. You think oh, my, those lovely people who are so nice, you don't want them to have these troubles but there are a lot of wonderful people who have come up against it.

Jean Harlow was one of them, too. Bless her heart, she was one girl I really loved and felt sorry for in a way because she had the same problem that I did. I mean hers was in a different way but I was considered quite sexy, too. I didn't try to be particularly but she did. She and I both liked each other. She told me, "If I ever have a little girl, I want her to be just like you, Anita." The girl was so much more sensitive than people realize. She was a dear, sweet girl in many, many ways and I think some women were just jealous of her. I know they were of me, too.

Jean became one of Metro's biggest stars and had an exclusive contract with them. In the beginning, I had one, too, and Metro wouldn't loan me to other studios. Charlie Chaplin told me that he'd asked them if he could borrow me for *City Lights* but they said no. They wouldn't loan me at all until we had the fuss with the contract. When I got the new contract, Metro began loaning me out. For instance, I did a picture with Marian Marsh at Warners, *Under Eighteen*. I liked her a lot and we got along just beautifully.

Later, I made pictures for Poverty Row studios like *I Have Lived* and *Jungle Bride* with Charlie Starrett who was a charming man. He loved his wife and he'd talk about her so nicely. I liked that. But I didn't want to make those pictures. That made me a little upset because I didn't go to Poverty Row. Metro sent me there. I think once I wanted to try out a certain make-up and that's the only reason I did the film. But I had no idea of ever playing in

With Clark Gable in *The Easiest Way*.

With (left to right) Clara Blandick, Constance Bennett, Clark Gable and J. Farrell MacDonald in *The Easiest Way.*

those pictures at all. So I rushed out of Metro. There was no "if," just "thank you very much" and out I went. Of course, that meant I was not going to be the biggest star on the lot. You know, these things are played around. You have to know where you want to go and just keep to it. So many women probably would have given it little thought. They would have said, "Oh, yes, I'd love to be the biggest star. Let's have a little champagne or something."

I just walked out when my contract was over. I probably could have negotiated another one but what had happened is I could do dramatic work beautifully without any help but when it came to comedy, I thought I should learn a little more about timing. I was in Billy Rose's *Crazy Quilt of 1933.* That was my only work on the stage and it was very fine money. Billy Rose was married to Fannie Brice at the time and later he started Esther Williams on her career. Charlie King was in this show, too. He'd been on the stage before he made his first movie, *The Broadway Melody,* and I don't know if he wanted to brush up or just wanted to get the job when he did this show with me. It was actually my personal appearances that drew crowds because more people knew me, of course. But Charlie was so good at plugging me. He said to me that if I wanted to get a good number in the show, he'd put in a word for me with the producer.

In one number, I had to stand up very high on a little bit of wood—you know, like a small piece of ladder or something—and I complained about it. There were a lot of girls in front of me with dresses so that it looked like it was me wearing all these

With Buster Keaton and Cliff Edwards in *The Sidewalks of New York.* (Courtesy of Cole Johnson.)

A holiday publicity still from MGM. (The Kobal Collection.)

dresses. When they opened up, I came down the walkway. I said, "This thing is so narrow," because I had to stand on it and it was so high. If I'd fallen, I'd have been killed.

I was furious at Billy for one thing. I had seen Franklin Roosevelt in a newsreel years before. He was the governor of New York at the time. I didn't see much of his face but he was in the Easter Parade and there was so much joy and life in that little figure that I thought, "Oh, he's something else." By the time I did the show, he was president. He was in the same city that I was in and as one of the two most important people in the city, I was asked to join his box. I was in seventh heaven. I thought, "Oh, I'm going to meet the president."

I already had myself at the White House and everything else but as luck would have it, dear Mr. Billy Rose said, "No, I can't let you go, Anita."

I said, "What do you mean?"

He said, "I mean that you can't go. You're in every number and we cannot let you go."

He could have shut down the theatre for one night but he wouldn't do it. Instead of that, he sent Eleanor Powell who was dancing in the show. Now I loved Eleanor. She was a dear little girl and I used to say to her, "I don't like tap dancing much but why do I love to look at you?"

She said, "Because I took ballet first, Anita, and I think that's why you like what I do." But if I couldn't go, I'd have been glad if none of them could go to meet the president. Oh, what a disappointment! I never got to see the World's Fair in Chicago, either. My mother and dad did. They were with me, of course. But all I saw was the four walls of the dressing room.

I thought the show was going to go for ten weeks when it started and it went on for seven months. But I had a run-of the-play contract and I had to do it. Then Billy wanted me to go South and I said, "Thank you, no. I've got to stop." I'd had to do five shows a day with sixteen costume changes per show for each number.

I stopped acting after that but I had never expected to stay in films for fifty years. I wanted to do just what I did—make a hit in pictures, stay in it and have a wonderful time. Then I wanted to stop and do things socially, hoping that I'd meet the man I would be in love with. Sure enough, that's exactly what happened to me. I did become a star and then I married but one man and he was my beloved for fifty-three years.

Dorothy Lee

With her infectious grin, roguish brown eyes and saucy "little girl" voice, Dorothy Lee was never cut out for a quiet, sedate life. Born on May 23, 1911, in Los Angeles, Dottie grew up a tomboy and when her mother attempted to turn her into a proper young lady at the Westlake School for Girls, she rebelled and found a natural outlet for her infinite vitality on the vaudeville stages of the twenties. She recalled in later years that her early theatrical experience was "great training. The best way for me to start was on stage where you get the feel of an audience because when you're in movies, they just say, 'Cut!' "

Her work in vaudeville in California soon led her to Broadway during its most fabulous era. When the diminutive Dottie hit the Great White Way, she brought down the house in the 1928 college musical, *Hello Yourself,* with Fred Waring's Pennsylvanians. *The New York Times'* theatrical critic, Brooks Atkinson, noted that "Miss Dorothy Lee, skilled in Ann Pennington gyrations and gesticulations, a scintillating little person, was a roving spot of light."[1]

Dottie then went on tour as a soloist with Fred Waring's Pennsylvanians, one of the early big bands that arose in the wake of Paul Whiteman's phenomenal success. The band caught the spirit of the young collegiate crowd with their jazzy dance rhythms and risque lyrical interpolations, a perfect accompaniment for the uninhibited Dorothy Lee. In 1929, Dottie and Waring appeared in one of the earliest movie musicals and RKO's first release, *Syncopation*, made shortly after MGM's *The Broadway Melody* had unleashed a craze for movie musicals. Dottie's appearance in the picture caught the attention of Bert Wheeler who was about to join Robert Woolsey in Hollywood for the film version of their 1927 Broadway smash hit, *Rio Rita.* Bert recommended Dottie for the role of his leading lady and the eighteen-year-old beauty was soon dancing on RKO's new sound stages to the lilting strains of Harry Tierney's music.

Rio Rita is, in essence, two films in one linked by a plot involving a mysterious bandit known as the Kinkajou. The colorful setting on the Texas-Mexico border provides a backdrop for the romance of a Mexican girl, played by Bebe Daniels, and a Texas Ranger, John Boles, while the zany comic story centers around Bert Wheeler as a harried bigamist, Dottie Lee as his new bride and Bob Woolsey as his conniving lawyer.

The teaming of Dorothy Lee with Wheeler and Woolsey in *Rio Rita* clicked at once with 1929 audiences, leading to a succession of comedy films in the early thirties that contributed significantly to the early growth of RKO-Radio. The secret of their success lay not only in their outrageous satire on pretension—with the military, divorce courts, South American revolutions and big business enterprises among their targets—but how the three played off each other. Neither Bert nor Bob were straight men so Dottie at times played "straight" for their antics. As funny as she was in the films with her spirited personality, she rarely had gag lines as such, but her dialogue tended to further the plot. Bert was a parody of the traditional romantic lover with his boyish, quavering voice, wavy hair, cherubic face and Cheshire grin while the slick, fast-talking Bob with horn-rimmed glasses, hair parted in the middle, a gargantuan cigar in his tiny mouth and his skinny physique in loud clothes was the epitome of the boastful, lecherous but good-natured all-American

With Robert Woolsey and Bert Wheeler in *Hook, Line and Sinker.* (The Museum of Modern Art.)

With Joe E. Brown in *Local Boy Makes Good.*

schemer. And there was Dottie, always playing Dottie, a vivacious, auburn-haired soubrette just five feet tall, the last of the flappers and completely natural. Her contribution to the team was quickly recognized by critics like Quinn Martin in *The New York World*. Reviewing the 1930 release, *Half Shot at Sunrise*, which he noted "attains a pitch of hilarity comparable to that of the Marx Brothers," he praised "the prettiness, the grace and the gifts as a young actress of Miss Dorothy Lee, the heroine."[2]

Dottie also appeared in a number of films without Wheeler and Woolsey and continued to perform on the stage. She had a memorable role in the Joe E. Brown comedy, *Local Boy Makes Good* (1931), as a pushy psychology student trying to cure the insecure Brown of his sexual problems. In addition to her personal appearances and singing engagements, she starred for six months in 1933–34 in the West Coast production of the Broadway hit play, *She Loves Me Not*.

Nevertheless, it was her work with the boys that stood out. Indeed, she was the only actress to be regularly co-starred with a comedy team, a factor that sharply distinguished Wheeler and Woolsey's comedic style. The other great teams of the Depression era tended to be misogynistic. Predatory women declared war on Laurel and Hardy while the Marx Brothers, for their part, led an assault on female society. But Bert and Bob were perfectly at home with the opposite sex. Bert would pair off with Dottie for romantic trysts and Bob would unleash his roguish lovemaking on women who were his match in the give-and-take of rough-and-tumble romance.

Dottie said in later years that she never had any grand ambition for dramatic roles. After all, in her work with Wheeler and Woolsey, she was often able to take center stage. As Fay Wray had discovered in the twenties, leading ladies in comedies were frequently little more than decoration, reacting to the comedians' antics. But Dottie could make things run. In *Half Shot at Sunrise*, Dottie, in the words of the critic for *The Theatre Magazine*, was "the outstanding performer apart from the two comics," playing "a boiling hot little spanker of vast beauty and incredible boldness."[3] A colonel's daughter, she uses her feminine wiles and intelligence to induce Bert and Bob, two AWOL doughboys, to undertake a dangerous mission delivering secret papers to the front. In *Hook, Line and Sinker* (1930), to get free of her dominating mother, she enlists the boys' aid in renovating and operating a hotel she has inherited.

In the tradition of silent comedy queen Mabel Normand, Dottie would do anything for a laugh, even risking life and limb for a dangerous stunt. She recalled that, when making *The Cuckoos* (1930), her second film with Wheeler and Woolsey, "I'd come back from lunch. I stood up against a board and they had a knife-thrower throwing real knives at my head—they'd come out the back of the board. But when the director, Paul Sloane, came on the set, he nearly died. He wouldn't let them do it, but I was willing to have them throw real knives at me."

Her musical numbers stand out, not only for their singing and dancing, but for their high jinks. In *Rio Rita*, she performs an acrobatic dance with

With Noah Beery, Bert Wheeler and Robert Woolsey in *Cockeyed Cavaliers*. (Courtesy of Edward Watz.)

Bert; another routine with both the boys and Follies girl Helen Kaiser ends with all four falling off a boat into the river. *Caught Plastered* (1931) has her going into a frenetic song-and-dance number with Bert after she gets "high" on soft drinks spiked with bootleg liquor. The mock ballet in *Hips, Hips, Hooray!* is masterful; Bert, Bob, Dottie and Thelma Todd first demolish a fancy office and then Bert and Bob toss Dottie in the air and spin her around as she swings from a chandelier.

In 1934, *Hips, Hips, Hooray!*, along with *Cockeyed Cavaliers*, climaxed the team's work together. The director, Mark Sandrich, who would go on to the Fred Astaire–Ginger Rogers musicals, succeeded in these zany, tuneful and rapid-paced films in his conscious effort to create "comic symphonies." Both films added Thelma Todd as Bob's seductive love interest. The second of these, *Cockeyed Cavaliers*, would be the last Wheeler and Woolsey film released before the Production Code went into effect, establishing a strict censorship. It uses a 17th century English costume setting to comment on class structures and the relation between the sexes. Thelma is married to a male chauvinist baron (Noah Beery) who believes a woman's place is in the home while a man can indulge in the "macho" sport of boar-hunting. Dottie is a peasant girl who, escaping from an impending forced marriage to a duke, disguises herself as a boy and helps two wandering vagabonds, Bert and Bob, evade the law. The three crash society with Bob romancing the baron's dissatisfied wife, Thelma, in the absence of her overbearing husband. The film, of course, ends in a comic victory for Bert, Bob, Dottie and Thelma after a wild chase involving a boar.

Too soon, however, the free-wheeling spirit of the early thirties was dampened by the new restrictions of the Code. Wheeler and Woolsey's style suffered because of it and, as Bob complained to a *New York Times* reporter, "Nothing gets by the censors."[4] Dottie, between her appearances with Bert and Bob, continued to make other films while the boys worked with various replacements including a beginner named Betty Grable. But Dottie brought a special sparkle to the team and when she left the act for the last time in 1936, something vital seemed to go with her. Bob began drinking heavily and his alcoholism led to an illness that proved fatal in 1938. Devastated by his partner's passing, Bert lost his enthusiasm for films, although he continued on as a performer for many years on the stage, radio and television. In 1968, he died in poverty, never regaining the heights of popularity he had enjoyed in the days when he was teamed with Bob and Dottie.

Meanwhile, the much-wedded Dottie had a final fling in show business that included a 1938 vaudeville appearance with Bert, several more films and a show with Gene Kelly in 1939, before settling down with her fifth husband, a businessman who owned a printing company in Chicago. The two had three sons and a daughter. Although she remained on friendly terms with all her ex-spouses and expressed no bitterness towards any of them, it was her sixth marriage to Charles Calderini, a lawyer, that brought her the most personal happiness and security. Her final marriage, it lasted until his passing, twenty years after they were wed.

Dottie lived in retirement in Galena, Illinois for a number of years before moving to San Diego. When I interviewed her in 1991 and 1992, she still had the vivacity that had brought her success on the screen and inspired Marcella Burke to write in *Screen Play Secrets* in 1930 that "Hollywood has produced a Peter Pan without Mr. Barrie."[5] As Dottie reminisced, she was matter-of-fact, lacking any pretension and displaying a dry wit that was often directed at herself. Although her speaking voice was more mature, it was still delightfully unique and now, curiously, with a hint of Bert Wheeler in its quality. She remembered the lyrics of the songs she did with Bert and Bob and could belt out a tune with the best of them. Living in comfortable but not resplendent circumstances, she seemed to be enjoying the new attention sparked by the revival of her classic comedies with Bert and Bob. Her warmth and maternal attributes endeared her to a new generation of film enthusiasts, some of whom had become her personal friends.

It was obvious that, in many ways, her screen persona was a projection of her off-screen personality. She was an extrovert, full of life and, as she said, like Bert and Bob, not at all shy: "We were so much alike that it's a wonder we didn't kill each other!" And indeed, in an intriguing way, the characters all three played on the screen were related to their real-life experiences. As Bert and Bob had overcome the limitations of an impoverished childhood, so Dottie triumphed over the attempts to clip her tomboyish wings. The mischievous, pint-sized beauty had found her own niche of immortality as the movies' best-loved soubrette.

I was born in Los Angeles. My real name is Marjorie Millsap. My father was a lawyer and my mother was just a housewife. My father was the youngest lawyer ever admitted to the bar in Iowa and he had his own law business in Los Angeles. It was funny—I mean strange—but my father wound up representing Barney Oldfield who was, as you know, a big race driver and W. C. Fields. I've heard that when W. C. Fields wrote a book, he mentioned Dorothy Lee and I guess it was only because he knew my father was his lawyer. I never read it or anything but somebody told me that. When W. C. Fields needed a lawyer, my father took care of him doing just what I don't know.

I first appeared on stage when I was two years old. A friend of my father and mother owned a big studio and stage where they taught dancing and singing and everything. They were putting on a show and my mother and I happened to be there. I watched them rehearse and I said, "Oh, Mama, I want to be on a stage."

So this friend of the family whom I called uncle said, "Oh, let her go out there."

Mother said, "Oh, for heaven's sakes, she'll get out there and be scared to death." Well, heck, I got out there and they almost had to get a hook to get me off. I still have my shoes from that first performance.

I was brought up very close to where they built the Ambassador Hotel on Wilshire Boulevard. I watched it being built. I had I would say a normal middle-class family life although my mother and father were divorced when I was about seven years old. They both remarried. I lived with my mother but I loved my stepmother and my half-sister Melissa and used to go see them on weekends. I adored them because they let me do anything I wanted to do when I'd come there. In fact—how I got on the roof I don't know but one time I went down the chimney and got stuck and they had to call the fire department. Can you imagine? I was crazy. But my mother was very strict and so was my grandmother who lived with us. My stepfather was divine—I loved him. However, I remained close to my father. I can't prove it but I think it was through him that my name was legally changed to Dorothy Lee when I went into show business. And it was my father who taught me how to drive a car. You won't believe it but I was fourteen when I started driving. You didn't have to take a driver's test then.

A photo from her years with RKO in the 1930s. (Courtesy of Dorothy Lee Calderini.)

I went to Virgil Junior High School, I did one year at L.A. High and then I went to the Westlake School for Girls. That was a finishing school, "very, very," of course. I am not the "very, very" type so I hated it. I was only about in the eighth or ninth grade then. It was right after that that I went into show business at the age of fourteen. I would say I was about a B and C average student. I didn't study very much. I think maybe English was my best subject. I wish I had studied it more. I'm not a "deze," "dem" and "dozer" but there was a lot more I could have learned had I continued in school. But when I started touring with the Orpheum Circuit, I would have to turn in my homework to my school. That's the way they did it in those days.

There were twelve boys on my street and I was the only girl so naturally, I was a tomboy and just hated being a girl until suddenly the ham in me came out about show business. In back of our houses, they built an athletic field where they taught me to high-jump, to pole-vault and all that crazy stuff. I high-jumped four-four which was pretty good. And I played on the United States Lacrosse Team at about the age of thirteen or fourteen at the Coliseum. I have pictures in my scrapbook to prove it which I can't believe. So I loved athletics and played tennis and golf all my life.

I also loved show business and the movies. In the silent days, my family would take me to the movies when I was little and I used to drive the audience crazy because I'd keep saying to my mother, "What's that say, what's that say?" I wasn't old enough to read the captions. Later, I was crazy about Douglas Fairbanks. I must have been ten or eleven when I had the mumps or something. I think my mother read in the paper that May 23 was his birthday, the same as mine. Of course, I was at the age when I was star-struck so I wrote him to please send me an autographed picture. It was so cute because he autographed it for me—my name was still Marjorie then or Midge—and I had it for years. Later on, I met his son, Junior, at some dance and I was so impressed. He was going to boarding school somewhere in L.A. and I was going to this fancy place I hated, the Westlake School for Girls.

In *Cockeyed Cavaliers*. (The Jamie Brotherton Collection.)

Homer Dickinson, the vaudevillian, was a friend of my family. His wife, Florence Tempest, was very ill and he needed someone to replace her in his act. He was at our house for dinner one night when I started acting up or something and he said, "Can you sing?"

I said, "Sure," so he went to the piano and played a few tunes.

Then he said to my mother, "Well, gee, she would be just great." My mother felt perfectly at ease about my working with him because he was like a father. So that's how I started. The act was sort of a Gracie Allen type of thing. I played a dumb little girl. We played the Orpheum Circuit so I certainly started A-class because the Orpheum Circuit was the top. We toured all over California and I'd stay in hotels or rooming houses. It was then that I changed my name. Homer Dickinson liked the name of Dorothy and my grandmother's name was Lee. But my sister and all my family continued to call me Midge for Marjorie. People who don't know me call me Dorothy but people who know me well call me Dottie.

After my stint with Homer Dickinson, I went with Fanchon and Marco who did shows for the theatre circuits. They were wonderful people to work for and they did some real cute things. They were doing a college thing—they would have different themes, you know—and because I was athletic, I would throw a basketball or a football out in the audience. Then I would come on the stage and sing with the master of ceremonies. One of them I remember was Rube Wolfe at Loew's in downtown Los Angeles. We'd play four shows a day and we would do a show in between the movie. That's what they did in those days long before you were born. I did two Fanchon and Marco tours which were travelling for five to six months. Sometimes we'd play a little town three days and two in another small one. When we'd play in a big town like San Francisco, it would be a week. We'd play in all the big theatres and it was a lot of fun and wonderful training because Fanchon and Marco were really the tops then.

I married for the first time when I was sixteen. My first husband was Robert Boothe whom I met in one of the Fanchon and Marco tours. He did an adagio dance with his sister in the show. He was a society boy from Pasadena and a health nut who'd taken up dancing in the summer for exercise.

Before I went to New York for a Broadway show in 1928, I made my first appearance in a movie. I had a scene with Bebe Daniels where I was playing in a chorus line in a Paramount picture called *Take Me Home.* In those days, the show girls who were tall were in the center and since I was the little one, I was at the end of the line. Bebe was the star and Mickey Neilan was the director. He pointed to me and said, "Come here, peanut"—he called me that because I was so small compared to the other girls—and he asked me, "How would you like to do a scene with Bebe Daniels?"

I said, "Oh, I'd love to." This was a silent movie but I did a line—I don't know, I probably said "yes" or "no" or something like that. A year later when I did *Rio Rita* with Bebe, I reminded her of it and, of course, she couldn't remember that it had been me but she remembered the incident. I didn't know Bebe and her husband, Ben Lyon, well but she was a darling person and so was he. Long after I was out of show business, I ran into them in London and it was just great to see them.

When I worked in this silent with her, Mickey Neilan told me I had talent. He gave me such confidence and he gave me good advice: "When you start in show business, it's a tough life. But don't be afraid—just do your best." I'll never forget, on the opening night of *Hello Yourself,* he sent me a wire. I'll never get over it, how he could have remembered. When I began working at RKO, he was a director there and he was going with Sally O'Neil. I never went out with him or anything. I just met him on sets and things but he was such a nice guy.

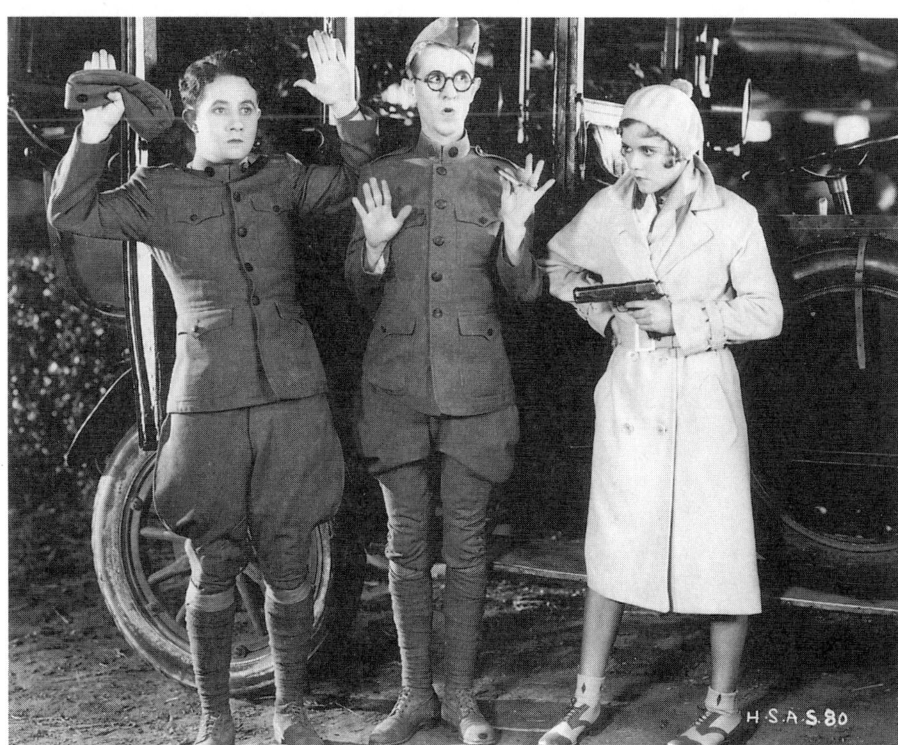

With Bert Wheeler and Robert Woolsey in *Half Shot at Sunrise.* (The Wisconsin Center for Film and Theater Research.)

I never got out of California when I was touring in vaudeville and with Fanchon and Marco. And it was in California where I auditioned for George Choos who was putting on this rah-rah college show in New York starring Fred Waring's Pennsylvanians. There were two hundred and fifty gals who auditioned and out of them, two were chosen. I was one so that's how I happened to go to New York at the age of seventeen for *Hello Yourself.* I was never in the chorus of the show. I played a featured part. I was one of the college girls on the campus and in the dorm and all that stuff. I started out with—oh, I think maybe one song in front of the chorus leading a number. Then, little by little, I wound up with about three numbers. Of course, I don't think I have much talent, never did, but Fred Waring is the one who saw the possibilities in me and he's the one who really brought me forward and helped me and coached me and things like that. I'd seen him on the stage before I worked with him. He was great with a show. He'd step in and do all the numbers. He'd just come back from a tour of Europe with his band when I joined *Hello Yourself.* It was wonderful training to work with Fred. For instance, he taught me how to phrase when singing.

With Fred Waring in the late 1920s. (The Museum of Modern Art.)

On opening night, I was doing a fast dance when my stocking started falling down. I kept pulling it up at the same time I was dancing. I hadn't planned it but the audience thought it was part of the show. They loved it so I had to do it every night. It wasn't easy, though.

There was one place in the show where I went into a fraternity house and they threw me in a blanket way up in the air. Finally, I got up so high I was out of sight. That was one of the big hits of the show when they hazed me as they called it. I mean, it brought down the house. Imagine tossing me clear up out of sight! I could have reached up and pulled a curtain or something and the show would have been closed. They finally put a flag up there and when I came down, I brought the flag with me.

Evelyn Nair and I roomed together in New York when we did the show and her mother came with us. Evelyn later married Fred Waring and she remained one of my best friends. In the daytime, we would rehearse the show and at night, we would rehearse our dancing. We would work from eight until nine, ten, eleven, twelve or one in the morning. We would walk home. In those days, you were safe. But boy, a couple of times we had to go barefoot because our heels were worn out from practicing tap-dancing. We were afraid to take the subway because the first week we were there, there was a terrible accident and we saw them bring out all these black bodies. And since we couldn't afford a taxi, we'd walk. We were very careful because our mothers had said, "Now don't go out with strangers or anything." There were a lot of stage-door Johnnies but I never went out on strange dates. Unfortunately, that time of my life was very dull but I guess smart. In those days, you were taught not to do that. Finally, some of the boys in Waring's band asked us, "Where do you live?" or something like that. They lived out of New York and when we found out that they were safe, we let them drive us home. We lived in a little tiny walk-up on—I don't know, Fiftieth Street, God knows where.

I didn't mix at all with the Broadway crowd. I usually had dinner with a group of us in the show

With Bobby Watson and Morton Downey in *Syncopation*. (The Museum of Modern Art.)

and then would go home with Evelyn. I never went out night-clubbing except a very few times. I did see many of the other Broadway shows of the time. I'll never forget that *Show Boat* was the first musical in New York I ever saw. I think Fred got me a ticket and I went by myself to a matinee to see it. Of course, I was never so thrilled in my life to see a show like that. I had an opportunity to meet Florenz Ziegfeld who produced *Show Boat* and I was impressed. He was a very nice gentleman. I also met George Gershwin at an audition. He was darling and very young—one of the nicest men I ever met. I forget what it was I auditioned for but I sang for him in his beautiful apartment in New York.

My husband had stayed in California when I went to New York. He came to visit me but it was just a matter of time when we were divorced after I came back to Hollywood. He was a wonderful, nice guy but I was interested in Fred Waring. Both of us were very much in love with each other. Thank heavens, we were finally smart enough to know it never really would have worked out because he wanted his life—naturally, being a success. He was a big star with his band and I was just coming up but I wanted to be in pictures. I was in love with him for years and years and years but it just never would have worked.

We took *Hello Yourself* on tour and went from New York to Chicago and Detroit. Back in New York, I did a picture called *Syncopation* for RKO in 1929 with Morton Downey and starring Waring's Pennsylvanians. It was one of the first musical pictures. I sang a number, "Do, Do Something" and Morton Downey did a song that became a hit, "I'll Always Be in Love with You." The studio in New York where we made it was destroyed in a fire a short time later. For years, Fred Waring tried to find a copy of *Syncopation* but I had guessed it just went with the fire. Now, they just found a copy in Russia. Isn't that a riot?

Morton Downey fell in love with Barbara Bennett who was in the cast of *Syncopation* and they were married and had quite a few kids. Downey used to use the most vile language and he did it because he knew I was such a young kid and naive. Oh, my gosh, the words he said—you know, I learned an awful lot about swear words through Downey although I never repeated it. And I think he got a kick out of it because I was so shocked. I'm not shocked by things today, though. I don't care for a lot of violence in today's movies but I don't mind the sex. As for people my age who are shocked by these movies—oh, hell! I'm old but I think young. How do we put it? If that's what they want to do, fine, it's none of my business. I haven't missed much.

Bert Wheeler and Robert Woolsey had just been signed to do *Rio Rita* in the movies when Bert saw me in *Syncopation*. He said to a young man he knew, "That's the little girl I want to play opposite me," when they met in a New York speakeasy. Bert thought I could work well with him because we were both short. The young man, who was working with me in *Hello Yourself*, introduced me to Bert and we had lunch. Bert told me he'd signed with RKO and said I should get my manager on the ball to inform RKO he'd found his leading lady. So I signed a contract with RKO. Of course, we had to finish the run of our play first and then I went out to Hollywood. I first met Bert's partner, Bob Woolsey, on the set of our first picture together, *Rio Rita*, and he was very nice.

Part of *Rio Rita* was filmed in black-and-white and part in color. When we made the picture, RKO did not own a color camera so we would start working between six and seven at night and work all night because the camera belonged to Warner Brothers. Why RKO didn't own one, I will never know. Maybe there was a question mark as to whether color would work or not. Bert, Bob, another girl and I had a number in color, "Sweetheart, We Need Each Other," where we ended up falling into the water. We had to make that in the middle of the night. It must have been about three or four in the morning when we fell over into the water and, believe me, it was cold. Then we had to get out and do it all over again. It's never one take—I don't know why.

Another thing I remember in *Rio Rita*, we went out into the San Fernando Valley where it was hot as the devil and they had a great big set where they built a stage for us to dance on. It was nothing but wood, of course, and because sound was just coming in, they sprinkled it with some black stuff. We had a chorus and I was doing "The Kinkajou." It was about a hundred and twenty in the sun and then on top of that, they had those big lights on us. They had a nurse on the set because I think about four or five of the gals fainted. Why I didn't, I don't know. Then when we'd finish the scene, we'd be

Dottie and the chorus performing "The Kinkajou" in *Rio Rita*. (The Jamie Brotherton Collection.)

all black because the stuff would come up all over us. That was to sort of calm down the sound or something. But oh, God, that's one of the toughest things I ever did in pictures. Why they wouldn't have us work on an indoor set I'll never know to this day. I guess they wanted a setting or something although there wasn't much of a setting that they couldn't have built inside the studio. But you don't ask questions if they say, "Report at five o'clock in the morning, get your face on." And then they'd have cars to take us out to hell and gone in the Valley where it naturally was twice as hot as it would be in town.

We used to go lots to the rushes of *Rio Rita* and I'll never forget, I went in and saw they were doing it in Spanish. I would swear it was my voice except I can't speak Spanish and neither could Bert and Bob. All of our voices were dubbed and the way they could copy our voices, I'd swear it was coming out of my own mouth. How they could do it and get those words like we speak English was just amazing to me. I think they dubbed it in German, too, but I did not see that.

Rio Rita was a big hit and that started a long series of pictures I did with Wheeler and Woolsey at RKO. I just thought it was wonderful. I mean, I was thrilled to death because they were both so talented and I was honored to be able to work with them. Bert was really easy to work with but Woolsey always wanted to run the show. Anything that you did with Woolsey, you sort of did it his way where Bert and I would talk it over and say, "Well, what do you think? Shall we do it this way or would you like it better that way?" So we were always in perfect agreement on everything we did. Bert was a very dear, sweet man. Sometimes he played the dumb part in the movies but, of course, he was not dumb in real life. I remember one of his favorite expressions was to say something was "peachy-keen."

Woolsey was always a little caustic, pulling your leg, or trying to be funny and take over. For instance, we'd sit down to lunch and he'd try to take over the conversation because he was just that way—real hambo—where Bert was more laid back. But they both had great senses of humor off-screen and were always saying something funny. Bob constantly used a cigar in his act. Half the time, he'd light them and I can remember how they'd smell but they wouldn't always be lit when we did the pictures. I never saw him smoke a cigar when he

A publicity photo with Bert and Bob from *Cracked Nuts*. (Courtesy of Edward Watz.)

was out anyplace. He only smoked them when he was working. There were no lenses in the glasses he wore in the movies. He actually did wear glasses off and on for reading. Although he was billed as Robert, we always called Woolsey "Bob." Everybody who worked on the set, as soon as we got to know each other, was on a first-name basis at all times. So I always knew them as Bert and Bob. Most of the people called me Dottie but Bert liked to call me "Lee." I don't recall that Bob had a particular nickname for me. He called me whatever it happened to be at the time that pleased him.

In the years when I worked with Wheeler and Woolsey, just about all we ever talked about when we got on the set was our lines. Sometimes we had a lot to learn. Before we'd do the scene, if there was something that bothered us and before it was time for them to shoot, we'd go on the side of the set, go over it and have someone give us cues. Bert and Bob would discuss gags or they would go to a director. It would all depend upon the director. Sometimes they knew exactly what they wanted but most of them would listen to any suggestions—and it was usually Bob who would have suggestions over Bert if he didn't like a scene or the way it was done—and they would say, "All right, we'll try it both ways." After we'd done a scene, Bob would ask Bert and me, "What do you think? Do you think it's funny?" Maybe we'd do two or three takes in two or three different ways and then when we'd go in to see the rushes, we'd pick which ones we liked the best. So that way it worked pretty well and very seldom did we have to take things over again.

Bert and Dottie performing the song and dance number, "Whistling the Blues Away," in *Half Shot at Sunrise.* (The Museum of Modern Art.)

Bert and Bob did fight a lot, mostly over changes in the script. I'd just stay out of it because I was sort of in the middle. Bert and I would just sort of go along with whatever we thought the director wanted or the way it was written. To us, that was business where Bob wanted it to be his way. But after all, Bert did have a say in it and he was starred over Woolsey. He made more money than Bob did because he was the one who had the big name first. I guess Bert and Betty Wheeler, his first wife, were famous in vaudeville long before Bert and Bob were teamed up in *Rio Rita* on the New York stage in 1927. But they never had any really bad arguments and remained friends off-screen. Being comedians, they enjoyed working together.

We didn't ad-lib too much. Now you can ad-lib on the stage but it's hard to ad-lib in movies. We had to know our lines, our cues and if they didn't give us the cue, sometimes we'd go up, we'd blow, but very seldom did we ad-lib.

I don't recall anything in particular about the sets on our pictures except for the big Paris set they built at the studio for *Half Shot at Sunrise.* I think I remember that because I hadn't yet visited Paris. When we went out on location—it was all in the Valley in those days—we'd get up very early, around two or three in the morning. We'd wait for the sun to come up so we'd have to be out there by the time they were ready to shoot and then we'd probably finish around five o'clock in the afternoon. Sometimes the shooting schedule for the location would be two or three days in a row depending upon what scene you were in.

We'd rehearse at least two weeks before we'd do the picture, sometimes longer than that. When we'd do any dancing scenes, we'd rehearse for almost a month. The musical numbers were recorded as we did them. Just as you see it on the screen, that's when we did it. We didn't do it afterwards with lip-synching or pre-recording like they did later. I think we really did it the easiest way because we knew exactly what we were doing. We had choreographers like Dave Gould and his assistant, Hermes Pan, but Bert really was the choreographer. He and I always did our own dances and he was great. Whenever the three of us did something, Bert was really the dancer. I saw Bob in a couple of things later and I was surprised. I didn't know he could dance as well as he did. But Bert was always the one who put it together and Bob and I followed his suggestions.

We dreamed up a cute thing in *Dixiana* but it was tough. I had to unhook my hoopskirt as I fell down. When I stood up, my dress was on the floor, I was in my pantaloons and then we did a crazy dance while Bob stood there watching us from behind a curtain.

If you can believe it, Oscar Levant was the piano player who would rehearse Bert and me in our songs when we first went into pictures. I can't remember whether Oscar Levant was under contract to RKO but I think that was a riot because he was a character and always funny. I look back on that and say, "My God!" He was just terrific and then he later became a great star. Max Steiner was the music director at RKO when I was under contract there and I think he did most of our Wheeler and Woolsey things. He was so kind and sweet. He would do it over and over and he was really a marvelous man.

We also had some great songwriters. Kalmar and Ruby not only did the songs but also wrote the scripts for our second picture, *The Cuckoos*—that's the one where we're sitting on the wings of a plane at the end—and a later one, *Hips, Hips, Hooray!* I remember they'd play the songs on the piano for us. Harry Tierney, who'd done the songs for *Rio Rita,* wrote the music for *Dixiana* and *Half Shot at Sunrise* and Anne Caldwell did the lyrics. My favorite song of any I've ever done was "My One Ambition Is You" which Bert and I did in *Dixiana*—that was cute. We sang that when we were coming down some stairs. Another song by Harry Tierney and Anne Caldwell we did was "Whistling the Blues Away" in *Half Shot at Sunrise.* Now I can whistle—that's my whistling in the number—but Bert couldn't whistle. Anne Caldwell also did some of the writing on the scripts of *Dixiana* and *Half Shot at Sunrise.* She was the sweetest lady, a darling woman and unusual. I was supposed to play the lead in *Babes in Toyland* with Bert and Bob which she was going to adapt for us but RKO never made it. She was very old but we became friends and she just loved us all and was wonderful to us.

I think all our directors were just wonderful, too. Eddie Cline directed us in *Hook, Line and Sinker* and *Cracked Nuts* and he was crazy, a comedian himself, a real character. Bill Seiter did *Caught Plastered*, *Peach O'Reno, Girl Crazy*, and a film I

With Bert, Hugh Herbert, Bob and Jobyna Howland in *Hook, Line and Sinker.*

made with Bert, *Too Many Cooks.* Bill Seiter was very sweet, very kind, and loved almost everything we did. I mean, he got as much of a kick out of us as I guess the audience did. When we'd do a scene that he liked, he would laugh right through it.

Then there were those wonderful character performers in our pictures like Edna May Oliver and Jobyna Howland. Edna May Oliver was in *Half Shot at Sunrise, Cracked Nuts* and a picture I did without Bert and Bob, *Laugh and Get Rich.* She was great, a very sweet lady. Jobyna Howland worked in *The Cuckoos, Dixiana* and *Hook, Line and Sinker.* She was really crazy and made us laugh all the time. I heard she'd been a Gibson Girl many years before. We also worked with the child star, Mitzi Green, in *Girl Crazy.* She was a darling little girl—very nice, mannered and polite.

There were many changes of producers at RKO. When I first came there, William LeBaron was in charge and he was the greatest man who ran RKO. Then David O. Selznick took over and he was terrible. Nobody liked him. I don't know too much about him but he wouldn't give anybody the time of day. His attitude was "How very, very." I mean, we were so beneath him. That's the impression he gave me and that's the way Bert and Bob felt, too. In fact, Wheeler and Woolsey thought they'd had it because when Selznick took over the studio, he said right in front of them, "Which one's Wheeler and which one's Woolsey?" Well, I think that was pretty lousy. I know we heard that remark because I remember Bert and Bob telling me that.

We were making *Girl Crazy* at the time. I didn't want to do it because they had written me out so that I was practically a walk-on. But Bert told me, "Look, Lee, we're on our way out so finish the movie, you're getting" whatever it was, I forget, over a thousand or something, "because we're all going to be thrown out seeing Selznick is taking over." We were like brother and sister and he was right so I did it and I didn't have much to do in it at all. But within a year, Selznick left and we came back when Merian C. Cooper took over. He was a very nice man married to Dorothy Jordan. After that, Pandro S. Berman became head of production at RKO. We got along fine although we had very little in common. I remember he would come on the set and bring people who wanted to see the

With Bert and Edna May Oliver in *Cracked Nuts.* (The Wisconsin Center for Film and Theater Research.)

pictures being made. We didn't care if ours was an open set but you were never allowed on Katharine Hepburn's set.

At the entrance to the studio, there were always billboards of RKO's new pictures. I'll never forget, I was coming into RKO driving my new Studebaker with free-wheeling or something and I looked up. There was a great big billboard of me, Dorothy Lee, starring in whatever the heck it was and, God, I took my foot off the gas pedal and the car just kept going straight. That was the first of my big expensive cars. Before that, I drove a Ford convertible with a rumble seat, the first car I ever bought.

We would park right in front of our building. I don't think it had our names on it but we automatically parked right in front of this long bungalow where all the dressing rooms were. We all had our own private dressing rooms. They were like motel rooms. Usually, the doors were open and we'd chat and say, "Good morning." Then of course, we'd have to go to make-up. Mel Berns was the make-up man on most of the pictures when I was there and Walter Plunkett, who was a real nice guy, designed many of the wonderful costumes. We'd all go to one place to have our make-up put on at about six or seven in the morning. There would be Ginger Rogers, there would be me, Irene

Top, Stanley Fields, Chris "Pin" Martin, unknown actor; left to right, Kitty Kelly, Mitzi Green, Bob, Dottie, Bert, Arline Judge and Eddie Quillan in *Girl Crazy.* (Courtesy of Edward Watz.)

Dunne and Hepburn and we'd all say, "Good morning." Hepburn, though—she'd naturally have to say "Good morning" but she just didn't want to be bothered with us so I never really got to know her. The thing that always made all of us mad was that Hepburn insisted on having a closed set where whenever anything else like *Flying Down to Rio* was going on next door—T. Freeland directed that—it was an open set, the more the merrier.

I remember I started at RKO at about four hundred and fifty dollars a week and went up to a thousand and twelve hundred which was good during the Depression, I'd say. But then that's not much money now—that's peanuts. I lived very simply. I never was impressed by keeping up with the Joneses even when I later married into a very wealthy family related to the Wrigleys. I continued to live the way I was brought up. I am a very normal person and I never was interested in great big mansions and all that. I mean, I couldn't care less. It's the same with clothes. I was never one to have to spend a fortune on clothes. I'm still the same way today. I'm not poor or I'm not broke but I've always been the casual type. When I'd have to go to an opening or something with Joel McCrea or whoever at the studio, I'd dress up but mostly I dressed very casually. I've been that way all my life. For instance, when slacks came in, I wore them and loved it.

When I began at RKO after I divorced my first husband, I stayed with my mother and stepfather. It was more fun to be at home and have them take care of me and cook for me and everything. In those days, you didn't live with people like you do now. So I was very happy being at home. It was convenient and it took me only about fifteen minutes to drive from our house to the studio.

Then I married Jimmie Fidler, the columnist. We were married for about six months. It was my fault. I was still in love with Fred Waring when Jimmie visited RKO and asked the publicity gal to introduce us. Jimmie took me to lunch at the Brown Derby and then he courted me quite a lot. I think two or three times I broke up with Fred. It was during that time that Jimmie asked me to marry him and dumb fool that I was—nineteen, I think—I married him. I remember Bert and Bob gave me a lovely dinner party. Well, the marriage lasted a hot ten minutes. Then I met Marshall Duffield

Bert and Dottie in the 1930s.

who played football for USC and married him in Tijuana. After the ceremony, the justice of the peace said to Marsh, "Now tackle her." Of course, when I'd get a divorce, Bert and Bob would kid me. Oh, God, they always gave me the business.

I was never involved with them. After all, they were both married. Bert and I were linked a couple of times in the columns but nothing serious. It wasn't true but you know how they make things up. I didn't know his first wife, Betty. When we did *Rio Rita*, Bert was married to Bernice Speer who was the mother of their daughter, Patricia. They had a house in the San Fernando Valley but I'd say it was nothing fancy. I saw a lot of Bert's third wife, Sally Haines, who was a great gal. His last wife, Pat, was a nice gal, too. I have no idea why Bert's marriages broke up. He was not a woman-chaser and didn't stray a bit. Maybe you just get tired of someone and want to move on.

Bob, of course, did chase the women—just like his screen character. We heard rumors about it. But he never tried to hide his affairs—he had such ego. There were some very cute chorus girls working in our pictures and Bob always made passes at all the babes on the set. Bert wasn't like that but Bob was. One time, Bob was poppin' a gal in the hay in his dressing room when they threw a shirt or something over the lamp and it caught on fire. Everybody was laughing about it at the studio including Bob.

In the very beginning, Bob made a couple of passes at me but I caught that. He was smart enough to stay away from me after that because anybody who got fresh with me, I'd really let him have it. But I liked him and he liked me. We all liked each other and were like a family. We got along fine all the years we were working together. He was always cordial with me and he never picked on me. Even when he'd made passes, he just did it to tease me. He wasn't being serious. He was probably trying to see if he could shock me. Of course, being as young as I was, I was so damned innocent, God, it was terrible.

I knew Bob's wife, Mignonne. They lived in a beautiful big house not right in Malibu but it was in a beautiful piece of property right on the ocean. I visited there several times. I think Mignonne was the type who didn't mind his having affairs. She had been a dancer and was a very nice gal. I remember whenever she'd had a few drinks at a party, she'd always get up and want to dance and bow and curtsy. I think Bob was a little startled because he'd say, "The old gal is stewed to the gills" or something like that.

Bob drank, too, at parties. He drank more heavily than Bert but I never saw him smashed. When you get up that early to go to the studio, unless you're an alcoholic, who in the h--- would have a drink? You know, you get there at seven in the morning if you're going to shoot at nine so none of our group were big drinkers like you've heard. When Bert and Bob were working, they never drank a drop and, of course, I didn't drink till I was over thirty-five. Neither of them ever used the kind of swear words that Morton Downey used, either. They were always gentlemen.

I remember one time that Bert played a joke on me. He said to me on the set, "Oh, Lee, this gal wants to meet you and talk to you." So then I met her and talked to her and I guess she sort of had the hots for me. I found out that she was a lesbian. It didn't take too long to find out when she started coming on to me. There wasn't anything wrong about it. It was just that it was funny. Bert was laughing about it. Anything that was funny or a little off-key or something, he got hysterical over. I don't know how this gal met Bert or knew him but he'd fixed it so that she could meet me. I think he had a rough idea that she was a lesbian but I was still a little naive. I wasn't quite as sharp as he was because, after all, he was older than I was.

With Joe E. Brown in *Local Boy Makes Good.*

I very seldom went out with Bert and Bob socially despite the many pictures we did together. We all went our own ways. Even Bert and Bob didn't go out together too much as I remember. After all, pictures are business—just like when you go home from the office, you don't always go out with the same people you see at work every day. The minute I finished at the studio, I'd play tennis or golf. I did not drink or smoke, I didn't like to go out to big fancy parties and I'd rather have been with my own group—a much younger crowd that included friends from my school days.

I wasn't one to go to premieres, either. In fact, until my dear friends started collecting my movies and sending them to me, I rarely saw any of them. Oh, once in a great while, I would go to see them in the theatres in the thirties but mostly I'd go to the rushes at the studio and that was about it. Sometimes I did go out when RKO wanted me to for publicity purposes. Joel McCrea and I were very good friends, not interested in each other but more like a brother and sister thing. We were told by the studio to go to openings together as publicity. He was well-known and I was beginning to be. We laughed at it but we did it. Those are the things that they don't do now. You did what the studio told you to then. Often the publicity wasn't anything to do with pictures. It was more our personal lives and you just had to accept it. But I can't say that I ever had anything said about me that would upset me terribly. Anytime I was interviewed personally, Louella Parsons and all of those were wonderful to me. And Jimmie Fidler, to whom, as I say, I was married for a hot ten minutes, did an awful lot of publicity on me, too.

Besides my work with Wheeler and Woolsey, I was doing other movies. In 1931, I was in *Laugh and Get Rich* with Edna May Oliver and Hugh Herbert. It was directed by Gregory La Cava who was very nice although I didn't really get close to him like I did Eddie Cline, Bill Seiter and Mark Sandrich. Then Bert and I did a film without Bob, *Too Many Cooks.* I saw it not too long ago and it was all right, it was cute. A lot of it was done on location in the Valley. When it was run on AMC, quite a few people called me and said, "Oh, we thought it was so cute." About that time, I was

With Lillian Roth and Charles "Buddy" Rogers in *Take a Chance*. (The Jamie Brotherton Collection.)

loaned to Warner Brothers to make a picture with Joe E. Brown, *Local Boy Makes Good.* Joe E. Brown was great. He was very kind and sweet and went out of his way to help you do scenes. And Mervyn LeRoy who directed us was wonderful, too. Of course, I never did work with any but very nice people. I guess I had a great break there.

I also did some short subjects but I almost draw a complete blank on all those. I did one with Hal LeRoy in New York when I was staying over there for a couple of weeks before I went to Europe with my husband, Marsh Duffield. Hal LeRoy was a dancer but I think we played straight parts which was so dumb. I think they just used us because of our names. All I can remember is we had something to do with flying in an airplane. I made another short with Chick Chandler. I think it was done at RKO in Hollywood. I can't remember it but it was sort of a political thing and it got quite good notices. I'd gone to Europe when it came out but I heard about it later. Then in 1933, when I came back from Europe, I made a feature at Paramount's studio on Long Island, *Take a Chance*, a musical with Buddy Rogers, James Dunn, Lillian Roth and Cliff Edwards. That was fun, too. My husband Marsh also worked briefly in pictures and was an assistant director on *Eight Girls in a Boat* for Paramount. I remember when they were on location near San Francisco, I drove my car up to see him.

Even after I was in pictures, I continued to perform for live audiences. In fact, I had it in my contract with RKO that when I was not working, I was free to go and sing with Fred Waring's band. I never did any of their phonograph records, however. Unfortunately or probably fortunately with my tinny voice, I was never around when they were recording. That was the style, though, in those days like Helen Kane. I knew her but not well. Maybe she influenced me without my realizing it. I admired her and I was kind of "boop-boop-a-doopy" then.

I think I was about to make my second picture with Bert and Bob, *The Cuckoos*, when Fred Waring brought his whole orchestra out to California and did a wonderful show called *Rah-rah Daze.* We did it in Los Angeles and I'll never forget, Gloria Swanson came to the theatre. She sent a note

With Cliff Edwards and James Dunn in *Take a Chance.*

back that she wanted to meet me. Well, that was the thrill of my life. She came backstage and said, "Oh, I just had to tell you how cute and adorable you were." Fred and I were falling over in a dead faint or at least I was. I was so impressed I was like someone who had her mouth hanging open and had never been around anyone in pictures.

I also went on the road. Bert, Bob and I took a tour in vaudeville playing all the big theatres in New York, Chicago, Ohio. We did it for about six weeks. There was just the three of us. We didn't have a musician, a piano player or anything like that. We would eat dinner together travelling on the train but I don't recall anything else we did en route. I think we were all readers. Of course, we always studied a script with all sorts of comedy stuff for our act and knew what we were doing. And I worked with Milton Berle for six weeks in vaudeville. His mother was a darling and used to cook for us. I'd never eaten Jewish food before and boy, was it good.

Around that time, an agent who was a friend of mine said, "How would you like to sing with Phil Harris at the Cocoanut Grove?"

And I said, "Oh, I'd love to," because I wasn't working then. I think that was when our contract with the three of us together must have run out at RKO. I don't know whether I had to audition—I don't think so. The Cocoanut Grove was in the Ambassador Hotel which was about ten blocks from where I was raised. That's where I met Art Jarrett who sang there. We became good friends and I introduced him to Eleanor Holm whom he married. Leah Ray was sort of starring at the Cocoanut Grove then. She sang with Phil Harris a lot. I just sang by myself. I think I only worked there for maybe a couple of months but the only bands I sang with were Phil Harris's and Fred Waring's. Phil Harris was a darling man to work with and had a good sense of humor.

Bert and Bob had gone on a world tour in 1933. They wanted me to go but I don't know—I guess I didn't want to go. But I rejoined them at RKO to make *Hips, Hips, Hooray!* and *Cockeyed Cavaliers.* We didn't have a party to celebrate but we were so happy to be back together. Mark Sandrich was the director on both pictures. I can't say anything except that he was one of the nicest and most thoughtful men I've ever met, really a wonderful man. In fact, I think he was a genius at directing. And if Bert and Bob were rehearsing a scene with me and if one didn't like what they were saying or vice versa, we'd go to Mark and say, "Could we do it this way? We like it better." Being comedians, they knew—not me but they knew which way the gag, the joke or whatever would go better.

He'd usually say, "Well, let's see it the way it's written. All right." Then he'd listen to the changes they wanted and say, "Yeah, that's fine. It gets the point across." So he was always agreeable and we remained friendly. I remember I saw him when I was playing in Chicago in 1939. He'd come through on the train and he sent me a note backstage: "Could I come back and see you?"

Thelma Todd was in both *Hips, Hips, Hooray!* and *Cockeyed Cavaliers.* Oh, how I loved her! God, what a great gal and how beautiful and outgoing! And how terrible about what happened to her—how she died. It was a shock to all of us. We always thought one of her lovers murdered her. That's something I guess will always remain a mystery. But I know as well as I know my daughter or my sons that she never committed suicide. I was always a happy person and so was she. If she drank in earlier years, I don't know but when she worked with us, she didn't. She was married to Pat DeCicco at the time she made those pictures with us and he was a constant visitor to the set. At the time she died, she had a cafe in Santa Monica. I never went in there but I had a house in Malibu at the time as well as a house next to Lakeside Golf Course and when I'd finish at the studio, I'd pass by Thelma's place on my way home to Malibu. It was a nice restaurant and I think she was doing very well.

Ruth Etting sang in *Hips, Hips, Hooray!* and she was a very sweet lady, too. Her husband, Marty the Gimp, was something. Boy, he was really telling the director how to direct her and oh, God, we just stood in awe at him, the nerve he had.

I never had a double throughout my career because I could do everything. As I say, I was brought up a tomboy and loved it. For instance, I remember there was something in *Half Shot at Sunrise* where I jumped off of the top of a car or some crazy thing. In *Hips, Hips, Hooray!*, Bert, Bob, Thelma and I did a Kalmar and Ruby song,

"Keep on Doin' What You're Doin'," and then we went into a dance. When Bert and Bob were twisting me around very rapidly, they used a mannequin but that was me hanging from the top in the scene. You see, what happened was I was swinging on a chandelier and Bert and Bob were supposed to catch me in a blanket which they did but it slipped out of their hands. That was about a twelve-foot drop. They broke the fall as you can see in the movie but still I hit the ground. At first, I was in sort of a state of shock but it didn't hurt because I danced off with them. But right after that, I couldn't move for about a week. My neck was stiff and I wound up with two slipped discs. Recently, I had a very severe back operation and I think that's what started it. But to think I lasted that long was pretty amazing.

In *Cockeyed Cavaliers*, I dressed as a boy and in one scene, I jumped out of a window onto a horse. I rode bareback from the time I was old enough to get on a horse so that was fun for me. They didn't want me to do it but I wanted to jump because I was really crazy. I loved to do stuff like that. Naturally, when I had that fight with a boy, you saw me rolling in the street with him. And I'll never forget another stunt when Bert and I fell out of a tree and he fell on top of me. Then Thelma Todd and Woolsey got into the scene where we did a dance. That was very interesting because it was one of the first slow-motion scenes they had ever made. Of course, it was done normally by us while they ran the camera at a faster speed. Thelma Todd and I were on a bench and then Bert and Bob jumped up on the bench with us.

While I was making *Hips, Hips, Hooray!*, I was also in a play, *She Loves Me Not*, in Los Angeles. Doing both at the same time, I never had so much dialogue to learn in my life and I never had a day off. One night after the show, as I was coming out of the theatre, two kids in their twenties came up to me and said, "Miss Lee, can we talk to you privately?" My husband Marsh and some friends of his

With Bob, Bert, and Thelma Todd in *Hips, Hips, Hooray!* (Courtesy of Cole Johnson and the Thelma Todd Society.)

With Thelma Todd, Bob and Bert in *Cockeyed Cavaliers.* (Courtesy of Cole Johnson and the Thelma Todd Society.)

were several feet away and couldn't see what was going on. These boys suddenly stuck a gun in my ribs and said, "We want your paycheck."

I'd been paid Thursday. This was a Friday so I said, "I don't have it with me and if I had, I wouldn't give it to you. I work hard for my living." Then they ran away. I started to cry and went to tell Marsh and his friends. They called the police who caught the gunmen as they were fleeing on a streetcar. The next day at the studio when I told Bert and Bob what had happened, they were shocked and said, "Don't you know you could have been shot?"

And I said, "Well, here I am, ready for a day's work."

I also made some pictures for the smaller companies at this time but I don't remember much about them. They were mostly only four or five days' work. The last two movies I did with Bert and Bob were *The Rainmakers* and *Silly Billies* but I hear they were dogs. However, Bert and I did have a nice song in *The Rainmakers*, "Isn't Love the Grandest Thing?" After those two pictures, I went to Reno to get a divorce from Marsh Duffield and in 1936, I married A. G. Atwater, a Wrigley brother-in-law. Then I left pictures and moved to Chicago.

All during the years I was teamed with Bert and Bob, I'd continued with my tennis and golf and I'd gotten to know a lot of people. One time I played tennis with Ellsworth Vines who was known for years to hit the hardest tennis ball in the world. It was when I was married to Marsh and we'd gone to England. Ellsworth Vines said it was an exhibition thing and told me, "Now stand right in the center of the court."

And I said, "Vinesy, what—" Well, of course, if he'd ever hit me in the head, it would have killed me and knocked me over the net. So that was one of the greatest thrills I've ever had, playing with Ellsworth Vines. I played Ping-Pong, too, and could beat Joel McCrea and Cary Grant.

I belonged to the Lakeside Golf Club for years. I remember Babe Hardy was always there playing bridge. I used to take my little son to school when I wasn't working and then I'd be over there on the practice tee about eight-thirty. Bing Crosby and

With Zelma O'Neal, Bob, Joseph Cawthorn and Bert in *Peach O'Reno*. (Courtesy of Edward Watz.)

Bob Hope were always there when they weren't working. They would both say, "Hi, Lee." They always called me "Lee."

I'd known Bing years before when I was married to Jimmie Fidler and he was starting to make his big success. I remember one night Bing was playing poker with Jimmie and me when he said, "God, I've got to go home and get up to make a record for a hundred and fifty bucks." That's nothing now but that was big money then.

I used to play golf with Ruby Keeler at Lakeside. She was married to Al Jolson then and he had to go to Hillcrest Country Club because they didn't allow Jewish people to play at Lakeside. I thought that was crazy but they were pretty stuffy at Lakeside. Years later, Ruby was doing *No, No, Nanette* and Patsy Kelly was in the show with her. I didn't know if Ruby would remember me from our golf days but the usher said, "Oh, please come back to see her." There was Ruby and Patsy Kelly. I hadn't seen Patsy in a thousand years and, my God, she almost broke my back we were hugging so. I loved the way show business backstage had changed because here were Ruby and Patsy in this lovely room and they had a bar set up. I couldn't get over it because in our day—well, my God, if you drank, you were thrown out of the show.

It was when I was playing in a golf tournament in Agua Caliente in the early thirties that I first met Howard Hughes. He was a wonderful man when I knew him and there's nothing I could say against him. It was so terrible towards the end how it all happened when he got on drugs. But in the thirties, Howard became a good friend of mine only like a sister so there was never any interest at all. Whenever he was in some kind of trouble, he'd call me up and I'd say, "All right now, knock it off, relax." That's the way it was. When I was singing with Phil Harris's band at the Ambassador for about six or eight weeks, Howard brought Jean Harlow and a big table of stars to my opening which I thought was just dear. Naturally, I went over to the table. That's the one and only time I ever met Jean Harlow and I was greatly impressed.

I was always in awe of stars like that even though I was in pictures myself. I remember when I first came out from New York to do *Rio Rita*, I was invited to go to two different places. One was Buster Keaton's house and the other was Harold Lloyd's. The man who invited me was sort of an agent. He wasn't mine but I'd known him for a long time. I don't know whether he was AC/DC or what but he was a very nice guy and he took me to both of those places. So that's how I met both Harold Lloyd and Buster Keaton for the first time. Of course, here I am, eighteen, I think. I'd always worshipped these stars and to be able to go to their houses—well, can you imagine if you were in my place what it would mean to you?

I loved Buster. He was great. We had mutual friends so we used to see a lot of each other. We remained friends for years. Once I invited him to some party. He started to slide down some stairs and rolled down the steps. It would kill you or me but being the acrobat that he was, it didn't bother him a bit. He was very quiet, though, when he'd go to a party. I guess for a while he had a drinking problem but afterwards, why, if somebody was having some people over in the afternoon to play gin rummy, backgammon or some crazy game, he'd sit in and watch and was always very quiet. But when he'd laugh, of course, we really would get a kick out of that.

Most of the stars I met were nice people and not stuffy at all. I knew a lot of them like Sally Blane and her sister, Loretta Young. I remember I met Spencer Tracy at a bar when he'd had a few. He went back to the bar to pick up something and somebody said to me, "Oh, boy, is he carrying a torch for Loretta!"

I met Alice Faye in a nightclub when she was married to Tony Martin. She was very lovely and had beautiful skin. I remember she wasn't very happy about her marriage so I said to her, "Well, honey, do the best you can. It'll all work out." Later, they divorced. She married Phil Harris and they were very happy for years.

Constance Talmadge was a friend of mine in those days. I used to go to her house to play tennis with her husband, T. Netcher. Connie was a very warm, very real, down-to-earth gal. She was fun, too, with a great sense of humor. I remember she loved to play the piano.

Naturally, I made friends with other stars at RKO. June Clyde worked with me in *The Cuckoos* and she was my best and dearest friend for years,

Playing tennis at her home in Hollywood in the 1930s. (The Jamie Brotherton Collection.)

she and her husband, T. Freeland, the director. When I went to Europe, I'd meet them in London where they were working at the time. Until she died, we were very close. She was just out of this world—darling, beautiful, talented. T. was great, too.

When we were filming at RKO, Fred Astaire and Ginger Rogers would often visit us on the set and we'd visit with them on their set. One night when I was at a party with Fred, he asked me to dance with him. That was fun but, of course, in a ballroom he danced like everyone else. And when Ginger was married to Lew Ayres and I was married to Marsh Duffield, we played tennis together a couple of times and they were both very sweet people.

When I married Mr. Atwater and moved to Chicago, I had a different life than I had had in Hollywood. I was now a young society lady going out to luncheons. My husband and I took up flying because it was easier to go to the Walgreens, for instance, in a plane. I got my license and I flew our little single-engine plane—a Stinson, I think.

I was living in Chicago when Bob Woolsey passed away from a kidney infection in 1938. We'd heard he was ill and when he got sick, I don't think it took too long. I hadn't seen him since our last picture together, *Silly Billies*, and I didn't think he was too well then. But he'd never been sick before during all the years I worked with him. I guess he'd begun drinking more than he should have but I must say again, he was not a big drinker when we made those pictures. I think I learned he had died from my family in California who had read or heard about it. Naturally, I felt terrible. I think that the newspapers called me in Chicago and asked me about it. It was sad because he was pretty young. Of course, he was a lot older than I was but in those days, nobody paid any attention as to how old you were or something. I didn't realize until both Bert and Bob died that they were twenty years older than I was. Well, what the heck, I was eighteen when I started with them.

In 1939, I returned to show business for a time. I think I had just divorced Atwater. God, I've been married so many times I do get confused. I made some more pictures but they were practically just walk-ons. And I worked on the stage again. I did a musical by Sigmund Romberg and Oscar Hammerstein. I auditioned in Beverly Hills at Romberg's house and so I got the part. We did it at the Muni Opera House in St. Louis, an open-air theatre which seats as many as ten thousand—it's really something—and I loved it. It was so cute when Hammerstein rehearsed me all the time. Of course, I was still young and there were a lot of good-looking men and everything, so when Hammerstein autographed my book, he wrote, "To my favorite troublemaker." Being foreign, Romberg was a little difficult when I went to him a couple of times and said, "Gee, this song that I'm singing, it's—couldn't we pep it up a little bit?" But when I'd go to Hammerstein on anything, he'd be wonderful.

I went back to Chicago in 1939 to work with Gene Kelly who was just darling. He was doing a show there, *One for the Money*, and Gracie McDonald, the gal who was playing opposite him, left because she had a film contract. Then somebody said to me, "Well, why don't you go and work opposite Gene Kelly?" Of course, he was not well-known then but I soon knew he was a great dancer and I think it was a great compliment that I danced with him. He was the choreographer and a perfectionist but patient and very easy to work with—just wonderful and always a happy guy. It was so fast—we rehearsed day and night. Gene knew my work. I remember he once remarked to me, "It must have been fun to work with Bert and Bob." So he was really delighted to have me. It was like a vaudeville show and we did sort of a jitterbug dance.

I met John Barrymore at this time. He was playing next door with Doris Dudley in *My Dear Children*. Our stage doors opened across from each other so they'd come over and watch our show and I'd come over and watch theirs in between. And every night we'd meet in the pump room at the Ambassador because that's where I was living east and west. I did not see it but Doris Dudley told me the worst thing that happened was at a matinee when they were playing some sort of serious scene. She was sitting on the couch and Barrymore was so drunk he fell on top of her and she couldn't get him off. They had to make up some kind of a story or fill in in order to lift him and get him off of her. It must have been very, very funny—not to her—but that's one of the things he did that was so crazy.

I finally left show business in 1941 when I married John Bersbach. My mother and I were driving back to Chicago from California when we heard that Pearl Harbor had been attacked. Although I had just rented my house and everything, I said to John, "I think we're crazy to get married."

But he said, "Well, why not?" Being a single guy, a lot of people thought that we probably got married to keep him out of the service which was not true. He wound up in the navy.

Bert and I remained friends all through the years I was living in Chicago. I remember Bert was playing in Chicago in *Show Boat* with Allan Jones in a theatre-in-the-round type thing. I was still married to John Bersbach who was the father of all my children. We went to see him and then we had him come over to the house. Bert was sort of on one of his downers then but he was just so sweet and always took it with a grain of salt. I think he'd been very generous with his money over the years. When I'd go out to lunch with Bert and Bob, it would be Bert who'd pick up the check. He was just a sweet and wonderful guy. Years later, I knew he was up against it. He was living at the Lamb's Club in New York and I knew he was broke because he was not a good businessman. We hadn't seen each other for some time so one Christmas, I said to my last husband, Charlie Calderini, "Let's call him up, offer to pay his ticket and have him come out and spend Christmas with us." But he was ill with emphysema then and he died shortly after that.

A publicity photo with Bert and Bob from *Caught Plastered*. (The Museum of Modern Art.)

I lived my life I think just the way I wanted to. I wanted to be in show business and I was. Then I always wanted to have a lot of children and I have four, three boys and a girl. And I wanted to raise them myself. I did not want to have children when I was in show business because I wanted to devote my time, my life to raising them which is exactly what I did.

My thoughts about both Bert and Bob are nothing but the nicest. I mean, it was just great working with them. It was a job, you just did it and, of course, I loved every minute of it. When you're doing something you love, it really helps make you a success or whatever. And I was a good golfer and a good tennis player and that was about it. In fact, before I had my back surgery, I shot a hundred and one on the golf course about three years ago. So what can I miss? I've been so lucky.

Walter Huston and Constance Cummings in *American Madness*. (The Kobal Collection.)

1931—FROM STAGE TO SCREEN

Appearing in the cast of the 1930 musical, *Whoopee!*, was a comely young actress billed as Marilyn Morgan. Soon after, the actress, who had been playing small parts in pictures for over a year, changed her name to Marian Marsh. Her chance meeting with director Edgar McGregor led to a leading role in a play. With that experience, she was cast opposite stage and screen legend John Barrymore in the 1931 production of *Svengali*. At about the same time, another young actress named Constance Cummings arrived in Hollywood from a stint on Broadway that took her from the chorus line to straight dramatic parts. Like Marian, she had originally wanted to be a dancer and also, like Marian, she found her first screen success opposite a distinguished stage veteran—Walter Huston in *The Criminal Code* (1931).

The inception of their film careers is indicative of the revivifying influence of the stage on the screen in the early 1930s. Studios looked for acting talent with theatrical experience, whether novices or veterans, as dramatic films succeeded the craze for song-and-dance on the screen. In addition, films reflected a reciprocal relationship between theatre and cinema, with directors drawing from the stage to depict contemporary life in a realistic manner while, in turn, playwrights benefited from adaptations of their works to the screen. Finally, producers imported dramatists from Broadway to collaborate with filmmaking veterans of the silents to create original works in the new medium of sound.

Although historians have often discounted the dramatic film in the early sound era as they have the first musicals, the screen work of such distinguished stage veterans as George Arliss and Ruth Chatterton demonstrates the evolution of sound films with performers increasingly accommodating their style of acting to the cinema. In 1929, for example, Ruth Chatterton's performance in a stagy version of *Madame X* for MGM, broadly played to the point of exaggeration at times, was decidedly ill-suited to the intimacy of the camera. Just four years later, she starred in *Frisco Jenny*, a virtual remake of *Madame X* directed by William Wellman for Warner Brothers. But in contrast to the earlier film, Chatterton is deeply moving as she underplays the role, showing the same sensitivity for the medium that characterizes most of her work in the thirties.

George Arliss's first talkie in 1929, *Disraeli*, earned him an Academy Award, yet despite the wit and charm of his portrayal, it tends to be slow-moving with lengthy scenes reflecting its theatrical origins. Arliss soon recognized, as he stated, "the danger of a hangover" from the stage with "long dialogues that are needless and which limit the possibilities of screen technique."[1] In *The Millionaire*, a more cinematic vehicle in 1931, Arliss's serene humor is well-suited to a breezy tale of a wealthy retiree who shows he is young in spirit when he takes a job incognito in a service station. As Arliss effortlessly moved in a contemporary realistic American setting, the stage yielded to the wider world of the screen.

While veteran stage performers became acclimatized to the talkies, the cinema was also enriched by the adaptation of stage plays. Some of these were inherently cinematic while others were enhanced when translated into the language of film. Two pictures produced by Warner Brothers and featuring Marian Marsh as the heroine exemplified these trends. The first, *Five Star Final* (1931), was adapted from a Broadway hit of the period written by Louis Weitzenkorn; the second, *Beauty and the Boss* (1932), was based on *A Church Mouse,* a Hungarian farce by Ladislaus Fodor that enjoyed considerable international popularity at that time, including a 1931 Broadway production with Ruth Gordon in the lead.

Mervyn LeRoy's version of *Five Star Final,* like two other 1931 releases, King Vidor's adaptation of Elmer Rice's *Street Scene* and Lewis Milestone's dramatization of *The Front Page* by Ben Hecht and Charles MacArthur, was based on a realistic drama. But whereas Vidor and Milestone had to overcome a static one-set original through cinematic techniques—Vidor through constantly changing camera set-ups and Milestone through a continually moving camera—LeRoy had the advantage of filming a play that had incorporated cinematic treatment in its staging. For Weitzenkorn, instead of telling his gripping story of the tragic effects of tabloid newspapers on ordinary people's lives through one or two settings, had devised a play with over twenty scenes for a three-part stage. This allowed for swift transitions with major scenes played center stage and more incidental ones on either side of the stage. Thus, Weitzenkorn's drama provided a ready-made blueprint for a successful, rapidly-moving film. Even the film's most technically-striking sequence with the divided screen showing the anguished mother in the center on the telephone to the managing editor on the left and the publisher on the right derived from the original play.[2] However, LeRoy accentuates the drama through his sensitive direction of the players and his use of visual symbols that go beyond the capacity of the stage—for example, the repeated close-ups of the conscience-stricken editor washing his hands.

Beauty and the Boss illustrates the creative alliance between stage and screen that was now possible with sound as filmmakers improved on the original by "opening up" a play while retaining much of its dialogue. When it was produced on the stage, *A Church Mouse* consisted of only two settings—the private office of a bank president in Act I and a swanky Paris hotel apartment in Acts II and III.[3] In the screen adaptation, the viewer also sees the entrance and other offices in the bank, the elevator and other rooms in the hotel as well as scenes in an airfield, a nightclub and a garden that take the film beyond the static confines of the stage. In addition, director Roy Del Ruth imbues the narrative with a sparkle not in the play, enlivening it by the use of cinematic techniques such as the high-angle shot of the bank president (Warren William) pursuing his secretary (Marian Marsh) in his hotel suite.

The ultimate result of the symbiosis of stage and screen is evident in the creation of original works in which dialogue was blended with a technical inventiveness that rivalled the freedom of the silent film at its best. Two 1932 films in which Constance Cummings appeared, *American Madness* and *Movie Crazy,* are among the best examples of the new autonomy enjoyed by the sound film.

American Madness was the first joint project of director Frank Capra and screenwriter Robert Riskin. Fay Wray, Riskin's wife, observed of their long association, "Each one did better when they were with the other." With no stage background, Capra had learned his craft as a filmmaker in the silent era and continued to direct for Columbia Pictures in the early thirties. Riskin was a rising young playwright in New York brought to Hollywood by the studio in 1931 to write scripts. Capitalizing on the economic unrest and bank failures of the early Depression years, Capra and Riskin collaborated on a film about an idealistic bank president whose faith in people is in conflict with the bank's conservative board of directors. Riskin brought to the script his uncanny ear for the rhythms of contemporary speech and his ability to draw character. Capra gave life to the script on the screen, utilizing all his genius as a filmmaker to heighten the drama. For example, Capra introduced overlapping dialogue, rapidly delivered, intensifying the naturalness of Riskin's lines and accelerating the tempo of the film. He uses a montage sequence of more than forty shots of people spreading rumors, mostly by telephone, of a robbery at the bank. With each retelling, the story is embellished, creating a mass panic that leads to the run on the bank. The integration of sound and image, dialogue and action reaches a dizzying pace, a uniquely filmic approach to talkies in which Capra had absorbed Riskin's theatrical skills to achieve an emotional force that could not be duplicated on the stage.[4]

If *American Madness* announced the emergence of a major directorial talent, *Movie Crazy,* another milestone in the evolution of the sound film, was

John Barrymore and Marian Marsh in *Svengali*.

arguably Harold Lloyd's culminating achievement as a filmmaker. Although the credited director was Clyde Bruckman, a longtime associate of Buster Keaton, Lloyd as star and producer was the film's ultimate creator. Like Capra, he drew on a theatrical talent for his script, in this case successful Broadway playwright Vincent Lawrence who wrote the screenplay and dialogue for *Movie Crazy*. Under Lloyd's supervision, the new film, as *Photoplay* noted in its review, "marks a great advance in the use of comedy dialogue. It never slows down the action nor interferes with the gags."[5] Lawrence's well-constructed screenplay unified a story by Lloyd's writers of a naive young man attempting to break into the movies and his interaction with an actress (Constance Cummings) with whom he falls in love. Lloyd's flair for visual gags and his use of dialogue to develop characterization combined with location shooting produced a hilarious yet realistic look at filmmaking and the pursuit of stardom in Hollywood. In one sequence, Harold, employed as an extra, with his earnest but bumbling ways creates utter chaos on a location shoot. Lloyd's parody of the more banal early talkie love scenes when his character, convinced of his own professional abilities, overplays his screen test to the point of absurdity demonstrates the comedian's brilliance at delivering dialogue for satiric effect. At a time when Chaplin clung to silence, Keaton and Langdon were floundering in sound films and Laurel and Hardy were not yet at ease in full-length films, Lloyd, blending Lawrence's theatrical craftmanship with his own comic sense, created a feature-length masterpiece—in sound.

As these examples illustrate, the influence of the stage on the sound film, far from being negative, injected fresh talent into a cinema that could have easily succumbed to an expanding studio system which, by its very nature, tended toward standardized, formulaic productions. Without overshadowing those silent filmmakers who continued to shape motion pictures, the theatrical imports were soon assimilated into the cinema. Fledgling actresses on the stage like Marian Marsh and Constance Cummings were snapped up by producers impressed by their youthful freshness and ability to handle dialogue. Marian and Constance quickly developed as actresses on the screen during those years when the talkies once again became the movies.

Marian Marsh

In spite of the hard-bitten, ultra-sophisticated milieu of Hollywood in the early thirties, innocence did not die with the coming of sound. Rather, it remained a precious treasure, a lost ideal to be cherished. No one more effectively projected this imagery on the screen than a petite blonde named Marian Marsh. In many of her best films of the thirties, she incarnated an unsullied spirit resisting the corruption of a world filled with predatory males. One expert on horror films, commenting on her 1935 classic with Boris Karloff, *The Black Room,* described her as "the perfect storybook heroine. Her innocence, delicate beauty and vulnerability made an audience want to protect her from the lascivious, lustful fiends who were drawn to her."

She was born Violet Krauth on the island of Trinidad on October 17, 1913 and came to the United States after World War I, settling on the East Coast with her German father, her British mother and three siblings. Although it would be Marian who would become the celebrity of the family, it was her sister who first broke into show business as Jeanne Morgan, appearing in the *Ziegfeld Follies* and a number of silent films including D. W. Griffith's *The Sorrows of Satan* (1926), perhaps the director's last really great contribution to the silent cinema. Indeed, it was Jeanne's pursuit of a film career that brought the entire family to California.

The untimely death of Marian's father left the family in a state of financial uncertainty, a circumstance which prompted Marian and her brothers to follow in their sister's footsteps by seeking work in show business. Bit parts in movies soon came her way. But it was her acting on the West Coast stage that attracted the attention of producers and landed her the role of Trilby opposite John Barrymore in *Svengali.* Marian's appearances with Barrymore in *Svengali* and a follow-up, *The Mad Genius* were striking—a romantic iconography of a beautiful blonde controlled by a mesmeric impresario. Marian's portrayal of Trilby, in the words of critic Hal Erickson, was "ethereally fascinating."[1] Gregory William Mank wrote that one of *Svengali*'s "greatest charms and powers" is Marian's "strange, bewitching little Trilby," one of the horror genre's "most unforgettable performances."[2] Marian remembered Barrymore fondly and gave him credit for his advice on acting. It was never better for Barrymore than at this time in both his personal and professional life. But some years later, when she saw him again, he said sadly, "I'm not what I used to be when I played in *Svengali* with you." Another scene-stealer in both Barrymore pictures was character actor Luis Alberni who she recalled "worked very hard, rehearsing by himself." Playing with such professionals proved an invaluable experience for the budding actress. Like fellow Warner Brothers contractee, Joan Blondell, Marian was chosen to be a Wampas Baby Star of 1931 and would soon be given even more challenging roles by her studio.

Named in honor of Griffith's star, Mae Marsh, Marian demonstrated that it was not only her name that was in the tradition of her revered predecessor but also the type of role she played. Not long after her films with Barrymore, she registered with a haunting performance as a girl whose life is devastated by scandal in Mervyn LeRoy's *Five Star Final,* a powerful indictment of yellow journalism, starring Edward G. Robinson. Marian's character is engaged to marry a socially prominent young

With Ramon Novarro in *A Desperate Adventure.*

In the title role of *A Girl of the Limberlost.* (The Museum of Modern Art.)

man when the tabloid newspaper edited by Robinson boosts its circulation by replaying a twenty-year-old murder case involving Marian's mother. The "exposé" drives Marian's mother and stepfather to suicide. In the climax, an emotionally-shattered Marian dressed in black, looking like an avenging angel of death, confronts the newspapers' publisher, demanding to know why he killed her parents. She denounces the publisher for his arrogance in telling women in his editorials how to live their lives, then cries out, "You omnipotent coward, raise my mother and father from the dead!" Perhaps drawing on her own personal pain over her father's death, the teenage actress was able to match her veteran co-star, Edward G. Robinson, in emotional power.

There were other choice parts for her at Warners. Although the incipient social realism of *Under Eighteen* was perhaps compromised by a happy ending in which Marian goes back to her fiancé, Regis Toomey, she is convincing as a poor girl rebelling against her shabby tenement environment and engaging in a flirtation with playboy Warren William. In *The Road to Singapore,* her character with her bogus sexual knowledge disguising a fundamental naiveté makes an amusing contrast to William Powell as a sophisticated seducer. Louis Calhern plays her brother, a cold, repellent doctor, and Doris Kenyon is his wife, a woman whose craving for sexual love is fulfilled by Powell in this handsomely-produced pre-Code film of 1931 with an unexpected ending.

Beauty and the Boss (1932) is a delightful bit of whimsy in which Marian, as Mordaunt Hall wrote in *The New York Times,* "gives a most appealing performance and her voice is charming. She is vivacious and attractive."[2] Again cast opposite Warren William as a wealthy European banker, Marian reveals her skill in comedy in the role of a plain but efficient secretary transformed into a seductive beauty. Pitting her wits and charm against all the sophisticates, she wins William's heart.

After completing *Beauty and the Boss,* Marian left Warners. Freelancing for the next few months, she did not have the same opportunities, for the most part, that she had at Warners, and within a year, she was making films in England. From there, she went to the Continent to appear in Luis Trenker's *The Prodigal Son* (1934), one of the finest German films of the thirties. It is the story of a mountaineer (Trenker) who falls in love with a vacationing American girl (Marian) in the Tyrol and travels to New York in a vain attempt to find her. Although it was widely acclaimed in Europe, it failed to gain an American audience.

When Marian resumed her career in Hollywood, she garnered two of her most memorable roles. At Monogram, she starred in her favorite picture, *A Girl of the Limberlost* (1934). Under contract to Columbia in 1935, she played Sonya opposite Peter Lorre's Raskolnikov in Josef von Sternberg's version of *Crime and Punishment,* perhaps the director's last outstanding achievement in Hollywood. She recalled that Edward Arnold, who portrayed the police inspector, Porfiry, was particularly helpful. He would ask, "If I did this or changed my playing in the scene, would it bother you?" Marian's performance brought out all the poignance and gentleness of Sonya in this notable, if often overlooked, film from the year when Hollywood went all out for adaptations of classic literature.

During those years, Marian, her siblings and her mother all lived together in a large hillside home on Doheny Drive in Hollywood. Her sister now worked in films under the name Jean Fenwick,

With Otto Kruger in *Lady of Secrets.*

while brothers Tony Marsh and George (also using the name Fenwick) had small parts in several pictures including the 1938 remake of *The Dawn Patrol* directed by Edmund Goulding and starring Errol Flynn, Basil Rathbone and David Niven.

Despite her somewhat fragile, doll-like appearance, Marian had the youth and physical stamina to keep up a demanding pace. Typically, when she was working in pictures, her idea of relaxation was to take Fridays off, get behind the wheel of her car and drive north up the coastal highway some four hundred miles in those pre-freeway days. Her weekend would be taken up with playing tennis with friends in San Jose, attending a football game at Stanford, or spending an evening at the opera in San Francisco. Then she would drive all the way back on Sunday, sometimes arriving home very late but ready to resume filming on Monday morning. (She recalled that she drank a lot of coffee in those days just to stay awake.)

Marian's frequent attendance at sporting events put her in contact with many prominent figures in Hollywood. Among them was Will Rogers, an enthusiastic polo player. She would often go horseback-riding on his ranch at Pacific Palisades and remembered seeing him flying kites on his polo field.

She first met Gloria Swanson at a polo game at the Riviera Country Club. The two became friends and Marian was an honored guest at Gloria's daughter's marriage. Gloria, as Marian said, was "a very alive sort of person, straightforward, warm and very caring. She was always aware of what was going on around her and liked intelligent men. She was a good conversationalist, too, never dull and lots of fun."

Marian also became acquainted with Billie Burke and her husband, Flo Ziegfeld, at the polo matches. She found Billie lovable and thought they looked like sisters. Billie liked to have Marian around as a companion to her daughter Patricia since the two girls were near in age and Marian often stayed at Billie's beach house in Santa Monica. When the veteran actress resumed her work in films, Marian had a vivid recollection of Billie piloting her small car with the top down heading for the studio miles away.

Even though she remained a part of the Hollywood social set throughout those years, her career began to lag in the late thirties when she was increasingly featured in B pictures. She was always a striking presence but, in an odd way, her screen image and "singular talent"[3] was better suited to the franker pre-Code era than the period after 1934 when family films were in vogue. Whereas Fay Wray's persona had juxtaposed her delicacy with bestial figures, Marian's innocence had been highlighted by contrast with sophisticated, sometimes corrupt characters, whether the hypnotic Barrymore, playboy Warren William, or the whole milieu of tabloid journalism in *Five Star Final* presided over by fallen idealist Edward G. Robinson and an assortment of cynical profiteers.

A year after her mother died in 1937, Marian wed Albert Parker Scott, a stockbroker who had previously been married to a friend of hers, silent star Colleen Moore. She had a few more leads in 1940–42 but new family responsibilities including two children soon took her out of acting altogether. After Al Scott died, she briefly returned to acting on television before remarrying, this time to Cliff Henderson, an aviator and director of the Cleveland Air Races.

When I interviewed her in February, 1992, she was still living in Palm Desert in the one-story ranch house set back from the road and surrounded by pine trees that had been the Hendersons' home since the early 1960s. Widowed since 1984, she had been able to maintain her independence. Nearly every day, she would go to her office at Desert Beautiful, the nonprofit conservation group she founded in the sixties to promote environmental causes including protection of the mountains and beautification programs. Among her many commitments was her attendance at the aviation events associated with Cliff Henderson that required her to travel east three or four times a year. Her self-reliance, she said, had been encouraged by her mother, who had always called her "an independent spirit" and advised her to "make up your own mind."

She spoke enthusiastically about her interest in cars and mechanics that began when she was a teenager helping her brothers repair jalopies. Because her hands were small, she was able to reach in and clean spark plugs. Among her cars was a 1909 Buick she had inherited from her husband. She was still taking it for a spin on occasion and despite its early vintage, said she found it very simple to operate—as she put it, "You just press on the gas and go." Once she replaced the crank with an electric starter, she planned to drive it more often.

She had retained her slender figure. While not given to ornamentation, she was meticulous in her attire, preferring dresses and high heels to the pantsuits so favored by many of her contemporaries. She spoke with a slightly British accent, a reminder of her origins on Trinidad.

It was obvious from our conversation that she was devoted to the old Hollywood and had little time for the modern trend towards explicitness in films which went far beyond the more suggestive frankness of the pre-Code cinema. An even-tempered person, she was not one to confront producers and directors, nor did she complain about her roles. Indeed, in a rarity for a film actress, she said, "I liked everything I did." Her memory was keen and replete with details of a career that ranged from the heyday of Warner Brothers in the early sound era to the German "Filmwelt" of the thirties.

I come from Trinidad in the British West Indies. Later, it became Trinidad and Tobago. My mother's father was an engineer who was sent to the island of Trinidad by order of the king to clean up the swamps and take charge of Pitch Lake. Pitch Lake is one of the wonders of the world. Within seventy-two hours, no matter how much they take out, it rises back up to the same place. In the early days of paving streets, America was the greatest user of pitch from Trinidad and many of the ships came there for refueling. It was quite a port for refueling and, of course, Trinidad is right at the mouth of the Oronoco River in Venezuela.

My mother spoke with a British accent but not really an English one. The island people speak a little differently because there's so many languages. My mother spoke Portuguese, French and pidgin English as they called it with a few Italian words thrown in. My father was born in Karlsruhe, Germany. He was in chocolate manufacturing and he spoke five or six languages because, as a boy, he had travelled around the world on an old freighter.

After the First World War—I'm really not clear on the date but I remember I hadn't seen my father because I was born on Trinidad and he had left there when the war had broken out. But I still have a vision of my mother pointing out my father and saying, "There's your father, there's your father." And I was rather frightened with this great big man. I thought I was going to be eaten.

Then she started to cry and I couldn't imagine why. I kept saying, "Why are you crying? Aren't you happy to see him?" or something of the kind though I was just a little girl. She said he'd changed his moustache and that was a tragedy which I've always found amusing.

I was the youngest of four children. The others included my sister Jeanne and my brothers George and Tony. I think I was around four or five when we all moved to the United States. We automatically became American citizens after my father had his citizenship. We settled in Medford, Massachusetts near Boston. In Medford, there was a Ball Park Square—I remember it well. It was a very

As Sonya in *Crime and Punishment.* (The Kobal Collection.)

good place with all the shops around it and those big trees. I remember one time we were swimming at Ralston Beach in Massachusetts. It's the coldest water in the world. My brothers threw me in and I was furious with them for doing that. Then as I was coming out, I cupped my hands together and I saw I had caught a little seahorse. I was so excited about it I started running in to show it when I fell and lost it. No one would believe me—they said there was no such thing. Some years later, when my father took us on the ferry from Boston to New York Harbor to see New York City for the first time, we went to the aquarium and there were the little seahorses. So I've always had a fondness for seahorses and made a bit of a collection of them.

I remember, too, we used to go to the matinees of the pictures. We didn't like sitting in the balcony so whenever we could, my brother and I would sneak down in the dark. A few times we were caught and then the fellow got to know us so well, he used to come up and say, "Well, there's some seats left. You can come on down now." And I remember being terribly sick when *Beau Geste* opened and I didn't tell anyone because I wanted to go so badly. When my mother got home and felt my head, I had a high temperature and she was so upset. But I had a keen feeling for pictures at that early age.

My sister Jeanne was so brilliant that she completed her high school education ahead of time. She thought she'd be a lawyer and she also knew a lot about politics at that early age. She was very beautiful and very tall and also had dancing ability. In 1926, Paramount was running a contest for the outstanding teenage boy and girl in America. A friend of my parents who admired Jeanne sent a picture of her to Jesse Lasky without our knowledge. Mr. Lasky chose her as the outstanding girl and Buddy Rogers was the boy. It was headlines throughout the United States about the two of them winning this contest and I think the friend told Father he'd sent in the picture after that.

Jeanne had parts in pictures that were made at Paramount's Long Island studio. She was billed as Jeanne Morgan. She was in a picture with Buddy Rogers, she worked with Richard Dix who was a big, charming fellow always smiling, and she had a part in *The Sorrows of Satan* directed by D. W. Griffith with Ricardo Cortez, Adolphe Menjou, Carol Dempster and Lya de Putti. I recall visiting the studio and meeting Adolphe Menjou. My sister and I became good friends of William Powell who was also working at the Long Island studio then in another picture.

Jeanne had only great praise for Mr. Griffith and was in awe of him because he was such a big man. He was wonderful and I know she felt it was a great privilege to have had the opportunity to meet him. She remembered he was always a gentleman. He was very interested in the fact that she wanted to be an actress. He admired her, too, for her lovely ways and her intelligence. He said to her, "If you weren't as beautiful as you are, you'd be a terrific businesswoman." He also told her, "You have the beauty and the talent to become a star but you don't know how to play the Hollywood game." Jeanne said he always worked in a straight line and was always decided about what he wanted to do and how to do it. I think he took two and a half months to make the film. She'd be called back for scenes. Things were slower then. They had longer waits while they rearranged scenes or changed sets.

About that time, Jeanne also appeared on stage in the *Ziegfeld Follies* where she did a solo dance. She did some graceful ballroom dancing and was very acrobatic, too, with her beautiful long legs. She would dance with a rose and at the end, she would throw it on the stage, bend over backward very slowly, and pick it up with her mouth and with her arms outstretched. Then the audience would stand up and applaud.

In 1927, Jeanne went to the West Coast with my mother to work in pictures. I remained in Boston with my father and two brothers and then we drove across the country in an old car that broke down frequently. Once, we were stranded in a little town called Delta in Utah. There was nothing there but a farmhouse or two and my father had to get a ride to the railroad track to get back to Salt Lake City to get parts for the car. We were left there at this farmhouse with these wonderful people who were all Mormons. They took care of us and I went on my first bareback ride with a fellow who was related to these people. He must have been quite young himself and he got turned around so we couldn't find our way back. They couldn't imagine where we had gone and they even had the fire department's one little truck going all over the place looking for us because it was getting dark. But we finally arrived before everybody got too excited.

Jeanne played leads in westerns and I could almost guess her salary was fifty or seventy-five dollars a week. We rented a home on De Longpre Avenue—I think it was 6220 De Longpre—in Hollywood right off of Vine Street and down at the corner just this side of Columbia Studio. It was a four-story flat and we were upstairs. We knew a lot of very nice people there. I used to go to the butcher right across on Vine Street to get liver for my cat and he used to tell me I was so beautiful I should be in pictures. He was my favorite butcher.

My father had become the vice-president of Sanpeco Chocolate Manufacturing Company. He had also made a recipe so that when you covered the raisins and nuts with chocolate, it didn't come off in your hands—that's where that started. He had come out here to California and he took my brother Tony with him when he met these people and decided on the property where he would have the chocolate company. In those days, all you did was look one another in the eye, shake hands and say, "It's a deal," and they'd have the papers ready for you. That's the way business was done—with one little piece of paper.

Then my father went back to Boston to clear up everything and he caught a cold and developed pneumonia. My mother got word that he was very ill in the hospital so they arranged for her to go on the Chief, the train, to Boston. I think it took four or five days then. She walked in the door, he called her name and he was gone. So there we were in this strange California just so short a time and all the plans were changed because he was gone. That was a very, very dramatic thing for all of the children.

Everybody went to work because the money was tied up right at first. Then we did receive his insurance and where did we put it? Into the Hollywood Savings and Loans because the priest at the Church of the Blessed Sacrament advised us that they paid the best interest and it was a very, very hefty sum for those days. Within three weeks, a man named Beasmeyer had absconded with the money. It was a dreadful thing. A lot of older people had put their money in it. People actually committed suicide by jumping off the Taft Building which was the tallest building in Hollywood, I believe—nine or ten stories. They finally found Beasmeyer after I think it must have been a couple of years or more. They paid off something like seventeen cents on the dollar and that was that.

I was interested in dancing and acting at this time. I was going to Le Conte Junior High School in Hollywood where I went out for anything that was a play. The first thing I tried out for was a French play and although it was really a girl's part, they passed me over for a boy instead. But he became ill so they decided I should do it. I was speaking French—parroting it is the word—and I remember the French consul came back and complimented me on my beautiful pronunciation. That was very encouraging.

Later, I attended Hollywood High School. My sister continued to work in pictures and I really owe my career to her because she took me everywhere and later helped me get bit parts in pictures. We went on an old rickety bus most of the time at first. Finally, we got an old car. It must have been a Ford that my brothers worked on all the time fix-

Marian and other cast members Edward Arnold, Peter Lorre and Tala Birell read the script of *Crime and Punishment.*

ing it up so it could run. Jeanne learned to drive, my older brother George learned, too, and that was our transportation other than the bus.

One day in about 1928, I was walking my puppy when Nance O'Neil and her husband, Alfred Hickman, passed me on the street. They told me I was a pretty girl and I had a nice voice and said, "Why don't you come and see us?" They taught speech and movement in their home.

I told my mother and she said, "Well, let's go and see them." So I took training from them. They were very nice and very decided about everything. They encouraged me to do things the way I wanted to do them.

I also developed a lot of early training when I worked in radio at this time. I played Clive Brook's daughter in a half-hour mystery show we did once a week at Warner Brothers' station on Hollywood Boulevard. It was a small station with only a couple of rooms. There was never much room to move around in. I had just happened to go to the station. They wanted a girl so much and then they said what about me? I got seventy-five dollars a week for the part. I was still in high school but the school permitted me to take a sewing class as a substitute for my day off. Clive Brook was a gentleman whom everybody liked and I remember they said he was doing the series during a "slacking-off time" in pictures. We did it for a whole season and it was so successful that it was renewed twice for a three-month deal.

I also started going around to various casting offices to see if I could get work in pictures. I had changed my name from Violet Krauth to Violet Adams. I did quite well as Violet Adams since my picture was featured in many of the movie magazines—little photographs they used as fill-ins. Then I was chosen by Edmund Goulding to make some tests at what was then the old Pathé Studios. I was given a contract with them and they changed my name to Marilyn Morgan. They had a school. Lew Ayres, who was a very nice and sincere man, was in it and Carole Lombard was there, too.

I made short subjects for Pathé and one of them was a four-reeler short with Carole Lombard. We played sisters and we were making each other up. It was supposed to teach women how to use make-up properly. I think it was made for Palmolive and

Thomas
A feather in her cap, indeed, for Violet Adams, at an honest seventeen, to be given a chance to become a star. But to our mind it's an even more vivid feather in the cap of those who induced her to try that they succeeded

This photo of the budding young actress appeared in the June 1929 issue of the movie magazine, *Motion Picture Classic*. (She was then actually 15, not 17 as the caption stated.)

I would imagine it was some of the first type of advertising in those early days of sound.

Carole was lovely, a very happy person and full of fun. My mother became acquainted with her mother and they were great friends for many years. I knew Carole, too, in later years when she was married to Clark Gable. Carole used bad language from an early age. I remember that because I was surprised. I didn't know that girls used such language.

One time, I was on my way to the Pathé Studio in Culver City. It was about the first time I was driving a car and I was speeding because I didn't want to be late. I was to make a short with James Gleason and his wife, Lucille. I had three policemen who followed me into the studio on their motorcycles. They all had motorcycles in those days. So they came in with me and Carole, bless her, was around. I immediately introduced them to her and that started to settle things pretty quickly. The wagon had just arrived and I ordered them coffee and doughnuts. Then a couple of the producers showed up—Ralph Block I believe was one of them—and they said, "Why are you here with Miss Morgan?"

The policemen said, "Oh, nothing very important. We just happened along." I never got a ticket or anything else. Those were the days when those things could happen and it wasn't thought of as a horrible thing.

I visited the Paramount studio to see about getting a part there on loan-out from Pathé. I didn't get it but I was introduced to Clara Bow. I think we just said "hello." She was a bit nervous and was seemingly in haste. She was there to act and perform and she wanted to get started. I remember she was very nice and not an "It" Girl at all. She was very quiet and not talkative. She wore a pleated skirt with a big belt around her waist and was very graceful. I could tell how talented she was because she could use her face so well. Whenever she spoke, her eyebrows would go up. She was very small with lovely hair over her forehead and great big eyes. She seemed insecure about the talkies and found the whole thing overwhelming. I remember hearing her say, "It's all so new to me." She was all alone there. She'd go into make-up alone and do it herself and she'd come on the set alone. She didn't depend on anybody. I didn't think the studio was supporting her. She was such a big star and I think she could have had a longer career if they had been more helpful. I was impressed with what a nice girl she really was.

I think it was the training at Pathé that led to my getting parts at other studios. My agent took me over and introduced me to Howard Hughes and I was chosen for a little bit part in *Hell's Angels*. It was with Ben Lyon and I'd always been a great admirer of his. I had met Bebe Daniels who became his wife. In the scene, I had to point to him as he walked by and say, "Oh, there's the man I want to kiss." He came over for his kiss and then they grabbed him and threw him in the army.

As a result of making *Hell's Angels,* I became a good friend of Howard Hughes. There was nothing romantic about it—Billie Dove was his great interest then. He was more like my third brother. In fact, he'd come over to our house for dinner. He loved my mother and was with my brothers a lot. He also took me out and tried to teach me to play golf. But I didn't like it and was never any good at it. He'd drive me in his beautiful white Cord which broke down frequently. I'd have to call my brothers who would come with one of our jalopies and tow us out.

About the time I was in *Hell's Angels,* I made a screen test for Charlie Chaplin who was doing *City Lights*. There was so much scandal about Chaplin and all the young girls and so forth in those days. It was the only time I can remember my mother never leaving the set and never taking her eyes off of me. I didn't get the part but I got along with Chaplin very, very well. I knew him in his later years when he was married to Paulette Goddard. We used to play tennis together up at his home and he did all kinds of mimicry. He'd say, "Look at a cow eating grass in the meadow and a train comes along." And I'd swear the way he did it, you could imagine he was the cow. He was amazing.

In 1930, I was in *Whoopee!,* a lavish Technicolor musical produced by Sam Goldwyn and starring Eddie Cantor. My sister Jeanne appeared in it as one of the chorus girls in the big dance numbers directed by Busby Berkeley. Betty Grable was also one of the girls. She was a very beautiful, outgoing type of girl. Although she was so young, you noticed her because she was more outgoing than the others. Virginia Bruce, an exquisite, beautiful person who should be mentioned more often, was another of the girls.

Jeanne had introduced me to Berkeley and I got the part through her. I was in the scenes that were directed by Thornton Freeland, the main director. But it was Berkeley who did the sensational shots of the chorus girls. He was like a second Griffith—a Griffith of musicals—because he came up with new ideas for photographing the dances. You always knew he was there on the set—he was quite vocal. Everybody called him "Mr. Berkeley" and he always seemed to have time for everyone. People felt free to ask him for suggestions and he was responsive to them.

I was in several scenes with Eddie Cantor and in one scene, he was having an argument with someone who got out of a car. Then I was supposed to get out of the car to read my line and when I did, I slammed the door on his line and he was infuriated that I'd done such a thing. He got so angry he turned on me and said something about my not being very smart—he might have even used the

Flanked by the Goldwyn Girls are, left to right, John Rutherford, Virginia Bruce (Goldwyn Girl), Eddie Cantor, Marian (then billed as Marilyn Morgan) and Spencer Charters in *Whoopee!* (The Academy of Motion Picture Arts and Sciences.)

word "stupid"—to do such a thing. And I simply abruptly turned and walked off the set. He had just sort of blown up. I think he was annoyed by a number of things earlier. But then he came over, put his arm around me and said, "I didn't mean to get you upset" and so forth.

I said, "Well, I'm sorry I didn't know you were going to say the line at that moment when I was getting out of the car. But I had been told to close the door of the car so I was doing what I was told by the director." We got it all straightened out and we got on very well during the rest of the picture.

Of course, I loved Eddie Cantor. I thought he was wonderful. I never felt he had all the acclaim that he should have had. Some months later, we both found ourselves in San Francisco. He was playing there and I was in *Young Sinners,* a stage play directed by Edgar McGregor. We took turns going over to each other's theatres and we went to the zoo together where one of the chimpanzees fell in love with me.

I met Douglas Fairbanks, Sr. and Mary Pickford through my sister Jeanne when we were making *Whoopee!* Doug took a liking to me and my brother Tony. He loved to call us. This was sort of an out-of-the-world thing. He'd send his limousine over to our little house on De Longpre, pick us up and bring us over to the studio. We'd sit and watch all these old films so I think I have probably seen more silent films than most people have in their lifetime. We saw many of Doug's earlier clips from all of the different pictures he was in. He'd just sit there and tell us about it—how it was made and why they did the things they did. He loved the stunts he did. I never saw him go up steps one at a time—it was always two or three. At Pickfair, he usually went over the bannister rather than on the steps when he came down. I knew Mary quite well, too, and she was always very delightful. As a matter of fact, my sister was at her wedding to Buddy Rogers and they remained friends and talked on the phone for many years.

I was still making the rounds of the studios and one time, I went to MGM to be interviewed for a part. No sooner had I walked in the gate than Minna Wallis, an agent who was Hal Wallis's sister, grabbed me and took me to see a test of a new young actor. I rushed up the high iron steps in my high heels to the projection room where I saw a scene from a forthcoming picture called *The Easiest Way.* It was a little scene between Anita Page with whom I later did a picture, *Under Eighteen,* and a laundryman coming into a house. It was just a simple scene but the young actor playing the laundryman, a fellow by the name of Clark Gable, was very handsome and had a terrific voice. When Minna asked my opinion of him, I said, "He's absolutely fascinating. But he must have his ears fixed." Of course, they tied his ears down and he became a sensation.

I didn't get the part at MGM. Instead, I was placed under contract to Warner Brothers but they weren't even aware of me. I was still using the name Marilyn Morgan and at the studio was the beautiful dancer, Marilyn Miller. Warner Brothers called to say they had Marilyn Miller and they didn't want someone else using Marilyn Morgan. It was too confusing and they wanted me to change my name. So before I did the play, *Young Sinners,* at the Belasco Theatre in Los Angeles, Warners changed my name. My mother came up with the Marsh because she liked Mae Marsh and the Marian was just to cut Marilyn short. Now I was Marian Marsh. I'll never forget going down and seeing my name at the Belasco Theatre, "Marian Marsh in *Young Sinners,*" and I didn't feel anything. I hadn't gotten accustomed to being Marian Marsh which was rather sad, I thought. But after a while, by the time we got to San Francisco and the name was up there in lights, why, I felt differently.

When we came back to Los Angeles, Darryl Zanuck and Jack Warner came to the theatre. They'd heard about me and I guess they came to see for themselves. The next day, they called and asked me and my mother to come up. They had to make a decision very quickly on who was to play Trilby with John Barrymore in *Svengali.* They would send a limousine for us, Mr. Zanuck would be there and they'd take us to John Barrymore's house because he was ill and in bed. When we got there, I recall walking in the room and Mr. Barrymore immediately sitting up in bed and saying, "Oh, she's lovely." We were introduced, we shook hands and he asked me to walk around the room. Then I sat down and we talked. He liked my voice and he liked my speech and he nodded his head like he was saying, "Yes, very good."

Then I was asked to leave and Zanuck came out and said, "Well, we're going to make some tests of you. As soon as Mr. Barrymore is well, we'll call you." Ten days later, I was called, we made the test,

With John Barrymore and Bramwell Fletcher in *Svengali.*

and I was chosen for the part. I knew it was going to be announced in the papers the next day. I was going to a big dinner party at Pickfair that night. I called Jack Warner and asked permission to announce at the banquet that I was to play Trilby and, of course, Warner thought that was terrific. So I made the announcement at Pickfair. I remember Louella Parsons was there and several other news reporters and it was like thunder had struck because so many famous people were after the role. Doug couldn't believe that this little girl was going to play a role so important with John Barrymore.

I made two pictures with John Barrymore, *Svengali* and then *The Mad Genius.* The second one was made right after the first but they held it for a while because they felt it was too close to the other one. It was possibly the best period in John Barrymore's life. He was a very fit man then—muscular and trim. He was very athletic with quick movements and a stylish man. He wasn't drinking and he seemed to be very happy with Dolores Costello. She came on the set many times with their little girl who was named for his sister Ethel. I met Ethel Barrymore later and became extremely friendly with Lionel. One time, we played chess. Having a German background, as you grow up, everybody plays chess.

John Barrymore was a very pleasant, concerned type of person. I had been warned he might have an outburst but he was very well-behaved throughout the filming. He was a soft-spoken man, in fact. He looked you right in the eye and made good eye contact. When we were working together, he was very, very interested in helping me. He was very sensitive about our love scene. Archie Mayo, the director of *Svengali,* wanted to uncover me a bit but Barrymore didn't want that. He never said anything about my being young, though. He wanted me to be good in the part. Many times I'd felt he'd sort of turned the scene for me. Often, he would say, "Just take it easy, take your time." That was one of his favorite bits of advice to me—"take your time"—which was good because it made the timing just right. Whenever anyone asks me who my favorite leading man was, I say "Mr. John Barrymore." I always called him "Mr. Barrymore" and he called me "Maid Marian" or "Little Maid Marian."

Once he noticed I was sitting there waiting and he asked me, "Are you tired or nervous?"

I said, "No, I'm fine."

He said, "Your veins on your pretty hands are sticking out. You should raise them in the air and wiggle them a bit. Then all the blueness in your veins will disappear." So I did that and it worked.

With Louis Calhern in *The Road to Singapore.*

Archie Mayo was a very outgoing, loud man. He couldn't give a direction without bellowing. Although I liked him very much, I didn't think he needed to be quite so loud but that was his style and I accepted it. The cast included Donald Crisp who was a wonderful person to know and Bramwell Fletcher who was not long from London, England. I must say that everyone of them was so accommodating to me. We were all very, very close and friendly. But that's the way the picture business was then.

We were on the film for quite a while. They didn't make them in ten days, two weeks or whatever. I recall that they sometimes had the camera on rollers. There was a scene when I was the great opera star leaving the theatre with Barrymore as Svengali to go to the carriage and my former sweetheart, Bramwell Fletcher, was there seeing me. That was one of those rolling scenes. In the picture, I was supposed to be hypnotized by Svengali. I remember Barrymore had a terrible time getting out the contact lenses that he used to open his eyes when he was hypnotizing me. They explained to me that in hypnotism when the person is going under, they momentarily close their eyes. Then they open them again and seem as though they know exactly what's going on but they're really not seeing. I tried to get that effect. In another scene, I was supposed to be posing in the nude for a painting but a double did the long shot as she ran out of the room because I was underage. She was in flesh-colored leotards, I think.

Michael Curtiz directed *The Mad Genius.* He was very colorful and very temperamental. He could swear up a storm, go stamping off the set and carry on all by himself somewhere on the stage. He and Barrymore got along fine and had no problem whatsoever. The things that would upset Curtiz would be the scene would be perfect and the cameraman would say something was wrong and they'd have to do it again. That would really set him off. He just didn't like that. Carmel Myers, who had been in *Svengali,* was also in *The Mad Genius.* She was very beautiful, very quiet and stayed very much to herself. I never really got to know her too well.

I never got to know Zanuck too well, either. After a day's work, we were always invited to the very special place where they showed the rushes. Mr. Zanuck would reach out, hold my hand and I didn't know what that meant, whether it was fatherly or what. John Barrymore always came to see the rushes and each time we'd go into the main projection room, I would sit in a different place. But Mr. Zanuck usually found me and sat next to me. The third time he held my hand, I simply took it away and nothing was said. The next time we saw the rushes, we were downstairs instead. Mr. Barrymore came walking alongside of me and said, "Good for you, my dear." That was all but I understood what he meant.

With Anthony Bushell in *Five Star Final.*

After I had finished the films with Mr. Barrymore, I was fairly well known in pictures and I became acquainted with Paul Kohner, the agent, and Willy Wyler who turned out to be an exceptional director. It was through them that I met all these great composers of the day. For instance, they'd take me over to Beverly Hills where Irving Berlin was living at that time. There, it was always just music, music, music, of course. Irving Berlin had two pianos. One or the other was going, the phonograph was always playing something and someone was always writing some music.

Paul and Willy were part of a definite group that got together every so often. They would call me up at the last minute and say, "We're going to have one of these get-togethers. So-and-so has come to town and will your mother give us permission to come over and pick you up?"

The two of them would always come and take me over there. I don't know why—I guess they just wanted to arrive with a girl. They'd introduce me as Marian Marsh, people would say, "Oh, you're the girl who played with John Barrymore," and that would be sort of the talk of the evening. They had the most delightful dinner—just a scrumptious feast. Then they'd all settle down into their music. Everyone would take a turn coming up with something and would say, "You know, I thought of something this morning. Do you want to hear this?" They'd go over to the piano and play the little thing. "What do you think? Do you think that has possibilities?" That would be the kind of evening it was. We'd talk and I learned so much about the Broadway stage and things that happened there and, of course, about European things from Paul and Willy.

I met Jerome Kern at these gatherings and that was a great pleasure. He'd sort of seek me out and we'd sit and talk a great deal. He'd ask me what young people liked and things like that. He'd come up with verses that he'd recite and say, "How does that sound to you? Would you buy a song if you heard those words?"

Then I'd say, "Oh, it's so romantic. That's beautiful." I met both Rodgers and Hart and the Gershwins, too, at these get-togethers. I knew Ira better. George was more quiet. I just would meet him and

With Louis Calhern and Doris Kenyon in *The Road to Singapore*. (Courtesy of Cole Johnson.)

say "Hello." But what a highlight that was in my life.

Warners put me in a number of pictures after the two I did with Barrymore. *Five Star Final* with Edward G. Robinson was about tabloid newspapers. Mervyn LeRoy directed that picture. He was a very quiet type of director, quite different from Archie Mayo. He'd let you know it was all right by just simply nodding his head. He had a big cigar always in his mouth unlighted. Years later, I realized he was very young then but to me, he was quite old when we were doing the picture.

There was quite a lot of discussion about it before the picture started. We had three or four sessions reading through the script and seeing if all the words ran together easily to use in that dramatic way. I know I made a change or two. I said it was easier for me to say one or two words a little differently than it was in the script and they found no trouble with that. It just filmed a little more easily.

Before we began the picture, I met Edward G. Robinson and his wife. We had lunch together on many occasions. What I was surprised about was what a gentleman he was. He played these rough, tough characters, the gangster type and so forth—that's all I knew about Edward G. Robinson. But he was quite a patient person. I had a very dramatic scene towards the end of the picture and he was so patient about it. A couple of times, he'd say, "Don't put everything into it while we're rehearsing. Save it for when the film is running in the camera." And Aline MacMahon who was also in it came to me and said, "Save your voice," because, of course, the scene required shouting in a crying type of way. They both had had enough experience to know that you had to save yourself for the big scene when it was actually being photographed.

I took their advice and then barely came through. You really had to work yourself into that situation and, of course, we did it over and over and over again because they didn't use two or three cameras like they do today. They used one camera. After you did it the first time, you'd have to wait for the next set-up in the opposite direction and then the third set-up in still another direction. So it meant doing the same thing over and over. I had to draw on myself for the scene. Developing the emotion, of course, was the main thing and to have tears come naturally which they did. It was draining. I know that night I was totally exhausted. After we finished at about seven or eight, I sat in a chair in my dressing room for a while to relax from the excitement, the strength and power of the scene. My mother, who had been on the set to fortify me while it was being filmed, was waiting in my car, a Chevrolet convertible. Then I took the wheel and drove myself home. It took me about forty-five minutes—I drove up some winding hills—and I no sooner got home than I just simply went to bed.

Making *The Road to Singapore* with Bill Powell was a bit of a relief. It was a very easy picture to do. It was somewhat of a comedy—at least my part was airy and quite free. It was fun to be more like my age, like myself. I was a young girl who thought she was in love with an older man played by Bill Powell. I remember he said, "I can't believe this. Here you are my leading lady—that little child I knew." He was most enjoyable to work with and we remained friends for years. Whenever my sister and I would visit him, he'd say, "Here come the Trinidads."

Doris Kenyon who was a beautiful person also had a leading role in *The Road to Singapore.* And Louis Calhern played my brother. We didn't look a bit like brother and sister. He was such a big fellow and a good actor, too. Al Green was the director and he was a funny man. He had a big stick and when he'd want you on the set, he'd bring the stick along and give you a poke, then move the stick towards the set with no words. That meant you were to come. I thought that was rather a strange way to do it.

At Warners, I did two pictures with Warren William—*Under Eighteen* and *Beauty and the Boss.* As an actor, Warren was very precise. He was always perfect. He knew every line, every movement and he rehearsed by himself. When they'd be setting up the lights, he'd walk through the scene. He worked very hard at it. It didn't come easy for him like other actors who'd run through it once or twice and know what they were going to do. But he would go over it many times.

He died from a strange illness. They couldn't find out what it was as I recall. He liked hard physical labor. He built a wall and I remember he insisted I had to come to his house to see it. It was beautiful. He did it all by himself and he was so proud of it. But lifting those great big rocks and everything—I remember his wife saying, "I don't know if that's what brought on his illness, whether he strained himself or something of that kind." He

With Anita Page in *Under 18.*

was certainly a gentleman. But I recall all the actors in those days were gentlemen. Possibly I could think of a couple a little bit later who weren't but not at that period in my life.

Beauty and the Boss was a comedy based on the play, *A Church Mouse*. I wore a funny hat and a black outfit in it. David Manners was in the picture and Charles Butterworth, who had been in *The Mad Genius*, was also in *Beauty and the Boss*. David Manners was such a handsome fellow, very quiet and soft-spoken. I found Charles Butterworth delightful and as clever as he could be. He could just suddenly give that look of his after hesitating, that expression of surprise as though he didn't know what was going on at all, and all of a sudden, he'd come to and say, "Oh, ah, yes." He used to go to the Brown Derby in Beverly Hills and I'd run into him there every once in a while.

The director of *Beauty and the Boss*, Roy Del Ruth, was very quick to make decisions. Although he was a quiet person, he was impatient. You'd better know your lines with him and know them well. Then he would change things and give you a few new lines when he was testing you on what he was doing. Just when they were about to say, "Camera's ready" and so on, he'd say, "Just change that a little. Make it easier." And somehow, you'd remember that.

I really am amazed to think how many pictures I made in so short a period. I did *Alias the Doctor* with Dick Barthelmess who was very solicitous of me. We were on location one night and all we did was sit in the car and read the lines through the script because neither one of us had had the script very long. It was from just one picture to the other in those days and no time really free. We read the whole script there to get the gist of it so we'd know just what we were to do. I remember I had to drive a horse and plow in the picture and they didn't know whether I knew about such things but I did. That surprised them and I could drive it better than Dick.

I had made tests with practically everybody at the studio when I began working there. I made a test with George Raft and one with Douglas Fairbanks, Jr. but I never made pictures with them. I became a very good friend of George Arliss and we always had wonderful conversations. I never worked with him, either. We often talked about that and that I should. Mr. Arliss was a gentleman of the old school and it was very, very pleasant to

With Warren William in *Beauty and the Boss*. (Courtesy of Cole Johnson.)

have known him. He had a sense of humor about everything in a quiet way it seemed to me. At my young age, I thought he was one of the most sophisticated men I knew.

When I started making pictures at Warners, my salary was three hundred and fifty dollars a week. I had a director's chair with my name on it and a beautiful dressing room on a raised stage. On my birthday, my family surprised me with a Chrysler with a folding top. It was delivered at the studio and I was permitted to park it on the Warners lot.

Thanks to the pictures I did for Warners, I was very famous right then. I think I hold a record. I was on the cover of eighteen movie magazines—*Photoplay, Screenland* and so on—in a three-month period. A couple of them were from South America and there were one or two from Europe. My brother Tony put the whole pile of them on the lawn and took a picture of them with me in the middle of them.

In 1932, though, I left Warner Brothers. At that time, Jimmy Cagney, I believe, had quit temporarily and there was quite an upset with several of the players. I think I just got shuffled around and it probably was a very good thing for me in the long run because then I went on to other things.

With Norman Foster in *Strange Justice.*

I did two pictures for RKO—*Strange Justice* and *The Sport Parade*. Reginald Denny was in *Strange Justice*. He had started a small company which made model airplanes out of balsa wood. I was an extremely active person and it was boring for me being on the set all the time with nothing to do. So I got these balsa wood airplanes and got the prop man to set up a table for me. I got all my things—a razorblade, a toothpick, a jackknife and a few things that you use to put them together. I started making these model airplanes and little by little, the prop men would come over, the cameraman who wasn't doing anything at the moment, the assistants and so on—you know, whoever visited on the set. They'd gather around and watch what I was doing. Then when I'd leave to do a scene, they'd take over and start making my airplanes. I had to fight my way back to get in and finish putting them together. You had to use the glue and so forth, then you rolled the propeller up with a rubber band. It got to be a big thing so everybody was making one. We had our own names on them showing which was which. At the end of the picture, we flew them out on the lot and they flew very well.

Joel McCrea and Bill Gargan were in *The Sport Parade*. Joel was a very wonderful fellow. He was in love with Frances Dee whom he later married and I used to play volleyball with them down at the Santa Monica Beach Club. I had a lot of fun being with Bill and Joel. We spent quite a lot of time together, the three of us, just as we did in the picture. Robert Benchley was in it, too. Oh, what a delightful man and such a sense of humor! He always played little jokes on everybody. Dudley Murphy was the director and it was one of his first pictures as far as I can remember. I don't think he had too much experience. He would get very upset about things. He was a bit of a perfectionist and he wanted things to be just right but he was pleasant enough.

While I was at RKO, Wheeler and Woolsey were there and I knew them quite well although I never worked with them. They were Brown Derby people and I used to meet them there. There were a number of stars of that time whom almost any evening or afternoon lunch you'd see at the Brown Derby. Wheeler and Woolsey were just like they were on the screen—go, go, go, talk, talk, talk! You never could get a word in edgewise with them because they were so busy telling you about vaudeville days and pranks that they had played on people. It seemed to me that they were always in friendly competition with each other. One of them would always end up getting the last word most of the time. Don't ask me which one it was.

I began making pictures for independent companies in 1933. In *Daring Daughters,* I worked with Joan Marsh. It was rather difficult because at that time Joan had her troubles. I'm afraid she was drinking a bit and I know that I rescued her a few times when I found her sitting on the curb on the street. I took her into my dressing room and had to get her ready. I did befriend her in that way and she never forgot it. Many years later, we ran into one another in Ojai and she said, "Oh, you were just like a sister to me, a true sister, all that you did for me. I'm perfectly happy and wonderful—none of that trouble anymore." That was all we ever said about it. We had dinner that evening together with her husband. He was a writer, a tall, lanky, nice-looking fellow and he was just crazy about her.

About this time, Darryl Zanuck called and asked me to come to the studio. He was then at 20th Century. I remember Ronald Colman was waiting there to see Zanuck. I'd known Ronnie way back when we were almost neighbors up in the Hollywood Hills and we used to see quite a lot of him. Zanuck called me in and told me that there was a picture they were deciding to make. He said, "You know, I looked at some old pictures of yours and you really were very, very good. So I'm going to ask you to see this director and then you must be in touch with the producer," a man by the name of Al Rockett.

So I went ahead and made a test with an excellent character actor. It was a beautiful, wonderful, dramatic scene that I loved doing. I saw the test when it was shown to people at the studio and it was outstanding. Everyone in the room applauded because it was that good.

Then Universal called me and Harry Lachman, the director, wanted to see me. He made the immediate decision that he liked me and I would be good for the part in *I Like It That Way,* the picture he was going to do. But could he see me in something? I mentioned to him I'd just finished this test and maybe he could go over to 20th Century and they might run it for him. Well, he did and within two days, he called me and said, "If you'll accept it, we'll have the contract and I'd like you to come and sign it. We're going to start within four days." They offered me a wonderful sum of money, the best money I made, and I accepted it.

In the meantime, the producer at 20th Century called and wanted to sign me to a contract. He heard I was making this picture with Lachman and he wanted it to be under contract to 20th Century. He knew Harry Lachman had come over and seen the test although I think he would have picked me for it anyway. But the producer made a big to-do and a big row about it. I simply stuck to my guns and told him, "I have already decided to do the picture for Universal." It meant a great deal to me because it was good money.

You know, I had such good fortune. People were always looking out for me. It was as though they had spread their wings and were always hovering to protect me. The man who was the film editor at 20th Century called me. He was terribly upset and he said, "That was one of the best tests I think I have ever put together. You were sensational in it and they ordered me to destroy it. And I didn't think that they should." "Well, don't destroy it," I said. "Make up a story about it in Pig Latin." But he wasn't able to save it because it was part of his job to dispose of tests they didn't use.

During the making of the picture at Universal, I remember we had dinner often with Harry Lachman and his wife, Tia, I think her name was. She was a Chinese lady and very attractive. She enjoyed my mother and my mother enjoyed her. Lachman was extremely temperamental. He was an artist and often he'd stop work and take off to paint with friends of his.

Despite this, things had not really gone well for me after I left Warners. Actually, no one was asking for me when British Gaumont sent a long telegram about all they would do for me if I would accept a part. I remember my mother and I opened it late in the evening. We looked at each other and we both said, "Let's go." It was that quick a decision. We

With Gloria Stuart in *I Like It That Way.* (Courtesy of Cole Johnson.)

immediately made arrangements and took off within a week. We left before Christmas of 1933.

It was the best and smartest thing I ever did, I think, because it turned out to be absolutely delightful. Immediately on my arrival, there were several other offers that I couldn't accept because it wouldn't work out. But I did do a second picture for British-International and, my, they really knew how to treat an actress beautifully. I stayed at the Grosvenor House across from Hyde Park. I had a car with a chauffeur whenever I wanted it. All I had to do was pick up the phone which I did on several occasions. When I was going out at night to any of the big prominent things, they always sent the car for me. They really treated me like a star.

I also had a car on loan from the studio that I drove myself. Several times I got lost in Soho when I was trying to get back to the place where I was staying. This one time, I was holding up traffic because I was right in the middle of the square and I couldn't find which way to go. So I called out to a man, "How do I get to the Grosvenor House? Where is that main street?" That's all I needed to know. This fellow came up to my car and you can't understand a word they say in that cockney English. He roared and screamed his head off at me and then all of a sudden, he stopped cold. I didn't know what to think. I thought something had happened to him physically. Anyway, he suddenly recognized me and then he was so nice and apologetic.

One of the pictures I did in England was a musical with Bobby Howes, *Over the Garden Wall.* I danced in that picture. At the beginning of my career, I had thought I would be a dancer so that was fun to do. Bobby Howes was the toast of London at that time. You couldn't go anywhere with him without everyone catering to him and so forth. He had a lovely wife and they sort of took us over. My mother was invited along with me for everything which was a little bit unusual. In America, they never particularly wanted the mother along but in England, that didn't seem to make any difference.

I met many, many famous people over there, among them Fred Astaire and Claire Luce when they were doing *The Gay Divorce* in London. I used to go backstage all the time and see them. It had been a hit in New York and then they took it to London where it was an overwhelming success and played for months and months.

I also knew the Duke of Sutherland. I used to ride horseback at his summer home which wasn't too far out of London so it was very convenient. It was beautiful. I'd ride along with the deer running alongside of me and all kinds of wildlife along the way.

In London, I literally bumped right into Paul Kohner who said, "Good heavens, when did you get here?"

I said, "Well, it's been in all the papers that I'm the first American actress this season to come over to London to make a picture for British Gaumont and then another one for British-International."

He said, "Well, what dates are those?" And he just tied me down to when was I working, when would I be through?

I asked, "Well, what are you getting at, Paul? What's all this?"

He replied, "Well, I have this picture we're going to make in Switzerland and Germany with Luis Trenker and there will be six weeks of skiing on location in the Alps."

That's about all he had to say. I'd become quite a skier at home. I asked, "When does it start?"

He said, "It's starting almost immediately."

I told him, "But I'm in the middle of this picture."

He said, "I know but I'll bet something could be arranged."

So up to the hotel we went where we found my mother. We talked it all out and I said, "Well, you know, he said it would be good money." And it was. It was very good, better than what I had from British Gaumont. I said, "I'd love to go to Switzerland. All my life I've wanted to go to St. Moritz."

On location in the Alps for *The Prodigal Son.* (The Luis Trenker-Zentral-Archiv-Kitzbuhel, Tyrolia.)

And Paul said, "Well, I'll talk to your producers here." I gave him the names of the different ones—Mr. Balcon was the head of British Gaumont at that time. The arrangements were made and in between the second picture I was making there, I had ten days so we went to Paris and then on to Berlin.

We started immediately with the interiors at UFA Studios in Berlin. I've been told by Paul Kohner that this picture I did with Luis Trenker, *Der verlorene Sohn* or *The Prodigal Son,* was the last one they made at the studio before Hitler took it over. It was a large studio—maybe not as large as some of the studios in Hollywood—but the place was so clean. They treated me as one of their stars and gave me an early call for filming. Before we completed it, I went back to London to finish what I was doing and once again went by way of Paris, mainly because I wanted to see Paris a second time. When I came back to Berlin, we filmed a couple of other things and after that, we went to Austria for what turned out to be eight weeks instead of six. Luis

Trenker also filmed part of *The Prodigal Son* in New York but I wasn't in anything they did there.

Luis Trenker both directed and starred in the picture. But I wasn't too aware that he was actually directing it. He did have someone else who was doing most of the outlay. When we were preparing the picture, we read the lines together and in great detail. He'd correct my pronunciation and then he'd want me to say it in English. Even in the picture, I would speak a little English and then say it in German though I had forgotten that I wasn't to speak German. That's the way he handled it.

Luis was simply loved as a great sports figure in those days. He had made many, many rescues in the Alps in his younger life. If people were lost or endangered, he'd risk his life to get them out—things of that kind. There were some great stories about him and, of course, he was famed as a skier. He was really a mountaineer as he called himself and such a great skier that he knew those mountains backwards and forwards. He was a delightful man. It was just happiness all the time being around him and with him. He was boyish and, in a way, shy.

Part of the time I stayed in St. Moritz but we did all the location filming in the Austrian Tyrol. It was absolutely sensational. We climbed all the way up into the actual mountain, the deep Alps you would call it. They had over sixty people carrying parts of a set and different things they would use such as reflectors. They didn't have a helicopter to put those things on top of the mountain like they do today. So everything was hand-carried—cameras, equipment and so on. Then I came up with a guide and also my stand-in who did some of the harder parts—the more difficult skiing and so forth. The only way to get there was on skis so they put the skins on the skis because it was uphill all the time. While we were there, we would stay in these big partitioned rooms they built for skiers. It was a terrific place and the greatest experience.

One time, Paul called me and wanted to know if I would do the translation of the German for an English version. I spoke German in it and I had picked up quite a bit of the language. I did very well with it. Of course, I had known some German since I was a child but we spoke it very little at home. They did play a trick on me one time. They gave me a script and told me to study it. They said I would have to do it with great endearment, just loving and beautiful and so forth, in all this German. I didn't even

With Luis Trenker in *The Prodigal Son*.

bother to ask for a translation but the rhythm of it was quite easy to follow to just read the German. So I did it and twice they showed it in the rushes one evening. Everyone was hysterical so I was probably saying something awful. I never did inquire. I said, "I don't want to know. Don't tell me what I was saying." But they had a lot of fun out of it.

The Prodigal Son was voted the most beautiful film at the Venice Film Festival in 1935. I stayed in touch with Luis through the years. He was in his lake home in Italy when he had his eightieth birthday and he was on the cover of a worldwide sports magazine. I was in Europe at the time and I talked to him on the phone. Just before Paul Kohner passed away, Luis was to send me a tape of *The Prodigal Son*. Paul had arranged it but somehow I never did get the film. Of course, I've seen it two or three times on the screen. And making it, as I said, was a delight.

We made the picture during the time that Hitler was coming to power in Germany. He had been made chancellor and I was on the streets of Berlin when everyone was standing there raising their hands and saying, "Heil, Hitler!" The amazing thing was that from the time we left Berlin, went to the Tyrol for eight weeks and came back, it was entirely different after Hitler had gone in and gotten more power. Every time you walked into a shop anywhere, they'd say, "Heil, Hitler!," the women with very high-pitched voices and rather nervous. I would pretend I didn't know what they meant so I wouldn't do anything because I immediately had decided I didn't like the idea of this "Heil, Hitler!" business. I don't know why I decided that but I did. And so I just wouldn't do it.

With Luis Trenker filming a scene for *The Prodigal Son* in the UFA Babelsberg studio near Berlin. (The Luis Trenker-Zentral-Archiv-Kitzbuhel, Tryolia.)

I never saw Hitler other than when he passed by me in his car in a parade. Then I did raise my hand because everybody had their hands up and I was told to raise mine. My brother Tony had come over so he could be with me for a time and he took a picture of me. He used to say, "Ah, now, I've got you. You do anything wrong and I'll turn this picture over to somebody."

I'm a Roman Catholic and so I always went to church. When I was in Germany the first time, I'd have someone from the hotel who would escort me to the church, a young fellow to guide me so I wouldn't get lost. Because I was in all the papers and easily recognized, they thought I should have someone with me instead of my just wandering along the streets alone. When I came back the second time and requested someone to go with me, no one wanted to go near a church. That was out as far as Hitler was concerned. And there were tanks coming along the street on Sunday—big, beautiful, handsome tanks. The children would all be beautifully dressed to go to church as they were in those days and the soldiers—young boys really, they weren't men but teenagers—would jump off the trucks in uniform, talk to the parents, say they would take the children and put them in the tank for a little drive. Then they'd start teaching the children songs right away and it was "Hitler, Hitler," something about Hitler every other word or two.

When I returned to London after finishing *The Prodigal Son*, I had announced I was going to leave to go home. So the Duke of Sutherland invited me and my mother for a good-bye dinner. He had some wonderful people there and everyone was making a little speech about how nice it was that this American girl had come to London and all this. Then I was asked to say a few words. I got up and after thanking everyone and so on, I got on the subject of Hitler. I don't know what made me do it but I said, "Do you know what's happening in Berlin and what I saw?" And I described what had happened, how the boy wouldn't walk me to church and that church was a no-no, only for women and old people. I said, "Hitler has all of these tanks and trucks and things. That's a man who's going to go to war. I think you people better do something about it." My mother was pulling at me. She thought I was absolutely mad to make such a statement and she was trying to shush me up.

Well, the next day it came out in the newspaper. The story said, "She may be a blonde but she's not dumb"—that was the beginning of it. You remember there were all those jokes about dumb blondes back then. Then they told the whole thing of what I'd said. That was all printed in the paper but I wasn't really aware that there were any reporters in the room. I don't think it ever went anywhere from there but isn't that rather an interesting thing?

When I got back to Hollywood, I played the lead in *A Girl of the Limberlost* which I did for Monogram. That was my favorite picture of any I made. I'd read the book when I was a youngster in school and I was always in love with the girl. I thought she was wonderful and the whole idea of it, living in the woods in that rural, rugged way. When it came along, Christy Cabanne was going to direct it and I went directly to him and said, "I think I can be that girl." He liked me and that's how I got the part. Louise Dresser was in it and she was an outstanding actress. Being in a scene with her was very comforting because you knew she was going to do exactly what she was supposed to and she always gave you the lines in a proper way. We were on location out in the San Fernando Valley most of the time when that was just rugged and rough. It was not far from where I owned a ranch later in my life near Chatsworth. That was a movie colony all through there for a while.

I went to Columbia for one picture in 1935 and then I was signed to an exclusive contract for two years. My relations with Harry Cohn, the head of the studio, were very good. I found him to be always cordial. He was a good friend of the director, Eddie Buzzell, who introduced me to him. We had our first conference, not in Harry Cohn's office but in his limousine driving around the studio lot. There was no place to park so Mr. Cohn had the chauffeur keep driving from place to place while we negotiated my contract.

Frank Capra was Columbia's leading director at that time. I never worked with him but I was on the set when he was directing. I remember he was very emphatic and not quiet about what he wanted in a scene. But he was always very kind in that he would never say to someone, "That's terrible."

The first picture I did for Columbia was *The Black Room*, a horror film with Boris Karloff with whom I'd worked before at Warners. Boris played identical twins and one was the good brother and

With Boris Karloff in *The Black Room.*

one the bad brother. An outstanding feature of the picture was their Great Dane who recognized which brother was which. The bad brother, of course, had killed the good brother and the dog really let the people know which was the bad one when it attacked him. It was an old story and probably has been done time and time again. The thing that was outstanding about it in a woman's mind was the costuming. I had the most beautiful clothes, old-fashioned but really beautiful.

Boris and I got along beautifully. He was married and lived on a little street off of Coldwater Canyon. After that picture, he invited me as he had done before for dinner one evening. I walked in the door and to my surprise, there was a full-grown pig in a child's playpen. I asked, "When did this happen?"

His wife said, "Oh, someone gave it to Boris when it was just a little thing. Then it's grown bigger and bigger and here it is."

I said, "Well, what's its name?" And the name was Violet. That was the name I was born with. I don't know whether he remembered that or not but I know we had discussed my many name changes before I was Marian Marsh. Then the car pulled in and the pig started to rock. It recognized the car and it would go from its front feet to its back feet and squeal. And in came Boris with his long, long legs. He stepped over it, petted it and had sort of a little romp with it in the playpen. All the guests were sitting there enjoying it. It was just the darndest thing.

I heard that Columbia was going to make Dostoyevsky's *Crime and Punishment* and that Josef von Sternberg would direct it. I'd read the book and I always thought Sonya was a great part for a girl—very dramatic yet very loving. I went to Harry Cohn and told him that it was a part I felt I could do well and I wished they'd consider me. He sent me to William Perlberg who was the producer and Mr. Perlberg said, "Well, if you can make Josef von Sternberg like you"—I'd never met him before—"it's all right with me if Harry Cohn thinks it's all right."

I said, "Oh, I think Mr. Cohn would approve because he sent me to you."

So down the way I went to von Sternberg's office, walked in the door and he said, "Well, what can I do for you?"

I said, "Give me the part of Sonya in your picture. I think I could do justice to it."

He said, "Now that's very interesting. Do you want to read anything?"

I said, "Of course, I'd be delighted to."

I sat there and read for about an hour and he said, "I think you're just beautiful. You are my new Marlene Dietrich." Of course, they were having something together at that time. She was crazy about him. In fact, she was on the set often when we were filming. It was almost as though she was making sure that he wasn't paying too much attention to me. Boy, she'd really watch me and watch everything that was happening. We had several conversations and one time we had a little lunch together. When she learned that I had had a German father, that broke the ice some more and we got on just fine.

Von Sternberg was a very demanding director. He'd film so many, many, many takes, one after another. I think we got up to thirty-seven one time for something that was extremely simple and there was no other way to do it that I could imagine. I was working with two little children who were supposed to be my little brother and sister. I remember the little boy turned to me and said, "Can't you do it right, Miss Marsh?"

I said, "Do you think I'm doing it wrong?"

He said, "No, but the director thinks you're doing it wrong."

I said, "Well, I'll try harder again," because he was the sweetest little boy and I couldn't figure out what von Sternberg wanted me to do. There was just nothing else you could do but he wasn't pleased with it. Later, I found out from one of the electricians that it was the lighting on the set he didn't like and he kept changing it. He was his own cameraman, you know. He did the lighting, he did everything. And I must say that in *Crime and Punishment,* there were some sensational scenes.

Peter Lorre played the lead, Raskolnikov, and he was strange, let's say he was different. But he was right there with his lines, he knew what to do. However, he had trouble with the language. He would get a little puzzled and ask, "Well, why do I say it in that way?" Then he and von Sternberg would have a few arguments about it in German and in English.

Mrs. Patrick Campbell was also in it and she was simply a good sport and a real pro. She got into

With Peter Lorre and Douglas Dumbrille in *Crime and Punishment.* (The Kobal Collection.)

that character—this miserly old woman in the pawnshop—and played it well. She was ugly enough to make you feel a little bit forgiving to the fellow who killed her, Raskolnikov. We really didn't have very much time together because the part she had took just a few days of filming.

In another picture I did for Columbia, *Lady of Secrets,* I played Ruth Chatterton's daughter. We first met when the whole cast more or less read through the script as was the custom then just to get acquainted with it together. The first day on the set we were doing the wedding scene and I was in the most beautiful gown. She was the mother of the bride and it was obvious that she wasn't very pleased about playing a mother at that time in her life. She came down, saw the beautiful gown I had and she turned around infuriated and left the set. Everyone was very shook up by her attitude and didn't know what to do. The reason was she thought her dress was dreadful in comparison to mine and she wouldn't come back until she had a suitable dress. So everything was held up for two days which was pretty bad. They did shoot around on some other scenes that neither one of us were in. After those two days went by, she came down in practically the same dress with only a few frills put on it. But she seemed calmed down and everything went very well. There was still a little stiffness and so on and I didn't know what we should do about it. The director, Marion Gering, spoke to me and no one knew quite what to do about it.

With Robert Allen, Ruth Chatterton and Otto Kruger in *Lady of Secrets.*

All through those years, I was riding a horse. My routine was to get up at the crack of dawn for a ride and whenever filming was over, the last thing at night I would go riding again, go home, read my script and go to bed. One day, I was out riding when who went whizzing by me on a horse but Ruth Chatterton. I thought, "Well, for heaven's sakes, she likes horses so if she knows I like horses, too, maybe we could become friends." I slowly cantered after her, she finally went into a walk and I caught up with her and went by her. Then I turned back, looked at her and said, "Oh, Miss Chatterton, I didn't know you liked horses." I slowed mine down, we walked along together and little by little the ice broke and we were friends. By the time we came to the studio the next day, no one could believe it. She was so pleasant and everything was fine.

In those days, I was going to all the football games. I knew everybody at USC and UCLA and so I always wanted to get off on Saturdays. I casually mentioned that and she insisted that my scenes must be finished on Friday and I should have Saturday off so I could go to the football game. She was a licensed pilot and in 1935, I think it was, she flew her own plane into Cleveland for the National Air Races and was the guest of honor. The man who was to become my husband many years later, Cliff Henderson, was the manager and director of the Races.

In 1937, after I left Columbia, I had the lead opposite Joe E. Brown in *When's Your Birthday?* The first time I ever met Joe E. Brown was when my brother Tony and I were trying to break into show business. We were at the Shrine Auditorium for a charity thing and they wanted people to come on and perform. My brother and I had a little act together. He played a violin, I did a dance and we talked a little teenage stuff. Joe E. was going on, too, and he said, "I'll tell you what you should do when you go on. You learn to do what I do." You know, he'd open his big mouth so wide and then just a little "hello" would come out. So he taught us behind the scenes how to do that. We went out and did it and people just loved it. They applauded it because here out came this little tiny "hello" and they were absolutely thrilled to hear it.

Years later when I did the picture with Joe E., you couldn't ask for anyone more fun to work with. Everything was always up with him. I was playing a lot of tennis in those days and I won a trophy. A fellow named Shields who was an excellent tennis player came over to the set to give it to me because I couldn't be at the Westside Tennis Club when they were giving the trophies. Joe E. set up a place where we could have the presentation. They

With Joe E. Brown in *When's Your Birthday?*

did it in front of the whole cast and made a big to-do about it.

The director on *When's Your Birthday?*, Harry Beaumont, was more like a businessman. He didn't seem like the normal director. His approach was "Let's get it done now. Come on, everybody, let's go." No ups, no downs, just a very plain and ordinary manner. But he got the job done and he certainly had a good sense of humor because working with Joe E. Brown, you had to have that.

Joe E. Brown and I remained great friends over the years. He had such a background at the schools, both UCLA and USC, and he'd appear at all of the ball games, do his act and all that. His adopted son, Mike Frankovitch, used to get me all my football tickets because Joe E. told him anything I wanted I should have. In fact, Joe E. confided in me in later years. He had been married to Catherine, his wife and the mother of his children, for many years. And he met this girl unexpectedly. He was going on a ship somewhere and it was just one of those things. He thought that he would ask for a divorce. His wife had become extremely heavy. Here he was such an athlete till the day he died. He was a tumbler—an acrobat is really what he was. He had been a clown in the circus and he could walk the tightrope. He was everything and his wife had sort of grown away from that. They still got along very well—it wasn't that. It was just this wonderful thing that had happened when he met this girl. He said it was the worst decision of his life that he had to say to her that they couldn't be together. He was going to stay with his wife. He told me he felt he owed it to everyone who thought of him just one way. We both cried together over it. I told him I thought that was the most beautiful decision and that he was a strong and very great man. So I gave him a hug and a big kiss and we just had that look between us.

I did some pictures for Republic in the late thirties and I had the chance to work with some great names from the silent days. *Prison Nurse* was directed by James Cruze. I remember he always wore a cap and I know that he wasn't happy because no one's happy when things haven't gone as well as you'd hoped. It was hard on him, I think, to be working for a smaller company like Republic. I didn't really learn too much about his career until later when I was told more about him. It just seemed I was so busy in those years, one picture after the other.

Ramon Novarro was my leading man in *A Desperate Adventure*. I had loved him in *Ben-Hur* which I saw when I was very young. But he was rather stand-offish when we did the picture. He was a homosexual and there was a lot of teasing if you want to call it that going on at his expense on the set because the prop-men were real he-manish. I didn't understand what it was all about and somebody had to give me an idea of what was going on. But he was just as handsome to me, he did his work well and he was pleasant to be with as far as working together was concerned.

The last picture I did was *House of Errors*, made for PRC in 1942. I played opposite Harry Langdon. I had known him before I made the picture so it was a bit of old home week. In real life, he was always Harry Langdon, no different than the character he played—simple and pleasant. You'd say something to him and you wouldn't get any words out of him. You know, he didn't talk very much. He sort of raised his eyebrows and when he did that, that meant everything was okay and you'd just go ahead. The director would say, "Did you feel okay in that?" and he'd raise his eyebrows, turn his head a little and that was that.

In 1937, my mother died and the following year, I married Al Scott. He was a stockbroker in earlier years and then he was in business for himself. But he became desperately ill with meningitis very soon after we were married. It was a miracle they saved his life. It was the first time they had used so much

With John Barrymore in *The Mad Genius.*

of the drug that was used for polio patients. He had to be in general hospital. It was a dreadful thing to go through but it was the only place that would take him. A very great doctor, Albert Bower, who was instrumental in having the hospital built in Honolulu for the burned boys from the battleships, cared for him. At least, I'd gotten him into the best of hands. He recovered but it took four or five years of recuperation.

We'd bought some property out in Chatsworth and had a ranch out there with cattle, horses, sixteen hundred chickens and fifteen hundred turkeys—a big, big ranch. I got into that kind of life and left pictures. It was hard to take me out of it for a while, especially having to care for my husband. Then when he fully recovered, we had our two children. Later we sold the ranch and moved to Pacific Palisades. He smoked a great deal—nobody had said not to in those days—and he was on a trip to Spain when he passed away from emphysema. Now I was alone with the children in the home in Pacific Palisades.

One day in the late fifties, I ran into Butch Romero—Cesar Romero—and he said, "Marian, my goodness, you're just as beautiful as ever. Why aren't you in pictures?"

I said, "Oh, I don't know. Why would I want to be doing it now? It's all so different."

He said, "Well, come and visit me at the set and you'll get that feeling and smell that powder again." Months went by and I was right near Universal so I took a chance, called and happened to catch Butch in his dressing room. He said, "Oh, wonderful, come on over. We'll have lunch."

As I was leaving the lot after lunch, I ran into

Mike Levee who had been my agent at one time for a couple of the pictures I did. He said, "You're the answer to a prayer."

I said, "Well, what did I do that I'm the answer to your prayer?"

He said, "We were supposed to start this television program tomorrow and the girl who was to fly in from New York can't come because she's ill. You're exactly the same type as she is and you've just got to say yes and do this show."

I told him I had to make arrangements for someone to take care of my children first. I thought, "Well, he did things for me so why not?" Later, I called him and said I'd do it. We didn't even talk money or anything.

Two days later, I was on the set and the leading man was John Forsythe. I played the mother of a boy who was causing me trouble. Forsythe was the man I'd fallen in love with and we were trying to figure things out. It was a homey kind of thing. I no sooner finished it than Mike Levee said almost bashfully, "I have another one you could do. Couldn't you keep the same arrangement with your children and do it?"

I said, "All right, I will."

It was with Gary Merrill, Bette Davis's husband at the time. I had an entirely different type of role—it was very interesting. I guess Merrill hadn't even told Bette who was in the show with him so she came on the set about the first day to find out. I'd met her over at Warners when she was starting out. She came over to me and said, "What in so-and-so"—oh, a lot of language—"are you doing here? You retired. What are you getting back in this rat race for?" Oh, she just bawled me out for being there.

I said, "Well, it all happened like magic," and told her about Mike Levee.

She said, "Oh, he can talk people into most anything. You do this and then don't you dare come back into pictures again. You went out at the right time and everything's awful now in comparison." She went on and on and Merrill was so embarrassed because all of this was at the top of her lungs.

A portrait from her days at Warner Bros. (The Kobal Collection.)

That was the last acting I did. Some time after, I married Cliff Henderson whom I'd known since 1937 when I was a guest of honor at the Cleveland Air Show. We moved to Palm Desert in 1960 where I founded Desert Beautiful, an organization devoted to the beautification of the Coachella Valley.

I feel that films, like nature, should be beautiful. Too many films today are totally overboard in their emphasis on the common and the cheap. I have a thought that the beauty of the early pictures was their ability to make people feel better. Their true artistry was that they did not show everything but left it to your imagination. Pictures should be like reading a book where you imagine what's happening. And I believe that the beauty of the world is what we should all be seeking.

(The Kobal Collection.)

Constance Cummings

Of the actresses whose careers spanned the decades, none enjoyed more sustained success than Constance Cummings, who mastered every medium in which she appeared. Remarkably, too, in a reversal of the usual trend, this woman of solidly American roots born and raised on the West Coast ripened into maturity as an actress on the other side of the Atlantic where she became one of the great ladies of the British stage and screen. And as if to refute the hoary myth that the Hollywood studio environment inevitably wasted talent, it was as a leading lady under contract to Columbia Pictures in the early thirties that Constance Cummings developed the acting skills that led to her long succession of achievements in the theatre.

She was born Constance Cummings Halverstadt in Seattle, Washington, on May 15, 1910 and grew up in Coronado, California. Her father, a lawyer, died when she was fourteen and her mother had the responsibility of raising the family. In the late twenties, Constance migrated to New York with her mother for the purpose of entering the theatre. She dropped "Halverstadt," a name she said nobody could spell, and used her mother's maiden name "Cummings" which she felt was "prettier."

Unlike many other actresses, Constance did not follow a planned path to stardom. Her early work in the choruses of musical shows led, not to the career she aimed for as a dancer, but to several dramatic parts on the stage. Before long, she was brought out to Hollywood after winning a test over such other young New York stage actresses as Bette Davis and Claire Trevor to appear opposite Ronald Colman in *The Devil to Pay.* Although the part was ultimately handed to established screen star Loretta Young, Constance was soon given the leading feminine role of the daughter of a warden (Walter Huston) in a major prison picture, *The Criminal Code,* directed by Howard Hawks. *The New York Times'* Mordaunt Hall called her performance "convincing" and her career was almost immediately on the upswing.[1] She was under contract to Columbia, a young and dynamic company ideal for an aspiring new artist seeking to learn her craft. There she came into contact with some of the finest talent in the industry, including the studio's major creative figure, Frank Capra, who directed her in *American Madness.*

She quickly gained critical recognition for her work at Columbia and was soon in demand by other producers, including Harold Lloyd. The quality which the small, beautiful strawberry blonde brought to the screen, a unique and enchanting combination of freshness and sophistication, made her the ideal choice to play opposite Lloyd in *Movie Crazy* in 1932. She took on the role of an "erratic" leading lady whose mercurial personality perfectly counterpoints Harold's earnest but bungling character who is determined to become a film star. Although it was not successful at a box office affected by the Depression, *Movie Crazy* was well-received by critics of the day. Not only was it Constance's own favorite among her films, it has grown in stature over the years with her performance contributing in no small measure to its present recognition as "an absolute masterpiece," "one of the most unfailingly hilarious films ever made" with "warm, distinctive human touches."[2]

That same year, she was again loaned out, this time to Paramount to co-star with George Raft in the Prohibition era comedy, *Night After Night.*

With Phillips Holmes in *The Criminal Code.*

The film is best known today as the screen debut of Mae West playing a rowdy old flame of Raft, a gangland speakeasy owner trying to make it in society. But Constance is equally impressive as the elegant society girl who inspires Raft's ambitions for the more cultured life. With a glance of her eyes, the slightest intonation of her voice, she conveys a sense of romantic excitement as she yearns from her upper-crust Park Avenue background to be in the company of what she calls "the pirates of today" embodied in Raft's character.

Off-screen, it would be the eminent playwright and screenwriter, Benn Wolf Levy, with whom Constance would share her life for forty years and who would be the catalyst that propelled her into the world of the theatre. The two met in Hollywood and were married in Levy's native England in 1933. Theirs became a notable theatrical partnership with Levy directing her in a number of his plays.

Shortly after their wedding, however, she returned to Hollywood to make several more films. Two of them, *Broadway Thru a Keyhole* and *Glamour,* paralleled her own rise to stardom. The 1933 musical *Broadway Thru a Keyhole,* with a sprightly score by Mack Gordon and Harry Revel and appearances by Texas Guinan in her last screen role and Lucille Ball in her first, features Constance as a chorus girl who becomes a star. The 1934 *Glamour* directed by William Wyler is adapted from an Edna Ferber story about a chorine bent on winning acclaim as a dancer. Constance's last Hollywood film, *Remember Last Night?,* made in 1935, is a stylish mystery-comedy directed by James Whale with Robert Young as her leading man.

By the end of 1934, Constance had established herself as a stage star with the hit Broadway play,

With George Raft in *Night After Night.*

Accent on Youth. Concentrating on the stage on both sides of the Atlantic, she was soon recognized as a major dramatic actress in the theatre. In the title role of *Madame Bovary* in 1937, she was hailed by *The New York Times*' dramatic critic, Brooks Atkinson, for giving "the finest performance of her career. Beautifully costumed and made up with a kind of cameo daintiness, she moves through the play with the loneliness of a woman whose hopes wither away wherever she places them. It is a deliberately planned study in the graces of despair."[3]

Her natural sophistication was well suited to her adopted country and she remained in England throughout all the difficult war years, working on both stage and screen. She appeared with Roddy McDowall shortly before he embarked on his Hollywood career in *This England,* a film made in support of the war effort. He remembered playing her son in a sequence set in the Middle Ages:

> Suddenly there we were in this Norman sequence in this movie, running back and forth from bomb shelters in these ancient costumes. I was twelve and proceeded to entertain this enormous crush for this truly beautiful woman. I recall she had long blonde plaits and wore a white satin creation that was to the floor . . . and extremely form-fitting. I thought the sun rose and set in her elegant beauty and poise. I expect Constance Cummings was the first beauty I carreened over.[4]

Her most famous British film is *Blithe Spirit,* a romp into the world of the supernatural, directed by David Lean in 1945 from the popular Noel Coward play. The perfect embodiment of Coward's wit, Constance plays with ease, grace and restraint a wife caught up in a bizarre "ménage à trois." She is driven to exasperation by her writer-husband Rex Harrison, who just happens to be visited daily by the ghost of his deceased first wife (Kay Hammond) after a séance with spiritualist Margaret Rutherford. Long established as a screen classic, the Technicolor production, which won an Academy Award for special effects, helped to usher in Britain's era of bright, literate cinema.

After the war, Constance devoted more and more of her time to the theatre. She shone in everything she did, an eclectic body of work ranging over the entire history of Western drama from Euripides and Aristophanes to Shakespeare and on to Chekhov and Shaw, Tennessee Williams and Edward Albee. Her British stage credits included plays written and directed by her husband, *Clutterbuck* (1946), *Return to Tyassi* (1950) and *The Rape of the Belt* (1957). On Broadway, she appeared in *One-Man Show* in 1945 and as Gertrude

With Emlyn Williams and Roddy McDowall in *This England.* (The Museum of Modern Art.)

in *Hamlet* in 1969. Her two greatest triumphs on the stage were Eugene O'Neill's *Long Day's Journey Into Night* and Arthur Kopit's *Wings,* roles which she recreated for television. As Mary Tyrone, the addicted wife of failed actor James Tyrone in Sir Laurence Olivier's National Theatre production of O'Neill's drama in 1971, Constance, in the words of Edward T. Jones in *Literature/Film Quarterly,* is "enchantingly beautiful and subtle . . . No other actress in my experience of numerous productions of the play . . . has ever achieved the poignance of Constance Cummings."[5]

A tour de force performance in *Wings,* produced on Broadway in 1979, won Constance a Tony Award for best actress in the role of Emily Stilson, a once-energetic woman flyer and wing-walker who, after suffering a stroke, makes a valiant effort to recover. She originated the part of the indomitable but lady-like Mrs. Stilson for the Yale Repertory Theatre in 1978. Richard Eder wrote in *The New York Times* that *Wings* "is one of those occasions where an actor and a role meet and strike an incandescent life out of each other."[6] As the stricken Mrs. Stilson, "Miss Cummings, white-faced and searching, shows the pain and bewilderment. But she conveys something subtle and most beautiful at the same time."[7]

Constance did not rest on her laurels but remained active in the theatre into the 1990s. She had just closed in a short London run of *The Chalk Garden* at the time I interviewed her in April, 1992. When I spoke to her in the spring of 1996, she was beginning rehearsals, playing Vanya's mother for a London revival of Chekhov's *Uncle Vanya.* She continued to divide her time between her country estate and her home in London which was designed for Constance and Benn Levy by the renowned architect, Walter Gropius, in 1938. After their two children were grown, the Levys sold the main part of the London house, keeping an upstairs flat which Constance still occupied at the time of our interview. When she wasn't working, she would get in her car and drive about seventy miles to her country home, a 450-acre dairy farm with a herd of Holstein/Friesians, a perfect getaway for a busy actress and a convivial place for entertaining friends. She lived in a small house on the estate, choosing to sell off the large, beautiful Tudor-Jacobean house after her husband's death in 1973 because she felt it was "not the house for a single lady—too big and full of memories."

Despite her American background, she spoke with a pronounced British accent, the result of years of performing in England. She talked not only about the theatre and the cinema from her storehouse of memories, but also about politics. Although she modestly claimed she was not much of a conversationalist, her discourse revealed an awareness of public issues as well as as a keen intellect and sensitivity to her craft. She had developed her interest in politics through Benn Levy who, after World War II, was elected to Parliament as a member of the Labour Party. Even after leaving Parliament, he was active in causes like nuclear disarmament. His commitment to progressive politics, views which Constance shared, was never more evident than in the McCarthy era when he helped American victims of the blacklist start new lives in England. Those who were aided by his beneficence included dancer Paul Draper, harmonica virtuoso Larry Adler, writer Carl Foreman, and director Joseph Losey. Constance portrayed a screen star in Losey's 1956 film, *Finger of Guilt,* also released as *The Intimate Stranger.* Although its main plot deals with marital problems, its subtext reflects the director's experiences with the blacklist.

For all of Constance's lack of ostentation and self-promotion, this unaffected lady with the finely-sculpted cheekbones and sylph-like figure was a conscious artist, a woman whose perceptions born of practical experience rather than systematic training or theorizing could be cited in textbooks on acting. And it was this combination of practicality and imagination along with a modesty mingled with pride in her craft that enabled the quiet-spoken American girl to become one of the world's great actresses.

I was born in Seattle, Washington. My father was a lawyer and my mother was a nonprofessional. She did sing and she had a lovely voice but it was always in amateur performances. She sang in church a great deal before she was married. Her parents really felt that it was all right for her to sing in church but not professionally. I mean, she was never encouraged to do it and I think she might have made a name for herself in the theatre as a singer if that had just been automatically open to her as the theatre was open to me when I was a young woman starting in New York.

My mother's brother was also a lawyer. He was a corporation lawyer but he worked in New York with Sullivan and Cromwell. I had a brother, too. He was four years older than I was. After we'd moved to California, he went back to school in Washington when I was about eleven. He went to the University there and then he went east and got into the newspaper business.

We moved to Coronado near San Diego when I was about seven or eight and we never went back except for my brother. Coronado was a placid, quiet little town across the bay from San Diego. I was very happy there and had many friends. But my father died when I was still living in Coronado. I was thirteen or fourteen and I think I didn't know that much about him. We had no money at all after my father died and my uncle—the one I spoke of who was the lawyer in New York—sent us all an allowance. My mother did go to work. She worked in a jewelry store, a small privately-owned shop called Millner's in Coronado—they imported Chinese and Japanese things. I know they were still in San Francisco when I was there doing *Hamlet*—there was a big store there.

Constance recreated her chorus girl background in *Broadway Thru a Keyhole*. (The Kobal Collection.)

I remember in the days we're now talking about, we used to go every Friday night to the little cinema in Coronado. Of course, they had special films then for children with Bill Hart, *The Perils of Pauline* and all that kind of thing. I had my first stage experience in Coronado, too—that was just in one play. I went over and got a nonspeaking part in *Seventh Heaven* at the stock company in San Diego. When anybody ever said, "What have you done?" I always used to build that up as a great thing. But it was really my one week in professional theatre there.

In many ways, I wish I'd gone to a university because there are lots of things I'm interested in but when I was sixteen, I couldn't wait to get out of high school and enter the theatre. My family were Presbyterians. Some Presbyterians were against the theatre in those days but they were not that strict about it. My mother was all for me and I think she probably had felt that she'd missed something in her youth. Suddenly, I was there wanting it and she was going to see that I got it. In fact, I can remember nobody at that time saying, "You don't want your daughter to go on the stage." What they said to her was, "Well, Kate, it's a mistake. All little girls of sixteen and seventeen are stage-struck and to go off to New York and devote this much time and energy and the rest of your life and possibly her life on the fact that she may have some talent is a risky thing to do." She did get that advice but, anyway, she went ahead with it.

I really had always wanted to be a dancer from the time I was very little. About three or four years after my father died, my mother and I went to New York so I could study dancing. But there wasn't much classical dancing going on in New York when I first went there—nothing like the wonderful ballet that they've got now, the New York City Ballet. There wasn't anything like that in those days—it was mostly dancing in choruses of musical comedies and that kind of thing.

I got one or two tiny jobs in the theatre and I really happened into acting. While we were living in New York, my mother went to work in a shop called Wanamaker's which doesn't exist any more. It was one of those big reliable stores like Altman's. I worked in the chorus of the Gershwin musical, *Oh, Kay!*—that was the first one I did. It was not the original production, of course, in New York but it was a touring show with Julia Sanderson and Frank Crummit.

Then in New York, I was in the chorus of *Treasure Girl* by the Gershwins with Gertrude Lawrence as the star. It was a very good cast and there was some lovely music in it but the show wasn't a success. I remember meeting George Gershwin who was there a lot for rehearsals. One of my really exciting memories is sitting on the footlights—three or four of us girls of the chorus—and George was in the pit where there was a rehearsal piano. He played *Rhapsody in Blue* to us and it was marvelous. I didn't know Gertrude Lawrence then, however. That happened later because in those days, a chorus always worked separately, then came in and was put together with the rest of the show. But you didn't mingle much.

My mother and I lived in an apartment down on West Eighth Street. If we were rehearsing before the show, I would be at the theatre from ten to five—that kind of thing. And during the show, we would be there from, say, seven to ten in the evening. Aside from that, I was still taking dancing lessons all the time.

After *Treasure Girl,* I was in the chorus of a musical revue, *The Little Show.* Kay Swift did the songs and Danny Dare did the dancing for it. That's where I met Peggy Conklin and she and I have been friends ever since. Fred Allen and his wife, Portland Hoffa, were in it, too, but I can't say I was very chummy with them because they were stars and I was still a chorus girl. Fred Allen was a very, very funny man—I used to listen to him a lot in later years on the radio. I can't remember who was the compere to begin with when we opened *The Little Show* in Washington, D.C. but that didn't work out very well and Tom Weatherby said, "We must get Allen." He came in before we opened in New York and I thought he was marvelous.

I had my first acting role in 1930 in something called *This Man's Town.* It was a play about New York by Willard Robertson with whom I later did a film. The straight theatre seemed to offer much more than dancing. As I say, there wasn't much of it then. Then I got to understudy and play a small part in a play by Ring Lardner called *June Moon.* I knew Lardner later but I don't know whether I met him then. Norman Foster was the lead, Linda Watkins played the girl and I understudied her. It was the part of a girl who comes on the stage with some bottles of booze. Toward the end of the run, I got to play the part and so did the boy who was understudying Norman Foster. We were both put on for one matinee day to play because they wanted to see if we could take it on tour. They had a long tour planned. There was a man who was a kind of roving reporter on *The New York Sun.* I can't remember his name which is awful. He came in, saw the show and wrote a very nice piece about two young understudies. I suppose there wasn't much else to write about in the theatre at that moment.

Well, at the time, scouts for Sam Goldwyn were looking for a leading lady for a picture with Ronald Colman. That was how the Goldwyn people said, "Well, let's make a test of her." So they took a test of me and in a few weeks, they whisked me out to Hollywood. The film was *The Devil to Pay* written by Freddie Londale but I didn't do it—I got thrown out. Loretta Young got the part instead. Irving Cummings was going to direct it originally but they changed him—George Fitzmaurice directed it finally—they changed me and I think they changed somebody else.

It was terrible—I thought, "This is the end of my career." Ronnie Colman, who was a very, very nice man and very sweet, really understood how devastated I was because at that age, you know, you think it's the end of the world. Now I wouldn't think that but I did then. He had a friend in Myron Selznick's office and he said to me, "I'm going to talk to Noll Gurney and tell him to get you one film before you go back to New York. Then, you see, you can say you did a film out here," which was terribly sweet of him. Well, that film was *The Criminal Code.* He got me a test for it at Columbia, I did it, and then I was there for two years under contract to them.

Howard Hawks directed *The Criminal Code.* His direction was all right for that film because it was a man's film, you know. He was a rather stern man as far as I can remember. I don't remember ever having any rows or difficulties with anybody in working. But Hawks was very serious and he was not what you'd call a cozy person. I had a good time, anyway. I had the leading girl's part, it was an important film and everything, so I was very happy doing that.

Phillips Holmes, who was in it, was a very nice young man. And Walter Huston, who was the star, was a lovely man and charming to act with. He was a very honest, straightforward person and actor. He was not a man who had any tricks really at all. What he did, he just did it right. He was always very interested in everything. He was like a small child in some ways. You would see him on the set talking to a carpenter or a grip or one of the technical people, frankly interested in their job and how they did it and wanting to know all about it. And that's rare, you know. You don't see that very often. He was like Abraham Lincoln in a sense—he'd just played him for D. W. Griffith.

I made an awful lot of films in those days because if Columbia wasn't using me, they were letting me out to somebody. They let me out all over the place. I worked for Paramount, I worked for RKO and I worked for Warner Brothers which they arranged—I had nothing to do with that. I remember when we went on location in those days, it seems to me it was always Griffith Park. When you went outside, whatever it was, you went up to Griffith Park and shot it there.

It was a busy, happy time in my life. There I was a young actress doing well and working. I liked people and liked working with them and I found the whole thing very pleasant. I even liked Harry Cohn. I don't want to be libellous but maybe I'm one of the few people who did. He could be a bully and he was a bit of a pirate, et cetera, et cetera. I would think he could be very tough to do business with but I didn't because my agent, Myron Selznick, arranged everything. In some ways, Harry Cohn was like—if I say he was like a big baby, that sounds silly. But he was like a chap who was being tough because he thought he had to be tough. He had to keep that up—he couldn't let the image slip. But I always liked him.

Boris Karloff was in three pictures I did at Columbia—*The Criminal Code, The Guilty Generation* and *Behind the Mask.* He was a nice, solid kind

With Walter Huston in *The Criminal Code.*

of man. He came back to London in later years and I used to see him. He and his wife lived not far from me and we used to meet walking up and down King's Road. Because he was always associated with rather stern or frightening parts, he was a man with a very unexpected and delightful sense of humor. He was fun. So was Jack Holt who was in *The Last Parade* and *Behind the Mask.* He was always very jokey and bouncy, very funny—quite unlike the rather straightforward, stern type of character he played.

Another picture I did at Columbia was *Big Timer* with Ben Lyon. In the film, I was training him to be a boxer which is a pretty silly idea. I knew Ben and his wife, Bebe Daniels, for many years afterwards in London where they had a successful radio show. I knew them all through the war and I was on their show quite a lot. They were a lovely couple who worked together and worked hard and I thought they were admirable.

Frank Capra directed me in *American Madness* which I did for Columbia in 1932. The film dealt with the bank failures during the Depression. I remember being terribly shocked by them at the time. There was a big bank in Hollywood—I think it was the Bank of America—that absolutely closed. That was a terrible shock to me because I always thought if it was the bank, it was safe as houses.

In *American Madness,* I worked with Walter Huston again, with Pat O'Brien and Kay Johnson, a lovely creature who was then married to the director John Cromwell. Frank Capra was very nice. He was very meticulous in getting things right. I remember there was a big scene where there was supposed to be a run on a bank. Walter Huston was a president, I was probably his secretary and there were a lot of people involved in it. I remember we took quite a long time to get it right. I think Frank was a bit of a perfectionist. Maybe because he was Italian, he was a bit cozier than Hawks. I remember him as being fairly calm—I mean, he was not an excitable man when he was directing.

Movie Crazy with Harold Lloyd was a loan-out. That was actually one time where I had an argument with Harry Cohn because—oh, this is all very complicated. The script was written by Vincent Lawrence. *Treasure Girl,* which I'd been in on Broadway, was his book. And he did *Night After Night,* another film I was to make. Now Vin Lawrence was a great friend of my future husband, Benn Levy. I had met Benn by now—we were not engaged or anything like that but I knew him. Vin had written a play called *Washington Fight* which was going to be done in New York. Benn had read it and when Vin asked him, "Who should I get for

With Harold Lloyd in *Movie Crazy.*

the girl?" Benn said, "You ought to get a young actress named Constance Cummings."

So Vincent sent me the play—now that was the first time I met him or had anything to do with him. And I said to Harry Cohn, "Could I go to New York and do a play?"

He said, "No, you can't." I mean he was quite definite about that because he wanted me to stay under contract and be at the studio.

So I said to Vin, "I'm sorry, I can't. They won't release me."

Well, time went by and Harold Lloyd was doing his third talkie. He wanted to change his format a little bit, you see, and he got Vin Lawrence to write this script, *Movie Crazy,* which really was very good. Harold and Vin were talking about who should play the girl and Vin said, "You ought to get Constance Cummings."

Harold sent it to me and then he got in touch with Harry Cohn who called me into his office and said, "I'd never let you do this part with Harold Lloyd. All his leading ladies are just dumb blondes. They don't do anything and this won't do you any good. You can't do it," et cetera, et cetera.

I said, "Look, I've read the script and it's very good. You're wrong. This is not just a dumb blonde." So we had a bit of an argument. Anyway, he gave in and that's how I did that film. I was right about it. Maybe Harry hadn't even read the script because it wasn't a dumb blonde. It was a charming relationship between Harold and the girl and I loved doing it.

I adored Harold and his wife, Mildred, who used to show up occasionally on the set—they were very sweet. Harold was great fun to work with and a very unpretentious man for such a big star. Of course, he had a wonderful sense of humor. Since he produced it for his own company, I would think he did a lot of directing but kind of behind the scenes. I'm sure he knew what he wanted and how it ought to go. But he didn't throw his weight about. That would have been embarrassing for Clyde Bruckman who was really directing it. Harold would have a gag which he would want to try out. He had a couple of property men who'd been with him for donkeys' years and he would say to them, "How did that go?"

They might say, "I don't think that's going to work, Harold. I don't think I'd do that." So he

With Harold Lloyd in *Movie Crazy.* (The Kobal Collection.)

would take advice from these chaps who'd been with him forever and ever and he'd cut the thing out. I don't remember that we did a lot of retakes when we were making it. I think, especially in a scene like when he gets into the magician's coat and all the little birds and things start coming out at the dance, he would rehearse and get it right the first time rather than getting it right through a number of takes if you know what I mean.

Some of it was filmed right on the streets—for instance, the bit where he says he'll fix my car, he ruins the top and we both get poured on with rain. That actually did happen out on a street corner somewhere. Of course, there wasn't any rain. They had to put up a sprinkling thing on it and if you look, you can see shadows because it was really a sunny morning when we filmed that. But for those shots, we were on actual streets in Los Angeles. I suppose they still do it but in those days, it was very easy to just ring up the police and say, "Will you block off the street? We want to film." And I think that's what they did.

Although it was a comedy, Harold wanted it to be realistic. For instance, the shot in my dressing room —I think that actually was my dressing room at United Artists. You could see the shots of him in the street outside and you could still recognize it as the United Artists studio. There's a big scene where he's sinking in the water and he and the villain have a fight in it. That was a huge tank of water that was built in the studio. The actress I played didn't have a lavish Hollywood lifestyle. The car I drove in the picture was similar to the one I had then and the little house I was living in was quite modest—it was very like the house I actually was living in at that time. Harold was pretty accurate about things like that.

I saw a reedited version of *Movie Crazy* not long ago and it all concentrated on Harold's escapades and there were really charming scenes between Harold and the girl which had been cut out. I suppose they figured that's all that the public wants to see. In fact, I think when the film was first shown, its reception was a bit of a disappointment to Harold. I don't think it was completely the success that he had hoped it would be. I think that's because he was trying something new and people were a bit disappointed because they didn't see him doing just exactly what he had done in other films.

Another film I made on loan-out was *Night After Night* which I did at Paramount with George Raft, Louis Calhern and Mae West. Paramount was quite a big studio with an enormous lot compared to Columbia which was a small studio at the time. I don't think Columbia ever made any big extravagant, expensive pictures in those days.

My memories of Mr. Raft are very pleasant. He was very nice to work with. I knew Louis Calhern better later because he was a great friend of Martin Gabel and Arlene Francis who were also great friends of mine. But Miss West was a bit of a wild one. I never met anybody quite like her before. I don't really know what to say—she came from a different theatre, a different world really. She was egotistical. I think she was really not greatly aware of other things but herself. Maybe I'm being unfair—I don't want to be—but she struck me like that. She was doing her own writing, doing her own thing and living in her own world. It was her first film and she was very funny in it, very good, absolutely. I would have thought that she knew exactly what she was doing all the time. Although Vin Lawrence did the script, I think she had a lot of her lines that she'd done on the stage in her plays. She knew they worked and she put them in the film. As I say, she was like somebody from an entirely different planet. I don't think anybody had a row with her or found her impossible—I'm not saying that at all. But it's just that she moved through the film like somebody from a different kind of theatre. I do remember once in a scene with Alison Skipworth, who was a distinguished English actress, that I thought Mae West just should have had better manners vis-à-vis Miss Skipworth. But I don't think she was aware that she wasn't behaving as well as she might. I think she concentrated on her own thing and what she did was very effective.

My salary when I started at Columbia was, I think, probably a hundred and twenty-five dollars a week. After two years when they didn't take up the contract and I could leave, I think it might have been something like two-fifty a week which really was not enough for the work I'd been doing. You know, I'd had a bit of a success, everybody was happy to have me and, of course, two hundred and fifty dollars was worth much more then than it is now. But it was not a big salary and Harry Cohn probably would have been smarter to have paid me more.

I was doing *The Mind Reader* with Warren William at Warner Brothers—that's the only film I ever did for them. Harry Cohn had forgotten to take up my option. He tried to say that he had taken it up verbally which apparently is legally quite all right. You're supposed to take it up in writing but if you can prove you've taken it up verbally, it's good. Well, it wasn't and he hadn't. I'd been under contract for about two years with him. I think I had a five or seven-year contract. He was loaning me out, making a great deal of money on me, and Myron Selznick was saying to him, "Look, you've got to pay her more money."

Harry said, "Well, you leave that to me. I'll do the right thing by her." Then he went off to New York and he didn't take up the option.

I was in the middle of doing this picture at Warner Brothers when Myron Selznick rang me up and said, "Look, you must not go to work tomorrow at Warners."

I was horrified. I had never missed a rehearsal, a performance or whatever was before me. I said,

With Mae West, Wynne Gibson and Alison Skipworth in *Night After Night*. (The Kobal Collection.)

With Warren William in *The Mind Reader*.

"Well, I couldn't do that. They'd be waiting for me. I'm in the first shot tomorrow."

He said, "I don't care. If you do that, then Harry Cohn will be able to establish that he took the option up verbally. You have got to act as if you have no contract with Warner Brothers."

So I stayed home for two days. It was agony, I can't tell you, because I thought I was doing the wrong thing. I felt I ought to be there. What happened, of course, was Warner Brothers got on to Harry Cohn, there was a big to-do, and then Warners made a contract with me to finish the film.

During my years in Hollywood, I lived very quietly. I never got up to any pranks and I never did any publicity stunts that would have invited attention. Some people did, you know. They would do anything to get a bit of publicity. But my mother and I lived quite simply in a very nice little house on Sunset Boulevard. We didn't live in the Hollywood style with great entertaining or anything like that. We didn't even have a maid or a cook—it was just me and my mother. I drove a little Ford car—I remember it distinctly. It was the first car I'd ever owned and I was very pleased with it because it was my first.

As for my friends in Hollywood, I knew Mae Clarke well. I was very sad to see just a week or so ago in the paper that she had died. I also knew Louella Parsons's daughter, Harriet, well. And I knew Carole Lombard. She was a nice creature, a very beautiful, wacky, funny girl. I knew her family, too. She had two brothers and a very nice mother called Bessie. I had other friends in Holly-

With Eddie Foy, Jr., in a big production number, "When You Were the Girl on a Scooter," in *Broadway Thru a Keyhole*. (The Kobal Collection.)

wood who were not film people. They were friends of the family somehow, daughters of people my mother knew. I've pretty well lost contact with the people whom I knew in my first days out there. Most of them have left the room like Mae Clarke.

I went out with Carl Laemmle, Jr. several times. I don't know whether he wanted to marry me and if his father objected on religious grounds—he was Jewish and I'm not—I never knew anything about it. I think he thought I was nice—let's leave it at that.

I also went out with Howard Hughes once and Harry Cohn was furious. I had a ring—it wasn't jade but there was a green stone in it. I believe that somebody who was writing a column in Hollywood said I'd been out with Howard Hughes and he'd given me a green emerald ring or something like that. Harry got in touch with me and he said, "What's all this?"

I said, "Well, it's nonsense. He didn't give me a diamond ring."

Harry said, "Well, have you been dating him?"

I said, "No, I just went to dinner with him the other night and that's about as far as it goes." Harry was furious because he never wanted any scandal about me or anything like that. He always thought I was such a nice girl with a nice reputation and he thought that Howard Hughes was kind of a wolf. But that's about all there was about Howard Hughes. I think I must have bored the pants off him because he never asked me out again.

I met Benn Levy for the first time when I was doing a film at RKO in 1931 and he was writing a film there, too. He said, "Well, I'm working at the studio with her. I'll go up and speak to her." I think we just started talking and I liked him from the start. He had made a point of meeting me to tell me, "I have a friend named Vincent Lawrence who's written a play he'd like you to read."

Benn was a successful playwright who'd been brought out to Hollywood to write scripts when I met him. Before I knew him, he wrote *Springtime for Henry* which Edward Everett Horton did on the stage for years. In England, he had done the book for the Rodgers and Hart musical, *Evergreen,* which Cochran put on with Jessie Matthews as the star.

Besides writing plays, Benn directed on the stage. At the beginning of her career, Katharine Hepburn was in *Art and Mrs. Bottle* with Jane Cowl which Benn directed. But that was a pity. Jane Cowl played Mrs. Bottle and then there's the daughter which Katharine Hepburn played. Benn hadn't really cast Katharine and there was somebody else I think he wanted. I don't know exactly what it was but I know Benn didn't find this out until a great deal later. Jane Cowl took Katharine on one side and said, "Look, don't pay any attention to the fact that the author who's directing this doesn't like you. I like you and I think you're very talented. I'll kind of direct you on the side if it will be any help to you"—something like this. So, of course, Katharine thought Benn didn't like her and I think she had a very unhappy time during the rehearsals.

When the opening night came, Benn always sent flowers to all the ladies in plays he was connected with. He saw some white lilies and he thought, "Oh, these are beautiful." He sent those to Katharine and I think she took this to mean "Well, it's your funeral." It was some extraordinary, very unhappy thing and I think she never liked Benn after that. I've seen her several times over the years. The last time I remember seeing her was when I was doing *Wings* in New York. She came to see the play, she came backstage and was very, very sweet to me, very complimentary.

Benn had a circle of writing friends in Hollywood in the thirties and I met them through him. I remember particularly Vin Lawrence and James Cain. Benn had met Vin in New York even before he went to Hollywood. Vin was unique—a surprising character. He was his own man. You couldn't put him into a category, I don't think. James Cain, who wrote *Double Indemnity* and *The Postman Always Rings Twice,* knew my mother, too. He used to beau her around a bit and she liked him very much but that was all.

It was early in 1933 and I'd just finished *The Mind Reader.* Now I had no contract with Harry Cohn but in the meantime, I'd been invited to come to England to do a film. I'd never been to England before—in fact, I'd never been out of America—and I thought, "Oh, yippee! That's just the tops." I went on a ship. I remember meeting David Niven on the boat going over—that was just before he got into films. In London, I did two films in 1933—the one I was brought over for, *Heads*

With Texas Guinan in *Broadway Thru a Keyhole*. (The Kobal Collection.)

We Go with Frank Lawton and then *Channel Crossing* with Matheson Lang for the British-Gaumont studio in Shepherd's Bush. Frankie Lawton was a good actor and a terribly nice young man. He was married to Evelyn Laye, a lady who could sing—she had a lovely voice. Matheson Lang was of the old school. He was an Edwardian and he might seem a bit stagy now but he was a very good actor and well-known.

The British film studios in the thirties were smaller than the American studios at that time. None had a roster of big stars like MGM. There were no long-term contracts in the British cinema then as I recall. They cast each picture as they were going to do it. I think my salary was bigger with the British studios than it had been with Columbia and I know I got excellent, red-carpet treatment from them. Michael Balcon, who ran British-Gaumont in those days, was very nice. I knew him personally as well as professionally. Both Benn and I were friends of his. And I've remained close to his daughter, Jill.

Benn and I were planning to marry when I came to England for the first time. He already had a house in London—the address was Number One Justice Walk which was very sweet. He'd lived in that house for a couple of years. When I first arrived over here, he was still in Hollywood so I lived there for a time. I had a car, too, that I drove myself around in. When he came back, I lived in a little Mews flat which somebody got for me—I suppose the studio got it for me. Then after I'd done the

With Russ Columbo in *Broadway Thru a Keyhole*. (The Kobal Collection.)

picture, Benn and I got married and I naturally moved into his house. It's not far from where I live now. If you go down Church Street and you turn left just before you get to the river, you get into Justice Walk, a tiny little street which runs into Lawrence Street. It's only a two-minute walk from here which is just a coincidence really because then we lived in one or two other houses before we built the house on Church Street.

Not long after I was married, my mother moved out of the house we had lived in in Hollywood into a smaller, more self-contained house because she was by herself and it was better. From then on, although I went back to New York and did plays and went back to Hollywood for films, Benn and I were more or less based in London. Benn did continue to go out to Hollywood for quite a number of years. He would go for about three months out of the year, they paid him very well and he would write these screenplays which, by and large, they never used. They always got somebody else to come in and rewrite it.

Shortly after we were married, I went back to Hollywood in the summer of 1933 to make *Broadway Thru a Keyhole* for Darryl Zanuck's 20th Century company. Lowell Sherman was the director and Russ Columbo and Texas Guinan were in the cast. All three of them died not long after—it was a pity. Lowell Sherman was a very sophisticated, funny man. Russ Columbo was a nice young chap, a good actor and I enjoyed acting with him. It was a terrible thing how he died, wasn't it? He was looking at a gun somebody had and it went off. I remember hearing that they didn't dare tell his mother about it. Texas Guinan was a different cup of tea completely from Mae West. She was a warm, nice, full-blooded woman. I remember I was very shocked when I heard that she died because it was a short time afterwards.

Broadway Thru a Keyhole was a musical. Walter Winchell wrote the story and it was based on the lives of Ruby Keeler and Al Jolson. I can't remember who the gangster was supposed to be based on but I believe Winchell's story was probably fairly true. I sang in that picture with Eddie Foy, Jr. and Russ Columbo but it was just a cozy little kind of getting-away-with-something. You see, when I did that film, I wasn't too long out of the chorus where I had done singing. I'd never sung solo but I'd belted out in the chorus.

I did three pictures in Hollywood in 1934. The first, *Looking for Trouble,* was made at 20th Century with Spencer Tracy who was a lovely actor, one of the greatest. Like Walter Huston, he was a very honest, straightforward character with no nonsense about him. This was long before he'd met Katie Hepburn. I don't remember any problems he had with drinking. I mean, he was always there and working as far as I knew. William Wellman, the director, was very nice, too, but I don't remember him awfully well.

Then I was in *This Man Is Mine* which was done at RKO with Irene Dunne, Ralph Bellamy and Kay Johnson. It was playing here on the television about three months ago and I thought, "Oh, my goodness, that's fun. I'll have a look at it." So I did and this is going to sound silly—I thought I was very good in it. I was surprised. I hadn't remembered a great deal about it except I liked making it, I liked John Cromwell who directed it, and then, of course, I loved Kay, his wife.

The thing that I remember about it is not actually making it but about going to one of the previews. They took it to Pasadena or somewhere and we all went to look. I played the scheming "other woman" and there's a point when Ralph Bellamy has really had enough of my shenanigans and he slaps me on the face. When he did that, several people in the audience gave a little applause. "Oh, that's right," they said. I was so thrilled because it

With Spencer Tracy in *Looking for Trouble.*

was the first time that I had ever played anything but a very nice young woman. When I was going to do *This Man is Mine,* someone said to me, "You can't play parts like that."

I said, "But I want to play it." At Columbia, Harry Cohn had never let me be cast as anything except somebody's young daughter or somebody's very respectable secretary. They were good parts but I kept thinking I'd like to try something else. So when I played this bad girl in the film and got this reaction from the audience who thought a slap in the face served me right, I was thrilled because I

With Ralph Bellamy and Irene Dunne in *This Man Is Mine.* (The Museum of Modern Art.)

thought I'd done it well. They really believed me. They think I'm a bitch and how nice to be able to do that instead of just be a nice thing. You see, in the thirties, you were either the heroine or the villainess and if you were a heroine, you didn't play baddies ever. And you've got to play all kinds of parts if you really like acting.

After *This Man is Mine,* I did *Glamour* at Universal. The leading man, Paul Lukas, was a delightful man and with all the charm that you saw on the screen. That was really like him—that wasn't put on. Willy Wyler was the director. I've always liked Willy and knew him for a long time afterwards. I knew his daughter, Kathy, too. When you've known people, it's very hard to say, "Well, my first impression was so-and-so" because it changes. But I don't remember him as ever being difficult.

I'll tell you what I do remember about making *Glamour.* Coming down to the studio one day, I found out there had to be a child in the film—I think it was a little girl. Anyway, I had a child of about three or four in it. Willy said to me, "Look, I want you to come over here on the set and help me decide something." So I went over and there were lots of mothers with children—one of these had to be chosen as my child. Willy said, "Which one do you fancy?" And I thought I could kill him because we were facing this array of mothers with their little babies on their laps wanting them to be picked. I thought, "This is a bloody awful job to ask anybody to do." In the end, I didn't pick any of them but it was a horrible moment.

I was known as an actress in films before I got good parts in the theatre. I finally returned to the stage in England in 1934 when I did Vin Lawrence's play, *Sour Grapes.* Then I went back to America and did Sam Raphelson's play, *Accent on Youth.* That ran for nearly a year on Broadway. That was the first play I did in New York in which I really had the leading part. It was a charming play. I think probably it could be revived. I don't know—I haven't read it for ages.

Following my appearance in *Accent on Youth,* I went back to Hollywood and Universal for *Remember Last Night?* in 1935. Jimmy Whale directed that film. I thought he was very good. He'd been a friend of Benn's, of course, in England before he went to Hollywood. Back in the late twenties, Jimmy was in a play with Charles Laughton, *The Man with Red Hair,* which Benn adapted from a book of Hugh Walpole's. I think that was Charles's first really big success here and Jimmy played his son, I believe. Then in Hollywood, Benn adapted *The Old Dark House* from J. B. Priestley's novel, a film with Charles which Jimmy directed.

Remember Last Night? was my final film for a Hollywood studio but I still get pictures sent to me that were taken in early days in Hollywood, pictures where the retoucher had been at them. That makes me very angry. They would cut the neckline down or they'd cut the skirt off and make it look like a miniskirt—I hate that. In fact, just the other day, somebody sent me a picture and said, "Miss Cummings, would you please sign this?" It was an early Hollywood picture so I signed it, sent it back and said, "I hope you don't mind me putting the neckline back where it originally was." I put the neckline up with a pen and ink because they'd cut it down so I looked like a—I don't know—it looked awful. But they did that at the time which was really so ridiculous, this fashion for taking the neckline and cutting it right down.

After *Remember Last Night?,* all the pictures I made were for British studios. I continued with the English half of Myron Selznick's firm. There really wasn't a great deal to choose between working in British and American films in those days—it was very much the same. When you're doing a film, you get up about six o'clock, six-thirty, whatever. Usually, you have to be at the studio at about seven to be made up and everything.

I did a couple of films for the studios at Elstree in the thirties—that's all television there now, of course. And for British Gaumont, I did *Seven Sinners,* a cozy little English film with Edmund Lowe who was a very nice chap—I made a picture with him before in Hollywood—and *Strangers on a Honeymoon,* a comedy with Hugh Sinclair. I remember with *Strangers on a Honeymoon,* we had two or three days' work on location and I brought my doggie down so he could get some exercise because it was in the country. He was a bulldog and because the location was just outside of London, I drove him down in my car. And Hugh Sinclair brought his doggie down, too. We shouldn't have done that because we both got in trouble. The doggies kept rushing in and out of the takes—they were having

Left to right: Constance, Robert Young, Reginald Denny, Sally Eilers, Edward Arnold and Louise Henry in *Remember Last Night*. (The Kobal Collection.)

a wonderful time. Finally, the director screamed at us and said, "Get those dogs out of here!"

I also appeared in plays in the thirties in both England and on Broadway including some my husband had written. In 1937, I played *Madame Bovary* for the Theatre Guild in New York and that really wasn't the happiest of productions as far as I was concerned. It's a very strange story as a matter of fact. The Theatre Guild saw the production in Paris which Gaston Baty produced. His wife was in it and I gather it was a marvelous production. It was in a tiny little theatre—really a two-by-four stage—and he got these wonderful effects because there were lots of different scenes in it. When the Theatre Guild came back to New York, they wanted to do it. They wanted me to play Emma and they wanted Benn to do an adaptation or translation into English. They had a literal translation so they sent him a copy of it to read. Benn then went to Paris where he saw the production. He said to the Theatre Guild, "I'll tell you what. I'm very interested in this and I would like to do it but it so happens I have never read the book. Give me some time to read the book and then I will tell you if I think I can do it because I don't think this play is really quite what Flaubert meant to write."

Benn then read the book and he said to them, "No. If I do a translation of this play, I'm not going to write Emma as a long-suffering, put-upon, tragic heroine because that is not what Flaubert wrote. He wrote about a very silly romantic woman and he was very anti-romantic." He had actually based it—I don't think Benn knew this at the time—on a woman who was a wife of a friend of his. It is a marvelous book but it is not a book that says, "Pity this poor woman." It is a book which says, "Well, this is the havoc that Victorian romanticism can cause in people's lives."

The Theatre Guild said to Benn, "Yes, all right, go ahead." So he wrote it and when he finished the script, they were not pleased with it. They felt that I was not being the traditional conception of the heroine. Putting it on wasn't an easy passage and it wasn't a great success because it sort of fell between two schools really. But Flaubert had not written her as a sympathetic character—this poor woman whom everybody should feel sorry for because everybody treated her badly. The fact was that she mucked up everybody else's life as well as her own. It's very interesting because even now, if you talk to people and ask, "Have you read *Madame Bovary?*" nine people out of ten or ninety-nine out of

With Edmund Lowe in *Seven Sinners*. (The Museum of Modern Art.)

a hundred will say, "Oh, yes, such a sad story, isn't it? That poor woman." And it's not what the book is about. Flaubert really doesn't give her one virtue. The only thing he allows her is that she's pretty but that's about all.

I know, though, that she's not a heavy or a villainess, either. There was the famous saying by Flaubert which is very, very interesting. Apparently, somebody said to Flaubert, "You're rather a tough cookie. How could you write this picture about this fragile woman who really needed somebody to look after her—so unlike you?"

And he said, "Non, Emma Bovary, c'est moi." And, of course, we've all got silliness and romanticism in us. I think that's what he meant and he must have understood it at the time he got to the end of the book or he couldn't have written it. I think you as an author would know you really cannot write a book about somebody you hate or somebody you have contempt for. Biographies can be different, it's true, but if you're writing a novel, it's like acting a part. I think however despicable the part is you're playing, at some point, you've got to be able to say, "Oh, God, yes, I've got a bit of that in me, too. I understand that."

But there are still those actors and actresses who don't want to play less sympathetic parts. I've known a lot of them. For instance, if they're asked to play the part of a bitch, they'll start softening it and making it nicer and they'll say, "No. I don't want to do that or I don't want to say it that way because the audience won't like me." They want to be liked. I never saw myself as playing just one kind of role. I never studied with any of the actors' schools, either. I feel that when you're acting, you should imagine. You imagine a lot about the character that isn't actually in the play. You just have to get to know the part and find it in yourself, I think.

I was one of the first actresses to appear on television when I did *Cyrano de Bergerac* the year before the war. I played Roxanne, James Mason played Christian and Leslie Banks was Cyrano. I'd known Leslie before. I think we did *Goodbye Mr. Chips* on the stage around about the same time. I remember that *Cyrano* was a tiny kind of production because it was right at the beginning of television. Nowadays, television is almost the same as doing a film but in those days, it was a much smaller, simpler production altogether.

I also did plays at the Old Vic in 1939. Juliet was one of my favorite parts and *Saint Joan* was another. I had to go and see Shaw which, of course, was a marvelous experience. He wanted to meet me before he would give permission for me to do it. That's the only time I ever met him but he was a fascinating man. I remember I said to him, "Have you ever seen me on the stage?" He said no, he hadn't, so I said, "Well, how do you know I'll be any good as *Saint Joan*?"

And he said, "Oh, I can tell, child, I can tell."

The people Benn and I mingled with in England were mostly theatre people really or people who were connected with the theatre. Indeed, we knew most of the English people in the theatre well including Laurence Olivier, Vivien Leigh and John Gielgud. I'd known Larry as soon as I was married because Benn had been acquainted with him since Larry was in a film which was shot in Germany in 1929 or '30, a film for which Benn had written the script. I knew Larry all the years he was married to Vivien Leigh and I worked with him years later in *Long Day's Journey Into Night.* Vivien was a delightful, charming person. She was very pretty, very bright and fun to be with. I never acted with her and I never acted with John Gielgud, either, but I've known John ever since I came to England—a very nice man and, of course, a very great actor.

Diana Wynyard was another of our very good friends always until she died so I'd known her for twenty or thirty years—something like that. She'd been at the Liverpool Rep before but I think the first play she did in London was one of Benn's. That was before I knew her. I can't remember why she left Hollywood—I know she was doing very well there. Like Vivien Leigh, she was a very intelligent woman and great fun to be with—a nice person, very sweet and very pretty to look at, of course—she was very beautiful.

Noel Coward and Benn knew each other well. They were the same age. They were born within a few months of each other in 1900 and they met in the theatre—I suppose in the middle of the twenties when they were both beginning to make a success. Naturally, I met Noel soon after I was married and I can't say that I was a great, great friend and saw that much of him but I did know him. There was a kind of careful suburban background about Noel and then on the other hand, he was very cheeky and very witty. He had these two sides to him which you've got to understand in order to do good productions of his shows. Noel had a very fast wit which was sometimes too near the bull's eye to be a great comfort to whomever was holding the target. But he was

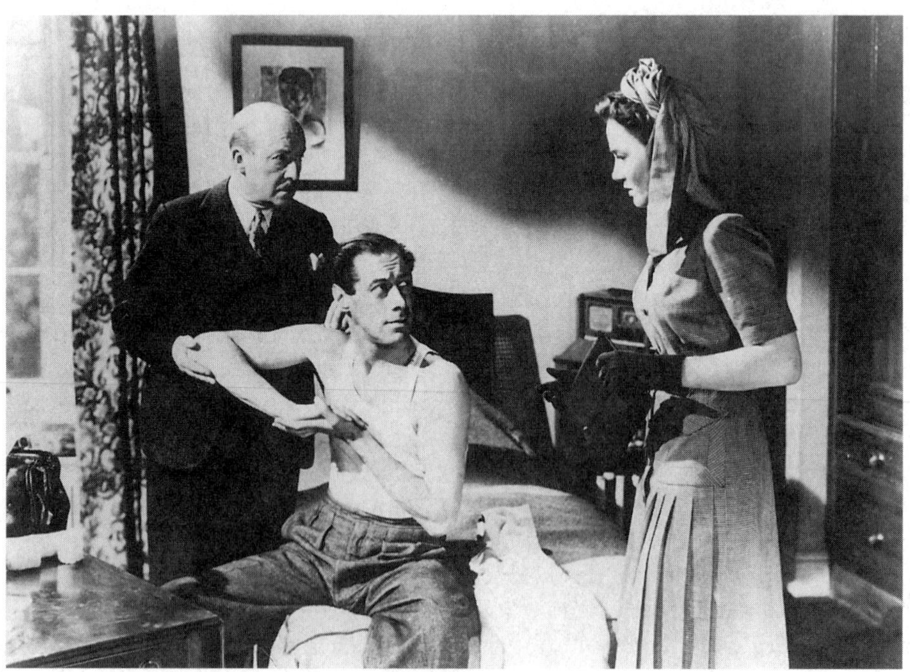

With Hugh Wakefield and Rex Harrison in *Blithe Spirit.*

not a vicious or harsh man. He was a sweet person and a gentle and kind friend to a lot of people in and out of the theatre. I have never heard an unpleasant word said about him. We should all be able to climb into our graves with that on our tombstones!

In the theatre, my God, he did everything—writing, composing, acting, directing. And he was marvelous in cabaret. I never saw him in an actual theatre—he could have done it there—but he could take the Cafe de Paris by storm. That was a nightclub where you went to dance and have dinner and all that and they used to have floorshows or entertainment. I've seen Noel there a couple of times and he'd spend an hour and a half just sitting at the piano, playing, singing and talking. Everybody was spellbound—he was a wonderful, wonderful entertainer all the time.

I can't remember if it was before or after I did the film version of his *Blithe Spirit* but I know he asked me to do *Design for Living* on the stage. I was interested in doing it but I couldn't because I was just embarking on a rehearsal for a play of my husband's. Noel was very sweet about it and said to me, "Well, obviously, Benn has first call on your services." So I never did that play.

Years later in the 1960s, I did one of his plays, *Fallen Angels,* with Joan Greenwood in the theatre. On the opening night, I received a charming bouquet—quite individual—something that had obviously been specially chosen. I opened the card which said, "Dear Cummings, go on the stage tonight and outshine Joan."

I thought, "He trusts me a lot to put that in writing!" A little later, I went to Joan's room to say something and saw on her dressing table the same bouquet but in a slightly different color scheme. I said, "What did he put on your card?" She giggled a bit and then showed me. It was exactly the same wording as mine with the names reversed. Wasn't that adorable? Despite all that, I don't honestly think I was very good in *Fallen Angels* but Noel was very sweet about it.

When I married Benn, I became a British citizen. It's just automatic so I've got both nationalities. I've always liked England. I like the English people and the life here. It's changed, of course—it's changed a lot in the years I've lived here. I think it's lost quite a bit of its original English character. Since the war, there has been such an influx of foreigners of all kinds which I think probably has been a good thing for England. But in the beginning of my life here, England was very quiet. It was very tranquil, very peaceful and I rather liked that. It's true, the Depression was still going on but that's always just bad wherever you are. And there was the abdication of Edward VIII but that really caused surprisingly little turmoil.

Benn and I used to go to France in the thirties, too. It was so much easier then. If you wanted to go somewhere, you just got in your car and off you went. You didn't have to make sure that you had a hotel reservation somewhere, et cetera, et cetera. It was just easy. Now, of course, everywhere you go is so crowded and not as much fun.

We had just finished building our new house on Church Street in 1939. Then the war came and I was over here all through the war. I felt it was dreadful we were at war but that it was the only thing that could be done as we had had a bad government under Chamberlain. Still, in some ways, the war was a marvelous experience although I wouldn't want it again. But there is no doubt that there was a wonderful atmosphere and attitude about things in England at that time. There was a lot of—oh, I don't know—people just dropped petty things and personal things, forgot about them and pulled together. There was an attitude which really was remarkable. It's just a pity we can't do it in peacetime. The English attitude to the Germans was very strange. What most people talked about was how do we treat the Germans after we'd won the war. Are we polite to them or what?—rather than any great apprehension about the fact that the English could lose the war.

Of course, the war was often quite frightening. Then the buzz bombs came later and they were even more frightening. What happened was that in the beginning, the siren would go off and you'd go down in the cellar and hide and hope you'd be all right. Then after some months of this, it really all became a bore and you just went on with your work or your life or whatever. If there'd been a particularly bad raid in some part of town and you knew somebody who lived there, you'd ring up if the phone was still working or try to get in touch with them and ask, "Are you all right?"

In one case, a couple I knew said, "Oh, we're fine. We were very lucky. We were in the country last night. We weren't in the flat which was a good thing because the apartment is absolutely finished. It's just demolished and we would have been finished, too, if we'd been there." And we all agreed that wasn't it great that they weren't in the flat. Nobody minded that the apartment was demolished. That was not really of any importance by then.

I was living in our house on 68 Old Church Street just as I am now—66 it was then—during the war. There was a land mine which landed just behind the house and blew out a lot of windows. It did a most peculiar thing which I've never forgotten. In Benn's study on the second floor, there was a big desk behind which was a bookcase full of books. The blast didn't disturb anything on his desk—there were papers and other things on it—but on the two top shelves of the bookcase, it pulled all the books out and threw them in the middle of the floor. It was most astonishing—I never could understand that.

My husband was in the Naval Reserve. They call it the Wavy Navy and he was there until near the end of the war when he was wounded. He was in a little boat, he got shot up rather badly and was sent back to England. The only thing I did in the war itself was to play to the troops for ENSA which was kind of the official body that arranged for shows—plays and music and things—for the troops. I didn't go abroad but I did quite a lot of that all over England.

I continued to work in plays and films during the war. One of the plays I did was *The Petrified Forest.* I met Leslie Howard through that because my friend, Peggy Conklin, had acted with him in it on Broadway. As for films, the war disrupted everything, of course. It depended mainly on where the bombs fell. Some of the studios were damaged and then houses and railroad tracks would also be damaged so you couldn't get where you wanted to go—that kind of thing. You just had to put up with that and do the best you could.

With Seymour Hicks and Robert Montgomery in *Haunted Honeymoon.*

I think the war had started when I made *Busman's Honeymoon* with Robert Montgomery. I believe he went to France after that. I don't think he was in uniform but he was doing some kind of war work there. Robert Newton was also in the film. We made it for MGM's British studio and I remember we did some of the locations in a little village called Beaconsfield which was not very far from the studio in Buckingham.

Robert Montgomery was a very serious actor. He took himself seriously and that easy-going chap he played so well took a lot of study although he was a very nice, easy-going man in real life. Bob Newton, on the other hand, was kind of an extrovert, a wild man who drank too much on his off time. He didn't drink when he was acting—I don't mean that. He was conscientious when he was working. But he didn't pay enough attention to the future. He was an excellent actor and if he'd taken his work more seriously, he could have done many more things and had a longer career.

This England was also made during the war. We made that out at Stanmore. There was a studio out there, strangely enough, which is just like a suburb of London. I worked with Roddy McDowall and I remember him very well. He was very young, very well-rehearsed and rather quiet. Of course, I have followed his career over the years with interest.

The Foreman Went to France was yet another film I did in the war. Some of it was done in the studio but a lot of it was done on location down in Penzance in Cornwall. Robert Morley played in it. He was always very shy about his acting ability. He would say, "I can play certain types of characters but not more challenging ones." He denied he could play the great classical roles. Still, for all his modesty, he was a very good actor.

The war must still have been on when I did *Blithe Spirit* because Noel was away. He was attached to the Navy and he was doing diplomatic work. He didn't come back until the film was over so he wasn't around when it was being filmed. It was made in Technicolor and I remember all the prints had to be sent back to Hollywood because they couldn't print it here.

David Lean directed it from Noel's play and the cast included Rex Harrison, Kay Hammond and Margaret Rutherford. Kay and Margaret, of course, were in the original play when it was done on the stage. Margaret was absolutely fascinating. She *was* Mme. Arcati, the medium. That wasn't a performance. We all said that who worked with her on the film. She was very unexpected, bouncy, full of ideas and great fun to be with. I don't know if she actually was a spiritualist but she took her work seriously and I would think she made a study of spiritualism. Perhaps like Mme. Arcati, she believed in it and also felt it was impressive.

I think David Lean was very, very good in his direction. He was quite thorough and had a very complete idea in his head about what he thought the film should be and what he was going to work towards. He didn't have to play about to try a lot of things he knew. I don't think we did many retakes. Of course, David started out as a cutter and so when he started to make a film, he had a pretty good idea of what he needed and what he was going to use.

There were not a lot of special effects as I recall. Of course, Kay was a ghost and then I had to look like a ghost. We wore pale green make-up and had different clothes and things on. But as a matter of fact, I remember Ronnie Neame who was the cameraman and I used to get together and say, "Oh, it would be such fun. You could do this, you could do that, you could do the other." He'd even talk to David Lean and tell him, "There'd be a great chance for doing trick effects and things."

But David said, "No, I'm not going to do any of that because Noel has said what he wanted me to do was to photograph the play as it was." Actually, I always felt that for a film there was a bit too much in that one sitting room.

There was one very funny thing that they put in which wasn't in the play. David, I suppose, felt one thing like that wouldn't matter. When Kay as the ghostly wife goes into Folkestone with Rex, she's driving the car as it goes by a patrolman who's on duty. The patrolman is amazed because he suddenly sees this car go by with a man sitting in the passenger's seat and nobody's sitting in the driver's seat. That was terribly funny and I really regretted that they didn't do a lot more of that.

I don't think Noel was a hundred per cent happy with the film but I may be wrong about that. I don't know why because David really photographed the play and there would have been opportunities for spreading it out. But when Noel was going away, he may have felt, "No, I'm going to ask them to just photograph the play because God knows what they'll get up to otherwise." So that's what was done. However, Noel always was complimentary about my work in *Blithe Spirit*. He thought I was very good in it.

Rex Harrison was a very self-concentrated actor. I'm not saying he was ungenerous or he was difficult or anything like that. But he was just so absorbed in his own part and what he was doing that he was really oblivious of what else was going on. I never acted with him on the stage but people who did have told me the same thing. I remember David and I giggled once or twice because Rex was so absolutely absorbed in what he was doing that you would think it was a solo performance. But it was just funny—it didn't make him difficult or not nice or anything.

In those days, Rex and his wife, Lilli Palmer, had a house down near Denham and she'd gone up to the London clinic to have their baby. Rex went up to see the baby as soon as it was born. Carey his name is—I think he's Rex's older son. At this time, everybody was very worried because they thought something was wrong with the whole first section of the film and they might have to reshoot it. We didn't know what it was but there was this talk and Rex was terribly worried because he didn't know what all of this meant.

Anyway, about this time, he went up to London to see Lilli and the baby. When he came back, we all asked, "Well, how's the baby?"

Rex said, "Oh, I don't know. Poor little beast—he's going to be a long tall drink of water like I am. He's a very long baby but I guess he's going to be all right, poor little thing."

So just as we were worrying about the film, we also thought, "What's the matter with the baby?"

Well, three or four days later, it turned out the main thing that had been the trouble with the film

With Kay Hammond and Rex Harrison in *Blithe Spirit.*

was simply a matter of color. But they had reprinted it in Hollywood and it was all right so the word went round that the first section was fine. It was splendid, it was marvelous and we wouldn't have to redo it. The next time we asked Rex how the baby was, he said, "Oh, he's a splendid little chap, you know, he really is." And he would go into ecstasies about this baby. But before, when he was worried that something was wrong with the film, even the baby wasn't all right. The baby was in for an unhappy life—nobody knew quite why. But when the scene was all right, the baby was fine. That's what I mean when I say everything for him was colored by the actual job he was doing at the moment—whether it was going well or not, was he doing it well or not. We all used to giggle about it to his face and say, "Well, there you are." But he didn't mind.

When Benn came back from the war, he was elected a member of Parliament with the Labour Party. That was a very exciting, marvelous time because in the first Parliament after the war, there was this terrific landslide to Labour. We were all very euphoric because we thought, "Well, we're in, we've got an enormous majority and we know how to put things right." But it didn't work out like that. I don't think anybody quite knows how to put things right. It doesn't look like it now, does it? What has happened is that there's a terrible apathy in England today which is really quite astonishing when one looks back at what the Thatcher government has done to this country in education, in health, in manufacturing—one department after another. And there's been no real outcry—it's quite astounding.

But, of course, back then at the end of the war, it was a very exciting time. I went round and made speeches when Benn was standing for Parliament. In fact, I got David Lean to vote for Labour. I think the majority of the theatrical people in England are liberal. I think it goes with the territory a bit here. I would say that was true of America, too. I think it's something to do with being an actor.

Of course, they had terrific long hours in the House of Commons. Benn used to get home at three and four o'clock in the morning because there was so much to be done. I hardly saw Benn at all while he was a member of Parliament. So I went to London University for a year and took courses in anthropology—social anthropology and physical anthropology. I'd always been interested in that.

Benn was very instrumental in beginning the end of theatre censorship in England when he was a member of Parliament. The bill actually came in when he was no longer a member. He didn't stand for a second term because he hadn't been able to do his writing which he wanted to get back to. But he was very much against theatre censorship as most of the authors were over here. He didn't believe in censorship in films, either. Many actors were opposed to censorship, too. You see again, it's this thing of actors being on the liberal side. It's true there are some people who, when they get older, do disagree. I think Katharine Hepburn's very like that now, isn't she? I heard her give a talk on the television once and she really surprised me because she seemed to be so cross about a lot of things that had happened in the theatre. I suppose there probably always has been a certain amount of things in the theatre I wouldn't have liked—it wouldn't have been my style or thing. But I don't think that the theatre or films—entertainment in general—is any worse than in the past. So many doors have been opened to the writing and what is accepted has been marvelous for the theatre.

I think you can have—well, I was going to say you can have codes of decency but even that is a bit difficult because it's all very subjective. When Hollywood established the censorship code in the thirties, there were a lot of busybodies who were saying, "Well, they shouldn't show this and they shouldn't say that." I think the reason behind the Code in Hollywood was probably the same thing that was behind the censorship in England in the theatre. The producers of the films felt safer if there was a code which they could work in and know that there wouldn't be any objection to their films. Otherwise, if no holds were barred, they would be very nervous about what the director would want to put in a film because they thought, "Well, now, some group might get up and say, 'This film should be banned!' "

Benn was always interested in politics—in democracy, in the left and all of that. He was certainly responsible for my political education because I don't think I ever thought about that until we were married. He put those issues in his plays, too, and I think he made a good contribution to the theatre. He was a very good director and he wrote some very good plays.

One play of his I did in the fifties was a big success in London but it wasn't a success in America. It was called *The Rape of the Belt.* We found out afterwards that the title shocked a lot of people in America because it had the word "rape" in it. That

With Robert Morley and Peter Sellers in *The Battle of the Sexes.* (The Kobal Collection.)

was astonishing. But, of course, it was one of the labors of Heracles. He had to get the belt of the queen of the Amazons because it was like the crown or the throne. Benn was very much a feminist and for women's rights and all that and that's what that play is really about although it's a comedy.

I'm for women's issues, too. I think women shouldn't be the Second Sex. Isn't that what Simone de Beauvoir calls them? But it still applies in the theatre. I think you could say that there are more good roles for men than there are for women in the theatre if you look. And, of course, in Shakespeare, there'd be twenty men's parts for two women's parts.

Although my son Johnny was born in 1949 and my daughter Jemina in 1951, I was still able to combine marriage and a home with a career because Benn and I were in the same realms and we worked together a lot. I've continued acting in the theatre all these years and I've also made a number of films, both for television and the big screen.

In the early fifties, I did a television film with Douglas Fairbanks, Jr. that he was producing in England. He did several and I did this one—it was called *The Scream*. They may have changed the title in the United States. I'd known Doug before and he's a very nice, charming, easygoing, delightful kind of person—I would think very like his father although I never met him.

Also in the fifties, Joseph Losey directed me in a theatrical film, *The Intimate Stranger*. I knew Joe very well because he and Benn were friends. There were quite a few people like Joe and Carl Foreman who came over during the McCarthy time and all that trouble. Joe was always very gloomy about everything or he sounded very gloomy. If you'd say, "Hello, Joe, what are you doing, what are you up to?" he'd say in a mournful tone, "Oh, I'm going to go to France. I'm going to make a picture with Michael Redgrave."

And you'd say, "Well, that sounds wonderful."

"Yes," he'd say, "it is." But the way he said it, you'd think it was a very sad story that he was telling you. It was very funny and we all used to tease him about that. It didn't affect his directing at all, of course. He was a very good director.

I worked with Peter Sellers in the films, *John and Julie* and *The Battle of the Sexes*. Peter was a very funny man and a great giggler. We used to get terrific giggles sometimes when we were doing a scene. I remember one scene in *The Battle of the Sexes* where a dog was supposed to go down a rickety staircase. It was a studio set and I've never seen a staircase like that before. This set of stairs was supposed to go down into a basement. It had slender bannisters and a handrail we could use. Astor had been trained as a police dog but he wasn't very fearless because he looked down this long staircase and then just sat there. He must have thought: "That's too bloody dangerous for me. I'm not going down those stairs." Peter and I started giggling. We were down at the bottom of the steps and we were all waiting for the dog to go down the stairs. We tried to look serious for the scene when the director said, "Action!" The trainer kept calling to the dog, "Seek, Astor, seek!" but the dog just wouldn't move. Peter and I went into hysterics and poor Charlie Crichton, the director—I never knew whether he got cross with us or pretended to be. He never got the dog to go down the steps but even if he had, we couldn't have done the scene by then—we were so helpless with laughter.

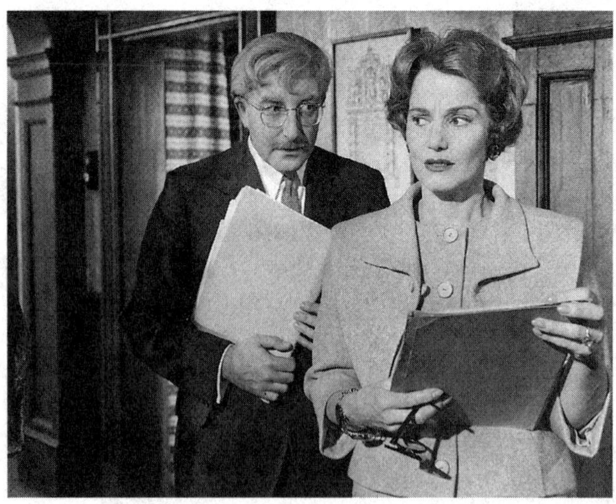

With Peter Sellers in *The Battle of the Sexes*. (The Kobal Collection.)

The time we did those films was at the beginning of Peter's career. I don't know what happened to him later. You know, he drank too much and sort of went to pieces. There was something eating him and bugging him. He was an unhappy man, a dissatisfied man. I don't quite know why or what it was because he was such an enormous success. But when we made *The Battle of the Sexes,* he was still very happy and very popular and, as I say, great fun to work with.

The last films I made in the sixties were *Sammy Going South* and *In the Cool of the Day. Sammy Going South* was released in the United States under the title, *A Boy Ten Feet Tall.* It wasn't really one of my favorite parts. I don't remember a great deal about that but I recall we were driving around in a car. I can't remember much about *In the Cool of the Day,* either, even though an actress I admire very much, Angela Lansbury, was in it. I didn't have a very big part in the film. I do recall that the studio where we did it was north of London.

By the sixties, I was concentrating on the theatre. I really preferred the stage to working in films—I still do. Partly, I may have been influenced by the fact that my husband really was a theatre man, not a film man. But the early films in Hollywood had been a great experience for me. Any acting you do is good training for the next bit of acting you're going to do and if it's the theatre or the stage, of course, it's a different technique because you have to project much more in the theatre. But the basic thing of creating a part helps you for the next one you're going to do, whether it's on the screen or on the stage.

I've done some radio, too. I can remember being interviewed on radio and I've done a lot of plays here on radio. I did some in America as well including one radio play with Cary Grant back in the thirties. But it's my least favorite medium. My favorite is the theatre, then second is television and films—I would link those together, there's not much difference—and third is radio.

I've done plays on the stage and then recreated them for television. I played Mary Tyrone opposite Larry Olivier in *Long Day's Journey Into Night* for the National Theatre in London and we performed it on television two years later. Larry was wonderful to work with, a man of great energy and imagination and very, very thorough when he acted or directed a play. Of course, he didn't direct *Long Day's Journey Into Night* but he was a hardworking man who was always thinking about whatever particular thing he was doing, a very concentrated man who studied a part a great deal. At the same time, he was a down-to-earth actor, a very realistic one and always with a sense of humor.

With Sir Laurence Olivier in the 1971 Royal National Theatre production of *Long Day's Journey Into Night.*

I think *Long Day's Journey Into Night* may have been my favorite part of everything I've done. That's a wonderful play. As a matter of fact, I felt I knew a lot about that woman, Mary Tyrone. It was interesting in a remote kind of way. I mean, she wasn't anything like my mother or my family but that girl was born in Columbus, Ohio and brought up there. My mother's family came from Springfield, Ohio and Columbus, Ohio, too. And the same Middle West kind of middle class mores that applied to what my mother thought was right—the way girls should behave and all that—applied to Mary Tyrone in the play. I have a feeling that—I don't know whether mothers still say this but my mother would say to me, "Well, you know, nice girls don't do that" or "That's not the way ladies behave, ladies don't put on a lot of make-up" or something which used to drive me crazy when I was young. Mary Tyrone talked to her two sons in the play rather in those terms and I don't know—it just struck little chords. I could remember my grandmother and my aunt and I just felt very familiar.

I thought, "I know this girl, I know what her childhood was like," although, of course, she was a very ardent Catholic and we were Presbyterians. There's a big difference there but there was just that same slightly buttoned-up feeling which from many points of view was what was Mary Tyrone's trouble, I think, in the play. So that, as I say, when I played that woman, I just kept saying, "Yes, I know her. I know the background." Not that I was like her or that my mother was like her but there was a lot I recognized and that, I think, always helps when you're playing a part. I think it's necessary, in fact.

In the original 1978 Yale Repertory Theatre production of *Wings*.

I did *Wings* on Broadway in 1979 and that was a fascinating play, very interesting to do and interesting in itself because we did a lot of swathing up on the state of what happens to the mind. We read books, we went to the rehabilitation center at White Plains, met people there and went to therapy sessions. From that point of view, it was absolutely fascinating. I mean, I learned a lot about what can happen to a human mind, what it's capable of and how different parts of it can be absolutely destroyed and other parts left intact. It seems anything can happen to the mind so, as I say, it was not just interesting to do as a part but it was an education in a way.

I also did a film version of *Wings* for PBS in 1983—that was the last time I went out to Hollywood. After all these years in England, I've gotten used to driving on the left side of the road. I was driving in Beverly Hills at one point during my stay there and I started driving down the wrong side of the street. There wasn't any traffic, there were no other cars on the road, but a police car came up and stopped me. The policeman said, "What do you think you're doing?"

I said, "What do you mean?"

He said, "You're driving down the wrong side of the street." And I said, "Oh, so I am." Through living over here and through acting here, I have something of an English accent and when he heard me speak, I think he thought I was a funny foreigner.

So he said, "Well, don't do it again."

I just keep on acting because I like working. I've worked all my life and I feel happier when I'm doing it. I just finished a short run of *The Chalk Garden*, a play of Enid Bagnold's which I did in New York about eight or ten years ago. Benn and I knew her quite well. She was a very powerful kind of lady. I think *The Chalk Garden* is her best play—she

A portrait from *Movie Crazy.* (The Kobal Collection.)

wrote about seven or eight. I think it was first done in America in '56. Gladys Cooper did it there and then Edith Evans did it over here the same year. Irene Selznick, of course, worked with Enid a lot on that play and Enid gave Irene a lot of credit for pulling it into the firm shape it was in.

I suppose I have a philosophy of life. I think I might say the rule that I go by is to say, "Have a go." You know, a lot of people are very cautious. They want to go slowly or steadily or they want to know what the outcome is going to be. They want to be sure something's going to work out well before they embark on it. I don't believe in that. I think it's better to go ahead and do something even if it's a failure because you can't know in advance. You know, people say the end justifies the means but you never know what the end is going to be. So I think it's just better to go ahead and try something that you want to do. If it doesn't work out, if it's a failure, all right, skip it and then try the next thing because you never know really where the goodies are coming from in life.

Evelyn Venable and Claire Trevor being directed by Lewis Seiler in *Star for a Night*. (Courtesy of Rosalia Woodson.)

1933—THE CLASS OF '33

As the newly-revived British cinema began recruiting such prominent young American actresses as Marian Marsh and Constance Cummings in 1933, Hollywood that same year was continuing to draw on fresh talent from the theatre. Among the new faces from the live stages of the East were Evelyn Venable, Jean Muir and Claire Trevor. Despite their youth, these actresses had attended college and received considerable professional training for at least three years before "going Hollywood." Evelyn Venable had learned her craft under the tutelage of the distinguished Shakespearean actor, Walter Hampden; Jean Muir studied the Stanislavsky method, then the rage in advanced theatrical circles, at Madame Maria Ouspenskaya's acting school; while Claire Trevor was a graduate of the venerable American Academy of Dramatic Arts. In effect, they were a graduate class of 1933 whose diplomas came in the coveted form of movie contracts.

Evelyn, Jean and Claire were part of a wave of young film players, often college-educated and with more formal training than most of their counterparts in the silent era and even some of the early talkie imports from Broadway such as Claudette Colbert and Barbara Stanwyck. Among the new arrivals, Margaret Lindsay and Rosalind Russell, like Claire Trevor, graduated from the American Academy of Dramatic Arts; Bette Davis and Lucille Ball studied at John Murray Anderson's acting school in New York; Sylvia Sidney and Marguerite Churchill attended the Theatre Guild School; John Garfield, like Jean Muir, went to Madame Ouspenskaya's school; Katharine Hepburn, Franchot Tone and Gloria Stuart first distinguished themselves in college dramatics; Henry Fonda, James Stewart and Margaret Sullavan were part of a stock company known as the University Players.

These performers were often spurred on by economic pressures that had not existed in the twenties. For the young stage player in the thirties, it was an uncertain future in a theatre that had been hit hard by the Great Depression. From the 240 Broadway productions staged in the 1929–30 season—plays planned before the stock market crash—the number dropped to 190 in the 1930–31 season and continued to fall each year in the thirties until there were only 89 in the 1938–39 season.[1] With many stage theatres half-filled or empty, producers facing bankruptcy and widespread unemployment, a ticket to Hollywood for the burgeoning theatrical talent became an economic necessity.

Unlike most silent stars as well as some of the early talkie performers who had believed in motion pictures and were fulfilling their own ambitions by going to Hollywood, the new stage imports were often faced with conflicting professional loyalties. They needed to find work within their craft, but in theatrical circles it was widely believed that the player was "selling out" by opting for the easy money of the movie industry. As a consequence, many of the new stage performers who were prevented by the Depression from rising to the top on Broadway and now had to adjust their professional skills to another medium initially came to Hollywood with an attitude of condescension.[2]

Armed with all their education and stage technique, the new emigrants settled in a film capital that, while still pioneering, was far from being a raw, unsophisticated village. Indeed, it was now the stage people who had to learn the technique of the screen rather than the reverse. Filmmakers had so fully assimilated the influences from the stage that they felt free to launch cinematic experiments which rivalled those in the silent era. 1933, for example, saw the release of *King Kong* as well as the great Busby Berkeley musicals for Warners—*42nd Street, Gold Diggers of 1933* and *Footlight Parade*—in which the choreographer dazzled audiences with his technical wizardry. And many of the smaller films concerned with the lives of ordinary people demonstrated a unity between cinematic technique and a fresh approach to acting in talkies that had evolved under the guidance of directors like Frank Capra and Mervyn LeRoy.

Nevertheless, the new group of performers from the stage enriched the screen with varied styles of acting shaped by their professional training. Thus, Evelyn Venable's absorption of Walter Hampden's classic romanticism seemed to imbue her often ethereal screen persona; Jean Muir's schooling in the naturalistic Stanislavsky method presaged her gravitation towards the more realistic films produced by her studio, Warner Brothers; and Claire Trevor's studies at the more traditional American Academy of Dramatic Arts prepared her for the wide range of roles she had to play in the Hollywood of the thirties.

In 1933, events in Hollywood were set in motion that would affect the three actresses' careers and overtake the industry as a whole. Not only had techniques become more sophisticated, the content of pictures was becoming more and more daring, provoking outrage from moralists and censors. For instance, despite an assertion of conventional attitudes in the films' denouements, audience expectations of what was proper for a woman in 1933 were upset by Barbara Stanwyck as the bitter, impoverished, man-hating girl who uses sex to get to the top in *Baby Face* and Ruth Chatterton as the powerful automobile executive for whom sex is both a perquisite and a means of manipulating men in her employ in *Female*.[3] And when Mae West's satiric jabs at sex and conventional gender roles were on display in two big box-office hits of 1933, *She Done Him Wrong* and *I'm No Angel*, the fuse was lit for an explosion that would eventually disrupt Hollywood's new freedom to explore previously taboo subjects.

The new movement to censor films was led by Roman Catholics who regarded as ineffectual the earlier efforts of largely Protestant reformers to regulate motion picture content through the Hays Office. In the fall of 1933, Catholic leaders set up a committee with the avowed aim of pressuring bankers to withhold money from the producers of "filthy" pictures. Spurred on by Joseph Breen, an ambitious Catholic layman in the Hays organization, the moral crusade gathered momentum. In 1934, the Episcopal Committee on Motion Pictures inaugurated an organization known as the Legion of Decency in order to pressure the studios to "clean up" their films. The campaign redirected the public's anxiety over their own sense of economic dislocation caused by the Depression to a moral crusade, soon attracting Protestant and even some Jewish support.[4]

Many of those who were concerned with the development of cinema as an art were appalled by the censorship demanded by the Legionnaires of Decency, including director Ernst Lubitsch who warned:

> The effect of this campaign will be to force artists to see life through pink glasses. . . . When the effect of the campaign is to fight the free and truthful expression of the artist . . . then the campaign becomes dangerous and the development of an artistic cinema is impeded.[5]

Nevertheless, despite opposition from some studio heads who perceived the censors as meddling in their business, the industry ended up capitulating to the new Puritans. At a time when the studios were trying to overcome the crippling financial effects of the Depression, they felt they could ill-afford to offend a powerful, well-organized, vocal minority.

In addition, the Depression and the advent of the New Deal along with the influx of stage people from the East led to revolts from actors, directors, writers, cameramen and other technicians, all of whom were organizing into unions. These activities caused panic among the producers who also feared the consequences of Upton Sinclair's 1934 campaign for governor of California on a platform promising radical reform. Feeling besieged on the left by the unions and on the right by the censors, the studio heads came to view a production code as a means of placating the public and containing potentially disruptive forces within formulaic films that would uphold traditional morality by emphasizing caution and clichés over chaos and creativity.

As a result, on July 1, 1934, the Motion Picture Production Code with its "dos" and "don'ts" (mostly the latter) was put into strict regulation under a new administration headed by Joseph Breen as a branch of the Hays Office. Their role was to oversee every script and every finished film of all the major studios in Hollywood. Almost overnight, the content of American films changed drastically. Instead of the more open approach of the early thirties, narratives now had to be cloaked in an evasive mantle of bourgeois respectability.

Yet, in this climate, directors—artists of the stature of John Ford, Frank Capra and William Wyler—once again became the most important figures in the cinema because it was primarily through their passion, commitment and imagination that films could overcome the attempts by censors to severely limit the subject matter of the scripts. The sweeping victory of Capra's 1934 *It Happened One Night* at the Academy Awards when it captured all the major Oscars and the succès d'estime the following year of Ford's *The Informer* did much to reestablish the power and prestige of directors that had been undermined by the industry's expansion of the late twenties. Without directly challenging the Code, Ford, Capra and Wyler were foremost among those who once again extended the emotional range and social conscience of the screen and decisively molded the careers of their players.

In the years immediately after the Code took effect, the talent in American films was still impressive. However, despite the extraordinary number of memorable achievements in the later thirties, there was a dearth of the good, honest "little" film that marked the pre-Code years. Unpretentious in terms of budget but often with unconventional, even startling ideas or narratives, these pictures had given filmmakers a chance to experiment with techniques and themes and players an opportunity to develop their acting skills. Under the Code, the smaller, so-called "B picture" increasingly became, not a valuable training ground for directors, writers and actors, but merely a formula for grinding out predictable films with stock characters, plots and situations.

The three actresses who came to Hollywood from the stage in the spring of 1933 would experience both joys and agonies, aesthetically, stemming from the industry's sea changes. Evelyn Venable and Jean Muir did have a number of opportunities to shine in quality productions. But

Jean Muir and Barton MacLane in *Draegerman Courage,* a 1937 Warners film.

within a few years, they wound up in B pictures that rarely displayed their talents to the fullest. Limited by the advent of the Code to her wholesome screen image and dissatisfied with much of her later work, Evelyn eventually retired from the screen to raise her family. Jean became equally dissatisfied but was far more rebellious and outspoken. At Warners, she had appeared in films with adult themes such as *Dr. Monica* in 1934 with its representation of adultery and pregnancy arousing the ire of censors, including Breen, who complained it included a lesbian, a nymphomaniac and a prostitute.[6] Jean's insistence on accurate cinematic portrayals gained her a reputation for being uncooperative, a view by the industry that culminated in her ultimate downfall.

Claire Trevor, for her part, less tied to a particular image or style of filmmaking than Evelyn and Jean, appeared in a wider variety of roles for Fox. Hoping to get out of B pictures, she would hang in, with her efforts over time rewarded during a long and successful career. Under the guidance of two great directors, she invested her portrayals of prostitutes in Wyler's *Dead End* and Ford's *Stagecoach* with an emotional truth that overcame attempts by the Code to impose a censorship on these characters. So in both their career setbacks and their unforgettable screen performances, Evelyn Venable, Jean Muir and Claire Trevor mirror the conflicts and the creativity of those years when Hollywood moved from a time of unpredictable fluidity to an age of both mediocrity and masterpieces.

(Courtesy of Rosalia Woodson.)

Evelyn Venable

Among the actresses who flocked to Hollywood in the early thirties, none had a more distinguished pedigree than Evelyn Venable. Born on October 18, 1913, in Cincinnati, Ohio to a family of educators, she was exposed at an early age to literature and the theatre. She portrayed Shakespeare's Juliet and Rosalind in her high school years and, after studying at Vassar, she joined the company of Walter Hampden, touring the country in *Cyrano de Bergerac* and *Hamlet.*

Responding to an offer by Paramount, Evelyn came to Hollywood to make her cinematic debut in *Cradle Song* in 1933. It was directed by Mitchell Leisen with Evelyn playing a young girl raised in a convent who yearns to go out into the world. In her second film, *Death Takes a Holiday* (1934), also directed by Leisen, she is a regal young Italian princess who falls in love with a handsome prince (Fredric March) who is Death in disguise on a vacation from his realm. Under Leisen's sensitive direction and against the backdrop of Paramount's elaborate, stylish recreation of an Italian palace, the strangely beautiful romance unfolds as the Princess Grazia overcomes the fear of death, and finally, out of love for him, elects to join Death in his kingdom.

In her films with Leisen, Evelyn manifested an ethereal persona with a beauty that seemed out of this world and a celestial voice that had a musical lilt. The young actress's performance in *Death Takes a Holiday* brought her immediate widespread acclaim and has continued to receive recognition through the decades. David Chierichetti writes in *Magill's Survey of Cinema:* "Evelyn Venable's interpretation of the difficult role of Grazia is sublime. . . . In person she was vivacious, robust, and almost as large as March, but Leisen was able to elicit from her a dreamy, ethereal quality which made Grazia believable."[1]

Evelyn's next film, *David Harum* with Will Rogers, made on loan-out to Fox, would change her life. During the making of this picture, she met the man she would spend the next forty years with, the noted cinematographer Hal Mohr whose credits included *The Marriage Clause, The Wedding March, The Jazz Singer* and *King of Jazz.* While they were filming, Evelyn invited the *David Harum* company to the preview of *Death Takes a Holiday* in Pasadena. Mohr later recalled, "I thought she was a cute kid but I never paid much attention to her until I saw her coming down the stairs (in the picture) . . . and that was it, I really fell."[2] With the sly encouragement of Will Rogers, Mohr and Evelyn began a courtship that led to marriage later that year. In Evelyn's memories, the filming of *David Harum* and her feelings for Rogers and James Cruze, their director, would remain evergreen. (Indeed, she would often take part in commemorations of Rogers including his centennial tributes in 1979.)

Evelyn continued making pictures for Paramount in 1934 including *Double Door,* a thriller with Evelyn, the young wife, and Anne Revere as "admirable foils" for a menacing spinster seeking to control the family fortune;[3] and *Mrs. Wiggs of the Cabbage Patch,* a remake of the popular Kate Douglas Wiggin story in which she worked with such veterans as Pauline Lord, ZaSu Pitts and W. C. Fields. But within a year, dissatisfied with their plans for her career, she left Paramount. She had fallen victim to Paramount's indifference at this time to developing the talents of their young actresses; they lost Ann Sheridan to Warners while gifted actresses,

With Robert Young in *Vagabond Lady.* (Courtesy of Rosalia Woodson.)

winsome Charlotte Henry and sultry Frances Drake, like Evelyn, wound up in B pictures.

Evelyn, however, was able for a time to stand out elsewhere. In the theatre, she appeared as Helena in Max Reinhardt's spectacular production of *A Midsummer Night's Dream* staged in the Hollywood Bowl in 1934. The play also featured a new young actress named Olivia de Havilland. The two became friends and Evelyn gave Olivia make-up tips. Olivia would go on to appear in the film version with Hal Mohr as cameraman, but Jean Muir inherited Evelyn's part. Evelyn's work in films at this time included *The County Chairman,* again with Will Rogers, *The Little Colonel,* in which she portrayed Shirley Temple's mother, and the classic version of Booth Tarkington's *Alice Adams* directed by George Stevens and starring Katharine Hepburn. Evelyn accepted a supporting role in this film primarily out of her admiration for Hepburn.

Off-screen as well as on, Evelyn was very much "the lady." But she became annoyed with some of the publicity that painted her as "the kissless girl," a demure image stemming in part from the roles she had played in films. So she was happy to cut loose in two screwball comedies made in 1935, *Vagabond Lady* for Hal Roach's studio distributed by MGM and *Streamline Express,* a Mascot production released by the newly-formed Republic Pictures. *Vagabond Lady,* directed by Harold Lloyd's longtime associate, Sam Taylor, cast Evelyn as the gumdrop-chewing employee of a department store and Robert Young as the ne'er-do-well son of the store's owner in what *The New York Times'* Frank S. Nugent called "a frothy, bubbling and sparkling farce." He noted:

> it is surprising to discover definite comedy talents in Robert Young and Evelyn Venable, who provide what is called the "love interest."
>
> Miss Venable . . . always has impressed us as an austere young lady who, after her first flights of cinematic romance, would settle down and join the ladies' sewing circle. In this picture, she barges off her pedestal and trades punches with [Robert Young] in a riotous scene that makes the Cagney tactics seem like a parlor game. The battle can be recommended particularly to those who expected something of the sort from the Baer-Braddock bout; they'll see lots more action. [4]

Streamline Express with Victor Jory and Esther Ralston was a takeoff on *Twentieth Century.* Like the John Barrymore–Carole Lombard screwball classic of the previous year, the zany Mascot production has an actress heroine (Evelyn) on a cross-country train trip with a wealthy fiancé (Ralph Forbes who had played a similar part in *Twentieth Century*) fleeing Broadway and her domineering director.

Not long after the film's release, Evelyn gave birth to her first child, Dolores, and left the screen for several months. In only two years, she had gone from being the most promising young actress on the Paramount lot to the leading lady in *Harmony Lane,* a Poverty Row picture about the life of Stephen Foster. However disappointing this turn in her career may have been, being a wife and mother was now more important to her than being a movie star. After a year's absence, however, she returned to the screen in leading lady roles to help

With Fredric March, Kent Taylor, Kathleen Howard and Sir Guy Standing in *Death Takes a Holiday*. (Courtesy of Rosalia Woodson.)

support the family when Hal Mohr was temporarily out of work due to the cameramens' union's strike. She worked steadily for the rest of the decade, taking time off only for the birth of her second daughter, Rosalia.

Evelyn was not proud of some of the B pictures she made in the later thirties, productions shot on modest budgets designed to make a quick profit on the second half of the now-established double feature program in theatres. Still, there were enjoyable films among them such as *The Hollywood Stadium Mystery,* a breezy little Republic comedy-mystery of 1938 which teamed her with Griffith veteran Neil Hamilton. Her beauty and talent continued to impress admirers including noted film and literary historian Edward Wagenknecht, who many years later compared her to Grace Kelly: "Evelyn Venable was certainly a lady—and probably a finer actress—but because she had a mind of her own she was soon cast aside, and nobody seems to remember her now."[5]

Ironically, she remained very familiar, albeit anonymously, to moviegoers over the decades. She was the model for Columbia Pictures' redesigned logo of the Lady with the Lamp although she did not receive compensation or even an official acknowledgment from the studio. And she is the Blue Fairy's voice in Walt Disney's classic animated feature, *Pinocchio* (1940), her supernal screen persona pivotal yet again in a cinematic landmark that continues to be revived for new generations.

Evelyn worked on into the early forties. Then in 1943, ten years after she had arrived in Hollywood, she made her last film, *He Hired the Boss,* a comedy for 20th Century–Fox co-starring Stuart Erwin, before retiring from acting altogether to raise her children.

In the fifties, she began a whole new career, becoming a professor of classics at UCLA, where she taught for more than twenty years. Her irrepressible personality combined with her scholarship endeared her to her students. She put her acting experience to good use when she convinced the classics department under her direction to let her students stage Greek and Roman plays complete with the appropriate costumes and make-up.

When I interviewed Evelyn in 1992, she had been retired from teaching for over a decade. Widowed since 1974, she spent part of her time in her Brentwood home and part with her younger

Left to right: Victor Jory, Evelyn, Ralph Forbes, Erin O'Brien Moore, Clay Clement, Allan Cavan, Esther Ralston, Sidney Blackmer and Vince Barnett in *Streamline Express.* (Courtesy of Rosalia Woodson.)

daughter in Idaho. (Her older daughter had become a regular tour guide at Will Rogers's home in Pacific Palisades.)

Evelyn fashioned her lifestyle to suit her personality. She loved animals and was a strict lifelong vegetarian. Cats, at one time as many as nineteen or twenty, had the run of the house and could be found everywhere, whether on chairs or preening themselves on the book-lined shelves. Talking to her was a continual delight as she punctuated her recollections of her days in films with spontaneous bursts of hearty laughter. Off-screen as well as on, Evelyn Venable glowed with the whimsical beauty that had enlivened even the least of her films and left its mark on cinema history.

I've quite an interesting family background. My maternal grandfather was the first generation from Scotland. His father had come over from Scotland. That was Walter Gay Cameron who married a lady named Eva Simpkinson whose ancestors came over from England. Dad's family originated in Normandy and there's a town called Venables with the "s" on the end of it from which they came. When they went to England at the time of William the Conqueror, the "s" got dropped somewhere. Although some very remote relatives in the East and out in California and probably across the country retained the "s" most of them dropped it. My paternal grandfather, William Henry Venable, was a scholar, a poet, a novelist, a historian. In those days, I guess a good writer did almost anything that occurred to him as interesting. He was a teacher and started the Chickering Institute. I have all sorts of books with Grandfather's name in them from the Chickering Institute. My father was Emerson Venable and he had a brother, Bryant. Grandfather had named them after his literary friends. Grandfather was the head of the Department of English at the classical high school, Walnut Hills High School in Cincinnati, and then Dad followed him. It's no longer called a classical high school but at that time there was what they called the annex which was the seventh and eighth grades and then the four years of high. So you went there for six years and you got Latin and Greek and all those other goodies. Dad himself also wrote but largely about Shakespeare and he lectured widely

A 1930s photo of Evelyn's "adoption" as "Laughing Eyes" into the Iroquois Nations. Left to right, Chief White Eagle, Iroquois; Running Deer, Iroquois; Red Star, Cherokee; Two Eagles, Sioux. (The Evelyn Venable Mohr Collection.)

on Shakespeare, too. My mother didn't work. Most ladies didn't work outside the home in those days unless they were poverty-stricken.

I was an only child and I was born in Cincinnati—normally, I think. I grew up there at Diana Place which Grandfather had built. Dad had been born there in the study in 1875. Later, he bought out his other brothers' and sisters' interests in the house and brought me and Mother and himself back there. We had the same German woman working for us who had practically raised Dad when he was a kid. There was a terrible influenza epidemic after World War I and my folks were scared because people were dying like flies all over the country—I suppose all over the Western World. So Dad and Mother decided to keep me home from school and just teach me what was necessary. Dad went down to the elementary school and said, "What things are required for the first years of elementary school?"

They said, "Well, a child must come out of the third grade knowing his multiplication tables, how to do long division—you know, the usual addition, subtraction, multiplication and division." So Dad and Mother taught me at home. When I went to school, they promoted me. They put me immediately into the fourth grade because I knew too much. They thought I'd be bored in the third grade so I went through school a year ahead of myself.

I went to the movies in those days but at that time I was only permitted to see Charlie Chaplin, Mary Pickford, Douglas Fairbanks and, until he got into that awful scandal, Fatty Arbuckle. After that, I wasn't taken to see him anymore. I was also allowed to see Tom Mix in westerns. He never even lost his hat and he never even kissed a girl. He acted as though he would have kissed his horse if the horse had been willing. I was a big girl before I was allowed to see any of those heavy lovers. Of course, I fell madly in love with Valentino as what woman didn't in those days but I never saw a film of his until after he had died. One of my favorite pictures was *Peter Pan* with Betty Bronson, Mary Brian and Esther Ralston. I remember them so well and I remember the dog Nana, too. I loved it. I saw it something like eighteen times. Mother had to take me all around town to catch them. If they'd only run it on TV, I'd watch it every time.

I also went to vaudeville shows. Once, I promised not to watch Gilda Gray shimmy. I guess she was the prime act on that vaudeville show and I was dying to see what a shimmy was—I hadn't any

With Robert Young, Reginald Denny and Berton Churchill in *Vagabond Lady.* (Courtesy of Rosalia Woodson.)

idea. They had a good program otherwise, too. I loved trained dogs and all those things. My mother, I suppose, knew what a shimmy was because she said, "We'll take you if you'll promise not to watch Gilda Gray."

I said, "All right." My cousin and I were in on this together. We're only a month apart in age to the day. We both did the same thing—we peeked through our fingers. We covered our eyes with our hands and then parted the fingers enough to see the whole act with Gilda Gray. That was a sneaky thing to do. I've been ashamed of it in a way but it amuses me, too.

I started acting in high school. Our high school was mainly scholarly kinds of things and we had kind of poor athletic teams in those days. The teachers in the meeting were trying to figure out what could be done that would attract public attention like the other high schools where all the parents and students would come and everybody would scream and yell. Dad said, "Why don't we do Shakespeare plays?"

The rest of the faculty said, "Oh, that's way beyond these students."

And Dad said, "No, we've got the brightest in the city. Let's try it. We don't have to put it on publicly if we don't want to." So they initiated it and by the time I came along, they had been going successfully for several years. The first year I had a chance to try out for a part was the first year they played in the public auditorium in downtown Cincinnati—Emory Auditorium which is still there.

I played Juliet and a boy played Romeo. There was a faculty committee who decided who should play what. Ordinarily, the two leads went to seniors but I was fourteen and a junior when I won the tryouts. I had just turned fifteen when the play was put on on December 7 of all days. I really was just a few months older than Juliet was supposed to be. The nurse says something about her being fourteen in two weeks. Being in a public theatre, *Romeo and Juliet* got the regular dramatic critics to come out and the reviews were absolutely stunning. You wouldn't believe how much they praised our performances. Then in my senior year at Walnut Hills, I played Rosalind in *As You Like It* which was quite a change from Juliet to this wonderful comedy.

Once Dad asked me, "What would you most like to play either on the stage or the screen?"

I said, "Well, I'd like most to play in both mediums Joan of Arc."

He said, "Is there a particular play you like?"

I said, "Well, yes." Percy Mackaye had written a very good play about Joan of Arc but there were a couple of things in it I didn't care for as much as I would have liked.

So Dad said, "Well, let me write one for you and see if you like that." And he did and it's wonderful.

Although I was young for my age in many ways, I went to Vassar at sixteen. I had a full four-year scholarship. The Vassar Club of Cincinnati gave it to me because my record was so good all through those six years of high school. When I got there, I was given a terrible little room. It was right in the corner of the building and the heating and water pipes went up through it so the pipes made noises when people would use the water. In those days, we had steamer trunks that stood on end. They hung things in them and they had drawers on the other side. When I'd open the trunk to get things out of those drawers or off the hangers, I couldn't get from the door to my room so I had to open and close the trunk to get across the room. That's how tiny it was.

A 1934 Paramount publicity photo of Evelyn driving her car near her Beverly Hills home. (The Evelyn Venable Mohr Collection.)

At Vassar, I went skiing for the first time. I had been sledding all my life at home on Vineyard Place. They called it that because it was originally in vineyards. It had lovely terraces and it was really great to sled down on them. So at Vassar, I thought, "Well, I'll go down there." I put the skis on—one of the older girls showed me how—I started out and I went faster and faster and faster. I saw a tree ahead of me and I didn't want to hit it, of course, so I tried to swerve and I succeeded in swerving right into a fence and crashed. I kind of came to. I was not totally knocked out but a little bit goofy in the head and I came to fully in the infirmary. I'd had a real accident and it's one of only two accidents I've ever had in my life. The other was out here in Southern California when I was thrown from my bicycle while I was out riding with my girls in Griffith Park.

At Vassar, they had a dramatic department but they didn't permit anybody to participate until they were juniors. Hearing Dad lecture before I was old enough to try out for those things, I kind of grew up breathing Shakespeare in one way or another. But as a freshman, I couldn't take all that. Besides, there were no male responses in class and I don't know—I was just used to being in a mixed group and I was quite unhappy so I left. I went back to Cincinnati and enrolled at the University of Cincinnati. I knew I was going to like that very much but then I got a telegram from Walter Hampden asking me to join his company. I had met him at Ridgefield, Connecticut in his home. Dad knew him because of the Shakespeare writings and all. I have a totally dried pomegranate shell—it rattles with the seeds dried inside—that Walter Hampden gave me when Dad took me backstage to meet him. He was playing in Cincinnati and he had a basket of fruit somebody had sent him. He reached in and said,

"Would you like this pomegranate? It has mythical connections with Persephone and so on."

I said, "Oh, I'd love it." And I've kept it all these years.

I guess I was about eighteen when I went with Hampden's company and I stayed about a year and a half. We never played Broadway but for a while, I joined a company in New York that was going to do an off-Broadway play. But it was dumb. It was a play called *Gas* and I can't even remember what it was about but it seemed awfully boring and stupid to me. I knew Jean Muir in New York at that time. She was known as Jean Fullarton then. We both were boarding at Jane Wyatt's mother's house. Jane had come from a wealthy family who went through the crash without a lot of damage and so Mrs. Wyatt was taking in select young ladies as boarders. This was before Jane had hit it very big. I shared a room with a girl named Alice Dalton and Alice and I would hear Jane declaiming as she rehearsed in her bedroom.

I was one of the youngest in Hampden's company. We went out in both *Cyrano de Bergerac* and Shakespeare. I just played a walk-on in *Cyrano* because they had another actress signed up for Roxanne but I felt beautiful as a nun walking across in the background when Cyrano was dying downstage. The company had about seventy-five people and of that, a dozen or so were women. Of the males, there were about eight who were not gay and were also single. A number of the women were older and married and had been with Hampden for years but the few of us who were young numbering maybe three or four were vastly interested in flirting with these few young men who were available. Nothing serious ever happened but it was kind of fun. It was normal, I guess, for teenagers in those days. We weren't as sophisticated at that age as they are now. At one point, I was collecting the dues for Actor's Equity Association. I'd knock on the dressing room door, people would say "come in," and you'd go in. One of the men who was playing a prominent role in *Cyrano* was there and he said, "Evelyn, I don't have the cash with me today. Can you come back at the end of the week when we get paid?"

I said, "Oh, you're just an old fairy." I was kidding. I didn't know what a fairy was. And he bridled and sputtered and I thought, "What's the matter with him?" Later, I realized why he had bridled.

When we hit Los Angeles, Richard Bennett was also playing *Cyrano* there. It just happened our

With Dorothea Wieck in *Cradle Song*. (Courtesy of Rosalia Woodson.)

programs overlapped at different theatres. When I wasn't on stage, I went over to see Richard Bennett and I thought, "Oh, boy, am I glad I'm with Hampden." It was such a different performance. Bennett was kind of drunk and he'd turn and make little comments to the audience that had nothing to do with the play. I thought, "Gosh, this sounds so unprofessional to me" and I guess it was. Bennett was his own boy and he did what he wanted to. He had a big name in those days.

A few weeks before we closed in *Cyrano,* Hampden had tryouts. He was going to do *Hamlet* the next season and, by golly, I worked real hard. Dad had taught me how to rehearse by myself so that I sounded the same way in my head that I did in reality. You know, we don't sound in our own heads the way that we sound to other people. He had rented what was called an Ediphone and I recorded every single syllable of Juliet before we did it and I did the same thing with Rosalind when I was in school. So I got an Ediphone in New York and I went over and over every scene as Ophelia till I got it the way I wanted it. That was why I think I went out there pretty well-prepared when Hampden gave me Ophelia. That was a thrill beyond thrills at that age to play the lead opposite the greatest Shakespearean actor in the world at that time. And he was wonderful to work for.

Paramount always had scouts around and the week after they had seen me in *Hamlet,* they began to pursue me all the way across the country back to New Jersey where we closed at Princeton. Each time there was an offer from Paramount to bring me out here, they raised it a little bit. I wanted to do Shakespeare but finally, the offer sounded stupendously big to me. I was getting fifty dollars a week to play Ophelia which was not horrible in those days but it was kind of the low point of the ladder because I was unknown really. Paramount came up with an offer—believe this—of three hundred and fifty dollars a week which looked like a fortune. Paramount, of course, knew exactly what they were doing but I didn't. I'd never had any movie experience. I didn't know they got fabulous salaries in those days just as they do now. So I signed with Paramount and they said, "Well, this is subject to tests for films." They flew me all the way back to Los Angeles during Holy Week when we were laying off and gave me a test. Strangely enough, it was a scene from *Mrs. Moonlight,* a modern play I had done opposite Stuart Walker who had had a stock company in Cincinnati. It was all coincidental. It was a good test, I guess—I looked okay to them. So they signed me up for this skimpy little three-fifty and it wasn't till I began working in pictures that I knew I had been had. At the same time, I enjoyed it but not nearly as much as the stage. I really missed doing the Shakespeare.

The first picture I did was *Cradle Song* in 1933 with Dorothea Wieck, who was a beautiful, beautiful actress until somebody started a rumor that her husband, who was a newspaperman in Germany, was a Nazi and that ruined her in this country. In the film, they found a baby at the door of the convent. Dorothea was the sister in this convent and when they couldn't find anything to do except take it to an orphanage, she said, "Oh, let me have the baby and raise it. We'll conform with every rule of the convent" and so forth. So I was that baby when she grew up and we had a lot of scenes together. I loved her. She was so lovely a woman as well as an actress. She had a very minimal accent. You weren't sure whether it was British or German it was so slight. Mischa Auer, who was in it, was in several pictures I did. And that was the first of several times I worked with Sir Guy Standing who was a lovely man with wonderful stories of the theatre. Gertrude Michael, who was also in the cast, was a great gal. I thought she was devastatingly beautiful and a damn good actress. I didn't know her intimately because in those days just a few years in age made a difference and she was, I think, two or three years older than I.

Cradle Song was also the beginning of my screen romance with Kent Taylor. We did six pictures together more or less as a team for the various studios we worked in. Maybe there were offers from others but we were pretty well tied up doing those six pictures—bang, bang, bang! Kent was a darling man. He had a wife and some kids and he wasn't a playboy at all—just a sweet man. There wasn't any off-screen interest although, of course, the press, not the studio, tried to make it that way. I always thought that was so silly because they also called me "the kissless girl" with this myth that my father had forbidden anybody ever to kiss me on the screen. Of course, I was kissed from *Cradle Song* on.

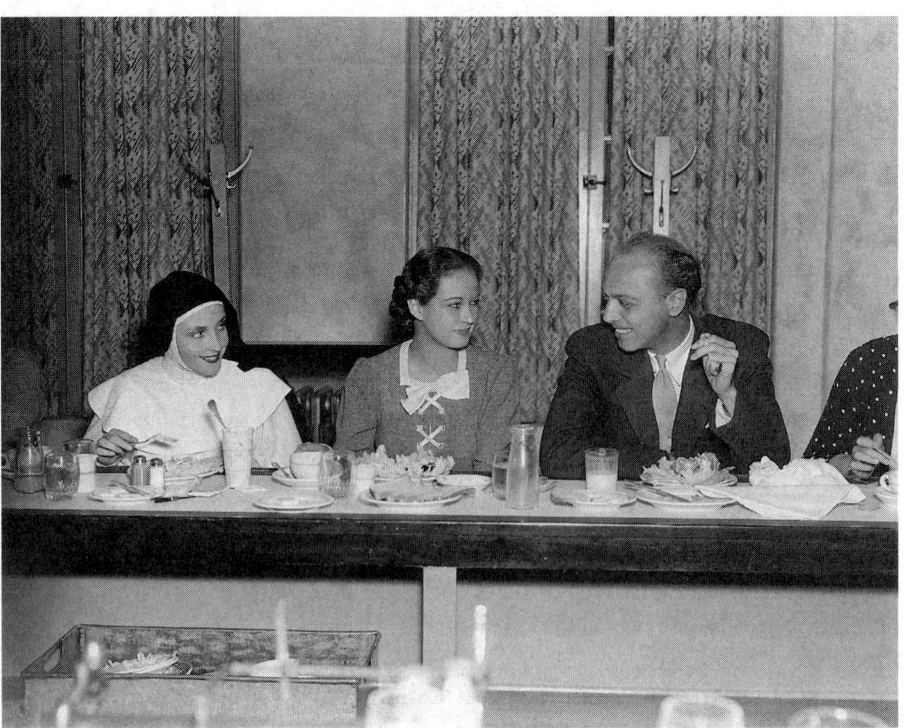

With Dorothea Wieck and Mitchell Leisen in the Paramount commissary. (Courtesy of Rosalia Woodson.)

Mitchell Leisen had been an art director and then an associate director before being promoted to a full director on *Cradle Song* and his next film and mine, *Death Takes a Holiday.* I thought Leisen was an excellent director with, of course, a fine artistic sense. He was very new to it but he was a darn good one. He was a very intelligent man and his artistic sense was a bonus, you know. We would rehearse a little but not much. He liked spontaneity to a certain extent and that's where it was helpful to all of us who had been in the theatre because we were able to work it out on our own and then come on the set ready to shoot. Of course, we were all a little bit hammy in those days because none of the directors were really quite used to the transition to talking films. People had to do more mugging in the silents and so some of the direction was a little spotty because of that. It wasn't that the director didn't know his job but it was just that it was a brand-new job. It worked out, though, all right and they're still running *Death Takes a Holiday* all over the world. I get clippings and fan letters still. In South America, they took all this seriously when they first showed the film there. People thought, "Oh, death must be wonderful." Bang! And they killed themselves. Now that was hearsay. I didn't go to South America to see for myself but I wouldn't be too surprised. Travis Banton did the beautiful costumes and changed one completely from what he had in mind for the final scene to that kind of frothy, more ethereal-looking one.

Fredric March was the lead and he was a sweet man but just absolutely girl-crazy. In one of the last scenes in *Death Takes a Holiday,* I was seated on a couch and Freddie sat down beside me. Gradually, as the romance developed, I was kind of moved backward until I was lying on the couch and he grabbed a handful of my bosom. Automatically, my fist came up from the floor—my arm had been dangling over that way—and I caught him on the chin and knocked him back on his fanny. I didn't really have anything in mind except getting out of there. Then he got up and looked at me with horror and stalked off to his dressing room. Leisen said, "I think you'd better go and apologize or we won't get this scene."

I said, "I don't think I'm the one to apologize. I think he is." And I stalked off to *my* dressing room.

Freddie finally came in and said, "I'm awfully sorry. I didn't mean to offend you. You're just a lovely woman."

With Fredric March in *Death Takes a Holiday.* (Courtesy of Rosalia Woodson.)

I said, "That has nothing to do with it. You offended me very much." It was all right, though. I said, "Okay, just let nothing like that ever happen again," and that was it. After that, we got along fine. I liked him. He was a nice man—he was married to Florence Eldridge—and I thought he was a very good actor, I really did.

When I went into pictures, my dad was unable to retire without notice and my mother had died so he insisted that I have a chaperone on the set and off. And if I went out socially, this woman had to go with me. I also employed a housekeeper who was a dear woman so we three women lived in a rented house first. It was not far from the studio and then I rented another one, a lovely place with a pretty view up on Crescent Heights north of where Franklin ends. Then I bought a house and after I met Hal Mohr, the cameraman I was to marry, I didn't need a chaperone or a housekeeper. My companion chaperone was the oldest sister of a girl from a large family, a girl who had been in the Hampden company. I had met this family and so had my father who approved of her as my chaperone. Her name was Dorothy Gardner and poor Hal had to take Dorothy with us when he first took me out to dinner. Finally, he decided it would be nice if Dorothy had an escort. Now she was six feet tall and a damn good bodyguard but the man she invited to be her escort on several occasions was about a foot and a half shorter than she. It was mildly embarrassing but not too much. Her younger sister, Edna Sallee, was my stand-in and I still see her.

Soon after I began working in pictures, I got my first car. Dorothy and I saw a used Pierce Arrow, a great big leviathan of a thing, and Dorothy said, "Oh, this car drives beautifully." It was a second-hand car but I found it drove like a dream and, by golly, we got it.

I bought my first Ford after I met Hal. He said, "You don't want that thing. It just gobbles gas and it's like driving a Mack truck." And it was so I got a Ford and I stayed with Fords for many years.

In those days, I used to get up at three a.m. as soon as the daylight was beginning to dawn and go out horseback riding every single morning. I'd wanted a horse all my life. The nearest I'd come to it was the pony track when Dad would hold the pony's bridle and run down the track with me on a pony. In Hollywood, I bought two horses so my companion chaperone could go out riding with me. They had some publicity from the studio that I had been arrested for riding a horse down Hollywood Boulevard without a parade permit, of all crazy things. I never rode down Hollywood Boulevard and I never would have dreamed of it but they had to keep things going in the press, I guess.

With her Ford. (The Evelyn Venable Mohr Collection.)

After *Death Takes a Holiday,* I was loaned to Fox to play in *David Harum* opposite Will Rogers. It wasn't 20th Century–Fox then, you know, just Fox. I'm really not quite sure how Fox borrowed me from Paramount. It was only my third picture and I assumed at the time and I suppose I still do that the studio to which you were under contract had the right to lend you. I'm sure they made a good profit on it, too, at the time. Not all of it was shot at the studio. We went to Riverside for the sulky races at the end—we used the racetrack down there. And we did some of the exterior scenes in Mandeville Canyon which is now all built up with beautiful homes and so forth, but at that time was largely wild. It seemed like an enormous trip all the way out from Hollywood almost to what is now Pacific Palisades but actually it's not very far.

I played the role of the city girl visiting in the small town in which David Harum was the principal banker. Really, the roles of the ingenues in the Will Rogers pictures were not too meaty dramatically. They were generally rather charming parts—the love interest really, you know. I had some lovely scenes with Will Rogers bantering back and forth. We were trying to, not really deceive each other, but horse-trade pretty smartly with one another in several scenes and we had an awfully good time. How he prepared for his parts, I haven't the vaguest idea. When he was not playing in the scene, he was generally at his typewriter working on his daily column for the newspapers. He didn't sit around and chat a great deal that I could see. He kept pretty busy—well, he was a busy man.

His relations with the director, James Cruze, were very warm. As a matter of fact, I met James Cruze and I met the man whom I was to marry, Hal Mohr, who was photographing it, and Will Rogers, all on that picture for the first time. And Jim Cruze became our closest friend, Hal's and mine, as long as he lived. Rogers and Cruze got along very well. Cruze was one of the directors who didn't like to fool around and waste time. He was known as alarmingly fast but, unlike some of the men who were alarmingly fast, Cruze knew exactly what he wanted and, better still, knew when he got it. That appealed, of course, to Rogers to whom time was also of the essence. I remember several days on that film we finished the day's scheduled shooting by one or two o'clock in the

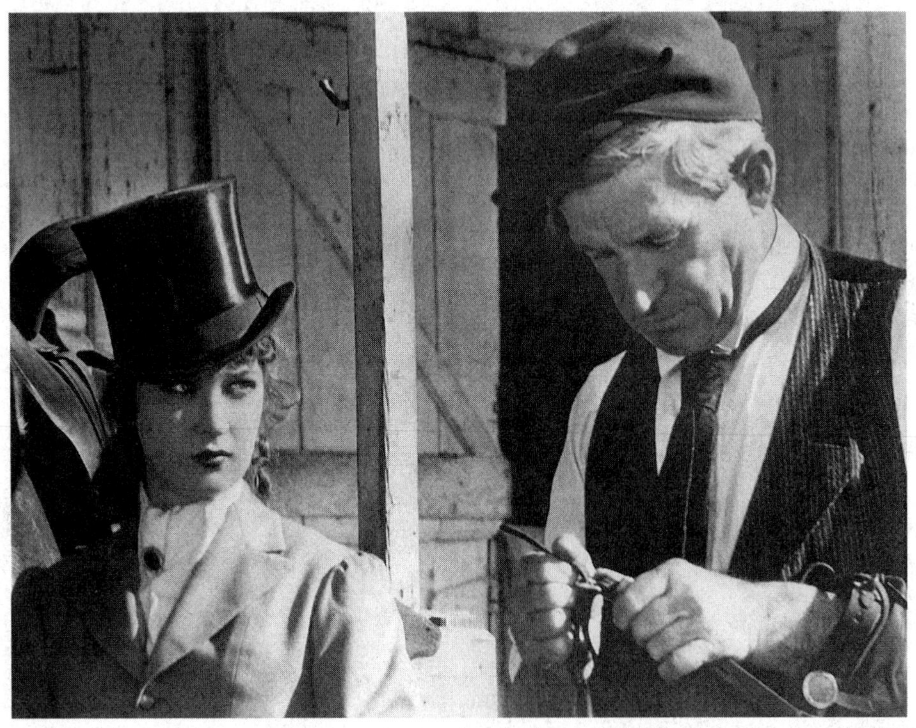

With Will Rogers in *David Harum*. (The Will Rogers Memorial Commission.)

afternoon. Cruze would say, "See, we can't go home now, Will. They'll think we aren't working."

And Rogers would say, "Well, let's fake it for a couple of hours." Then we'd have to quit because there was nothing left ready for us to shoot—you know, the next set or whatever. But it was a marvelous team, Rogers and Cruze. And my husband, although he was twice an Academy Award winner for his photography, was also fast in arranging the lights and setting the scene up and also knew when he got it and didn't have to fool around with extra retakes. So they got along famously.

Will Rogers ad-libbed, of course—oh, did he ever! I had my script and I had my lines down pat—that was part of the old stage-training. And as you're well aware, I'm sure, on the stage, actors simply don't rewrite the lines in mid-scene before the audience, not in the sort of thing I had done, anyway. I had played Shakespeare, *Cyrano de Bergerac* and that sort of thing and nobody could quite improve on those. But Will—he always kept to the story line but very often, he'd say something that was quite different from the line in the script though it tended in the same direction dramatically. And you just had to be awfully attentive. This was where I was awfully pleased to have had the stage background that I'd had. I had learned that it was important to convey sincerity to an audience. It was important to listen just as you would to a person you were having a social chat with. It was only by listening to what Rogers was saying that you could divine when he had come to the end of this line and pick up the cue. Sometimes, you had to modify your own line to fit the context but it was great because it kept his performance always fresh.

I absolutely loved it. Of course, I was a great admirer of Rogers. He was about thirty-five years my senior so we didn't have any particular social interplay off the set. But he was so kind and so warm, so easy to work with. If he felt that you were ill at ease, he'd do some little gag even if he wasted a shot, to put you at ease, to make you laugh and then you could go on. I remember he used to have fun with my name. He'd call me "Evelyn Venerable," or, because I'm a vegetarian, "Evelyn Vegetable."

There is one thing I have from Will in connection with that film. As I just said a moment ago, I met my husband on that picture and it wasn't three weeks before we were engaged. Will gave us an autographed picture. I asked him for a photograph

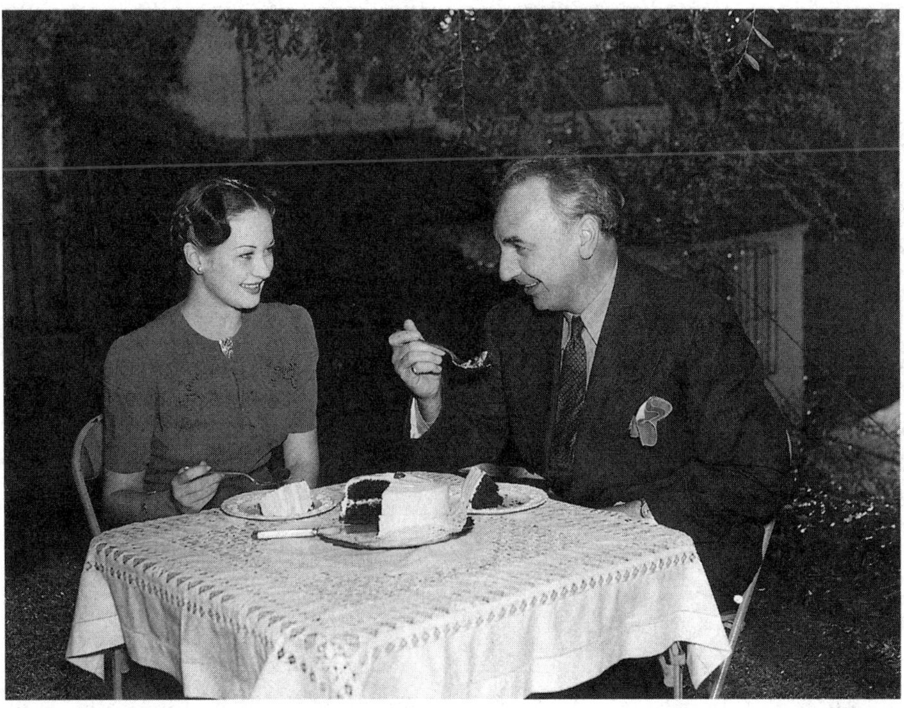

With her husband Hal Mohr at their home in the Hollywood Hills in the 1930s. (The Evelyn Venable Mohr Collection.)

before the picture was finished and he wrote on it, "To Evelyn and Hal from the old matchmaker," and I have that hanging on my library wall now. It was very sweet of him to claim that but he didn't have to make any match. I think Hal and I knew which way we were heading right away. But, of course, it's a cherished memento of our meeting.

Hal had proposed to me the first time we took a drive when we were down in Riverside on the picture. He had his interlocutory decree at that time and he said, "If I were free, would you marry me?"

I said, "Yes. When do you get your final decree?"

He said, "It's a little short of a year."

And I said, "Well, I want to wait a full year because I want to be awfully, awfully sure. I don't want any of these 'marry and divorce,' 'marry and divorce' experiences." And it worked out very well. We were both even more sure at the end of that year than we had been before.

I'm not sure I'm right but I've been told that *David Harum* was the biggest moneymaker of that year. And it's been quoted to me—and again, I haven't checked it, I have no reason to—that it was one of the very top if not *the* top of the Will Rogers moneymakers. So it was a very successful picture. I don't really have any anecdotes about it. Nothing drastic happened at all. It was just lovely, almost like a vacation it was so pleasant to make that picture. I remember one thing that struck me awfully vividly from the beginning of the picture until the end. When Will would decide that the day's work had gone on long enough, and it was never very much after 4:30 or 5 o'clock, he'd suddenly stop in the middle of whatever was going on, in the middle of a scene if need be, turn around, look at the director and say, "Santa Monica Canyon!" That meant we're going home and he went home to that lovely ranch in Santa Monica which was merciful. It's true that sometimes scenes he wasn't in were shot later on. There had to be some night things, too, of course.

Jimmy Cruze was the sweetest man in the world outside of Hal and they loved each other like brothers. I have his autographed picture hanging up here beside the one of Will Rogers because they were my two great admirations. We didn't know Will in the way we knew Jimmy who, as I've said, became our dearest, dearest friend. He was having a hard time in his later years and he still had those open houses on Saturday nights out in his lovely estate at Flintridge. But the place was deteriorating physically. He couldn't afford the gardeners, the household help and all the things he had had. We would bring out pure grade alcohol. He liked just that and water as a highball. I never saw him get drunk but he'd sit there and drink it all evening. He'd sit in a great big chair that he left to me. His furniture was all antique Spanish—it was beautiful stuff—and I have several pieces that he left to us. He adored his daughter Julie. His first wife, Peggy Snow, was her mother. Julie was a highly gifted gal. She was musical and wrote wonderful, charming songs. But she was a lesbian and she got on drugs and died young. It was tragic. His second wife, Betty Compson, was always coming out and borrowing money with her charm. She was a lovely gal—a very charming woman socially—and Jimmy, I think, was always kind of in love with her even after they had divorced.

He didn't have much money in his last years. Sometimes if he'd have a ten-dollar bill, he'd put it in a book—he had a rather large library. Then he'd forget which book he put it in. He was saving it for a really terrible day and he never could find it, the poor thing. Hal tried to get the industry to help him but nobody would do a thing, not even the people who were indebted to him. He was a has-been, you know. He married Alberta McCoy. Her father had been a veterinarian. I can't quite remember how she showed up at Flintridge one day. Some friend of Jimmy's brought her as his guest, I guess, and she was very much concerned about the straits Jimmy was in, both physically and financially. My golly, he asked her to marry him and she did. She took care of him like a mother in his last years. We called Alberta "Tots," the nickname her father had given her when she was a little tot. They moved out to Amalfi Drive in Pacific Palisades just as we had done. They were on the other side of Sunset and lived there very, very happily.

Back at Paramount after *David Harum,* I was in *Double Door* and *Mrs. Wiggs of the Cabbage Patch.* Charles Vidor, who was married to Karen Morley at the time, directed *Double Door.* I didn't like him. It wasn't that he made moves on people but he was just a nasty little man, the "knife-in-the-back" kind. But I enjoyed the film. It was a good cast. There were several people in it I'd worked with before. And they brought out Anne Revere and Mary Morris from New York.

I didn't have very much to do in *Mrs. Wiggs of the Cabbage Patch* except be the ingenue. Pauline Lord, W. C. Fields and ZaSu Pitts were in the cast. Poor Pauline Lord could not remember her lines. She had camera-fright so badly that they had to have what they called at that time "idiot boards" or cue cards today. W. C. Fields was always fried before noon. When we started shooting at eight a.m., he had his drink already half-gone. I don't know how many he'd had before he came on the set. I had very little contact with him but he was always very pleasant. He wasn't a falling-down drunk because when he got to that point, he wasn't in the scene. In some of the films he hated children but I was a little bit surprised—he wasn't like that at all. He was perfectly nice to the children in the picture. As long as he was aware of who he was and what he was doing, he was very nice to everybody. I loved ZaSu Pitts. I had seen her in *The Wedding March* which Hal had shot for von Stroheim. She played a crippled princess and she was great as a tragedienne, I thought. And here she was playing comedy just as well. I'll never forget those hands that she used to such effect, twisting her fingers and all that.

I went back to Fox and Will Rogers for *The County Chairman*. It was released in '35 but I wasn't yet married when I made it and Hal and I were married in December of '34. When I did it, I was so much in love. I don't know whether you've ever been in that state but it's a very serious preoccupation. We now knew that we would be married on the first day we were both free of a shooting schedule. I was exceedingly preoccupied with Hal Mohr then and I really was kind of concentrating on my personal life. So I don't remember *The County Chairman* that well. It wasn't by far the picture that *David Harum* was from the point of view of story and so forth. I have a feeling I played a schoolteacher but I'm not even sure of that. It was about a small-town politician—the county chairman—and the involvements with the bad guys and the good guys. It was a period setting. I don't know whether it was the Gay Nineties or early turn-of-the-century but around in there somewhere. I had my first ride in one of those old

With Kent Taylor in *Mrs. Wiggs of the Cabbage Patch.* (Courtesy of Rosalia Woodson.)

flivvers where you wear a duster and a big veil tied over your wide-brimmed hat and go like a bat about fifteen miles an hour down the street.

I haven't any idea how I came to do *The County Chairman.* I was lent again by Paramount so the chances are that somebody asked for me. It may have been Will—I just don't know. Louise Dresser was in both *David Harum* and *The County Chairman.* Oh, I loved that woman. She was one of the loveliest, kindest, most gracious, cultivated ladies I think I ever met. She and Will did a number of films together. They knew each other so well. Louise had difficulty with her hearing at that time. Will knew it so he always managed to maneuver where he would be in her line of vision unless there was to be a cut. When he'd be speaking right to her, of course, she could hear it but, otherwise, she'd follow his lips or his gestures or something. Nobody, I think, was aware of it at all.

Mickey Rooney was also in *The County Chairman.* He was older than he looked because he was little so he was still playing kids younger than he was. I think he was a decent guy but he was just crazy about girls which showed later when he married over and over and over. We'd take him to a meal with us at Musso and Frank's between pictures or between scenes and he was always fun. I remember his head was spinning around watching all the pretty ladies in the place.

For the locations in *The County Chairman,* we went to Sonora, California, up to the top of the Mother Lode country and shot for—oh, I think it was probably a couple of weeks—I don't recall too clearly how long we were there. There was one thing that happened while we were in Sonora that may be a worthwhile anecdote. It was quite a small community. I imagine it's grown like everything else in California but it was small then and surrounded by fairly large ranches on one of which we did a number of our locations. When it was learned, as it was almost immediately after our arrival, that Will Rogers was there, he received an appeal from the police department of Sonora. They were presenting a benefit for the families of men who had died in the course of their duty and they asked Mr. Rogers whether he would be good enough to make an appearance. They knew it would bring in a houseful. So he said, "Why, certainly." He went up there and this was after a practically dawn-till-dark shooting day because on lo-

With Will Rogers in *The County Chairman.* (Courtesy of Rosalia Woodson.)

cation, you know, they started with the sun so they could take full advantage of the exterior time. He went on at the very beginning of that show and he gave a one-man show. The place was packed from wall to wall and he literally brought down the house. He was just magnificent—as though he were fresh as a daisy out of bed and he must have been a very tired man at that point. But the gratitude of the police department and, of course, of the whole community was incalculable.

I believe the last time I saw him was strangely enough, again, a police benefit for the same purpose—for the wives and children of men who had died in action. But this time it was for the city of Santa Monica and quite a large benefit performance. Of course, Will Rogers's Santa Monica Canyon ranch is right there and it was known he was coming so the thing was tremendous. They had a huge parade, he rode his horse, I rode a horse in western costume and lots of things like that—Leo Carrillo with his palomino and so on and so forth. And again Will gave his everything. It obviously didn't matter to him whether he was paid or whether he was doing it for free for a good cause. He put his whole being into it and that was pretty much.

With Shirley Temple and Hattie McDaniel in *The Little Colonel.* (The Kobal Collection.)

I remember when I heard about the crash in Alaska with Wiley Post. It was not long before my first baby was born. I was driving my husband out to Warner Brothers. We lived in the Hollywood Hills and, as we were going over the Cahuenga Pass, the word came on the car radio. I remember it felt as though somebody had said, "The world has just ended." You know, the shock was such because when Will Rogers went off with a man like Wiley Post, who would ever dream there would be a plane accident? Hal and I were both stunned. Then I just pulled off to the side which you could on the road in those days and I remember bursting into tears and so did my husband. It was just terrible. I think most people in the country who knew Will Rogers at all felt he belonged to them personally. I just wish he were around, that he had stayed with us longer. I think maybe our political problems would have been a lot less burdensome if he'd been here to make his comments. I think the country would be more sane and more happy.

As I said before, the Will Rogers pictures were made on loan-out. I had signed with Paramount for a seven-year contract at their option, not mine, but I suddenly knew I didn't want to do some of the things that they had in mind for me. My agent found a loophole. My contract had not been approved either by the court or by my father who was my legal guardian. I was still underage when I signed the contract—you had to be twenty-one in those days. So I got out of the contract and immediately, I think, went to Fox to do *The Little Colonel* with Shirley Temple, Lionel Barrymore and Bill Robinson. My salary jumped—wow!—to a very excellent one in those days. I think it was something like seven hundred and fifty a week but I could be wrong.

Making *The Little Colonel* was wonderful. I had read *The Little Colonel* books when I was a little girl. And oh, that Shirley Temple—she was the exception that I ever met to the child actor syndrome. She was just a charmer because she had a very wise pair of parents. She didn't know she was a star and she wasn't spoiled at all that I could see. She just thought this was a game. She was talented as she could be. She could learn her songs and her dances right away. Lionel Barrymore was an interesting man. I didn't know him personally off the set but I thought he was the best actor of the two brothers.

Bill Robinson or "Bojangles," who danced with Shirley in the picture, was one of many black performers with whom I worked in Hollywood. Others included Stepin Fetchit, Clarence Muse, Hattie McDaniel and Louise Beavers. They were all wonderful and I loved them. There wasn't a whole lot of discrimination on the set. But I grew up in Cincinnati, a city which had been one of the outlets of the underground railroad so black people were not looked down on at all there. All the actors, black or white, were very friendly at the studio and on a first-name basis. There was no subservient thing at all when speaking to each other. Once, Eddie Anderson who played Rochester on Jack Benny's show took us down to the Central Avenue district which was all black. He took us to a wonderful club where black performers went to entertain and to be entertained. There were maybe only two or three white people in the audience and they had a great show. After that, Eddie said, "I want you to come to my house if you'd like to. I'm having a little party." And he sure enough was. They had a buffet spread that you couldn't believe with everything under the sun. After everybody had eaten his fill, he said, "Would you like to learn how to shuffle and do some of our natural dances?"

We said, "Sure." So one black took one of us and one took another and taught us to shuffle. It was such fun.

I did *Vagabond Lady* with Bob Young and Reginald Denny for the Hal Roach studio, a comedy that was completely screwball. I think that was the first one I did that wasn't a costume picture. Bob Young, who was the leading man, was a heck of a nice man. He was really a charmer. I think he later became an alcoholic. We saw him, though, after he had joined AA and he was all clean and so nice. Hal had taken me to the fights. I wanted to see what a prizefight was like. It was pretty bloody. Bob came down the aisle, came over and spoke to us. Speaking of fights, Bob and I had a knockdown, dragout fight in the picture and that fight was for real. We weren't pulling any punches. Bob was trying to but I kept hitting so hard and I was enjoying it. It was physical activity which was fun. I hadn't done much of that on screen. Reginald Denny was a very entertaining guy. I was a fan of his to start with and when he was in the picture, I thought, "Oh, boy, this is great."

With Robert Young in *Vagabond Lady*. (Courtesy of Rosalia Woodson.)

After that, I had a supporting part at RKO in *Alice Adams* with Katharine Hepburn and Fred MacMurray who was a lovely man. I was such a fan of Hepburn's—I still am—that I thought, "Oh, I would do anything. I would bring her coffee in the morning if I could just meet her." When this offer came along, I was pregnant and I knew I couldn't work very much longer because I think I was already in the eighth month or something. So I got, I think, a six out of eight consecutive days kind of contract and a heck of a lot of money for it. The thing was to have worked with Hepburn. Oh, gosh, she was exactly—what you see is what you get. She was wonderful. Not what I would call any friendship developed. For one thing, there wasn't time and also she's a very private lady. But it was such a thrill to me, I'll never forget it. She was very, very nice and very cooperative theatrical-wise. We both had the advantages of an education but we didn't really socialize at all. I just admired her from afar as it were and loved having had the chance to meet her. George Stevens, the director, was as nice as he could be, too. He was not as celebrated as he later became. I think Hepburn kind of followed her own lead and a director would have been a fool that didn't appreciate it.

About the same time while I was still pregnant, I did *Streamline Express* with Victor Jory and Esther Ralston for one of the smaller companies, Mascot. I admired Vic as an actor and we got to know him pretty well when Hal did *A Midsummer Night's Dream* because he played Oberon. Esther Ralston was the most beautiful lady. People probably thought it was make-up and all that made her so beautiful but she really was just as lovely off the screen. And a very sweet lady, very nice to work with.

After my first child was born, I really began to lose interest in doing movies. But Hal was blackballed because he had taken the wrong side in the union thing. It was later proved that he had not. He had been trying to solve the problem but they blamed him for having called the strike. Actually, he had opposed it. He said, "This is biting the hand that feeds us." So I just took whatever came along because we needed the dough at the time. I worked at Mascot, I worked at Columbia and Republic. A lot of them were forgettable pictures. The main thing I remember about *North of Nome* with Jack Holt at Columbia was being in the swimming pool at night which was supposed to be the ocean. It was icy cold and I thought, "I'm not going to live through this. I'm going to die of pneumonia." But I didn't.

It was around this time that Columbia used my face as the model for their logo of the lady with the

With Katharine Hepburn in *Alice Adams.* (Courtesy of Rosalia Woodson.)

lamp. I had met with Harry Cohn in his office and he asked me permission to borrow my photo from Paramount to use as the model for the design. I said sure. But there was never anything in writing and for that reason, I never got any royalties for it.

In 1937, I was in a musical at Republic, *Happy Go Lucky,* with Phil Regan and oh, God, that was a horror picture. Regan was another of those grab-you guys. He was what I call a professional Irishman and they're kind of smug in a way. A lot of them are nice guys like Pat O'Brien and Edmund O'Brien. But some of them are kind of cocky and self-assured and smart-alecky and Regan struck me as that way. Between scenes, we went to rest in the seat of a car—the door was open and everything. He tried to get me down on the seat but I managed to escape because I'm pretty agile.

In another picture for Republic, *The Hollywood Stadium Mystery,* Neil Hamilton was my leading man and Barbara Pepper and Reed Hadley were in the supporting cast. Barbara married Craig Reynolds and she asked us if we'd stand up with them at their wedding. We remained really good friends and saw a lot of them. I think Craig was killed in a motorcycle accident and Barbara raised their two kids by herself. Reed Hadley's name was originally Reed Herring and I suggested changing it because it sounded like a dead fish. I think I suggested him for another picture. He wasn't really a great actor but he looked good for the part. He did a number of other films and improved as an actor.

With director Aubrey Scotto and Phil Regan during the filming of *Happy Go Lucky.* (Courtesy of Rosalia Woodson.)

Back at Paramount in 1938, I was in *The Frontiersman,* one of the *Hopalong Cassidy* pictures with Bill Boyd and Gabby Hayes. Bill was quiet and very sweet and Gabby kind of kept to himself. I loved Clara Kimball Young who was in it. We roomed together when we went on location up in Kernville in Kern County. I got a lot of early movie lore from her—she was able to tell me so much about the silent era. I was so much of a fan that I was just fascinated with her and she was really a warm and wonderful lady.

What I remember about the filming was a scene in which I was supposed to take a running leap, land astride a horse and ride away into the distance. Well, I was a good rider but I did not know how to take a running leap in a costume and land on the saddle. I gave it a couple of tries and then I said, "No, get the double. She'll have to do the mounting." But then we switched and I did the riding off in all directions, it seemed. I remember the horse got the bit between his teeth before I got on it, it took off and we rode and rode and rode until it was exhausted. Actually, I found it kind of exciting because I was confident I could stay on—it was a western saddle, you see. Even though I had these period clothes on, I was sure I wouldn't have an accident and I didn't.

At one time, there was a tendency to just list the cameramen among the credits. Hal got his own union card as soon as it became possible to do so and that made him feel a lot better. Later, they began to notice everything at the Academy and gave awards all over the place including two to Hal. Of course, I think "colorization" is a terrible thing because a good cameraman designed the photography in order to enhance the story. Hal said, "If you hear the music in a film, it's a bad film and if you particularly notice the photography, it's bad photography. It ought to just be in harmony with the story."

He had wanted to direct. It wasn't a matter of high rank or something. He just wanted to do it and he had a chance to direct *When Love Is Young*, a lovely picture with Virginia Bruce and Kent Taylor. That turned into a wonderful friendship after we happened to move next door to Virginia and her Turkish husband on Amalfi Drive. We lived in a charming English provincial house there. We would alternate going to each other's house for cocktails each evening. This one day, we went to Virginia's. Her house was on a vise. We were sitting out on her patio and there was a little house-gate blocking the view of the patio from the street. Virginia, of course, was the most beautiful woman I think I ever saw. She was perfection—her skin was just exquisite. She had a seamstress come to her house each week to make the clothes she wanted designed for her. On this occasion, she was wearing a beautiful linen dress that had no sleeves and a deep collar—not a "V" but a square neck. It wasn't cold but it was breezy and suddenly Virginia said, "Please somebody close that gate. It's getting kind of chilly out here." And it was just this little bum house-gate that came up to your waist. We were sitting down but it didn't protect us at all. Everybody burst out laughing and Virginia looked wounded. She said, "Why are you laughing?" Nobody tried to explain it—it was really funny. But Virginia was like that sometimes. She had been married to John Gilbert who had this big beautiful bed in his home. When she saw it after he took her there, she asked, "Is this the bed that Garbo slept in?" It was odd for a new bride to hark back to something like that.

In 1939, I made personal appearances here and there on a train across the country for Paramount. Cecil B. DeMille was also on this tour. I met him and he was courteous but he was very much involved with one of the gals on the train. Then I got terribly sick in New York and had to be flown back to my own doctor in California. I insisted on that—I thought I was dying. They had called three separate doctors in New York for me and I was certain that they were ignoring something and giving a wrong diagnosis.

Sure enough, I had amoebic dysentery which should have been deadly because, when I got back to the hospital here and my own doctor identified it, he said it was the highest amoebic count they had ever had and have a patient survive. There's two possibilities as to how I got it. When we played in Chicago, the plumbing was old in the theatre and it could have been in the water. But before we hit Chicago, we were in the Southwest. They were bringing in vegetables from Mexico where they were grown with human fertilizer and they may not have been washed properly and cleaned in the places we ate. I think a banquet was the only place I ate anything of a salad nature uncooked when we were there. So which place I picked it up in I don't know. But oh, brother, I literally died twice and my doctor brought me back both times.

I was still playing leads in films. In 1940, Fox put me in *Lucky Cisco Kid* opposite Cesar Romero. He was a close friend of Virginia Bruce and we remet at her house and were really good friends. Dana Andrews made his screen debut in that picture and I became a fan of his, too.

It was about the same time that I was the voice of the Blue Fairy in Walt Disney's *Pinocchio*. I also took part in deciding what color the Fairy's hair should be in the picture. There was a voice tryout but with no camera, of course—they didn't need that. They did have some of the cels that they planned on using hanging on the wall in the little room where I did the voice recording. I was supposed to kind of keep my eye on those cels so I'd know what the Blue Fairy was doing at the time she said such-and-such a line. And I did that. There was no direction really on how to read the lines, just the cels to show me what the action was going to be. It didn't take very long but it was a very interesting job. I just worked alone. I imagine some of the voices had to work together. I remember Cliff Edwards who was the voice of Jiminy Cricket came up to the house—we were still living in the Hollywood Hills then—and drank a lot and was very entertaining as he played his ukulele. I met Disney, too, but it was only a scant "how do you do." He had chosen me from two hundred voices that had been tested for the Blue Fairy. But there wasn't much publicity about it because they weren't broadcasting who the voices were. After the film was finished, it was mentioned here and there. I've gotten envelopes from the Disney outfit lately over and over again,

With Neil Hamilton in *The Hollywood Stadium Mystery.* (The Evelyn Venable Mohr Collection.)

some of them duplicates of what was sent before with the reviews when it was re-released and some of them with a picture that shows the Blue Fairy. I was invited to come and make an appearance this past year. A couple of their writers came out to my home and gave me these huge posters. They said, "Well, Miss Venable, we've missed having you there but we thought it was so nice of you to have done this picture and to have been sweet to us that we thought you might like to have these posters."

I finally left films because I wanted to raise my family, run my home and be with Hal. When I was working, there were times when we were like ships in the night almost because his schedule would be so different from mine. Additionally, I worked with the Red Cross because I wanted to make some contribution to the war effort. So I joined the Motor Corps and worked in the night shifts. I had a station wagon of my own and they fitted it with stretchers in case we were attacked on the West Coast. I never got overseas because I wanted to be with my family by day.

I had always wanted to go back and finish my degree that I had abandoned when I left college to join Hampden. So when the older of my two girls was ready to start college—she wanted to go to UCLA and I wanted her close to home, too—I decided, "Well, I'll see if I can go into UCLA just before her." I talked to a counsellor in the College of Letters and Science at UCLA, a lovely, lovely man who was the dean at the time, and he saw I'd really not completed the year at Vassar. But he said, "Well, you were there attending classes till the very last of the year."

I said, "I would appreciate it. I just didn't want to enter as a freshman because that'll be in the same class as my daughter. I want to beat her through college, anyway."

So he said, "Well, let's give you credit for a full year because certainly your life experience in the meantime should count for education." That's true but I thought it was generous of him because it wasn't by the book.

Then I enrolled as a sophomore and she as a freshman. I had had the classical high Greek and Latin—six years of Latin and three of Greek—and I was afraid I would have forgotten everything. But

With Stuart Erwin in *He Hired the Boss.* (Courtesy of Rosalia Woodson.)

With Will Rogers in *David Harum*. (Courtesy of Rosalia Woodson.)

A 1934 portrait from *Death Takes a Holiday*. (The Evelyn Venable Mohr Collection.)

they asked me something at UCLA that in the days at Vassar, nobody talked about—a major and a minor. They said, "What will be your major?"

I thought, "Oh, my Lord." Dad had told me never to teach English because you'd go blind grading compositions in awful handwriting. So I said, "Well, I had six years of Latin. Let's say Latin. I hope it'll come back to me." By golly, I remembered everything but vocabulary and that came back fast. I remembered the grammar, the structure, the sentences, the declensions, the conjugations and all that. Strangely enough, there had been twenty-two years in between but I had had enough of it. And I taught classics at UCLA for just short of twenty-five years. So, in two words, I had two whole separate careers.

(Courtesy of David Jaffe.)

Jean Muir

In 1934, André Sennwald, the film critic for *The New York Times,* hailed Jean Muir, a rising star in Hollywood, in a review of Warner Brothers' new release, *Desirable:*

> A pale, blonde girl, with a touching honesty and directness of manner, and a throaty voice which adds a new emotion to her words, Miss Muir immediately becomes one of the most attractive and skillful of Hollywood's younger players. Her portrait of a famous actress's lonely daughter in *Desirable* is a delightfully fresh and truthful piece of acting. Watching her apparently artless progress through the moods of a sensitive girl in late adolescence, the spectator is lured out of his customary embarrassment. For Miss Muir touches the imagination. She is an excellent young actress, she is fair of face and she is free of the mannerisms which accompany girlish charm. It is a privilege to toast her.[1]

The actress who inspired this unusual tribute was born in New York City on February 13, 1911, and grew up in a middle-class family in New Jersey. Her early ambitions to be an actress led her to study drama at the Sorbonne in Paris and with Maria Ouspenskaya in New York. A succession of parts on Broadway brought her to Hollywood under contract to Warner Brothers. Despite her initial reluctance to abandon the theatre for the movies, she quickly advanced from bits to featured supporting parts, beginning with *The World Changes* opposite Paul Muni in 1933.

Along with the growing critical recognition that greeted her promotion to leads in 1934 was a reputation in the press for outspokenness. An honest, candid person by nature, the tall, beautiful blonde, who was unusually serious about her work as an actress, sought to bring to her roles a realism born of her sense of truth. This commitment would cause continual conflict with the powers-that-be at Warners. For example, she balked at an attempt to glamourize the farm girl she played in *As the Earth Turns* (1934). While she failed to persuade the studio to let her wear a plainer costume and make-up, she more than compensated with the "charm and ability" of her performance.[2]

This same concern for the truth and an emotional awareness of her role was reflected in *Desirable* in which she plays the 19-year-old daughter of a prominent stage actress (Veree Teasdale). The actress regards the lovely girl as a dangerous rival and has her fears confirmed when her daughter develops a crush on one of the actress's admirers (played by George Brent). Jean, who in her personal life had conflicted with her own mother, effectively conveys the confusion of a girl at odds with her mother and struggling with her emotions when she becomes aware that her feelings for George Brent are much deeper than a schoolgirl crush.

Jean's career was at its peak in 1934 despite her much-publicized disputes with Warners causing her to be labeled "the studio pest." Even though she often felt she had compromised with her pursuit of realism, she had the advantage of working in a studio that was foremost in dramatizing social issues. For instance, her final film of 1934, *Gentlemen Are Born,* is a study of the corrosive effects of the Depression on male college graduates and the women they love. But her career as well as Warner Brothers itself would soon be affected by the imposition of censorship with the Production Code and the response by studio heads to the radicalism they perceived in the attempts to unionize the

With George Brent in *Desirable*.

industry and Upton Sinclair's gubernatorial campaign.

This more conservative trend was evident in Jean's 1935 film, *Oil for the Lamps of China,* in which she played in support of Pat O'Brien and Josephine Hutchinson. Alice Tisdale Hobart's original novel was an indictment of the oil industry's treatment of its employees in China. But Mervyn LeRoy's film version, despite excellent performances by Jean and other cast members, so altered the story that the oil companies are shown as essentially beneficent employers. Only two years before, Jean had worked with LeRoy on *The World Changes,* in which the director presents a naturalistic view of how the pursuit of capitalistic wealth leads to decadence and destroys families. Now suddenly, the studio had changed course and Jean's complaints about the compromises in the new film, while supported by critics at the time, did little to endear her to producers already vexed with her frankness.[3]

Because of her clashes with the studio, she would make only a few more major films at Warners. In the spectacular all-star production of *A Midsummer Night's Dream,* she is a memorable Helena to newcomer Olivia de Havilland playing her rival, Hermia. A landmark of Hollywood history, it was a notable, pioneering attempt at filming Shakespeare. In her last film of 1935, *Stars Over Broadway,* a musical co-starring Pat O'Brien and James Melton, she is a girl aspiring to be a singer and pursuing her ambition with the same dogged determination that had marked Jean's own drive to be an actress.

All too soon, Jean's film career took a nosedive from which it would never recover. Although in the fall of 1935 she was promising to be more cooperative with the studio in exchange for better parts, the producers did not live up to their end of the bargain. Instead, they packed her off to England for a film at Warners' Teddington studio intended for British distribution, not American release, and farmed her out to Fox for *White Fang* before again featuring her in a film at their Burbank studio. Jean's last films for Warners were a succession of B pictures quickly produced to finish out her contract.

Jean, for her part, was heavily involved in the union movement and supported a number of progressive causes including the Spanish Loyalists who were combating the forces of Franco in the Spanish Civil War. Activities like these caused her to be listed as one of Hollywood's leading leftists in a 1938 internal report by the censorship group, the Legion of Decency. She made only a few more films after 1937; her last, *The Constant Nymph* was released in 1943. Perhaps the best of her later films was *And One Was Beautiful* (1940) in which she gives an outstanding performance as Laraine Day's social climbing sister. When she refuses to take responsibility for a fatal hit-and-run accident, playboy Robert Cummings is unjustly convicted for the crime.

Beginning in the late thirties, she concentrated on the stage, particularly summer stock on the East Coast. For example, she toured with Phillips Holmes in the summer stock production of *Golden Boy,* playing the part originated on Broadway by

With Dorothy Burgess and Clara Blandick in *As the Earth Turns.* (Courtesy of Cole Johnson.)

another blonde rebel, Frances Farmer. That same season, she worked with the new young actor, José Ferrer, in *Arms and the Man* at the Ridgefield, Connecticut theatre managed by Gertrude Lawrence's husband. She headed up the Suffern, New York summer stock company for two years in the forties, on one occasion directing Madge Evans. She produced the Russian comedy, *Listen, Professor!* starring veteran actor Dudley Digges, on Broadway in 1943 and in 1947 appeared in a contemporary American comedy, *Tenting Tonight.*

Increasingly, however, her personal life was consuming more of her time and attention than acting. In 1940, she married Henry Jaffe, a show business attorney who in later years was the national counsel for the American Federation of Television and Radio Artists, finally becoming a prominent television producer in the late fifties. The couple had three children, two boys and a girl.

In 1950, Jean was about to embark on a career in the brand-new medium of television, playing the part of the mother in *The Aldrich Family* series, when she found herself caught up in the political maelstrom of the time. The show's fall premiere on NBC was "abruptly cancelled . . . after the network and the sponsor had received protests" against her appearance as *The New York Times* reported.[4] It immediately became a front-page story around the country and a watershed in the onslaught of McCarthyism. Jean had been labelled a Communist by various right-wing groups who listed her in their organ, the booklet *Red Channels,* as one of a number of radio and television artists with alleged Communist ties. The only American actress ever fired from a television show for her political views, Jean became a symbolic victim of the times. "Her dismissal," commented Eddie Cantor, "is one of the most tragic things that ever happened in show business."[5] Others who came to her support included her friend and colleague from the old days at Warners, Margaret Lindsay.

Jean vigorously denied she had ever been a Communist.[6] Her true political allegiance was to a very liberal wing of the Democratic Party and she had been an impassioned supporter of Roosevelt when the Communists were still dismissing him as a "bourgeois" or even "fascist" lackey of capitalism. But the rightists of 1950 who had

A publicity photo from her years at Warner Bros. (Courtesy of David Jaffe.)

found her guilty without a hearing were not interested in the truth. Indeed, an official in the American Legion proudly took credit for her dismissal.[7] Liberals and moderates were aghast. *The New York Times* editorialized that she had been the victim of "trial by character assassination";[8] playwright Howard Lindsay compared her treatment to the Stalinist purges;[9] letters to the editor reminded readers of how Hitler had come to power and suggested a boycott of General Foods, the sponsor.[10] Merle Miller headed an inquiry by the American Civil Liberties Union that resulted in his book on the case, *The Judges and the Judged.*[11] But all in vain: Jean Muir had been offered up as a sacrificial lamb to the postwar forces of repression and paranoia. General Foods did not reinstate her. They formally declared her "a controversial person" whose appearance on television "might adversely affect the sale" of their products.[12] And in Hollywood, where her conflicts with the studio in the thirties were well-remembered, she could count on no support from a Screen Actors Guild now headed by the politically ambitious, born-again conservative, Ronald Reagan, who reportedly years later still considered Jean a Communist.

Meanwhile, with her marriage disintegrating, Jean's personal life fell apart and she began drinking heavily. While she never hit the depths experienced by Frances Farmer, the fifties were a void in her life. The few bright spots were her friendships, including one with a new star by the name of Grace Kelly. On several occasions, Grace spent weekends with the Jaffes and Jean was an invited guest at Grace's wedding to Prince Rainier in 1956.

After she divorced Jaffe in 1959, she picked up the pieces, stopped drinking and made a comeback on the stage and in television. In 1960, she appeared on Broadway with Ed Begley and Frank Silvera in *Semi-Detached,* a drama which flopped although her personal notices were good. Her ban from television lifted by producer David Susskind, she appeared in several shows including the *Naked City* and *Route 66* series.

Her interest now, however, was focused on teaching drama. And in 1968, after several previous teaching stints, she began an eight-year association with Stephens College, years which were the happiest, most fulfilling of her life. When she left Stephens, she taught at other colleges for another five years until her retirement in the early eighties.

Jean continued to live independently for most of the eighties until health problems caused her to move to a retirement home in the Los Angeles area, where she was staying at the time I interviewed her in September, 1992. Her integrity,

With Clara Blandick, Warren Hullund and Beverly Roberts in *Her Husband's Secretary.*

while it had caused her much grief, had at the same time enabled her to maintain a circle of lifelong friends throughout her stormy career. One of them was George Baxt, the president of her fan club in the thirties and later a well-known mystery novelist who always managed to include a reference to her in his books. He first met her in 1938 when he invited her to speak at his high school in Brooklyn. He followed her stage career faithfully in succeeding years and in 1950, when she was blacklisted, he and Margaret Lindsay were the first to call Jean and offer her their support.

Despite all her vicissitudes, Jean had retained her sense of humor and her dedication to activist politics. She was introspective, acknowledging her own shortcomings and, considering the difficulties she had had in the industry, surprisingly devoid of bitterness. Yet her feelings about commercialism in the industry and the elements who had blacklisted her were still strong. A maverick in her time and one of the last survivors of Warner Brothers' golden age in the thirties, Jean Muir continued to display the independent spirit that had been her hallmark when, for a few short years, she advanced the art of acting in motion pictures.

I'm an only child. I spent my childhood in Ridgewood, New Jersey although I was born in New York City. I think I had one year in high school in Ridgewood but I went to boarding school after that—Dwight School in Englewood, New Jersey. My father was an accountant for a firm down on Front Street. He was a Scotsman and he had been trained in accountancy in Scotland and was always in demand because those accountants are better than ours—at least, they were then. My mother took part in everything in the community. She was the president of the Women's Club at one time and she directed plays. But she stayed home, she was a mother.

When I was nine years old, Mother took me to see *The Merchant of Venice* and when I walked out of the theatre, I said to Mother, "When I grow up, I'm going to be an actress and I'm going to play Portia in *The Merchant of Venice*." Well, of course, I never did because at the time I was acting in New York, Hitler was around in Germany and the whole first part of the play was such a run-down of Jews that they just didn't do it.

With Frank McHugh and James Melton in *Stars Over Broadway*.

I was a very serious person in school—I would talk Shakespeare, for instance. After I graduated at eighteen or so, my family sent me over to Scotland in the summer of 1929 where I visited my aunts, uncles, cousins, second cousins and so forth. My father had saved the money to send me over to meet all his family and mine. He had several brothers and a sister, Aunt Margaret, who was a darling. They were most all in Scotland so I stayed there for most of the summer. But I finally did go down to England where one of them was and had a nice time there. Then in the fall, the stock market crash came but I didn't know anything about it. One of my aunts and an uncle who was an invalid took me over to St. Jean de Luz in the south of France and I stayed there for the winter. But I got bored stiff down there because I wasn't learning French. And what the hell was the use of being anywhere when I wasn't learning anything? I was supposed to generally help with my uncle. I took him out on the *plage* or boardwalk during the day for a walk. Then he'd sit and I'd go on walking. I had on my Scottish kilts and the funny thing is that twice in my future while I was in Hollywood, I heard stories about this girl who would walk up and down the *plage* in St. Jean de Luz. I embarrassed them terribly by saying it was I in my kilt. (I never played a Scottish part except in real life sometimes when I wouldn't let the kids have their allowances.)

I lived in France for about six to nine months in 1930. I went to the Sorbonne, the very fine university in Paris. They took me in so quickly. They just talked to me for a few minutes and said, "Well, if you think you know enough French to learn the language."

I said, "Yes." I had had French and Spanish at school but I never learned Spanish any better. Well, they were very nice at the Sorbonne. My father sent me twenty-five dollars a week to live on and pay for my schooling and books, too. I was on my own and it was heaven. I lived with—believe it or not—a Catholic royalist family. They still wanted the king back—the king was around someplace, I forget his name, a Louis something probably. They were a very sweet couple, very nice to me, and I loved every minute of my time in France. But my father didn't have enough money anymore to keep me there. When I left, I hadn't spoken English in six months and I had learned French so well—of course, I was learning all the Racine plays and Molière. So by the time I was coming home on the boat, I found it very difficult to change to English.

When I got back to the States, I began working in the theatre in New York. I had one or two walk-on parts at first. I was trained and filled with the Stanislavsky method of approaching a part. I studied under Madame Maria Ouspenskaya who was a magnificent actress and a tiny little creature—you know, I towered over her. She was about fifty-five years old when I went to classes with her but she seemed much older with her white hair pulled back in a knot on the back of her head. Once, a child was sitting on a piano doing the balcony scene from *Romeo and Juliet* and the boy playing Romeo was down below her on the floor when Madame Ouspenskaya got up. She was so angry at this girl that she pulled her off there, climbed up and sat on top of that piano—it wasn't a grand but one of those uprights—and said to the boy, "Now, start the scene." So he did and I've never seen a Juliet as good as she was.

I didn't have any really big parts in anything on Broadway. I was looking for jobs in New York and I always seemed to get something even if it was a sick woman lying in a hospital bed in *Life Begins.* I tried to get into some of the summer stock companies but I never made it until I got away from Hollywood four years after I went there and then I did a lot of summer stock.

The first play I did on Broadway in 1930 was *The Truth Game.* Ivor Novello was the star, Billie Burke played the feminine lead and Viola Tree was the second woman. Viola Tree was so funny—tall and gangling and very English—she was really a riot. I was playing a maid, I believe. I forgot my entrance once and Billie Burke was very sweet and forgave me. Then I forgot it another time and that time she didn't forgive me. She was furious and I don't blame her. I also did *Peter Ibbetson* with Dennis King and Jessie Royce Landis. I played Peter Ibbetson's mother in the dream sequences. It was a nice part—I liked it. As I said before, I only played one small part in *Life Begins* in 1932 and Glenda Farrell and Mildred Dunnock had the leads. And there was *Troilus and Cressida,* a Players' Club production. It was only done for two or three nights and I don't know whether I even had a speaking part. Unfortunately, I have not read the play since which I should.

I thought I was going to get my break when I understudied Marguerite Churchill in *Dinner at Eight* and I understudied the other vampish part. I wanted so badly to play that. The actress didn't turn up one day for a matinee and I'd gotten into the bed all ready for the curtain to go up when in she ran still in her nightgown she'd slept in. She pushed me out of the bed and there she was. So I never did get to play it although I met George Kaufman, the author, whom I adored. But I did get a good part in *Saint Wench.* Helen Menken was the star and I played the mad sister sitting by the fireplace staring at her the whole time.

I think it was because of *Saint Wench* that I was brought out to Hollywood. They did screen tests of me and then suddenly Warner Brothers called me up for an interview and I went to see Jake Wilk, the casting director in the New York office. I walked in and said, "I'm very sorry. I'm a little late but I had to walk. I didn't have money for carfare." They immediately had the contract that they were going to give me. They were going to give me a hundred and fifty dollars a week to go out to Hollywood instead of which, of course, I started at seventy-five dollars a week. Never give away that you're poor.

My full name was Jean Muir Fullarton and they said, "We're going to change your name to Fullar." And I said, "Oh, no, you're not. You can use my middle name if you want." So that's how I became Jean Muir. I felt I was committing suicide when I signed a contract to go to Hollywood because the theatre was so serious to me. I think now my attitude about it was rather absurd but then I thought I was selling out when I went into pictures. So much so that instead of going out there by train, I went from New York to California by boat right through the Canal Zone. I wanted to delay my arrival in Hollywood as long as possible.

I was twenty-something so nobody in my family came with me. My father, who still had a Scottish accent, said only, "I wish you'd be a writer, dear, so you could stay at home." But my parents were backing me in whatever I wanted to do. My father died about six months after I was in pictures. I always figured that he said, "Well, Jean is all right. She'll take care of her mother, I don't have to worry" when he died. He'd had TB three times in his life and I'm sure subconsciously he was ready to die. I couldn't grieve for him too much because I had just begun to learn to know him unfortunately. My mother died many years later when she was eighty-seven. I don't think she was too supportive of me during the political troubles of the McCarthy era. She was a woman on her own, she had her own

With Veree Teasdale and George Brent in *Desirable.*

opinions and a lot of them didn't agree with mine. She was an amazing woman but, you know, l-o-v-e didn't seem to be in her vocabulary.

I arrived in Hollywood in the spring of 1933—I think in June. I stayed at the Knickerbocker Hotel when I first got out there. One night, I woke up. My bed was trembling and I thought somebody was under it. So I got up to rush to the telephone and suddenly realized it was an earthquake, my first earthquake. This was in the fall within six months after I moved there. I called the man at the desk downstairs and asked, "What's happening?"

He said, "Oh, nothing, don't worry. Nothing's happening at all. It's perfectly all right. It's all gone now."

I said, "Well, thank you," and I guess I went back to bed and went to sleep. The next morning when I went downstairs, that whole huge, very highly and badly decorated ceiling of the hotel lobby was on the floor and I said to him, "What do you mean telling me that nothing happened?"

He said, "Well, we didn't want to worry you." I've never been able to get upset about earthquakes since.

The Knickerbocker Hotel was in Hollywood itself right across from the Valley. I just had to go up to Cahuenga Pass right across to Warner Brothers, so it was about fifteen or twenty minutes drive. I'd begun driving in New Jersey as soon as the law allowed—sixteen, I think. Once in California, I realized I had to have a car out there and I spent my first salary in getting one. I got myself a little Ford and I later got a better one. (At the peak, my salary got to four-fifty when they dropped me.) I moved out of the Knickerbocker about three or four weeks before Christmas in 1933. After that, I lived in four different apartments, I think. I had one on Crescent Drive, one of those streets that went down from Hollywood Boulevard to Sunset and so forth, and then I had one somewhere else in Hollywood.

With Paul Muni in *The World Changes.* (The Academy of Motion Picture Arts and Sciences.)

I had small parts in my first pictures at Warners. In *Bureau of Missing Persons,* I played a girl about to commit suicide on a park bench. The only thing I remember about that is I was supposed to be crying before I go and commit suicide—jump in the lake or whatever it was—and one of the stage managers came up with a little thing in his hand and said, "Here are some tears for you."

I looked at him and said, "What?"

He said, "Tears, you want tears. You're going to be crying."

I said, "Excuse me but I'm an actress. If you want me crying, I'll cry"—which they didn't like, of course. I got off on the wrong foot from the very beginning.

In *Female* with Ruth Chatterton, I think I played a secretary or something, a very small part. She was very sophisticated and I was a little scared of her, I think. The first film in which I was really featured in a part was *The World Changes* with Paul Muni. I played two parts in that, in fact. I played his sweetheart whom he left behind and her daughter. That was funny because he was quite short and I'm very tall so for this walk down the lane, they dug a trench about six inches deep. I had to walk in the trench and he walked beside me so he would look taller than I. It's always amused me. I get a big kick out of it but Paul Muni didn't think it was so funny.

Muni was very kind to me, an impressionable young lady, and I adored him. He was a perfectionist. More than that, everything was just so and he got it so well-rehearsed and learned with each intonation. I thought he was a genius. He was really a technical actor if I ever saw one but he could raise the tears, too. Muni and his wife were very, very apart from the whole moving picture community and I was, too, in a certain sense. I was not at parties and stuff like that. I really didn't meet very many of the people in the industry except those I worked with. Aline MacMahon also played in *The*

With Joe E. Brown and Johnny Mack Brown in *Son of a Sailor*.

World Changes. She was such a wonderful actress. But I just had so much awe of her as an actress that I never got to really know her as a human being.

Mervyn LeRoy directed the film. As a moving picture director, I guess he was one of the best. But very few of the moving picture directors at that time understood what the actor was beginning to do on Broadway with the whole Stanislavsky system. However, LeRoy was very good. I didn't like him at first but then I realized he was giving me some very good advice. The first time I said, "No, that's not the way to do it," he was very sweet. He explained to me the difference between acting on the stage and screen: "I don't have time. No director in pictures who has three weeks to make a picture in has time to go into depth of character. You have to depend on the actor for that. I can give you clues and give you ideas to work on." I remember he was a short man. But after that, I looked up to him and paid attention to what he said. I guess he'd say maybe I didn't, that I was arguing or something. I was a pretty pesky person, I think. I'm amazed they kept me so long.

In the beginning, I used to go to the previews of my pictures and then I said, "Oh, to hell with it." The first time I saw myself on the screen was in *The World Changes*. I went to see the preview in a full theatre downtown. I sat on a step up in the balcony, I watched this thing and when I came on screen, you could hear my voice all over the theatre, "My God, I'm beautiful!" First, I got a reputation as being egotistical and then when people knew me better, they realized it was surprise that was in my tone.

After *The World Changes*, I was in *Son of a Sailor* with Joe E. Brown which was exactly what it sounds like. Joe E. Brown was not famous for his acting, he was famous for his comedy and comedy can be done by somebody without ever making contact with anybody else on the stage or on the screen. So I kind of felt as if I were all alone out there. But he was a dear, just a sweet person, and I loved working with him. I think we went down on a ship once—that's the one location I remember.

I had the feminine lead in *Bedside* with Warren William. I played a nurse. The director, Robert Florey, was very nice and very quiet. He'd pull you aside and talk to you quietly if he wanted to give you direction. I recall that Warren William was very quiet, too. I don't think any of them liked me very much because I came showing off all my acting things from the theatre and I was an aggressive little bitch, you know.

With Marjorie Rambeau and Richard Barthelmess in *A Modern Hero.*

The first picture in which they starred me was *As the Earth Turns.* It was taken from a very fine novel written by Gladys Hasty Carroll. She lived in Maine and she had drawn this beautiful picture of a farmhouse and farming in Maine. Of course, it was "moviefied" so that you barely saw that part of it. You know, they called me "the studio pest" because I had a lot of conflicts with the studio. In one scene in *As the Earth Turns,* they wanted me to get all dressed up like a moving picture star and I refused. Well, how much glamour would a farm girl in Maine have? But Hollywood glamour was what they were talking about. Alfred Green was the director and he was a very sweet guy. I never had any trouble with him but I don't remember him giving me any direction that inspired me. His directions were all very physical and I finally sat down and said, "Look, I'm a little lost here because I wasn't trained this way and I have to learn it."

I don't really remember very much about G. W. Pabst who directed Richard Barthelmess and me in *A Modern Hero.* Pabst was supposed to be such a great director and so I was waiting to be directed by him. But he spoke German and I think he had somebody translate for him. I do remember Dick Barthelmess because he chased every skirt in town off-screen. He tried it with me but very quickly I let him know that I was not interested, that I was a virgin and that put him off immediately. That was my biggest defense, you know. We got along very well other than that. He really was basically a very sweet man.

They were starting to censor everything when we did *A Modern Hero.* In one scene when Dick was making love to me, we were sitting together on a grass knoll or something and he grabbed me in his arms, lay there and then he's supposed to push me down. The last close-up you see is of his head above mine, so obviously we were lying down, right? Well, that was cut out by the censors of that period so they had to fade that picture out as we went down. That was the kind of thing they did and when the Code came in shortly after, it was worse because there wasn't any such thing as sex. There was no organized protest against the censorship then even though it was terrible. But when you look at a movie today, on the other hand, you might not mind having some restraint.

In my pictures, I graduated from the virgin to the wronged woman. In *Dr. Monica* with Kay Francis, I was an unmarried woman who had a child and at the end, I flew off into the sunset to commit suicide. I guess Kay Francis was very unhappy at the time we did it. She came in with her wrists bound up once and the rumor spread that she tried to commit suicide. Another time—I don't know what was the matter—I couldn't reach her and I guess I didn't try too much.

I had the lead in *Desirable.* I got very excellent reviews but the studio didn't do a big job on publicity for it. They could have to help it along but by that time, they were a little angry at me. I was still basically antagonistic to the whole idea of being in Hollywood. I didn't want to be there. I wanted to be back in New York where the theatre was. Verree Teasdale played my mother in *Desirable* and she disliked entirely playing my mother. George Brent was my leading man. I was very impressed with him but he wasn't impressed with me so there was a little bit of friction sometimes. Not outward friction but shy and turning away on my part—pushing away, I guess. But it was a fun film to make. I enjoyed making it because I liked the part.

Then I made *Gentlemen Are Born* with Franchot Tone and Ross Alexander. It was about young college people in the Depression. I never discussed anything with Franchot Tone—I don't know why. We had met in New York when we'd made a screen-test together. In fact, I think the test with him brought both of us out here but to different studios. I was basically afraid—not afraid *of* him but frightened *by* him because he had such a sexual drive. I was scared to death of that. But I thought he was a splendid actor. I'd seen him in one or two things in New York and he'd been just marvelous. I never saw him do anything in pictures that was like that. Ross Alexander was a good friend. He committed suicide just a few years after that picture was made. I didn't know what was happening to him and it was such a shock because I admired him. People didn't talk to me very much about their problems. They do now. I go out on the porch here and people come over and tell me their whole life story. But then I was so involved with Jean Muir and I was, I think, a very selfish young woman. I was sensitive but selfish.

With Kay Francis in *Doctor Monica.* (The Museum of Modern Art.)

In 1935, I did *The White Cockatoo* with Ricardo Cortez who was the best upstager in pictures. He knew just how to lean on his upstage foot. On the stage, you have to take a big step to upstage somebody but all you have to do in pictures is to move back on one foot. You just shift your weight onto your back foot and you're upstaging the other actor. Ricardo Cortez had been doing this to me regularly and I was getting a little mad when I caught on to it. I was complaining about it to a cameraman who knew what was happening between Ricardo Cortez and myself: "I know what you do on stage but I don't know what to do in movies."

The cameraman said, "Look, I'll tell you what you do. You very simply move back on your one foot, your downstage foot."

"Back?" I said.

"Yes, back," he said. "That will force you around with your backs to the camera."

"What good is that?" I asked.

"Wait a minute," he said. "With your back slightly to the camera, it will be an over-shoulder shot of Ricardo Cortez. Then when they come to make the over-shoulder shots, they'll skip him because they'll say that we had it already."

I said, "All right, I'll try it."

So I moved back. You just have to move your body to be a lot on camera and one cameraman who wasn't in on this little thing, when he finished taking the shot said, "All right, Mr. Cortez, that was an over-shoulder shot for you. I'll take Jean's now." Ricardo Cortez was going to the nightly rushes when he suddenly saw himself cut out because he had moved forward and the camera was focused on the same place where he had been. He went out of focus, I came into focus and he was furious. What could he do? It was his own fault. He was the one

With Ricardo Cortez and Ruth Connelly in *The White Cockatoo.*

who was moving back. He never upstaged me again although we didn't get along. You don't make up with the Ricardo Cortezes of this world. But the cameraman had fixed it and it was fun.

Oil for the Lamps of China was supposed to be an exposé of the dealings of the oil industry in China and it turned out to be a pat on the back for them. That made me mad and I suppose I talked about it. Pat O'Brien was the leading man but I didn't really know him. It was a very strange relationship.

Then I was loaned out to Fox to make *Orchids to You.* That was fun because it was a different studio, everybody was very nice and I enjoyed it as far as I remember. John Boles was the leading man and he was amazing. He couldn't act as much as a kitty-cat. But he could sing—he really had a beautiful voice. Charles Butterworth was in it and he was marvelous. He was a dear and so funny offscreen as well as on. And Spring Byington was a doll, always fluttering around in real life the way she did on the screen.

I went back to Warners to play Helena in the most ambitious film I did for them, the Max Reinhardt production of Shakespeare's *A Midsummer Night's Dream.* I was really looking forward to Mr. Reinhardt, one of the great directors of the world and, of course, the theatre. But he never gave me a direction that had to do with the inside character. He'd say, "Put your hand in front of you on your bosom at this speech."

And I said, "Why?" And so I wasn't in favor with him, either. I liked William Dieterle who co-directed very much. Whatever I got out of the character, I got from him and not from Reinhardt who acted like a dictator. But I'm proud of having been in the film. It was the first really successful adaptation of Shakespeare on the screen. I have great admiration for Mary Pickford and Douglas Fairbanks but I didn't think their version of *The Taming of the Shrew* was good Shakespeare. The production of *A Midsummer Night's Dream* was very spectacular. I wasn't conscious of the sets on most of the Warners pictures. They were average—there wasn't anything special about them the way there was in *A Midsummer Night's Dream.* There was just an office, an apartment or walking along the street—I don't really remember what they were. But for *A Midsummer Night's Dream,* Reinhardt spent money right and left and Warner Brothers went along with it. They did everything Reinhardt wanted and what Reinhardt wanted was the earth.

With Mickey Rooney in *A Midsummer Night's Dream.*

There were some splendid performances in the film. Jimmy Cagney was wonderful as Bottom. I'll never forget his delivery of the speech when he awakens. And Mickey Rooney was just like Puck, the character he played. I didn't really get to know him but I remember how he climbed a tree. His body was so nimble and he was very fast. I envied him because he was so free and I was tied up in knots in those days. He was really a mischief-maker always playing practical jokes.

The little girl who played Hermia, Olivia de Havilland, was going places. There's no doubt that girl was going to be a star. There was so much energy, so much putting out and by this time, I was a little quelled, I must say. I just wanted to get the hell out of there. But she just came on that screen like a bombshell and I could see it right then. Even when I played a scene with her, she brought me up, you know. I think she's one of the finest actresses Hollywood ever got. I'm sorry that she didn't go back to the theatre because she would have been a wow. She would have been the biggest star we had in the theatre.

I was in a musical, *Stars Over Broadway,* with Pat O'Brien and James Melton, the singer. I think James Melton had a beautiful voice but I don't think he could act. Obviously, he couldn't because he didn't stay in pictures. Another famous singer, Jane Froman, made her screen debut in that picture. She lived in Columbia, Missouri in later years and when I was teaching at Stephens College, I knew her quite well. Bill Keighley was the director and I liked him very much, one of the very few gentlemen in the business.

Busby Berkeley was directing the dance numbers and what happened during the making of the film was all very bad. Berkeley drank too much, got into an accident and killed one or two people on the road going home from a cocktail party at which I happened to be. I don't know why I was there—I didn't drink at the time. The next morning when I got on the set, they were all complaining about Berkeley having killed somebody. But that afternoon, when I got back on the set, they said, "It wasn't his fault, you know."

I said, "What the blazes are you talking about? It isn't the fault of a drunken man to run sideways along the street, hit somebody and kill them?"

They said, "Oh, that isn't what happened." They had to rearrange the whole story. The publicity went out from Warners right away and everybody on the set had been told about this except me so I didn't know what was going on. The whole thing was arranged so that the poor man would be proved innocent. I don't think he even went to jail for a night nor on to a conviction in a courtroom.

With Ross Alexander, Dick Powell and Olivia de Havilland in *A Midsummer Night's Dream.*

Generally, I wasn't one to go to Hollywood parties so I didn't know too many of the people in the industry. I did know Joan Crawford who was married to Franchot Tone at the time. She was a real glamour woman and very dramatic. She and I were friends but not on a really close basis because she worked at another studio, MGM.

Most of the actors and actresses I knew in those days were at Warners. Margaret Lindsay and I became quite good friends. I didn't know Ann Dvorak as well. We talked confidentially to each other and everything but I wouldn't call her as close a friend since I didn't see her away from the studio. Bette Davis was coming up very fast as a star. We were friends the way people are in a studio. She knew I wasn't trying to do her out of her place and she knew that I admired her so that she was a little warmer to me than she was to most people of her generation who were making pictures at Warners. She was very, very tight about her position, you know. I enjoyed her very much. I thought she was a real professional who worked awfully hard. I met John Garfield when he was with the Group Theatre back in New York. We never were dear friends but we always recognized each other. We might be sitting at the same table in the cafeteria for lunch and we would talk.

I have a very funny story about Dick Powell. Once, I took a vacation at a very fashionable place on the way down to Palm Springs. This small hotel up on the mountain above the highway looked right across the railroad tracks and way over the other mountains. So I went down there for a weekend and Dick called and asked if he could stop by. I said, "Sure," so he came by, we had dinner and we went out to sit on the lawn. I'm thinking, "Oh, my goodness, isn't this romantic? Here I am with a moving picture star and oh, oh, dear, it's wonderful."

And suddenly, I heard him muttering to himself, "A hundred and two, a hundred and three, a hundred and four. What do you know, Jean? There are a hundred and four cars on that freight train." It was going by down in the valley below, so that wrecked the romance. It's enough to wreck any romance. Anyway, it couldn't have gone very far because he wasn't my kind of person. He was a sweet guy but I don't think he read a book. He married Joan Blondell not long after and I don't think she could have been very happy because she was a bright woman. I didn't know her well—I just admired her tremendously. You know, we golfed or we had lunch when we met in the dining room at the studio—things like that. But she knew I admired her and she was very nice about it.

With (top) Dick Foran and Robert Light and (bottom) Ann Dvorak, Franchot Tone, and Margaret Lindsay in *Gentlemen Are Born*. (The Museum of Modern Art.)

For the most part, I didn't meet any skirt-chasers. I suppose Jimmy Cagney was one but he recognized that I was nobody to chase. In fact, one day, he asked me into his dressing-room for a cup of coffee or something. He opened the door, I went ahead of him and he slapped my rear-end and said, "Don't worry, I don't like virgins." My overall favorite person was Jimmy Cagney whom I admired more than anybody else in that town—he had such intelligence. I worshipped him. We became very, very good friends. He was always teasing me—it didn't matter what. If I said, "I'm going to wear a red dress," he'd say something like "Who the hell cares?" I don't know if he said that but that was the type of thing he'd say. He treated me like an uncle would a teenage niece. He wasn't that much older than me. The difference was actually because I was naive and rather stupid then. I mean, I had a brain but I wasn't using it yet and he was very kind to me.

I didn't see him in later years because he just retired from the whole business. As a matter of fact, I don't think there were many people in the industry at Warners that I stayed friends with over the years. There was one hairdresser with whom I got on very well. She was always devising new hairstyles for me and we were very good friends. I went to her wedding and when she had her first baby, it was very exciting. And then there was a woman of whom I was very fond who was in the publicity department. I tried making the acquaintance of one or two of the cameramen who were actually on the floor and who impressed me as being very talented at the camera. But I don't know why—I didn't seem to know many of them.

With Charles Butterworth in *Orchids to You.*

As for my leisure activities away from the studio, I was never particularly athletic, certainly not like my parents. My father was a wonderful golfer and my mother was excellent at tennis. I had gone to summer camp when I was a girl and I did like to go hiking in the mountains. I did some horseback riding, too, over the years but I didn't keep it up. I think I was afraid I'd be too reckless. So when I was in Hollywood, I generally spent my days off doing a lot of reading, particularly of plays.

While I was working at Warners, I started a kind of actor's workshop where young actors could get a chance at playing on a stage and getting some decent direction, a little stage studio that we set up to teach. Our first show was *Green Grow the Lilacs* by Lynn Riggs. I worked with a girl who later became a big star. I did it for about six to nine months but Warner Brothers didn't like it at all.

When I'd get through with a picture, I'd usually get in my car and drive up to San Francisco to see Paul Smith, a newspaperman with whom I was in love at the time. He was a columnist for *The San Francisco Chronicle* and he really had a great mind. I still have letters he wrote me. He wasn't in love with me—I think he may have been gay—but he got me mentally jumping and that inspired me to go back to college which I did later on.

I suppose I always had a slight knowledge of public events. I was very young but I remember the day after the First World War ended. I went out to pick up the paper in the morning as I usually do and I asked my mother, "Why aren't there any big black headlines anymore?"

Mother said, "Because the war is over," but that didn't make any sense to me then.

Most actors in those days were not very socially conscious nor country-conscious nor conscious of

With John Boles in *Orchids to You.* (Courtesy of Coles Johnson.)

anything but Hollywood and their careers. A lot of them were very, very dumb in that sense. I'm sure I was, too. I include myself in that because several times Jimmy Cagney said, "Oh, Muir, shut up. You're not a kid anymore." I hadn't taken much interest in politics up until then. I think it was one of Roosevelt's elections that got me excited. I liked what he said and that was the first time I voted, I think. When I was in high school, I used to go around saying how marvelous Hoover was so I had grown up. I remember when I was still in New York and Roosevelt came in, the first thing he did when he got inside the White House was to order all the banks in America to be closed. This was on a Friday—Thursday would have made it worse because you get paid on Friday. So they closed over the whole weekend and the minute they closed, everybody relaxed and the weekend was marvelous. One person had ten dollars cash, another person had two cents, somebody else had twenty-five—everybody shared everything. And then the New Deal put about a million men to work cleaning up all the streets of the United States—it was something. Roosevelt had a way of speaking. I've never forgotten his first inaugural address—"The only thing we have to fear is fear itself." It seemed so apt to the situation at that time.

The reason I got the reputation for being a left-winger was I was involved in the creation of the Screen Actors Guild. We were going out on strike when they recognized us. It was a deal they made. I was the working secretary of the strike committee when we were gathering all the people together for the threatened strike. Every night for a week in a different star's house, we would have each actor from a certain studio talk to the group. I can't tell you who they all were but it was about a hundred people in a star's house every night. Fredric March, I can tell you, was one and Jimmy, of course, Jim Cagney. All the actors had signed agreements to go out on strike. We were having a meeting and were looking for people to go on a picket line on Monday morning when the strike was supposed to begin. Except for one or two very right-wingers, we had voted a hundred per cent for the strike. We had to plan a picket line around MGM for Monday morning. At 7 a.m., no one would appear for work at MGM, none of the artists, I mean. (They call the actors artists and everybody else who does equally hard work they call workmen or technicians.) So I was told to start calling people. They gave me a little list of names alphabetically listed I had to call. I got very good reception—ninety-nine per cent of the people said they'd be there on strike. Then I came to the name "Greta Garbo" on the list. I was such a fan of hers that with trepidation I dialed and I heard this low voice say, "Hello."

I said, "May I speak to Miss Garbo, please?" Strange calling her "Miss Garbo" since everybody refers to her as "Garbo."

She answered, "This is she," and I thought, "Marvelous grammar." And she did—she used the correct tense instead of saying "I'm her" or something like that. I told her what was going on and she said, "I know." I had introduced myself first. I said my name was Jean Muir and she said, "I know about you, I know you."

I thought, "Oh, you know me, I know you." Anyway, I didn't go into it at that moment. I was under shock because I had an adoration for her. She was my favorite actress and it made me kind of shy to have to call her to ask her this. But I said, "You know that the actors are going out on strike on Monday."

She said, "Yes," "yaas" or however she pronounced it—I've forgotten now.

I said, "We need people on the picket line outside the entrances to MGM. Particularly we would like to have all the actors who are under contract to MGM to be there."

And she said, "I be there. What time?"

I said, "About—we'd want to start the picket line at seven in the morning, you know, because pictures—"

She said, "I know, I'll be there seven o'clock. At what gate?" So I told her which gate we had assigned to her. You know, MGM had an enormous number of gates all over. She said, "All right, Jean, I be there."

I said, "Thank you very much." I couldn't say "Miss Garbo" and I couldn't say "Garbo" and she said, "Goodbye" and hung up.

She was very polite with a very simple and abrupt manner of speaking. But I was quite thrilled that I had spoken to her because she'd always been my favorite actress in pictures. I qualify that because there were a lot of people who were very, very great at that time and Ethel Barrymore was my favorite

With Michael Whalen in *White Fang*.

actress on the stage. I saw her in practically everything she ever did.

Of course, Garbo never had to be on the picket line because the strike was called off. They sold themselves short, you know. They didn't really want to go on strike—so much so that they made a deal with some man whose name I can't remember but it was a friend of the executive secretary connected with the Longshoreman's Union in Los Angeles. It wasn't a very left-wing union there unlike the one in San Francisco headed by Harry Bridges whom I met. I didn't have to call Garbo back to tell her that the strike was off because it was announced in all the papers, it was on the radio and I knew she'd see it—it was so publicized. I think they sold out in the end which infuriated me.

About this time, after I did *Stars Over Broadway*, I went to England in the fall of 1935 to make *Faithful* for Warner Brothers' British studio at Teddington. I remember they didn't want me to drive because they said, "After all, you're an American and we drive differently."

I said, "Give me a test." Of course, I had driven in England sometime before and I had learned to drive on the left side of the road very quickly. So it was all right. I drove out to the studio from London every day and I took my dresser who was a sweetheart with me and anyone else who wanted a lift to the studio.

After I made the picture in England, I went to France where I gave an interview to the newsmen from all the Paris newspapers. It was a big success with big applause and big everything. So I sat up there and said, "Messieurs, mesdames, j'avais beaucoup d'honneur de travailler sous Professeur Reinhardt," at which the whole house came down. They laughed and I didn't catch it for a second. Then I thought, "Oh, my God." I had said, "I had a great deal of honor working under Professor Reinhardt," which would be perfect in

In *White Bondage*.

English but in French, it meant physically under. The correct way to say it would be "sous la direction de Professeur Reinhardt." (I didn't have much honor working with him, by the way, as you know.) But that story swept all of Paris. Everybody roared and then the fact that I had corrected myself immediately afterward started another roar of laughter and applause. So it was a very embarrassing day for me.

When I got back to the United States, I was loaned out to Fox to make *White Fang* with Michael Whalen and Jane Darwell—she was such a wonderful person. Then I went back to Warners for more films but now I was being featured in B pictures. In the beginning, they had given me a lot of publicity and I think I was in every photoplay magazine there was for a while. But it soon died down when they got a little bit disgusted with me. They had turned me into a star overnight and after they realized I wasn't a star, they wanted to let me go.

I don't remember very much about the last films I did for Warners or the people involved. I did one every three weeks and they were all done in preparation for letting me go. I think they were all done in the first part of 1937. I do remember making *White Bondage* which was about sharecroppers in the South. That was the one time I got a line changed. I had a line in which I had to say something like "We all gotta get together." So when it came to the take, I said, "Look, we all got to organize." I got my little union word in.

Warners was just keeping me there until they were ready to let me go. I had a seven-year contract with options every year but they gave it up after four years. They were happy and I was happier. Everybody said I was stupid, that I should stay there in Hollywood and look around for another job but I thought to myself, "I want to go to New York."

I was going out of the studio for the last time, packed up my last things, put the dog in the back of the car, and off I went in my little Ford. I was getting out of there the day after my contract was over. Jack Warner was standing near the gate and he said, "Well, goodbye. I hope you're successful somewhere else."

I said, "Oh, I will be, thank you, Mr. Warner."

So I drove to New York in June of 1937. I always felt safe driving alone with dear Mima, my boxer, in the back seat. I remember once I parked the car by the side of the road and a man came up. Mima put her paws on my shoulder, growled, and the man ran away.

I left Warners just before Ronald Reagan began working there. That's one more reason to be thankful that I left them when I did. That's about as stiff an actor as there is, even more than the stiff ones I played with. Excuse me, I'm being an awful cat, aren't I? But how in the world the American people were dumb enough to elect him president, I don't know. I guess they got taken in by the charm. He claims to have helped found the Screen Actors Guild. I was in that fight and I don't remember him there at all.

When I came to New York, I played in summer stock including one of my favorite parts and I still reread the book sometimes, *Pride and Prejudice*. I went out with Dick Watts, a very well-known critic of moving pictures for *The New York Herald-Tribune*. We were around a lot together at places like "21." He fell in love with every young starlet that was around so he thought he was in love with me but that was ridiculous. Anyway, he introduced me to someone who knew Auriol Lee, the British female director, who was looking for a woman to play a part in a London play. So he recommended me, I saw her and I went to London in the fall.

We opened just around Christmas week in Manchester and the play was a failure so there I was out of work again. But I was in England and since all my family was in Scotland, that was fun. I had time to study at London University where I took a wonderful course in economics taught by Harold Laski, the distinguished political scientist. I also made a film called *Jane Steps Out* for a British company and then I came back to the United States in the fall of 1938. That was because I had a feeling about Hitler. I knew there was going to be a war and everybody in England laughed at me. They didn't think he would dare attack them. They were absolutely unconscious of what was going on, the most politically unconscious people I had ever known in my life because they didn't see this war coming and prepare themselves. They were so un-

With Robert Cummings, Billie Burke and Laraine Day in *And One Was Beautiful.*

prepared it was ridiculous. But, of course, England woke up politically during the war.

After I came back to the United States, I met Henry Jaffe who was to be my future husband. We were living together for about two years before we were married in the fall of 1940. I don't remember what I did professionally during that time. I think I did a lot of summer stock. I went back to Hollywood to make *And One Was Beautiful* for MGM with Bob Cummings and a little new girl, Laraine Day. And I did *The Lone Wolf Meets a Lady* for Columbia with Warren William.

My husband was drafted during the war and I proceeded to follow him around from camp to camp to get pregnant. I have three children but the youngest one was born after he was let loose. He was a lieutenant in the judge-advocate's office, the legal arm of the military. He brought the soldiers in to remove a big famous capitalist—I think it was the president of Montgomery Ward—who wouldn't move out of his big chair in his office. The government was going after him so they went in there, lifted him up chair and all, took him out of the office and threw him out.

For the most part, I really wasn't working very much in the forties and I wasn't looking for it too much. I was too busy having children. There were two years between the first and second and two and a half years between the second and third. I did do a couple of radio shows and I did a play, I think, which was a flop.

In 1942, I was back at Warner Brothers for my last film appearance, *The Constant Nymph.* I found out I was pregnant while I was there. It would have been a larger part except that they had to cut out some of my scenes. They rushed me to the hospital to save the baby from being born prematurely and I went back just to do one scene. The doctor said I wasn't to stand around a lot. It was the death-bed scene, I think, of the father and I was propped up against the wall behind by his head. I was propped on a big wooden board so that I wouldn't have to stand up.

I also did some lecturing about this time. I was lucky enough to speak on the same platform as Eleanor Roosevelt. I was making a speech at a place where she was supposed to have come after me. I was talking mostly about the role of the black in

With Joyce Reynolds, Charles Boyer and Joan Fontaine in *The Constant Nymph.*

moving pictures, how he could barely make it and how hard it was. Mrs. Roosevelt came in late and, of course, everybody stood up and everybody stopped. Then I stopped and she came up to the platform and said, "I ask your forgiveness, Miss Muir, for being late and I wonder if you would do me a favor."

I said, "Anything."

She said, "Would you start your speech again so I could hear the whole thing?" Now, there's a generous lady. I just adored her. And then she spoke to me afterwards about how she enjoyed what I was saying.

In 1950, I was to play the mother in *The Aldrich Family* series in the new medium of television. The political lines were pretty clearly drawn at that point, the mad, hungry Communist chases were out in full force and everybody was rushing around being patriotic with a capital P. We were all called on to the set after the dress rehearsal for our first show by a young boy of nineteen or twenty. We were all ready to go on. It was about six o'clock, the show was at seven, and he said, "I will have no questions after I read this announcement." The announcement was: "The show for tonight has been cancelled."

I went home and when I got back, my husband Henry said, "What are you doing here?"

I said, "I don't know. The show was cancelled."

He looked at me, I looked at him and both of us had the same idea. So he called Jack Gould, the TV reviewer for *The New York Times,* who was a friend of Henry's. Jack said, "I'll check it right away." And he called back in half an hour and said, "That's what it is." I had been listed in *Red Channels* as a dirty Communist and so forth.

We went up to see the head of General Foods who was the sponsor. His role was to say, "Sorry, Miss Muir, but that was that." My husband almost blew his top and I proclaimed it the way I felt it. Henry was trying to calm me down and convince the man that this whole story was a pack of lies. He said, "Well, I'm sorry, very sorry, goodbye." I don't think it was because it was a family show. They weren't that deep-thinking. All they thought about was that it would be blacklisted. It was a period that anyone who had been related to any cause which was always trying to re-elect Roosevelt—then that person was a Communist and should be thrown out.

Then we went down and applied to be heard by the Committee that set itself up as God, that Committee that set itself up to say who was a Communist and who wasn't. I went there, I testified and told them under oath that I was not and never had been a Communist—you know, the whole routine. But they never cleared me publicly. I refused to name names. In fact, my husband told them ahead of time, "Don't ask her for names. She won't give you any because she doesn't think any of them were Communists and she's not going to give names of people who were friends of hers and liberals."

I don't remember anything after that happened. I think I was absolutely struck dumb in my brains and my voice. I didn't understand it. I said, "I thought we live in America." That was the only expression I could make. And they were riding high then, those men in Congress—they were the tops. But every one of them lost his seat very soon after that. I was out of work, of course, for a long time in the fifties. Slowly, I became an alcoholic—more than a quart a day—and it wasn't until the end of that decade that I suddenly came to. Henry had moved out to the Coast by that time. He couldn't take it anymore and my eldest son went with him because he didn't like me either, and now he's so wonderful. Anyway, I was sort of on my own in this big house in White Plains—we had a beautiful house there—and it was just misery. I wasn't a very good mother as you can imagine but, actually, I'm very lucky. They all love me very much now and I'm surprised sometimes.

In 1959, I was going on a train to Reno to get a divorce. I was thinking about all this business. I had the two younger children on my hands. I was responsible for them and I don't know what thoughts went through my head—the fact that I was an idiot and I'd better stop if I wanted my life to be anything and since I was getting a divorce, I could start a whole new life. The waiter came up and said, "Would you have a cocktail?"

I said, "No, thank you." And that was the end of that. I haven't had any alcohol since.

I guess it must have been right after the divorce that I got a job from David Susskind, a television producer who was against that Committee and who was very, very good. He asked me to appear on a show called *The Witness* and that was one of the few TV shows I did. He had a different person on every week who was the witness at some kind of a trial or some kind of a crime.

Suddenly, out of the clear blue sky, Stephens College which is a women's college in Columbia, Missouri asked me to come and teach acting. I'd been doing some odd teaching around and to this day, I don't know who suggested me. Anyway, when I got out there, I found that I was in charge of the freshman drama class. I was not just a teacher but I was in charge of the other freshman drama teachers and the various sections of the class which is always big, you know. Everybody else was so nice and they took it for granted that I should be head. I was kind of surprised and pleased and honored and I took it over.

We had a very, very good policy with freshmen. The first policy I made was they were not allowed to be on the stage. Ooh, they hated me for a while but they finally understood why. The reason is because they can't act—I mean, they don't know even the basic techniques. They just want to be actresses. And so first, they have to learn something about themselves. You have to know yourself a little bit in order to be a good actress because you're using yourself all the time and you have to know how to create these things. There are techniques for creating a certain emotion or a certain character and so forth. They got used to it. Some of them appeared in the big musical show they did every year—everybody could apply for that. And one of them who had been in it came back to class after the thing was finished and she said, "May I say something, Jean?"

I said, "You certainly may." I had a feeling it would be good for me.

She said to the other girls in class, "Don't ever try to act when you're a freshman." So that policy was maintained and I think it still is there.

I loved Stephens. It was wonderful and my teaching years there went on until I was sixty-five. Stephens then retires you. So I went around to various colleges. I had a good reputation from Stephens and people would hire me for a year or for a semester. I was at the University of North Carolina, I was at the University of Iowa, I was at the University of New York at Albany, I was at Loyola Marymount here in Los Angeles—I had a good friend who had been at Warners who hired me and I stayed there for two and a half or three years—and I was at the University of New Mexico. Then slowly I said I don't want to look anymore

With Laraine Day and Robert Cumming in *And One Was Beautiful.*

As Helena in *A Midsummer Night's Dream.*

and I just decided I would not go out on the road again looking for work.

I've always been a feminist. I don't know that it had too much to do with my work in films except that it angered the producers who didn't like anybody that independent. I wasn't as strong out there then. I was twenty-two but I was still a kid and very unsophisticated. But as I got older, I began to talk on the subject of feminism a lot. I'd go out on the lecturing field for Roosevelt, for instance, when women weren't doing much lecturing. Here, I'm in a home with old men and old women and I'm fighting to see that the women are treated equally. In some cases, they're not. They're treated like children and so they turn into children. So I guess I've always been that way. I'm going to start something again. I don't know what yet but I'll be involved.

Claire Trevor

Throughout the history of film, there have been stars who have represented the changing moods of their culture. Such an artist is Claire Trevor. This consummate, versatile performer appeared in film after film ranging from the brisk optimism of her early pictures in the 1930s to the evocations of a heroic past and a corrupt present in the roles of her maturity. During the course of a career that spanned decades, Claire earned the respect and affection of her colleagues with films that embraced not only minor B pictures but also major works that changed the course of American cinema history. Noted filmmaker Robert Wise, who directed her in the film noir classic, *Born to Kill*, recalled:

> Working with Claire Trevor was one of the best experiences I have had directing a female star. Claire was highly professional, very receptive to suggestions from the director to improve her performance. But also with a keen mind and instinct of how to improve the scene.
>
> She was working with Lawrence Tierney who was not the most stable person from time to time. Claire handled him beautifully and helped me handle him as well.
>
> I always wanted to do another picture with Claire but things didn't work out for us to get together again. I've always regretted that.[1]

An only child, Claire was born on March 8, 1910 in Bensonhurst, New York, to immigrant parents. Her father, a custom tailor working for some of the most prominent business executives in New York City, earned a good living until the Depression. Up to that time, Claire had enjoyed a happy childhood into her teens living in comfortable circumstances. But now, with her plans for a college education interrupted by the family's financial situation, Claire, fascinated by the theatre and films since her earliest years, began to pursue an acting career. Two years of work on the stage plus appearances in three Vitaphone shorts preceded her leading feminine role in the 1932 Broadway hit, *Whistling in the Dark*. Although film producers soon expressed interest, it would be the adverse effects of the Depression on the theatre that finally caused Claire to accept an offer from the Fox studio the following year.

She immediately went to work as a leading lady opposite western star George O'Brien in *Life in the Raw* and *The Last Trail*. But it was a later appearance in 1933 with Spencer Tracy in *The Mad Game* that first won her critical attention. André Senwald wrote in *The New York Times* that "Claire Trevor is quietly effective as a girl reporter"[2] while the critic for *Variety* commented that she gave "about the best portrayal of a newspaper gal which the studios have submitted."[3]

Although Claire played a variety of parts in a succession of films at Fox, the strength of her performance in *The Mad Game* caused her to be most often featured as an American working girl striving to make her way during the Depression. It was a characterization that had enormous contemporary resonance and Claire's working-girl heroines were generally up-tempo, determined women in keeping with the feminism of the era—bright, emancipated spirits seen as capable of surmounting the economic hard times. In *Jimmy and Sally* (1933), Claire plays a clever secretary who rises from her position with a meat-packing firm to head its publicity department, demonstrating far greater skills

In *Born to Kill.*

than her ineffectual sweetheart, James Dunn. She returned to the role of a newspaper reporter in several other films including *Hold That Girl* (1934), a breezy comedy-adventure again opposite James Dunn with the daring Claire involved in one escapade after another. In *Wild Gold* (1934), she is cast as a nightclub singer. And in *Career Woman* (1936), based on an actual contemporary case, she plays a woman lawyer whose dedication and intelligence helps acquit a girl accused of murdering her father. Claire was able to invest these women with a sense of truth in part engendered by her real-life situation as a hard-working actress who had turned to stage and screen out of economic necessity.

Claire survived the change-over when the old Fox studio headed by Sol Wurtzel and Winfield Sheehan merged in 1935 with Darryl F. Zanuck's 20th Century company. Yet despite her early success, Fox continued to cast her in B pictures, discouraging for an ambitious, talented actress. She longed for the more challenging roles that were being essayed by actresses like Bette Davis and Katharine Hepburn. Looking for a fresh medium to express her abilities, she branched into radio, starring for years with Edward G. Robinson in the series, *Big Town,* as well as appearing on many other shows.

Meantime, she continued with her film career. In 1937, she was loaned out to Samuel Goldwyn for *Dead End,* William Wyler's powerful adaptation of Sidney Kingsley's hit play about the social inequities of contemporary urban life. Submerging her blonde beauty in a part requiring her to portray an unkempt, diseased prostitute and former sweetheart of gangster Humphrey Bogart, Claire made an indelible impression with a poignant, electrifying performance in a scene with Bogart that brought out the sensitivity of both players and earned her an Oscar nomination.

In 1938, she left 20th Century–Fox and was featured in two films for Warner Brothers, *The Amaz-*

With Spencer Tracy in *The Mad Game.*

With John Wayne in *Allegheny Uprising.*

ing Dr. Clitterhouse and *The Valley of the Giants.* The latter film was a Technicolor version of the Peter B. Kyne story of the redwoods that had previously been the subject of two silents. More unusual was *The Amazing Dr. Clitterhouse,* co-starring Edward G. Robinson and Humphrey Bogart with Claire once again as a woman of dubious morals. Directed by Anatole Litvak and scripted by John Huston and John Wexley, the film is a black comedy about a doctor who joins a gang in order to test his theories about crime and ends up committing murder himself. Claire is a glamourous gang leader masterminding robberies of furs, a character far removed in appearance and manner from the tawdry, defeated streetwalker of *Dead End.* But her vigorous portrayal in *The Amazing Dr. Clitterhouse* is as much a departure from the wholesome heroines of the Code era as her role in *Dead End*—and is just as trenchant in its criticism of society. When Robinson asks her if she ever feels pangs of conscience about the wrongful effects of her "business" on society, she snaps back, "Would you ask that same question of a stock-promoter who robs widows and orphans or one of them society mugs who owns a lot of fire-trap tenement houses where the rats and bugs eat you alive—the kind of place I was born in? No, the way I look at it, professor, me, you, all of us here are more on the level than those guys."

Claire's profound, intuitive grasp of the characters she played commended her to John Ford, who was preparing to direct a new film called *Stagecoach.* He had bought the rights to a magazine story, "Stage to Lordsburg," that had impressed him. When he and Merian Cooper went to David O. Selznick for financing, the producer wanted established box-office names Marlene Dietrich and Gary Cooper for the starring roles but Ford insisted on his own choices, Claire Trevor and John Wayne. Ford and Cooper formed a company and then contracted with Walter Wanger, an independent, to produce the film.[4]

Validating Ford's faith in her, Claire was brilliant as Dallas, a prostitute cast out of a town in Arizona by the local puritans. Together with other outcasts and social misfits, one of them an escaped convict known as the Ringo Kid, played by John Wayne, Claire survives the siege of the stagecoach by Geronimo's Apache warriors. In the end, she leaves the corrupt town of Lordsburg, her original destination, to start a new life in the wilderness with Wayne. In contrast to the seamy modern urban environments of *Dead End* and *The Amazing Dr. Clitterhouse,* both of which had doomed her characters to a sordid life, the open western landscapes in *Stagecoach* symbolize the freedom that provides a salvation for the woman with the past so movingly enacted by Claire. Ford, who felt she had played the role with understated eloquence, told her she was so good that the audience wouldn't even know it. In that same vein, she recalled he once eliminated a whole page of dialogue to get to the essence of the scene, a trait of understatement sometimes mistaken for casualness that concealed the power of Ford as a director. A major creative achievement in his long career, *Stagecoach* inaugurated the director's most brilliant period of sustained artistry and remains one of the great works of cinema.

Although *Stagecoach* is always remembered as the film that made John Wayne a top star, it is equally significant in Claire Trevor's career. Indeed, in this and two follow-up films, *Allegheny Uprising* (1939) and *Dark Command* (1940), reteaming Wayne and Claire, the actress was billed above the Duke. So effectively had Claire registered as the feminine lead in *Stagecoach* that she was cast in a long series of westerns well into the fifties, the strong feminine image she had projected in her working-girl roles now directed to her portrayals of the pioneering women of the Old West.

Simultaneous with Claire's roles in westerns were her appearances in those extraordinary works of the forties later known as "film noir." As early as 1939, Claire had co-starred with George Raft in *I Stole a Million,* a film scripted by Nathanael West that anticipated the "noir" genre. In the picture, Raft attempts to go straight after being forced into a life of crime when he loses his life's savings, but returns to his career as a gangster because his wife, played by Claire, has been thrown into jail for shielding him. The mood of fatalistic despair and social criticism in *I Stole a Million* reappeared in the "noir" films of the war and postwar years and Claire became a central figure in the genre.

However, she was scarcely typecast in "film noir." In *Crack-Up* (1946) opposite Pat O'Brien whom she recalled as "a dear man, warm and wonderful off-screen," she is his supportive romantic interest as he attempts to recover from a nightmare world of amnesia. In *Murder, My Sweet* (1945), one of the most significant films of the decade, she is the scheming femme fatale who resorts to murder to maintain her social position. In *Raw Deal* (1948), directed by Anthony Mann, she is gangster Dennis O'Keefe's loyal moll who helps him to escape prison only to lose him, first to good girl Marsha Hunt and finally to the bullets of a rival mobster. She won an Oscar as best supporting actress for her remarkable performance in *Key Largo* (1948), playing a former nightclub singer and the pathetic, boozy mistress of gangster Edward G. Robinson. Perhaps most striking of all is her role in *Born to Kill* (1947) as a woman whose desire for material wealth leads her into an unholy partnership with a cold-blooded murderer. Torn between her good impulses and her fatal attraction to gangster Lawrence Tierney, she belatedly tries to break free only to perish at his hands in the end. In all of these films, Claire's blonde beauty, sometimes sympathetic, sometimes sinister, illuminates the dark, moody works exploring a corrupt, violent society, a far cry from the thirties optimism of her Fox films and the epic heroism of her westerns.

Claire's career went on non-stop until the late 1960s. Her work in westerns included King Vidor's *Man without a Star* (1955). Her co-star in the film was Kirk Douglas whom she characterized as "a very serious dramatic actor, very dedicated and star-struck at that time." Besides western and crime films, she now ventured into domestic roles, memorably as the manipulative mother of a tennis pro in Ida Lupino's *Hard, Fast and Beautiful* (1951). Eventually, the mother's schemes destroy the relationships with her daughter and her husband, leaving her alone in the end. Claire also made many television appearances, winning an Emmy Award for her outstanding portrayal of Fran, the social-climbing wife in *Dodsworth* oppo-

With Basil Rathbone in *Crossroads.*

site Fredric March.

Her personal life had weathered two failed marriages, first to producer Clark Andrews and then to Cylos William Dunsmoore, before she found a long-lasting and happy relationship with her third husband, producer Milton Bren. She placed a high priority on her family, never letting her acting career dominate her life.

Twin tragedies struck in 1978 when she lost Charles, her son by her marriage to Cylos William Dunsmoore, in the crash of an airliner, and Milton Bren, who died from a brain tumor. Although this nearly destroyed her, she was able to overcome her grief through her resoluteness and inner strength.

To cope with her loss, she moved to New York City and built a new life, surrounding herself with old friends and making new ones including Claudette Colbert. She would briefly return to acting with a featured role in a 1982 comedy film, *Kiss Me Goodbye* and particularly enjoyed working with the film's star, Sally Field, whom she adored like a daughter and described as "very disciplined, very sincere about her work." There was also a stint on *Murder She Wrote* in 1987 and the same year a made-for-TV feature, *Breaking Home Ties,* shot on location in Texas.

At the time I first interviewed her in June, 1992, Claire was living in a suite she maintained at the Hotel Pierre in New York City. When I completed the interview in June, 1994, she had moved to a spacious new home, complete with a saltwater pool, in Newport Beach, California. There, she kept a busy schedule of social activities when she wasn't dashing around town at the wheel of her Mercedes. In her eighties, she seemed to have an inexhaustible vitality, the same appetite for life and openness to experience that she had brought to her screen roles. Her voice had a youthful quality as beguiling and distinctive as when she had made her mark in films and on radio. Insisting she had no interest in returning to acting, she tended to be unassuming about most of her films, reserving her highest accolades for her work with such masters as Wyler, Ford and Huston. Nevertheless, for all of her modesty, the entire course of her career is significant in cinema annals. The petite blonde from New York became a superlative actress who incarnated the history of her country and its women on film.

I was born in Bensonhurst, New York, but I only stayed there for two years or a year and a half. I don't know exactly how old I was when my parents moved me to Manhattan. We later moved up to Larchmont where I graduated from Mamaroneck High School. Our house was within a block of the water and I was able to walk to school.

My father was a custom tailor and had his own shop on Fifth Avenue. My real name was Claire Wemlinger. My father's parents came from Alsace-Lorraine and I guess that was on the German border. I don't know exactly where they were from—I wish I had found out about these things. I know that they came to Paris and my father was born there. My mother's family name was Morrison. She was born in Belfast, Ireland and she came to this country when she was ten.

I was an only child but I had a wonderful childhood. I was about ten years old when I first worked on the stage in *The Blue Bird.* I was in a chorus or whatever—I took several different parts, danced across the stage and played one of several children in the production. It was a professional production in New York. I think they did it every year at that time just at Christmas. And I loved it. It was like a fantasy, simply wonderful. I didn't consider it work at all. It was very glamourous being on the stage with the colored lights, the dancing, getting into costumes and things like that. I thought it was marvelous.

As for the movies, I was going to them at a young age. I went with my father and mother maybe once a week to the neighborhood theatre. I remember seeing Rudolph Valentino in *The Sheik* and falling madly in love with him. Norma Talmadge was another of my favorites. I thought she was beautiful. And the girl who was in *The Sheik,* Agnes Ayres, also made a big impression on me at the time.

I had wonderful teenage years, too, and was involved with all the teenage activities. I went to a lot of dances and parties, studied hard, and just loved my life. I went to all the different proms at different colleges. I was lucky enough to meet boys in prep school who would come to Larchmont where I lived for weekends with a family there. The boy in this family went to Choate Prep School and so I

In *Star for a Night*.

went to a Choate house-party with this boy. Then when he went to Yale, I went to a lot of the games, the crew-races, proms and house-parties there.

I was very anxious to go to college but I never made it. I did take extension courses at Columbia University. I studied art and I majored in conversational French. I was very good in French in high school. When my father and his brothers would take me to lunch, they'd speak only French and I wanted desperately to speak French.

I only went to Columbia for six months because my father had lost almost everything in the stock market crash and he couldn't afford the second half of the term. He told me, "You'll have to go to work and do something to help." The only thing I knew how to do was to be on the stage. I had never forgotten the experience in *The Blue Bird* and I had done church plays and school plays all along through my high school years. So I started to work on the stage. First, I went for six months to the American Academy of Dramatic Arts where you learned how to fall gracefully, you learned body motion, you did little exercises to get the walk and things like that. In the second half at the Academy, you took part in plays they put on but I thought I might as well do it for real.

I made my debut in *The Sea Gull* with Robert Henderson's Repertory Players in Ann Arbor, Michigan. Robert Henderson, the head of the drama department at Ann Arbor, came to New York to cast the company for the summer festival in Ann Arbor. They had a brand-new theatre which looked very glamourous and the whole thing sounded marvelous. By this time, I had made up a line in a brochure of what I had done on the stage. I pretended to be a New York actress and for every interview, I gave the same line—you know, I was in this play, I was in that play (short runs and not important parts)—hoping that nobody would catch me or find me out.

I had also gathered a name for myself—Claire St. Clair. I had a good friend, Martha Sleeper, an experienced, marvelous actress who had worked professionally in movies and on the stage. She was a cousin of this boy in Larchmont, John Murdock. His father was J. J. Murdock, a very rich man who had owned Pathé, I think, and then just retired at that time. Mr. and Mrs. Murdock were the richest people in Larchmont and owned about twelve cars. Martha would spend lots of times at their house in Larchmont on vacation and we had great parties then. We went to plays together, too, and I remember she took me downtown to New York in her aunt's car with a driver to an agent's office. She and I decided I had to have some other kind of name so that's what we chose.

When I pretended I was a New York actress, Mr. Henderson was very impressed and he wanted me to do the ingenue lead in all these plays. I think they did four or five plays in the summer, one of which was *The Sea Gull*. They wanted me to go see the very good actress who was in *The Sea Gull* in New York at the time. I gave him the salary I wanted which was outrageous then—a hundred and twenty-five dollars a week. He said, "Oh, I can't pay that much."

I said, "I'm sorry, that's my salary."

He left town and went back to Michigan. In

about a week or two, he sent me a telegram saying, "All I can pay is seventy-five a week."

I said, "Okay." So my mother and I went out there and I did those plays.

I think it was after that that I changed my name for the last time. I was in the office of the agent Chamberlain Brown in New York and I said, "My name is no good, it's terrible." One of the men who worked there took a telephone book, flipped through it, put his finger down and it landed on "Trevor." I said I liked that so there it was.

New York was going through the Depression then and there was no theatre, there was no anything, so I did anything I could to earn some money. I posed for Stetson hats at that time—they were making women's hats then—and I did a lot of modelling for photographers. Whatever came up, I would do. When the people at the Vitaphone Studio asked me, "Would you make a short?" I said, "Sure." So I went out to their studio in Brooklyn and did these shorts. One was with Jack Haley, I know, and another with Jack Pearl, I think. I didn't like it but it was something to do and I got paid for it.

Vitaphone was owned by Warner Brothers and I guess they saw me in these shorts. At that time, Warner Brothers was trying to train young people to be actors and actresses. They opened a stock company in St. Louis and they sent me out there as the ingenue lead for eight or ten weeks or maybe twelve—I forget how long it was. We did a new play every week, ten performances a week. We opened Monday night and Tuesday morning, we started rehearsing the next week's show. It was a very horrendous experience because it was not only physically draining but mentally, too. I had to stay up till two or three in the morning memorizing lines and at that time, you only got lines on what they called sides. You'd get the last three words of the speech behind your speech and that was the way you'd memorize it.

I think the director was sadistic because he did everything but beat me physically. He'd yell and scream and make me feel miserable. He'd come back after the first act and say, "Why did you cross in front of the sofa? I told you to cross in back of the sofa." He'd make me cry and I don't cry easily. I lost a lot of weight, too. My mother was with me and she was priceless. She heard my lines at two in the morning and so forth. It was ghastly but I think I probably learned something.

After this work with the Warner Brothers Stock Company, I came back to New York. I did a play

With Dennis O'Keefe in *Raw Deal*.

in Bayonne, New Jersey which never reached New York. I can't remember the name of it but my leading man was John Emery who was a very good actor. Rosalind Russell was also starting out as an actress and she was very much in love with John Emery at the time. She would come to the theatre and meet him backstage. Years later, I worked with Roz in *The Velvet Touch,* a picture that she and her husband, Freddie Brisson, produced. And she couldn't have been nicer to me.

I knew Connie Cummings, too, in those early days in New York. We both made tests for Sam Goldwyn to play opposite Ronald Colman in a picture. She was chosen for the part and I was green with envy—I thought he was so divine. She didn't do it, I know, but she started it. We've remained friends and I still see her when I'm in London. I met Colman at a big party years later, I danced with him, and I almost fainted he was so beautiful.

Every day, I would make the rounds of the offices of all the producers and directors who were planning on doing a play. I heard about the Hampton Players so I went to see them. Hank Potter was in charge—he was the director. He and his wife had rented this big old house—sort of a Victorian house three or four stories high—in Southampton. Lucille Potter was a sensational lady. She hired a cook to prepare our meals, we lived there and we got five dollars a week for the summer. At the end of the summer, if there was any profit, the Potters would divide it with the actors. Additionally, the actors made the scenery and put the chairs out. It was a communal experience—it was wonderful. They did four new plays every summer. I don't remember the names of them at all. All I know is that all the producers, directors and writers would come down to see these plays looking for new talent.

With Pat O'Brien and Herbert Marshall in *Crack-Up.*

I got a lot of leads and offers after that summer in 1931 that I followed up. Alexander McKaig offered me a comedy called *Whistling in the Dark* but he was the last one I paid any attention to. I had sort of neglected to call him which I should have until he sent me a couple of telegrams. Then I went to see him, had a reading and got the part. Edward Arnold was in it, Ernest Truex was the star and they were wonderful. We rehearsed and opened out of town in a couple of places, then came into New York and I knew it was a hit on opening night because the laughs were so full and often. It was a very exciting night. We ran for nine months in New York when every play was closing in about two days. You know, the Depression had really hit the theatre. Then they asked me if I wanted to go on the road with it—the national tour—and, of course, I did. That's the first time I was away from my mother and father.

When I landed in Hollywood during my tour with the play, they still were impressed by a stage actress so I made tests at virtually every major studio. They offered me five-year and seven-year contracts and I turned them all down. My heart was in the theatre. At MGM, I made a test with Lionel Barrymore from a scene out of a picture. They used to take all afternoon then when they made tests like a scene shot right in a movie. It must have been a very good test because Irving Thalberg said he wanted to see me. So I made an appointment and went to his office. He said, "Now why don't you want to sign, Miss Trevor? Why don't you want a seven-year contract here?"

I said, "Seven years of my life is like an eternity. I want to go back to the theatre and maybe do a picture a year or something like that."

He said, "Don't you know it takes seven years to make a star?"

But I thought, "No, I'm a New York actress, I can do what I want. I can get plays and so forth." How stupid could you be? I think that's the biggest mistake I ever made in my life—not signing with Thalberg—because he was that interested that he had an interview with me.

With Gene Lockhart and Edward Brophy in *Career Woman.*

After not being able to get work for a long time, I was back on Broadway in *The Party's Over* with Ross Alexander, Katharine Alexander, Peggy Conklin—all good people. Ross Alexander got a contract with Warner Brothers after that. It was very sad—he died very young, a suicide. My God, he was good-looking and he had everything. He was fun to be with—a charming man with a lot of pep and jollity.

The Party's Over was not my choice of a play, however. I hated the part mainly because it was about a waitress in New Haven. All the years that I'd gone to parties at New Haven, I knew all the boys there. At one point—I think it was when I was in *Whistling in the Dark*—the senior class voted their favorite actresses. They voted Helen Hayes, Lynn Fontanne and Claire Trevor and nobody else had ever heard of Claire Trevor. So I was tied to that wonderful school—I hate to think of women there now, it just spoils the whole thing for me—and I was ashamed to play a waitress in a New Haven cafe, sort of an easy girl. I just didn't like the whole thing but it was a good part and I got a lot of laughs even though I felt inferior in it.

I was in it for about two weeks when Fox sent me a telegram offering me a five-year contract. I think it was three-fifty a week which sounded enormous and solid. I said to my mother, "In six months, we don't have to worry." You know, they paid you these six-month options. They wanted me out there immediately so we went out on the Super Chief and I got right on a horse and did a western, *Life in the Raw*. Life in the raw is right! When I had arrived in Hollywood—I think it was in April of 1933—the agent, Vic Orsatti, met me at the station, went back to the office and said, "We don't have to worry about her. She won't be around very long."

Then they took me around and introduced me to everyone at the studio which was on Western Avenue. I met the head of the studio and the different departments' heads, I was taken to the wardrobe department and was fitted for clothes. The producer of the picture said, "I've got advice for you. Save your money and don't fall in love with your leading man."

I said, "Are you kidding? A western actor, George O'Brien?" Later, of course, I fell in love with him. I thought he was divine, a charmer and a perfect gentleman. He was so sweet to my mother and me. He'd give us a lot of good advice, he'd take us to dinner and we went to his charming house in Malibu which was brand-new to me. I mean it was right on the water.

But doing the picture was so hard for me. First of all, I didn't know anything about the technique of movies. Making two shorts is not worth anything and so it was a whole new technique. I'd studied on the stage and that was what I thought I knew something about. The calls were for five-thirty in the morning which was entirely opposite from the theatre's hours. It just seemed all foreign and awkward and a western out on location all the time—I wasn't used to that. Of course, I didn't know how to ride a horse, either. I came straight from New York City and I'd only seen a horse in Central Park. So I had to learn how to ride. I was in almost every shot in the picture and we worked six days a week. We had Sunday off but almost every Saturday night, we'd work till two or three in the morning. It was very, very hard work.

About that time, I met Clara Bow and her husband, Rex Bell, when I was on location. They were living near there and they came on the set one day. I was thrilled to meet them.

Not long after I made my debut with Fox, I played opposite Spencer Tracy for the first time in *The Mad Game*. I got wonderful reviews in that and I thought he was a wonderful actor. I adored working with him and he thought I was terrific. He said, "Where'd this kid come from?" He didn't believe that I knew how to read lines.

With Harvey Stephen and James Dunn in *Jimmy and Sally.*

He asked me out to dinner a couple of times and I refused because I said, "You're married. I don't go out with married men."

He said, "Don't ever change."

In one scene in *The Mad Game,* I had to run and jump on the running board of a moving car but they had me run from where the car was coming towards me and pick it up. So I was trying to jump in the wrong direction. I should have run from in back of the car and caught up with it. That was kind of a rough stunt I did but they didn't consider it a stunt.

My father had decided to remain in New York but he insisted that my mother come with me when I went to California. I rented a house after staying in the Hollywood Hotel when I first got there and then we rented a little apartment. Then I rented a house up in the Valley—Sunswept Drive just a little past Laurel Canyon which then had four corners filled. There was a general store, a gas station, a bank and a drugstore and that's all there was. There was hardly anything from Laurel Canyon and Ventura Boulevard all the way up to the Valley and all the way down to Hollywood. In those days, the Valley was full of trees and horses and it was beautiful. I rented this charming house with a beautiful view of snow-capped mountains and orange groves—it looked very Californian—for sixty-five dollars a month, fully furnished, three bedrooms and two baths, maid's room and bath. Then I got a maid to help my mother and I thought everything was great.

I took taxis to work in the beginning but soon I thought, "I've got to have a car." So I bought a Ford right out of the window and the salesman had to drive it home for me. I just practiced with it and learned to drive it. It was a Ford convertible—I wish I had it now. It looked so cute.

With Shirley Temple in *Baby Take a Bow.*

At Fox, I just did one picture on top of the other. I made about six or seven a year and since I did all the leads, that meant working, working, working. I played every kind of role. In one film, I played a gangster's moll, in another picture, I played a mother, and I did a musical. I didn't sing so they dubbed it while I mouthed it to the playback.

I wanted parts that were believable. Instead, I was often doing sort of crazy characters, the kinds of people that I'd never met. *Fifteen Maiden Lane* with Cesar Romero was a good picture but about diamond cutters and jewel thieves and it was all very grotesque to me. I would have given anything to play a really marvelous part like Bette Davis had.

I was in *Baby Take a Bow* with Shirley Temple in 1934 and the studio took very good care of her. There were definite rules about children working and, of course, they babied her. And she was sensational. It was my third picture with James Dunn. He played Shirley's father and he was really crazy about her. He was a real song-and-dance man with an Irish sense of humor.

I did another picture with Spencer Tracy in 1935, *Dante's Inferno.* They tried to make it an A-film—they spent a lot of money on it—but I thought it was a poor film. The same year, I was in a picture with ZaSu Pitts and Lew Ayres, *Spring Tonic.* I adored ZaSu and Lew is a marvelous man but when we all saw the picture, we seriously got together and said, "Let's combine our money, buy the picture and burn it." We couldn't believe how bad it was. Later, I was in *One Mile from Heaven* with Bill "Bojangles" Robinson and he was marvelous. I loved knowing him and just enjoyed every minute I was with him. He was so talented.

I made several pictures with Allan Dwan and he was a wonderful director, a fabulous man and very intelligent. We all went to Hawaii together with his wife and the casting director of the outfit at the time—Bryan, I think his name was—and his wife and my mother and I. We were going to film background shots for the next film we were to make, *Navy Wife.* Allan Dwan's wife never got out of her cabin and I found out that she was an alcoholic. He was marvelous to her, really babied her and took care of her. He had tried to hide everything. I always enjoyed him and working with him was a most intelligent, wonderful experience.

Rita Hayworth was in a couple of pictures with me at this time. As a matter of fact, her first film was *Dante's Inferno* where she did a dance number with her father in the cafe. I think Fox signed her up then. I don't remember what happened but, anyway, she was under contract there. I believed in Rita as an actress and thought she had real potential. They were going to make a film called

With Spencer Tracy and Henry B. Walthall in *Dante's Inferno.*

Ramona at Fox and they were looking for someone to play the lead. I said, "You have the girl right here on the lot. Rita Cansino" (which was her real name) "is perfect." But they didn't pay any attention to me and they got Loretta Young for the part. Rita wasn't the glamourous figure she later became when she went to Columbia. Her name was changed to Hayworth and Helen Hunt did a remake on her. She did the electrolysis that put the hairline back and changed the color of her hair. Oh, a million things happened and a metamorphosis took place.

Making pictures in those days was often uncomfortable. When you're dressed in velvets and boots and costumes and have to ride a horse and you're out in the sun, it's just excruciating. Also bear in mind, none of the sound stages at that time had air conditioning so between takes, they'd fling open the doors and let the hot air in to cool it off. That was pretty excruciating, too. They'd have a big fan there and blow some air in but the stages would get red hot with the lights and especially if it was in color because the lights they used for color were much more potent and radiated much more heat. And, of course, I didn't particularly like locations. You'd have to traipse around in the forest and up hills.

I didn't care for premieres, either, and I avoided several. And after a certain time, I stopped going to the dailies because I'd look at them and be ready to kill myself. I'd worry about this scene or that one that wasn't done properly and I was always disappointed. I'd beg them to do it over or something and, of course, they'd always say no. So I thought, "What good is this?" Instead of concentrating on what I was doing that day, I worried about what I had done yesterday. And I said, "I'm not going to go to any more rushes."

I was always trying to get out of B pictures at Fox. I thought, "Here's my big chance." And then the parts were so insignificant it didn't make any difference. In *To Mary—with Love* with Warner Baxter and Myrna Loy, however, my part was very good. At least, it was very cute even if it was a supporting role. I remember I had a line that was sort of far-out then. I said, "I'm getting quietly cockeyed." Warner and Myrna were darling, sweet people and I was thrilled to work with them. I remember Myrna's mascara was smudged under her eye in one scene and I thought, "Oh, my God, she ought to fix that." She didn't fix it. It didn't bother her at all and she looked great.

I had another supporting part in *Second Honeymoon* with Loretta Young and Tyrone Power. Loretta was a marvelous movie star. She'd have her hair combed in just a certain way and then walk without moving an eyelash so her hair would stay

With Warner Baxter and Myrna Loy in *To Mary—with Love.*

just so all the way from a dressing table or her dressing room onto the set. She knew exactly how to get every camera angle to her benefit and make every angle count. I admired her very much.

When they'd say to me, "Miss Trevor, you're finished for the day," I'd tear my eyelashes off and get in my car. One day—I will never forget—when they said, "Miss Young and Miss Trevor, you're finished for the day," she called up the portrait gallery and said, "I'm free. Do you want to make some portraits?"—which was my idea of absolute torture. I thought, "Wow!" What I really didn't do all the years I had a chance to was work with the publicity department along those lines. I should have devoted much more time to it but I would skirt them and try to get out of everything they set up for me. I hated that part of the business which was stupid because if you're in a public business like that, you should cater to it and I didn't—not nearly enough.

Tyrone Power and I started going out together at that time—that was before he met Annabella—and he was darling. I met his mother and it was getting serious, you know. In those days, we took dating very slowly compared to now. I thought, "If I get serious about him, I could fall in love with him in two seconds. But if I get serious, my heart's going to be broken because he's so handsome, he's going to be a big star and I'm going to be left crying." So I said, "Tyrone, I can't go out with you anymore." But we stayed friends for years and he spent the last year of his life in Newport Beach. He was at our house all the time. I painted a picture of him. His last wife said she gave it to Keenan Wynn's ex-wife, Evie, who married Van Johnson. Evie and she were two of a kind and close friends and she gave it to her because Evie said she once had an affair with Tyrone. I was furious. I thought, "If she's going to give it away, why doesn't she ask me if I want it?" because I loved Tyrone. We were really close friends.

I met Howard Hughes at a big party in Malibu in the thirties. He sort of looked sideways at me and then had one of his henchmen call me up. He said, "Mr. Hughes wants to take you to dinner."

I said, "Have Mr. Hughes call me," which he never did. So I never went out with him. But I had very strong morals then. I can't remember any actors in films making a pass at me. We always had respect for each other's abilities and were charming in our off-screen relations. That did happen to me once earlier in the theatre and I fought it off. The director went on the make. He grabbed me in the dressing room, tried to kiss me and I said, "Hey, are you kidding?" He was an old man as far as I was concerned.

With Tyrone Power, J. Edward Bromberg and Loretta Young in *Second Honeymoon*.

I went out with Oscar Levant several times because he was so amusing. He had been signed by Fox. They didn't know what to do with him but they gave him an office with a piano in it. Once, I went with him to a party where I met George Gershwin as well as Harpo Marx and Sam Behrman, the playwright. They were all good friends of Oscar and he was the darling of that set.

I loved that whole group but I didn't continue seeing them. You see, my social life was very small. You'd have to appear at certain functions because you were supposed to do it. But we worked six days of the week so you couldn't make a dinner date for Saturday night. I only had Sundays off which I usually spent at the Westside Tennis Club trying to play tennis—and trying was the word for it. I went on only a few vacations in the thirties. It was marvelous going to Palm Springs in those days because everyone walked around in sandals and shorts, nobody dressed up and it was just easy living. My mother and I would go down and stay at a ranch where there were horses and you wore boots and blue jeans. That's about as much as you dressed up. Now it's all furs and diamonds down there.

The studio gave me a nice dressing room at Western Avenue. They built me an apartment with a kitchen and everything, a big living room, and a beautiful dressing room furnished sort of Art Deco. And when I wanted to buy a house in Westwood, the studio loaned me the down payment or something and took it out of my salary every week. I got bonuses, too, at the end of the year or maybe twice a year—I don't know now. I never felt strapped for money because everything was done nicely for me. I hired a couple to take care of my new house. The man briefly doubled as a driver but I didn't like his driving and I don't like people waiting for me so I quit that. I drove myself always.

In 1937, 20th Century–Fox loaned me out to Paramount to make *King of Gamblers*. There, I had the opportunity to meet Stravinsky. He knew the director Robert Florey, who was a Frenchman, very well. He came on the set, had lunch with us and I had my picture taken with him. That was the thrill of my life because Stravinsky was something—in another world to me.

That same year, Fox also loaned me to Sam Goldwyn to do *Dead End*. At that time, I'd done twenty films and I thought William Wyler had called me because he saw me in one of the films. But during the interview, he asked, "What have you done, Miss Trevor?"

Lois Wilson (the star of *The Covered Wagon*) and Claire (the future star of *Stagecoach*) with Jean Parker and Cesar Romero (one of Claire's leading men) at a 1936 Hollywood party.

I said, "You mean you've never seen me on the screen?"

He said, "No."

I said, "Well, I thought that's why you wanted this interview."

He said, "No."

I was interviewed for the part of the secretary which became Wendy Barrie's part. But on the way out of his office, I turned and asked, "Who's going to do Francey?"

He said, "You would be great for Francey."

I said, "Well, that's just a bit part." I wasn't used to that. However, I'd never been in a real "A" picture and I was thrilled to be in one with William Wyler who I thought was a marvelous director. I said, "Well, let me read the script. If there's something I can do with the part, I'll take it." So I read it and I thought, "Yes, I can do this. I can do something good with it." There are many parts that are longer but you can't do anything with them.

The night before we were to film it, he called me about eight o'clock and said, "I just finished work. You're going to start shooting tomorrow." It only took a day and a half to film the scene with Humphrey Bogart and me. I don't think Wyler knew that then when he called me but it was a very small part—about two pages, you know. He said, "Come down to the studio now and I'll meet you at the wardrobe department. We'll pick out something to wear." No more care than that. So we went to the wardrobe department and, of course, they're huge. You press a button and the whole string comes out like cleaners only miles long and every era that you can think of. So he picked out a black satin dress and said, "Try that on." I put it on and he said, "That's great. Now we have to get some kind of a hat." He got one like a beret and said, "I want stockings with runs in them. Don't comb your hair. Go to bed tonight and do not touch it with a comb or a brush. Come down as is." At that time, I had longer than shoulder-length blonde hair. I came to the studio without combing my hair and without make-up, without anything. Wyler wouln't let me wear any make-up except eye make-up, beaded eyelashes and lipstick which I thought made me look terrible. Nothing really stood out about the filming except that I felt messy and dirty and unattractive. I didn't want anyone to see me, I just wanted to hide. Joel McCrea who was so beautiful and darling and was in the picture—I didn't want to see him, either. But when I saw the picture recently, I thought I looked wonderful. I wish I looked like that now. I don't know what I was so ashamed of but you feel so naked, you know.

With Allen Jenkins and Humphrey Bogart in *Dead End*.

Wyler gave me explicit direction about where to turn my eyes, my head, not about the feeling or the mood of the scene. He didn't discuss that—that was obvious. He was exacting in his technique but I appreciated that tremendously because I was still really a new kid on the block about picture technique and his direction was helpful in putting over a scene.

I was hoping that I'd get across something that would be memorable. I went to the opening or the preview. Usually, whenever I'd see myself on the screen, I'd squirm down in the seat and practically get on the floor I'd hate it so. I did the same thing with this and Randy Scott, who was sitting in front of me, turned around after the scene and said, "That was wonderful."

I said, "Oh, God." I was nominated for an Academy Award for the first time as best supporting actress for *Dead End* and I said, "Well, I can't win that one." Alice Brady won it and, of course, I was disappointed. But I was amazed and thrilled that I had been nominated. Then I went back to Fox and did the same old B pictures. Today if this happened, they would take a young actress and go zoom with her. But in those days, they didn't think someone who was nominated became a star.

In 1937, I also began working in a weekly radio series at CBS with Edward G. Robinson, *Big Town*, which was the best half-hour dramatic show on the air for years. I did it for five years, all except the last year it was on the air. And besides that, I was on almost every radio show you can name. I adored radio. It was heaven because you didn't have to be photographed and you had an audience. You didn't have to memorize anything, you just read it, and it was just the voice so you didn't have to be fitted for clothes, pose for stills, put on make-up and do the close-ups. So I think radio was my favorite medium. Of course, there were goofs all the time on radio and we'd fall on the floor laughing. The goofs were really hilarious but I don't remember any specific one.

In the years I was doing *Big Town*, the studios had to make a rule to let me go at noon on Tuesdays, I think, so I could rush down to CBS and

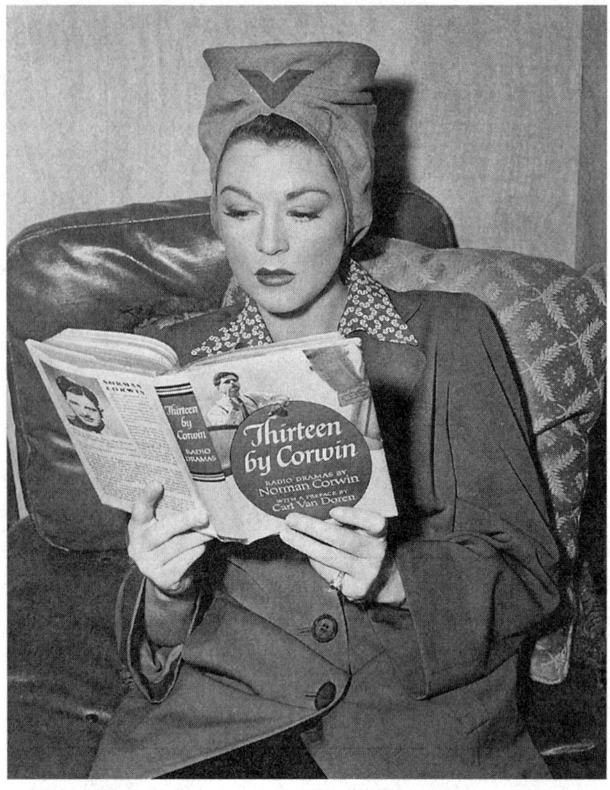

Claire, between scenes on a 1940s Columbia film, reading a book of radio dramas by her friend, Norman Corwin. (The Kobal Collection.)

start rehearsing the big show which went on at eight o'clock. And then we'd go to New York for three weeks every winter to do the show which was a great chance for me to go back again and see where I was born and raised. I loved that.

Big Town was about a newspaper called *The Illustrated Press* and Edward G. Robinson was the editor, Steve Wilson, and I was Lorelei, the society editor. In the beginning, each actor had a wonderful characterization. Robinson would be playing the piano and talking about music and things and it had real depth. Irving Caesar wrote that. But later, Robinson took over and gobbled up the show. It got to be the joke in the radio industry that he'd say, "Wait for me in the car, Lorelei."

He'd go in and play this big scene with a dozen people, then he'd come back to the car, I'd say, "What happened, Steve?" and he'd tell me. It became a soapbox in which Robinson got on and spouted forth all his views. When it got more and more into politics, it turned me off. I was never involved in any sort of organization or movement—I was never that kind of a person.

Besides, I thought I was being smothered and my part was getting smaller and smaller. I think my salary for the show was a thousand dollars a week. My contract called for a raise but they wanted me to go on for the same amount of money. Robinson was supposed to get a raise, too, and he wouldn't go on without it. I said, "Why should I go on for the same amount when Robinson won't? You can have your show." That's when I got off.

Not long after I left the show, I went to visit my then-husband, a Navy pilot, in Kansas City where he was stationed. I was in a butcher shop and I said, "Those lamb chops look good. How much are they?"

And before the butcher looked up at me, he said, "Lorelei Kilbourne!" He remembered the show and I realized I shouldn't have quit it. I thought, "My God, it had an impact."

My relations with Robinson were never unfriendly—nothing to fight about. We did several pictures together, too. I thought he was a fine, fine actor. He had great technique and such an expressive face.

He was well-known for his art collection. When we were doing the show, he'd say, "I want to show you a new painting I just got today." I remember vividly he was very proud of this one Picasso and I hated it. It was a whole group of people standing around a coffin, just wispy figures all grays and blacks. He said he'd paid twelve thousand for it which I thought was outrageous.

At Fox, Darryl F. Zanuck and I did not see eye-to-eye because I don't think I was his type at all. He liked the musical stars and the real glamour girls and I don't think he ever thought of me for any picture. He wasn't making the kind of pictures that I could do. My contract with Fox expired in 1938. They wanted me to sign a new one but I said, "Never again."

I made two pictures for Warner Brothers in 1938. *The Amazing Dr. Clitterhouse* was a good picture with Edward G. Robinson and Humphrey Bogart. It was directed by Anatole Litvak. But making *The Valley of the Giants* up in Eureka was ghastly. I hated locations because we'd stay in a very inferior hotel or motel, then drive for about an hour up near the woods and spend the whole day

With Edward G. Robinson and Humphrey Bogart in *The Amazing Dr. Clitterhouse.*

there. Men loved making locations. They felt like big strong outdoor guys.

Warner Brothers had a promotional thing going at the time and they wanted me to be the "Oomph Girl." They wanted me to sign for five years but I turned them down. I said, "I'm not going to be under contract again." That may have been foolish, too, because I would have been the "Oomph Girl" rather than Ann Sheridan and also Warners did more of the kind of thing that was suitable to me.

When I'd been at Fox, John Ford was on the lot and would speak to me every once in a while about doing a picture for him. He had one picture in mind, *Salome Where She Danced,* I think. I remember one time he wanted to see me about something and I had fever-blisters all over my mouth. I wouldn't let anyone see them so I had a whole handkerchief in front of my mouth and that sort of spoiled the interview.

After I left Fox, John Ford told me he wanted me for the lead in this picture he was doing called *Stagecoach* and I accepted. He asked me if I'd make a test with John Wayne. He was going to sell him to Walter Wanger and the studio who were producing the film. So I said, "Sure." I had never met Wayne before or even heard of him. He was a friend of Loretta Young's and his wife was in with that whole group. We rehearsed a scene from the picture and shot it, the one where we're standing against the railing outside of the inn where the baby was born and we're talking about our history, our past—that tender scene. It was a good test, I guess, because Ford sold Wayne to Wanger and the part of Dallas was handed to me.

The whole thing was a joy to me. It was absolute lush, plush pleasure compared to all of the other pictures I'd been making with the eighteen-day schedules. We stopped for tea every afternoon. It was such a joy to work for Ford—he was gorgeous. The whole cast was so brilliant, the script was so brilliant—not one extra word—and it was just the joy of my life to work on it. I wish it had gone on forever. I didn't think Ford was a genius then but I thought he was almost and if he had said, "Claire, walk to the edge of the cliff and jump off," I think I would have done it. I had such confidence in him. He was not really very verbal in his direction. He would give you a feeling of how he wanted you to play a scene. He would do it with gestures. I got sort of a radio message from him, an electronic exchange between people. So we had a very good relationship and he had respect for me. Only one time I remember I came on the set and they were shooting somewhere. But the red light wasn't on and I walked across in back of some set and I was whistling. Ford yelled out, "Who's that whistling? Stop it!" And I

With John Wayne in *Stagecoach.*

kept right on whistling. I thought he was joking and he got furious. But he was always wonderful to me and that's the only time he screamed at me. He would scream for a lot of things—he was a nervous, high-wire man, you know.

Ford was ruthless with Wayne who took a lot of beatings and embarrassment from him. Ford would grab his chin, shake his head in front of the whole cast and say, "What are you doing with your chin? You don't act with your chin, you act with your eyes. I want to see it in the eyes, not in your mouth and chin." It was embarrassing but, boy, it worked. He'd never had good direction before. He'd done a lot of B westerns and even "C" sometimes. Of course, he was very athletic and could have done the big stunts that Yakima Canutt did in the film. He adored Yakima—they were good friends and I guess he had worked in a lot of his pictures.

During the filming, we were all friendly. We were a family. We were together all the time because we were in the stagecoach all the time. So we were all called at the same time, worked closely together and respected each other's talents. John Carradine was so hipped on the Bacon-Shakespeare theory we'd have arguments about that all the time. One day, he came with a whole suitcase filled with books on Bacon to prove his point. He was a very erudite and strange kind of man. I never thought he'd have successful sons like he did.

Thomas Mitchell was a fabulous actor and Donald Meek was meek and darling. I mean everyone was terrific. All the people on the production were marvelous, in fact. Walter Plunkett did my costume—there's only one outfit—and he did Louise's, too. I adored Louise Platt. She married Jed Harris, the "boy genius" producer who had about three smash hits going on Broadway at one time. He was a madman and Louise was so New England and intelligent. It was a strange combination.

We had the ordinary amount of rehearsal on *Stagecoach*. I don't think it was overdone but it was well-planned and beautifully directed. I didn't go to the locations that were filmed in Monument Valley. Everybody who was inside the stagecoach didn't go. Only the people on top who were seen had to be there so I missed that gorgeous country. But when they came back from shooting it, I asked Ford about it and he said, "Perfect. We got sensational shots." He was very pleased. We were on location very often but usually close by, getting out of the stagecoach, entering or leaving a building—that's about what it amounted to.

The interiors, of course, were shot in Wanger's studio which was also Sam Goldwyn's studio in Santa Monica. I remember there was a close-up they wanted to get of me holding the newly-born baby and smiling across at Duke. It was an important eye-to-eye contact in the movie. John Ford always did that. He promoted more sex that way and I thought those close-ups were filled with better sex images than they show today when you see two heaving bodies. That's not sexy at all. Anyway, he wanted to get this close-up and the camera crew had slowed down in order to get the lighting just right. I was doing the radio show and I had to be at CBS at one o'clock for rehearsal. They were supposed to let me go at twelve o'clock sharp so I could have lunch and drive down there. At about five of twelve, they said, "We're ready now."

With Thomas Mitchell in *Stagecoach*.

I said, "Jeez, I don't have time to do this."

They said, "Oh, but we've been setting up the lighting for two hours for this shot. Please, you can't run off now. It'll only take a minute. We're all ready to go. Let's do it." So I did it and then I'd get hell for being late at CBS. I really developed a kind of ulcer from that.

We were told we were going to have to be in a benefit one night. We had been shooting close-ups and whatnot of the stagecoach. It was a fake stagecoach on stage with background shots and we had dust thrown on our faces all day, shaking of the stagecoach and so forth. The benefit was right after dinner so we quit work in the late afternoon—I don't know what time. Louise and I decided we had to get new make-up, new hairdos and everything because we were so dirty. So we went back to the make-up department at the studio. We were going to meet the boys in a restaurant where we would have some dinner before the benefit. This was to be at the Shrine Auditorium which had a very big stage. We would all be in a stagecoach with six horses which would pull out on the stage and was supposed to stop as we got out and were introduced. That was the whole program we were going to take part in.

Well, by the time we got to the restaurant—Lucey's, I think it was, right near the studio—the men had been drinking and everyone kind of swacked after working all day to the point where they got up and made these silly speeches. It was hysterical. Donald Meek I remember got up, ordered crepe of some kind and used it as a powder-puff—he was that swacked. Normally, he was very, very straight and very conservative. When we got to the theatre, nobody wanted to sit inside the stagecoach with the girls. Everyone wanted to be on top. And John Carradine was weeping at this point—he had a weeping jag. We were off on one side of the stage and I think Duke or somebody shot off a gun or something. The whole stagecoach

With Andy Devine, George Bancroft, John Carradine, Donald Meek, Louise Platt and John Wayne in *Stagecoach*.

with the six horses then ran straight across the stage like a flash. I'm sure the audience didn't know what had happened.

I'll never forget the preview of *Stagecoach* because I sat riveted. Usually, I can't look at myself on the screen but this time I forgot I was in the picture. The whole thing was so electric to me—the music and the way it started, the motion of the picture. It was a real motion picture and the characters came on like gangbusters. I was so caught up in the story that I forgot I was in it and I was thrilled to death with the whole thing. Afterwards, we were walking up the aisle and I said to a columnist, "Wasn't that terrific?"

He said, "That's a darn good western." I could have hit him right over the head because I thought it was a masterpiece. I wouldn't have called it a western somehow just because it had a western background. Later, they opened in Radio City Music Hall and it was a big, big picture although not as big as it's grown to be. I think it's the best film I did and the best example of a motion picture. There's no other medium that could capture all that. The stage can't do it, a book can't do it because you don't hear the music. To me, it's a perfect motion picture.

I felt the same way about Orson Welles's *Citizen Kane*. I never worked with Welles—I wish I had—but I met him and I saw the Mercury Theatre when it first started in New York. I heard that Welles learned a lot from John Ford and *Stagecoach*—camera angles and so forth—but he was a genius, too. I'll never forget the opening of *Citizen Kane*—I could hardly get up and walk out of the theatre I was so overcome by that movie. I said to myself and to other people around me, "*Citizen Kane* is the best picture I have ever seen and it's going to stay that way for a long time." It was fabulous.

My agent went to South America for six months after *Stagecoach* was finished in 1939 and nothing happened. I mean, I just sat there. So I was really upset about that. Then I went to Universal to make *I Stole a Million* opposite George Raft. Nathanael West wrote the script. It was directed by Frank Tuttle who was a very intellectual, sweet man. George Raft was exactly what you'd expect him to be. He'd say, "Saturday night is the night to howl." He always had his bodyguard or henchman with him, Mack Gray. He told me at that time that he was a grandfather but he was very young looking, very, very virile and full of fun. He had his own style. I wouldn't call him a sterling actor but he was cute. He was a good dancer and he had to dance in the movie, I think. He told me that when he started dancing in nightclubs in New York, he

With George Raft in *I Stole a Million.*

wore wire shoelaces to keep his shoes on tight and his feet would bleed. So he worked hard.

After that, they put me in two quick pictures with John Wayne, *Allegheny Uprising* and *Dark Command*—boom, boom—and not very important or very good. I think they messed up *Allegheny Uprising* by not paying enough attention to the personal story. There was too much production in it with all the soldiers marching in the big scenes. But I'll never forget that RKO built a whole town out in Thousand Oaks for the picture and at that time we all lived there for six weeks instead of going into the studio. Now with the freeway, you'd get to the studio in half an hour. But then we were out in the wilderness which is unbelievable when I see what's happened up there now. Each one had his own tent with a bedroom, a bathroom, a little sitting room and a porch with wooden floors so it wasn't a hardship living there. The street was composed of two rows of these tents built along a dirt road.

While we were staying in this village, Wayne got news of the birth of his fourth child so he said, "This calls for a celebration." And they celebrated! It was the only time I saw Duke waver from the straight and narrow as far as acting is concerned. The next day he had to shoot but I think they were up all night carousing. They came strolling down the street at two in the morning or something singing like crazy. They used to send out movies every night so we could look at movies outdoors. We had seen a Shirley Temple movie the night before where she became blood brothers with an Indian—they cut thumbs or something and pressed them together. I don't remember exactly how it happened in the movie but Duke and the others said, "Let's become blood brothers." They went into the tent next to mine and I could look through and see them. They were trying to cut their fingers with a beer can and put their thumbs together—blood brothers, you know.

Dark Command was directed by Raoul Walsh for Republic. He was the most casual director I've ever been with. He would shoot a scene and turn his back while it was being done. While we were filming it, I came down with a very severe case of the flu and I think they closed it down for six weeks until I recovered.

Wayne improved as an actor with every picture but he was very sincere. You can't help falling in love with guys like that but Wayne's fourth child was just born and I had married so there was no off-screen interest. By falling in love with him, I mean having a crush on him. Besides Wayne, the cast of *Dark Command* included Roy Rogers and Walter Pidgeon. Roy played my kid brother and he was darling. Walter was a good actor and a charming gentleman. Unlike the others in the picture, we were not western types so I remember we talked a little about the theatre.

In 1941, I worked at MGM with Clark Gable and Lana Turner in *Honky Tonk.* It used to be that Lana Turner and I would walk on the set and until we got close to the crew, they didn't know which was which. So I had to wear brown powder in my hair which I despised. That's what they did to make your hair darker. I thought I looked terrible and I felt inferior. However, Clark Gable was divine. He was so sweet and he seemed to me like a teenager. He was full of life and interesting but not mature. As for Lana, she was very young then and absolutely beautiful. She was very easy to work with and got along with everyone on the set. But that picture broke my heart because in the beginning, I had a much bigger part. Then when I went to the preview in Huntington Beach, I came out, burst into tears and cried all the way home. I thought my career was ended. They had cut so much of it that it seemed to me it didn't ring any bell anywhere.

After that, I got frightened and thought I'd better sign with someone. If not, my career was going

With Lana Turner and Clark Gable in *Honky Tonk*.

nowhere. So I signed a contract with Columbia for maybe two years. I had a couple of run-ins with Harry Cohn there because I fought about the script. He gave me one script and I said, "I just can't do it."

He said, "Why not?"

I said, "Because I'll become ill. I'll throw up as soon as I start doing that part—it's so ghastly."

I did anything they handed me. I would have preferred the kind of dramas and wonderful stories that Bette Davis had—that's what I would have loved, *Now Voyager, Mrs. Skeffington,* anything that had real body to it. But while I was at Columbia, I got trapped into westerns like *Texas* and *The Desperadoes.* They were all inconsequential pictures and I don't think they set anybody on fire. But I did get to work with Randolph Scott, Glenn Ford and Bill Holden. I went out with Randy Scott a couple of times after I made a picture with him. We went to several white-tie things—everyone wore white-tie then. I didn't think much of him as an actor. But I thought Glenn Ford was marvelous in romantic leads. He did a picture with Margaret Sullavan and I thought he was wonderful. Then he sort of went into westerns and action things and I thought he was wasted in that.

I adored Bill Holden—that was a darling man. He did everything well and I knew he had great potential. He was really a naive young boy when he did *Texas* and happily married to Brenda Marshall. I never thought his life would end as it did. I thought he was all set to have a happy marriage and a great career. He did have a great career.

Columbia loaned me out to other studios. In 1942, I was back at MGM in *Crossroads* with Bill

With William Holden and Glenn Ford in *Texas.*

With Hedy Lamarr, William Powell and Basil Rathbone in *Crossroads.*

Powell, Hedy Lamarr and Basil Rathbone. I was happy about the way I looked in that picture and that seldom happened to me. Bill Powell was wonderful and Hedy was the most beautiful thing I've ever seen. I loved working at Metro and I knew the head of the music department, Bronislau Kaper. He and Basil Rathbone and I had lunch together almost every day in the commissary. We had a wonderful time because they were both brilliant and full of wit and it was a great, great luncheon hour.

Then I went to Paramount to do *Street of Chance* with Burgess Meredith. He used to tell me stories about Paulette Goddard whom he married. He was nuts about her and he told me about her beaus who would come in and out. She'd juggle them all around and he thought that was fascinating.

Some time later after I left Columbia, I was in *Murder, My Sweet* at RKO with Dick Powell. It was based on Raymond Chandler's story, *Farewell, My Lovely.* I thought that picture was very good, very well-directed by Edward Dmytryk. I had a crush on Dick Powell and he later became a good friend of mine. To change from a singer in musicals to a dramatic actor was a big jump for him and it made a whole new career for him. I thought he was sensational in *Murder, My Sweet.* He couldn't have been happier because that's when he started going with Junie—June Allyson whom he married.

I did a lot of other noir films in the forties and *Born to Kill* I remember as one of the best. That was one of Robert Wise's first pictures and he was wonderful. I had not worked with a top director very often and I thought he was tops. He had great taste and inspired confidence. He was very articulate and anything he said was pure gold although the picture was not that complicated and didn't require a lot of explanation. Lawrence Tierney was my leading man and he was kind of kooky but entirely different from the killer he played in the film. He was a creative, poetic kind of man who would write marvelous letters.

I played villainesses in many of these films but it never entered my mind if people thought I was like the characters I portrayed. If they did, that was their hard luck. It never bothered me. You had to make those parts believable and some of them were written in a way that was not really true to life. They were concoctions of a dreaming author so that was the difficulty. Nothing is any good unless it's believable and some of these were sort of "outré" characters. However colorful they might

With Dick Powell in *Murder My Sweet.*

have been, they didn't excite me because you never met people like that in real life.

I didn't begin my life till I married Milton Bren. He had been my agent when I first came out from New York in 1933. Bren-Orsatti were assigned to me as an agency by my New York agent who said they were going to be my representatives in California. I met the whole office at that time but I didn't see him often because he handled mostly writers and directors and I soon had a different agent. He didn't handle actors and actresses and was not in that part of the agency.

I had known him all these years but I didn't see him again till after both of us had been divorced and we were at a tennis round robin thing. We went to Ed Lasker's house after the tournament for dinner and dancing and everything else. I danced with him and he was a wonderful dancer. He wanted my telephone number. He said, "I want to see you," and that started it.

I had been married and divorced twice and I was through with marriage. I felt no good as a wife—something's wrong, you know—so I didn't want any part of marriage. But we started going out dancing at Ciro's and Mocambo and all those places. We had a wonderful time, then he drove me down to see his boat and he courted me. We went together for two years before we were married in 1948 because we wanted his children to get used to us being together and so forth. The minute we were married, his children moved in with us, we were an immediate family, my son and his two boys, and I raised them. They were my sons.

In 1948, I was in *Key Largo* and I enjoyed that the same way I had *Stagecoach.* Now that could have gone on forever as far as I was concerned. John Huston was a dream as a director. Like Ford, there was something intuitive about his direction. He wasn't that detailed in his suggestions. He would say something like, "You know, this girl that does that," but you knew what he wanted. We had a week's rehearsal on the set which was a plum. I mean to get that was so unusual and that cast was terrific—Humphrey Bogart, Betty Bacall, Edward G. Robinson and Lionel Barrymore who was wonderful, a very sensitive man and very musical.

Bogart named the boat that appears in the film the *Santana* after his own boat. There was one outdoor shot that was taken in Florida with Bogart getting off a bus at the beginning of the picture. But the rest of us never did get to Florida. Most of it was filmed at the Warner Brothers studio. We all had two rows of dressing rooms on the stage. We had one whole stage just for the dressing room, we

With Lawrence Tierney in *Born to Kill.*

shot on another stage, and Huston had a third stage to himself where he had his office and he was reading new scripts and everything. Every day, we'd all have lunch at the country club out there—Bogart, Betty, Huston, myself and maybe one or two other people. Huston would call everybody in the world he thought of that he could rib and put Bogart on. It was a party—it was wonderful.

There was a scene in the picture where I was supposed to sing and I was very concerned about rehearsing with the music department. I wanted to get the gestures of an old nightclub singer—the old-fashioned style and how they put the song over. I wanted to rehearse it with the playback so I'd be able to mouth it very well when we synched it. I kept asking Huston, "When am I going to go to the music department? I want to go to the music department to rehearse the song."

He kept saying, "There's plenty of time, plenty of time." So one day we came back from a long lunch at the country club and he said, "I think we'll shoot the song this afternoon."

I said, "What?" I hadn't done any rehearsing at all.

But he said, "Yeah."

I said, "Well, I haven't heard the playback."

He said, "You're going to sing it."

I said, "I can't sing."

He said, "You'll do fine." And Lionel Barrymore also said, "You'll do fine." They both said it would be great. So Huston put me in the middle of the room and there was a piano off-stage. They hit one note and he said, "Okay, go." And the whole crew was standing around watching with the whole cast and everybody in there. I had to sing it. I did know the lyrics but that was a tough, tough thing to do. I was terrified and embarrassed like the girl I was playing so Huston was right about not rehearsing it.

I won the Oscar as best supporting actress for *Key Largo.* I remember at the Academy Awards, John Huston and Walter Huston had just been awarded Oscars for *The Treasure of the Sierra Madre.* Walter Huston said when he accepted, "I hope my kid gives his old man another job."

That was a cue for me so I said, "Well, I hope my three boys grow up and give me a job later on."

By this time, Bogart and I had become very good friends. I never had a crush on him—we never felt that way about each other. I always felt like he was my buddy and I appreciated his humor and appreciated him so much. I called him "Bogart." You'd say "Bogie" once in a while but in referring to him with other people, I always say "Bogart." All his sailing friends would call him "Bogart," not "Bogie." No one called him "Humphrey" except as a joke.

My husband was a yachtsman and always had boats so we became very close to him because of his boat, the *Santana.* Bogart loved his boat and I think any man with a yacht loves the yacht more than his wife. We had a longer boat than the *Santana.* Our boat was eighty-three feet long, a sloop with one mast. Bogart's was a ketch, fifty-five feet long. We'd spend every weekend in Catalina and we had adjacent moorings in Moonstone Beach. Every Sunday, we'd race back to San Pedro where the boats were berthed and my husband said, "You have such a slow boat. We'll give you a half-hour start." Now when you pass a boat on the windward side, you take all the wind from the boat on the leeward side so when you pass, it's like putting on the brakes right on the boat. This one time, we were ready to pass Bogart mid-channel with a sailboat. Our son could then steer this big boat and Milton said, "Everyone get below. Just leave this child at the wheel." So all Bogart saw then was this boat passing him with a tow-headed youngster of five at the wheel.

Bogart respected me and was very careful with me although I remember he teased me one time years before. Just after *Dead End,* we were at some

With Edward G. Robinson, Thomas Gomez, Lionel Barrymore, Humphrey Bogart, Harry Lewis and Lauren Bacall in *Key Largo*.

big party together. I was dancing with him and he would stop a lot of people and say, "You know, she has a disease."

I'd say, "Bogart, nobody believes that." He said that was a rib.

I knew the stories about him and his wife, Mayo Methot, the "Battling Bogarts," but I didn't see that. The stories, of course, were all over the place—how they'd come to Catalina in their little putt-putt, run it up on the beach and both pass out. But by the time we became very close pals, their marriage had ended, he had married Betty Bacall and I had married Milton Bren.

When I first worked with Bogart in the thirties, I thought he was a good actor but I didn't think he was a Laurence Olivier. Later, because of films like *The Treasure of the Sierra Madre* and *The African Queen* and because he was so dedicated, I realized he was a fabulous actor. But I had no idea—neither did anyone—that he'd become this legend and there'd be this cult about Bogart.

Milton and I weren't part of Bogart's Holmby Hills Rat Pack although we saw them. We lived in Beverly Hills then. But we were with Bogart and Betty all the time. We went to Romanoff's together many times, we were in New York together, and, of course, we were on the boat together. He'd always say to my husband, "Miltie, I'm your friend, Miltie."

We had dinner at their house one night, the four of us—Betty, Bogart, Milton and myself—and the three boxers under the table on the floor. After dinner, they got in some kind of an argument—I don't know what it was. They were always ribbing each other and they were just terrific. Bogart was sitting in a chair in the living room and it got to be pretty rough. Milton went on over and said, "Come on outside, Bogart. You're such a wimp, get up."

And he looked up and said, "Lift me, Miltie."

The whole last year of Bogart's life I saw him almost every weekend because he'd come on the boat alone. He'd come right over to our boat as soon as we'd pull in and he'd say, "Let's get Betty on the phone." We had a better ship-to-shore radio than he had. I was in the last race he was in in his boat. He was in terrible pain the whole of the last year. It got worse and worse the last month or so. I don't know how long it took but finally he couldn't sail. He used to come over to our boat all the time and it got harder and harder for him to climb up the porting ladder. It was a very hard time for me and I hated the whole thing.

With Humphrey Bogart and Lauren Bacall in *Key Largo.* (The Kobal Collection.)

Then I started a painting of Betty and the baby and I wanted to get it to him before he—while he could still see it, you know. So I used to go over to his home when the crowd would gather for a drink and he'd be brought down in the elevator in his wheelchair—he was skin and bones. I brought the painting one day while it was still wet and he looked at it and his whole face lit up. So that was terrific. He loved it.

All this time, I'd continued to work in pictures. I never had a chance to work again with Wyler, Ford and Huston but that's life, isn't it? I would have liked to have continued with those guys but, unfortunately, I didn't. My husband and I did become social friends of John Ford's. We were on his boat, the *Araner,* quite often. He'd bring it over to Catalina once in a while. I knew his wife and daughter, too.

In 1948, I played opposite William Bendix in *The Babe Ruth Story.* I met the Babe and his wife whom I portrayed in the picture. It was during the shooting of the movie so it wasn't a lasting social friendship. We met them at the railroad station when they arrived in California and took them to the Beverly Hills hotels and bungalows. We had lunch together and things like that. He was not well. He had lost his voice almost by then and died not long after of cancer. But he couldn't have been sweeter and more intent, earnest and hard-working—really a darling man. And his wife was very sweet and very attractive.

Jack Benny produced a picture I did called *The Lucky Stiff* in 1949. Jack and his wife were very good friends of mine and I'd visit them in Palm Springs. I was crazy about Jack Benny as everybody was. He was one of the dearest men. He asked me right after the war to go with him on a tour of the battlefields and entertain the troops. I had been on bond tours and had left my young son for quite a long period of time so I said, "I can't do it, Jack. I can't go and leave him again."

My husband had always wanted to be a producer, too. He had started as an agent when he was a young boy and become a top agent in Hollywood. But he hated it. He wanted to get into show biz so he quit the agency business and became a producer. In 1950, he produced *Borderline* which I did with Fred MacMurray. The director, Bill Seiter, and his wife, Marion Nixon, were close friends of ours. But I thought it didn't turn out as well as it should have. I don't think Bill Seiter was a strong director and the script didn't click. Bill

With Sally Forrest in *Hard, Fast and Beautiful.*

Seiter was not very deep. He was a fun guy to be with and warm and genial and I think he could have done the crazy kind of comedy earlier. But I think time had passed him by a little bit when we did the picture. In later years, I would often get directors after they had passed their peak and were starving for some kind of work.

Ida Lupino directed me in *Hard, Fast and Beautiful* in 1951. She was wonderful and a very intelligent woman. We had great rapport. I think she was completely supportive of a woman and her needs as an actress. Having been one herself, she knew exactly what an actress would like and was very, very intuitive. I guess she was softer than a lot of men would have been but she wasn't wishy-washy at all. I don't know what word to use—she was more understanding.

I was still doing westerns. I can't remember the name of the picture but when one of my sons was six years old and another sixteen, I thought they'd like to go with me on location and see the horses, the stunts and the train robberies. Well, the sixteen-year-old found some girls in town who went rabbit-hunting at night on the back of a truck so he didn't come out to location—he wasn't interested. The six-year-old found a horse. He loved to ride and he would go off on little toots by himself. One time, the cameraman was looking through the finder and he said, "There's something moving on that mountain over there." So they sent the cowboys out and it was my son on his horse.

William Wellman directed me in *My Man and I* and *The High and the Mighty.* He was a tough man—too tough. I remember that Ricardo Montalban who was in *My Man and I* was the dearest man. His wife was taken to the hospital about to give birth and he asked Wellman if he could leave the set. He said, "I've got to be in the hospital. I've been with my wife every time the baby's been born. I've got to be there." But Wellman wouldn't let him go.

I did *The High and the Mighty* with John Wayne in 1954. That was a boring film to make because we were sequestered on the set of an airplane for days. Phil Harris was making his debut in a dramatic picture and he hated it. But we had some fun when we played scrabble together between takes. I was nominated for an Oscar for it as best supporting actress but I thought my part was ruined when the preamble to my character was cut out during the editing of the picture.

I did a lot of television drama in the fifties. That was an experience to be doing an hour and a half live on television. It was terrifying but very exciting. I did *Dodsworth* opposite Fredric March for *Producer's Showcase* in 1956 and that was my favorite performance of any I ever did. That's the one

With Kirk Douglas in *Man Without a Star.*

time I'm almost proud of what I did. To me, that was such a beautiful play. There, I played a real woman. We rehearsed, I think, two weeks before we did it and it turned out to be great. I remember we were standing on the set during the countdown ready to start—"ten," "nine," "eight"—and the perspiration was just pouring off me I was so nervous. It was a frightening experience because somebody would grab your hand at the end of a scene and pull you through, you'd change clothes and you'd be in another set before you knew what had happened. That was the only time I worked with Fredric March and he was wonderful.

I replaced Bette Davis in *If You Knew Elizabeth* on *Playhouse 90* in 1957. I don't know what the reason was for her not doing it but that was another terrifying thing. Gary Merrill was looking for this character and he'd go to her friends and her parents. Each one remembered her in a different way so the part I played seemed to have six different lives. And that was interesting and exciting.

I also worked on the stage. In 1947, I had starred on Broadway in *The Big Two.* Robert Montgomery directed that. I was in summer stock, too. I did a play in Laguna, *The Time of the Cuckoo.* In later years, I did *John Brown's Body* with Rock Hudson. We went on tour with it and it was very, very exhausting. I was sorry I had ever done it. The stage is not for me anymore. But Rock was such a good friend of mine and I thought it would be nice to do something with him. He'd always wanted to work with me.

Frank Capra asked me to play the part of Apple Annie in his last picture, *A Pocketful of Miracles,* which he made in the early sixties but I just couldn't do it. It would have turned me into an old hag and I thought, "I've never been a really glamourous person in the theatre or the movies. Why should I be an old hag now before my time?" He tried to convince me to do it but Bette Davis did the part instead. It's a shame that I had to turn it down because I missed the experience of working with Capra. I would have loved that.

In my later films, I had the opportunity to work with younger stars—Natalie Wood in *Marjorie Morningstar,* Jack Lemmon in *How to Murder Your Wife,* Joanne Woodward in *The Stripper*—and they were all absolutely wonderful. Natalie Wood was a dream girl. I loved her like my daughter. Jack Lemmon was such a dear—I just adored working with him. And Joanne Woodward—I taught Joanne how to crochet.

I mostly stopped working after the sixties. There

With Sally Field in *Kiss Me Goodbye.*

A photo from the 1940s.

are no scripts being written for older women so you don't get the parts. I didn't continue on like Bette Davis and Barbara Stanwyck. The only time I would have worked was if something irresistible had been offered me. Bette Davis had nothing in her life except her career. I had many other interests and a happy marriage and she didn't have that. She was only happy when she was working and that's not true of me.

Barbara Stanwyck, of course, I knew. She embarrassed me one time when I was at Ciro's or some restaurant like that. She came in the ladies' room when I was in there, got down on her knees and said, "Claire Trevor!"

I said, "Get up, get up!"

She was marvelous. She said, "I really have to bow to you."

I said, "No, I have to get on the floor with you." Anyway, we became good friends after that.

After a long time away from acting, I appeared in an episode of *Murder She Wrote* with Angela Lansbury some years ago. That was just like early movies to me. First of all, they said, "You're going to stay in a hotel right near the studio."

I said, "Great. I can roll out of bed and go to the studio in nothing flat."

Well, we never shot anything in the studio until the last day. Everything was on location so they said, "Your call will be for five o'clock in the morning. We'll pick you up in the lobby of the hotel." Five in the morning! I'd been retired a long time and got up when I felt like it. This was a jolt. So we'd stay on location all day and I'd get home at nine o'clock at night.

It was very, very rugged and I said, "Never again," although I enjoyed working with Angela. But a TV series is something I could not do. I'm way out of training. Angela is in the routine of it and it's no easy job for her, either, although everything's made as simple as can be for her. She has a big trailer, a caravan thing where the dressing room is. She gets made up in there, she gets dressed in there, she can take naps in there. But she carries cards around. Right before a take, she has to go over them. We'd finish shooting Wednesday evening nine o'clock. She had two more shots after I left and I was exhausted. I said to her, "I don't know how you do it." She's amazing and also a fabulous woman. On Wednesday, she goes home and Thursday morning, she starts a whole new episode with a new director, new script, new clothes which all had to have fittings the week before while she's shooting. I mean it's just unbelievable.

Looking back on Hollywood, I think the demise of the studio system is just too bad because they knew how to make stars. They weren't businessmen like they are today. To be the head of a big corporation doesn't mean you know show business. They were showmen in those days and they were marvelous.

I've great respect for the technicians of those days, too. It breaks my heart when films are "colorized" because the whole mood is lost. Each cameraman took great pride in black-and-white effects, in getting the mood right, the people lit correctly and so forth. It took hours and hours to light and Karl Freund, the cameraman on *Key Largo,* took forever.

Most of the films I did, though, were just daily work and I didn't get really excited about anything except something like *Stagecoach.* When you work with a director of that magnitude, you're in heaven. By the same token, I enjoyed *Dead End* but that was a day and a half and *Stagecoach* was just a projection of that enjoyment for a much longer time.

Acting wasn't the main impetus in my life. Working to me started from necessity. I never based my whole life and dreams on a career. I had many other things. I had many friends, a wonderful family and a marvelously happy marriage. But when I worked, I gave it everything I had because that's the way I do everything.

Claire Trevor and John Wayne with Moroni Olsen, John F. Hamilton, Wilfred Lawson and Robert Bassat in *Allegheny Uprising*, filmed in the summer of 1939.

1939—THE SUMMER OF DREAMS

"Now that Europe is tumbling about our ears . . . it is an escape into a lavish, romantic past that perhaps will not come again into our time."

—F. Scott Fitzgerald in a September 27, 1939, letter to his publisher outlining a projected novel depicting the Hollywood of the 1930s[1]

In popular history, the year 1939 has taken on a legendary aura unique in film annals. It has often been called "Hollywood's Best Year"[2] although many earlier years may have actually produced a greater number of outstanding achievements. But 1939, nevertheless, remains extraordinary as simultaneously an end, a beginning and a revival in cinematic trends in that peculiar nexus where art and history meet, a year in which film artists, like the world as a whole, enjoyed one last season of hope, one last time for dreaming great dreams.

Contributing in no small measure to the mythic status of 1939 was the release of what would become America's two most beloved films, *The Wizard of Oz* and *Gone With the Wind,* both shot in Technicolor and based on novels that were popular modern classics. Although Victor Fleming was the accredited director for both, they were ultimately triumphs of the collaborative studio style that had supplanted the reign of the autonomous director in the late twenties. The two films perfectly embodied the national mood of the time which balanced the ideals of the past with the dreams of the future. Dorothy caught between the nostalgic pull of her gray Kansas farm and the glittering attractions of Oz's Emerald City and Scarlett O'Hara divided between the red earth of her farm, Tara, and the worldliness of Atlanta were emblematic of an America emerging from the Great Depression and oscillating between its simple agrarian past and the technological marvels of the World of Tomorrow, the fabulous featured exhibit of the 1939 New York World's Fair forecasting the country two decades hence.

Although 1939 thus saw a culmination in the ability of the studio system to address the experiences, aspirations and yearnings of a mass audience, the year was also impressive for the reassertion of directorial authority. Frank Capra with *Mr. Smith Goes to Washington,* Ernst Lubitsch with *Ninotchka* and William Wyler with *Wuthering Heights* were among the year's preeminent directors who stamped their personalities on their achievements. But the dominant figure by far in American films at this time was John Ford, who began the year with *Stagecoach* and quickly followed it in the same year with *Young Mr. Lincoln, Drums Along the Mohawk* and *The Grapes of Wrath.* With these explorations of American history from the Revolutionary War to the Depression, Ford became the cinematic spokesman for the ideals of the New Deal era as the nation climbed out of the economic collapse of the thirties to confront future challenges posed by events overseas.

Ford was also a source of inspiration to a 24-year-old tyro of theatre and radio brought out from the East in the summer of 1939 to work for

RKO in Hollywood under conditions of unprecedented freedom. Before embarking on his own directorial career, Orson Welles ran and reran *Stagecoach* in order to study cinematic technique. Released in 1941, Welles's first film, *Citizen Kane,* like D. W. Griffith's *Intolerance* and Abel Gance's *Napoléon,* would reinvent the cinema as Welles explored unusual visual and narrative techniques, reviving experiments from the silent era and introducing audio effects from his work in radio. But after the studio cut scenes from his second film, *The Magnificent Ambersons,* over his objections, Welles began a long and often frustrating struggle with commercial interests to make films in his own highly individualistic style.

Welles's fate had been foretold by many of his predecessors in the silent era including the man whom he revered as the cinema's greatest figure, D. W. Griffith. Griffith had been inactive as a director since the release of his final film, *The Struggle,* in 1931. Growing restive in his Kentucky exile, he resurfaced in 1939 with an article in *Liberty Magazine* in which he excoriated contemporary Hollywood as "a sterile Detroit where emotions are as standardized as automobile parts."[3] Yet despite his criticism of the industry, he still longed to plunge back into directing to realize his dream of making more epic films. The article led to the first serious offer Griffith had received in years to work in Hollywood. Filled with renewed confidence, he departed for the film capital in the summer of 1939 to work for the Hal Roach studio. He ended up not directing, however, but assisting Roach on *One Million B.C.*, released the next year. Unhappy with the finished product, Griffith did not wish to have his name publicized in connection with the film, and, although he continued to reside in Hollywood until his death in 1948, he never again worked in a film studio.

Erich von Stroheim was planning a return to directing in France in 1939. After his *Walking Down Broadway* was reedited and reshot by Fox as *Hello, Sister* in 1933, von Stroheim resumed acting and writing in Hollywood before moving to France, where he became a popular star. With Jean Renoir's encouragement, von Stroheim that summer was preparing to direct *La Dame Blanche,* a film that would return to the setting and themes of *The Wedding March.* The project was cancelled, however, with the outbreak of the war in September. Von Stroheim, who never again came so close to reviving his directorial career, remained an actor for the rest of his life.

The war would also affect the career of Abel Gance. After a dry period of comparatively minor films in the early and middle thirties, Gance had reappeared as a major directorial figure in France with such powerful films as *Beethoven* (1937) and *J'accuse* (1938). In this summer of 1939, he was making preparations for a new epic film depicting the life of Christopher Columbus. But his plans to explore new worlds of cinematic art were dealt a fatal blow by the war. Gance, who described his life as "an office of lost dreams," would work only intermittently in the French cinema in later years. For the rest of his life, he would be haunted by the Columbus epic he sought unsuccessfully to bring to the screen.

For two pioneer visionaries of the silent screen, 1939 would prove to be the final chapter. It had been five years since Lois Weber had directed her last film, an independent production entitled *White Heat.* Although the film had been entered at the Venice Film Festival, it had brought her no other offers and she was replaced by William Wyler as the director of *Glamour,* a 1934 release starring Constance Cummings. Weber drifted into poverty and obscurity. She died in Hollywood in November of 1939, her funeral expenses paid by her friend, screenwriter Frances Marion. Once a major, often controversial force in American films, Weber received little mention in the press at the time of her passing. One month later, Douglas Fairbanks, Sr. died. It had also been five years since his last film, *The Private Life of Don Juan;* in contrast to Weber, however, his obituary was headlined throughout the world. The deaths of these two artists in the waning weeks of 1939 as the world began to rush into war seemed a fitting epitaph for the era of creative vitality and optimism in filmmaking.

Hollywood, keenly aware of its own aging, became increasingly retrospective. Silent western star William S. Hart filmed a poignant farewell to the screen to introduce a reissue of his last picture, the 1925 *Tumbleweeds. Hollywood Cavalcade,* a fictionalized depiction of the silent era, was filmed that summer with Alice Faye in the lead and Buster Keaton in a role that brought him back into prominence after a decade of personal difficulties. F. Scott Fitzgerald, now a screenwriter, was also recovering from a "lost decade," making plans for a novel recreating the Hollywood of the thirties. But with the author's death in December, 1940, *The Last Tycoon,* like many of the dreams of 1939, would remain unfinished.

For all the looking back at past glories, 1939 nevertheless stands out as a time when filmmakers were boldly forging ahead with new productions, refining cinematic techniques and taking up provocative themes. Indeed, the work of such veterans as Ford, Capra, Lubitsch and Wyler along with the brief fluorescence of Orson Welles and the directorial debuts of screenwriters Preston Sturges and John Huston marked a watershed in the revival of directorial authority in the late thirties and early forties. But with the war and many of the leading directors in uniform, the studio system was able to reassert itself as films became a wartime industry to boost morale and entertain the public. As Capra wrote in his autobiography, "Assembly-line products were manufactured not only cheaper and faster than the independent producers' quality films, but . . . they made more money."[4] Individual creativity would now find its most distinctive expression in those dark, pessimistic, smaller-budgeted productions later known as "film noir," works which launched the careers of newer directors like Edward Dmytryk and Robert Wise. These films, reflecting the somber mood of the war and post-war years, were a far cry from the brighter atmosphere of most American films of 1939, whether the creations of individual "auteurs" or the products of the large studios' factory system.

With Hollywood poised at the end of an era and the beginning of another, the actresses whose careers have been documented in this volume were caught up in the prevailing euphoria during the temporary calm of the summer of 1939. By then, some had channeled their energies into their personal lives; others were still endeavoring to fulfill professional ambitions, although only one would enjoy further triumphs in Hollywood.

For Billie Dove and Anita Page, 1939 proved to be another year in which they were content to devote their time to their families far removed from the hustle and bustle of their glamourous past. Billie had just passed up the opportunity to revive her career with a flourish by turning down a tempting offer to play Belle Watling in the year's most anticipated film, *Gone With the Wind.* Anita, as in the past several years, spent the summer traveling with her naval officer husband.

For Dorothy Lee, however, the year brought a brief resumption in a career that marriage seemed to have ended in early 1936 after her final film with Wheeler and Woolsey. With her fourth marriage failing by the end of 1938, one month after Bob Woolsey's passing, she came back to Hollywood from Chicago to appear in a supporting role in *Twelve Crowded Hours,* made for her old studio, RKO, and starring Richard Dix and Lucille Ball. Its release in early 1939 was followed by the Republic film, *S.O.S.-Tidal Wave,* in which Dottie had another supporting, nonmusical part. During the summer, the performer who had brightened the earliest cycle of movie musicals danced with newcomer Gene Kelly on stage in Chicago in *One for the Money.* While Dottie would retire within two years, Kelly would take first Broadway and then Hollywood by storm. As the new king of movie musicals, he would later star in *Singin' in the Rain,* his most famous film and a recreation of the era that had brought celebrity to both Dottie and Anita Page.

Marian Marsh garnered a part in only one film in 1939, a supporting role in *Missing Daughters,* produced by Columbia with Richard Arlen and Rochelle Hudson in the leads. But Marian, as always, was happy to be working and was proud of the fact that she was tapped that summer to appear in a skit at the Golden Gate International Exposition, the great San Francisco fair on Treasure Island which rivalled the New York World's Fair. Marian and veteran silent star Neil Hamilton wowed audiences at the Exposition, demonstrating how movies were made with a director staging the whole scene as if it were an actual production.

Evelyn Venable that year played the lead in a Paramount remake of the Zane Grey western story, *Heritage of the Desert,* co-starring Donald Woods. She was nearing the end of her career with just two more leads in the offing—one in 1940 and another in 1943. Nevertheless, she would soon gain a new kind of immortality as she recorded the Blue Fairy's voice for Walt Disney's classic, *Pinocchio,* released in early 1940.

For Jean Muir, it was a year of missed opportunities despite her continuing work on the stage and radio. She had been considered for the role of Melanie in *Gone With the Wind,* a plum part she lost to her friend and co-star at Warners, Olivia de Havilland. But two years after she left Warners, she was back in Hollywood in the summer of 1939, testing for another choice role in a major film—the part of Mae in *Of Mice and Men* which went to Betty Field instead. In August, Jean was prominent in a West Coast delegation of film actors to the American Federation of Labor's council meeting in Atlantic City protesting the attempted take-over of the Screen Actors Guild by the mob-controlled International Alliance of Theatrical Stage Employees. Her return to Hollywood that summer also led to co-starring roles in two 1940 productions and a final supporting one in 1943.

If many of the actresses had begun to recede from the forefront of public consciousness in 1939, no one was more in the limelight in that year than Annabella. Her one film of the year, *Bridal Suite,* co-starring Robert Young and released in the spring by MGM, received its title from a studio eager to capitalize on the celebrity of her marriage to Hollywood's leading heartthrob, Tyrone Power. For Annabella, the summer was one of enchantment and love as she and Tyrone honeymooned in Europe. But, as they were returning to America, the season of dreams was abruptly terminated by the outbreak of war, a drama that would affect their lives and careers thereafter.

The summer was also a transitional time in Fay Wray's life. Once the busiest actress in Hollywood, she appeared in only one film in 1939, *Navy Secrets,* released early in the year by Monogram. Finally separated from John Monk Saunders, she spent the season doing summer stock in Skowhagen, Maine. She later recalled she had felt this experience would be valuable because of the serious nature of many plays. However, she was disappointed to discover that plays could be as superficial as some of her lesser film efforts and soon realized that she never could crave the theatre the way she did her first and truest love, the movies. Yet the summer was not without its rewards: she formed lasting friendships with people in the theatre; observed an up-and-coming actor named Hume Cronyn in rehearsal in Skowhagen; went on picnics with her daughter; and met and fell in love with Clifford Odets.

In England, Constance Cummings was concentrating on the theatre, fulfilling a lifelong ambition. She made no films that year; instead, she starred in *Romeo and Juliet* and *Saint Joan* for the Old Vic. Her company opened the season in Buxton up in Derbyshire and planned to open in London in September, but were forced to relocate in Streatham Hill across the river from the city when the outbreak of the war put a temporary embargo on plays in London. Her Romeo was played by Robert Donat, then at the peak of his career and fresh from the title role in one of the year's top films, *Goodbye Mr. Chips,* which would soon earn him an Oscar as the best actor of 1939. He was, as she remembered, a very nice chap who was not physically strong but was able to conserve his energy for his work. She recalled a September day she was with Donat on a picnic when they heard over the radio they had taken with them Prime Minister Neville Chamberlain's announcement that war had broken out.

Meanwhile, in California, Claire Trevor and John Wayne were refighting the violent aftermath of an earlier conflict, the French and Indian War of the 1700s, in *Allegheny Uprising,* made for RKO. Although several months elapsed between the completion of *Stagecoach* in early 1939 and her next picture, by summer Claire was very busy indeed, continuing her work on radio, finishing *I Stole a Million* with George Raft in early July and, within a few days, beginning the shoot on *Allegheny Uprising.* Claire would never work again with Ford, yet *Stagecoach* had proved that she could play complex, mature women whose struggles and emotions were far greater than those of formulaic heroines in B pictures and her career prospered in Hollywood right up to the end of the studio era.

While all of the actresses in this book eventually chose a life away from the camera, each had made a vital contribution to the cinema. As these interviews have demonstrated, their individual experiences were reflective of the creativity, the upheavals and the trends in filmmaking in the 1920s and 1930s. Those years saw the cinema attain an astonishing level of perfection as a visual narrative art, only to be shaken to its foundations by the introduction of recorded speech, then revitalized by absorbing new creative talent from the theatre to evolve once again into an autonomous art.

Through it all, these actresses had been among those at the center of the frame when the cinema was in flux in the years from 1927 to 1933. Some had been part of the period when the director shaped the picture. All who began in silents survived the change-over to sound and became part of the collaborative environment of the studio system. Most were there when, with the imposition of censorship, the director reemerged as the artist indispensable in guiding cast and crew to bring life to narratives that had often been laundered by the censors during the scripting phase.

The studio system, like Janus, had two faces for these actresses. Without the support of large, well-equipped studios employing gifted people at every level, it would have been impossible for them to have sustained their careers for any length of time, much less express their individual talents in a medium that brought them recognition throughout the world. Although they were never truly hapless victims of the studio system, they were, in a sense, engulfed by it. A career, like the films themselves, was shelved once its money-making potential was exhausted. The actresses chronicled in these pages, while all were talented, popular and ambitious, differed from such actresses as Joan Crawford, Bette Davis and Barbara Stanwyck who maintained their stellar positions for decades through a knack for publicity and an ability to combine the skills of diplomat, executive and streetfighter.

It is perhaps significant that for most of the actresses in this book, 1939, a year of nostalgia for the past mingled with hopes and fears for the future, was the dividing line in their personal and professional lives. But whether realized or not, the dreams of that summer of 1939—dreams shared by these actresses—had the power to resonate on succeeding generations. Viewed through the prism of time, it was a season of promise in an age of creative ferment, a moment of achievement and striving that left its mark on the imagination. Its sense of renewal had been anticipated at the beginning of the year with the completion of *Stagecoach*. Much as Billie Dove, Fay Wray and Annabella had been guided in the twenties by their directors, so at the end of the thirties, Claire Trevor became the ultimate survivor through her work with John Ford. Once again, a creative director was working independently on a story and theme of his choosing and with an actress he had personally selected, one in consonance with his vision. Once again, the mystic partnership between the director, the player, the camera and the audience had created magic on the screen, wedding image to sound to explore new frontiers of the art.

Filmographies

Billie Dove

1917–19: Appeared as an extra and bit player in films including *Joan of Plattsburg* (1918, Goldwyn); 1920: Leading lady in Johnny Hines comedy shorts for First National; 1921: *Get-Rich-Quick Wallingford* (Cosmopolitan-Paramount); *At the Stage Door* (Robertson-Cole); 1922: *Polly of the Follies* (First National); *Beyond the Rainbow* (Robertson-Cole); *Youth to Youth* (Metro); 1923: *All the Brothers Were Valiant* (Metro); *Madness of Youth* (Fox); *Soft Boiled* (Fox); *The Lone Star Ranger* (Fox); *The Thrill Chaser* (Universal); 1924: *On Time* (Truart); *Try and Get It* (Producers Distributing Corp.); *Yankee Madness* (Film Booking Offices); *Wanderer of the Wasteland* (Paramount); *The Roughneck* (Fox); *The Folly of Vanity* (Fox); 1925: *The Air Mail* (Paramount); *The Light of Western Stars* (Paramount); *The Lucky Horseshoe* (Fox); *Wild Horse Mesa* (Paramount); *The Fighting Heart* (Fox); *The Ancient Highway* (Paramount); 1926: *The Black Pirate* (United Artists); *The Lone Wolf Returns* (Columbia); *The Marriage Clause* (Universal); *Kid Boots* (Paramount); 1927: *An Affair of the Follies* (First National); *Sensation Seekers* (Universal); *The Tender Hour* (First National); *The Stolen Bride* (First National); *American Beauty* (First National); *The Love Mart* (First National); 1928: *The Heart of a Follies Girl* (First National); *The Yellow Lily* (First National); *The Night Watch* (First National); *Adoration* (First National); 1929: *Careers* (Part-talking; First National); *The Man and the Moment* (All-talking; First National); *Her Private Life* (All-talking; First National); *The Painted Angel* (All-talking; First National); 1930: *The Other Tomorrow* (First National); *A Notorious Affair* (First National); *Sweethearts and Wives* (First National); *One Night at Susie's* (First National); 1931: *The Lady Who Dared* (First National-Warner Bros.); *The Age for Love* (Caddo-United Artists); 1932: *Cock of the Air* (Caddo-United Artists); *Blondie of the Follies* (Metro-Goldwyn-Mayer); 1962: *Diamond Head* (Columbia).

Fay Wray

1923–24: Appeared in comedy shorts for Century Studios and Fox including *Gasoline Love* (1923, Century); 1925: Feature debut: *The Coast Patrol* (Bud Barsky Corp.); Appeared in comedy shorts for Hal Roach-Pathé including *Isn't Life Terrible, What Price Goofy?, No Father to Guide Him, Unfriendly Enemies, Moonlight and Noses* and *Madam Sans Jane;* 1926: Leading lady in Universal western shorts including *The Saddle Tramp* and *Hearts and Spurs;* Features—*The Man in the Saddle* (Universal); *The Wild Horse Stampede* (Universal); *Lazy Lightning* (Universal); 1927: *Loco Luck* (Universal); *A One Man Game* (Universal); *Spurs and Saddles* (Universal); 1928: *The Legion of the Condemned* (Paramount); *The Street of Sin* (Paramount); *The First Kiss* (Paramount); *The Wedding March* (Paramount); 1929: *The Four Feathers* (Silent; Paramount); *Thunderbolt* (All-talking; Paramount); *Pointed Heels* (All-talking; Paramount); 1930: *Behind the Make-up* (Paramount); *Paramount on Parade* (Paramount); *The Border Legion* (Paramount); *The Texan* (Paramount); *The Sea God* (Paramount); *Captain Thunder* (Warner Brothers); 1931: *The Conquering Horde* (Paramount); *Not Exactly Gentlemen* aka *Three Rogues* (Fox); *The Finger Points* (First National-Warner Bros.); *Dirigible* (Columbia); *The Lawyer's Secret* (Paramount); *The Unholy Garden* (Goldwyn-United Artists); 1932: *Stowaway* (Universal); *Doctor X* (Warner Bros.); *The Most Dangerous Game* (RKO-Radio); 1933: *The Vampire Bat* (Majestic); *The Mystery of the Wax Museum* (Warner Bros.); *King Kong* (RKO); *Below the Sea* (Columbia); *Ann Carver's Profession* (Columbia); *The Woman I Stole* (Columbia); *The Big Brain* (RKO); *One Sunday Afternoon* (Paramount); *Shanghai Madness* (Fox); *The Bowery* (20th Century-United Artists); *Master of Men* (Columbia); 1934: *Madame Spy* (Universal); *Once to Every Woman* (Columbia); *The Countess of Monte Cristo* (Universal); *Viva Villa!* (Metro-Goldwyn-Mayer); *The Af-*

fairs of Cellini (20th Century-United Artists); *Black Moon* (Columbia); *Woman in the Dark* (RKO); *The Richest Girl in the World* (RKO); *Cheating Cheaters* (Universal); *White Lies* (Columbia); *Mills of the Gods* (Columbia); 1935: *Bulldog Jack* (Gaumont-British); *The Clairvoyant* (Gaumont-British); *Come Out of the Pantry* (United Artists); 1936: *Roaming Lady* (Columbia); *When Knights Were Bold* (General Film Distributors); *They Met in a Taxi* (Columbia); 1937: *It Happened in Hollywood* (Columbia); *Murder in Greenwich Village* (Columbia); 1938: *The Jury's Secret* (Universal); *Smashing the Spy Ring* (Columbia); 1939: *Navy Secrets* (Monogram); 1940: *Wildcat Bus* (RKO); 1941: *Adam Had Four Sons* (Columbia); *Melody for Three* (RKO); 1942: *Not a Ladies' Man* (Columbia); 1953: *The Treasure of the Golden Condor* (20th Century–Fox); *Small Town Girl* (MGM); 1955: *The Cobweb* (MGM); *Queen Bee* (Columbia); 1956: *Hell on Frisco Bay* (Warner Bros.); 1957: *Rock Pretty Baby* (Universal); *Crime of Passion* (United Artists); *Tammy and the Bachelor* (Universal); 1958: *Summer Love* (Universal); *Dragstrip Riot* (American-International); 1980: *Gideon's Trumpet* (TV feature film).

Annabella

1927: *Napoléon* (Westi-Société Générale de Films-MGM); *Maldone* (Société des Films Charles Dullin); 1928: *Trois jeunes filles nues* (Integral Film); 1930: *La Maison de la Flèche* (Prod. Jacques Haik); *Barcarolle d'amour* (Films P. J. de Venloo); *Deux fois vingt ans* (Gaumont-Franco-Film-Aubert); *Romance a l'inconnue* (Gaumont-Franco-Film-Aubert); 1931: *Le Million* (Tobis); *Un soir de rafle* (Films Osso); *Autour d'une enquête* (U.F.A.); *Son Altesse l'amour* (Pathé-Natan); 1932: *Paris-Mediterranée* (Pathé-Natan); *Un fils d'Amérique* (Osso); *Marie, Légende Hongroise* (Osso); 1933: *Quatorze Juillet* (Tobis); *Mademoiselle Josette, ma femme* (Films de France); *Gardez le sourire* aka *Sonnenstrahl* (French-Austrian Prod.); 1934: *La Bataille* (Nicolas Farkas Film); *Caravane* (Fox); *Les Nuits Moscovites* (Alexis Granowsky Film); 1935: *Variétés* (Pathé Consortium Cinema); *La Bandera* (Société Nouvelle de Production); *L'Equipage* (Pathé-Natan); *Veille d'armes* (Pathé-Natan); 1936: *Anne-Marie* (Aurea Films); 1937: *La citadelle du silence* (Imperial Films); *Wings of the Morning* (20th Century–Fox); *Under the Red Robe* (20th Century–Fox); *Dinner at the Ritz* (20th Century–Fox); 1938: *The Baroness and the Butler* (20th Century–Fox); *Suez* (20th Century–Fox); *Hotel du Nord* (Marcel Carne Film); 1939: *Bridal Suite* (Metro-Goldwyn-Mayer); 1943: *Tonight We Raid Calais* (20th Century–Fox); *Bomber's Moon* (20th Century–Fox); 1946: *13 Rue Madeleine* (20th Century–Fox); 1948: *Eternel conflit* (France); 1949: *Dernier amour* (France); *L'Homme qui revient de loin* (France); 1950: *Le plus bel amour de Don Juan* (Spain); *Quema el suelo* (Spain); 1982: *Elizabeth* (French TV feature film).

Anita Page

1926: *A Kiss for Cinderella* (Paramount); *Love 'Em and Leave 'Em* (Paramount); *Beach Nuts* (Kenilworth Prod.; short never released); 1928: *Telling the World* (Metro-Goldwyn-Mayer); *Our Dancing Daughters* (MGM); *While the City Sleeps* (MGM); 1929: *The Broadway Melody* (All-talking; MGM); *The Flying Fleet* (Silent; MGM); *The Hollywood Revue of 1929* (All-talking; MGM); *Our Modern Maidens* (Silent; MGM); *Speedway* (Silent; MGM); 1930: *Navy Blues* (MGM); *Free and Easy* (MGM); *Caught Short* (MGM); *Our Blushing Brides* (MGM); *The Little Accident* (Universal); *War Nurse* (MGM); 1931: *Reducing* (MGM); *The Easiest Way* (MGM); *Gentleman's Fate* (MGM); *Under Eighteen* (Warner Brothers); *The Sidewalks of New York* (MGM); 1932: *Are You Listening?* (MGM); *Night Court* (MGM); *Prosperity* (MGM); *Skyscraper Souls* (MGM); 1933: *The Big Cage* (Universal); *Jungle Bride* (Monogram); *Soldiers of the Storm* (Columbia); *I Have Lived* (Chesterfield); 1936: *Hitch Hike to Heaven* (Chesterfield); 1996: *Sunset After Dark* (Wild Cat Entertainment).

Dorothy Lee

1928: *Take Me Home* (Paramount); 1929: *Syncopation* (All-talking; RKO-Radio); *Rio Rita* (All-talking; RKO); 1930: *The Cuckoos* (RKO); *Dixiana* (RKO); *Half Shot at Sunrise* (RKO); *Hook, Line and Sinker* (RKO); 1931: *Laugh and Get Rich* (RKO); *Cracked Nuts* (RKO); *Too Many Cooks* (RKO); *Local Boy Makes Good* (Warner Brothers); *Peach O'Reno* (RKO); 1932: *Girl Crazy* (RKO); 1933: *Plane Crazy* (Short; Warner Bros.); *A Preferred List* (Short; RKO); *Mazie* (Plymouth Pictures); *Take a Chance* (Paramount); 1934: *Hips, Hips, Hooray!* (RKO); *Cockeyed Cavaliers* (RKO); *School for Girls* (Liberty); 1935: *In the Spotlight* (Short; Warner Bros.); *The Curtain Falls* (Chesterfield); *The Old Homestead* (Liberty); *The Rainmakers* (RKO); 1936: *Penthouse Party* aka *Without Children* (Liberty); *Silly Billies* (RKO); 1939: *Twelve Crowded Hours* (RKO); *S.O.S.-Tidal Wave* (Republic); 1941: *Roar of the Press* (Monogram); *Too Many Blondes* (Universal); *Repent at Leisure* (RKO).

Marian Marsh

1929: Appeared in sound shorts for Pathé including a comedy series with James and Lucille Gleason; Feature debut: *The Sophomore* (Pathé); 1930: *Hell's Angels* (Caddo-United Artists); *Whoopee!* (Goldwyn-United Artists); 1931: *Svengali* (Warner Brothers); *Five Star Final* (Warner Bros.); *The Road to Singapore* (Warner Bros.); *The Mad Genius* (Warner Bros.); *Under Eighteen* (Warner Bros.); 1932: *Alias the Doctor* (Warner Bros.); *Beauty and the Boss* (Warner Bros.); *Strange Justice* (RKO); *The Sport Parade* (RKO); 1933: *Daring Daughters* (Tower); *The Eleventh Commandment* (Allied); *A Man of Sentiment* (Chesterfield); *Notorious But Nice* (Chesterfield); 1934: *I Like It That Way* (Universal); *Over the Garden Wall* (Wardour); *The Girl Thief* aka *Love at Second Sight* (Associated British Films); *Der verlorene Sohn* (*The Prodigal Son*) (Deutsche Universal); *A Girl of the Limberlost* (Monogram); 1935: *The Black Room* (Columbia); *Crime and Punishment* (Columbia); *In Spite of Danger* (Columbia); *Unknown Woman* (Columbia); 1936: *Lady of Secrets* (Columbia); *Counterfeit* (Columbia); *The Man Who Lived Twice* (Columbia); *Come Closer, Folks* (Columbia); 1937: *When's Your Birthday?* (RKO); *The Great Gambini* (Paramount); *Saturday's Heroes* (RKO); *Youth on Parole* (Republic); 1938: *Prison Nurse* (Republic); *A Desperate Adventure* (Republic); 1939: *Missing Daughters* (Columbia); 1940: *Fugitive from a Prison Camp* (Columbia); 1941: *A Gentleman from Dixie* (Monogram); *Murder by Invitation* (Monogram); 1942: *House of Errors* (Producers Releasing Corp.).

Constance Cummings

1931: *The Criminal Code* (Columbia); *The Last Parade* (Columbia); *Lover Come Back* (Columbia); *Traveling Husbands* (RKO); *The Guilty Generation* (Columbia); 1932: *Behind the Mask* (Columbia); *Big Timer* (Columbia); *Attorney for the Defense* (Columbia); *American Madness* (Columbia); *Movie Crazy* (Paramount); *The Last Man* (Columbia); *Washington Merry-Go-Round* (Columbia); *Night After Night* (Paramount); 1933: *The Billion Dollar Scandal* (Paramount); *The Mind Reader* (Warner Bros.); *Heads We Go* aka *The Charming Deceiver* (British International Pictures); *Channel Crossing* (Gaumont-British); *Broadway Thru a Keyhole* (20th Century-United Artists); 1934: *Looking for Trouble* (20th Century-United Artists); *This Man Is Mine* (RKO); *Glamour* (Universal); 1935: *Remember Last Night?* (Universal); 1936: *Seven Sinners* aka *Doomed Cargo* (Gaumont-British); 1937: *Strangers on a Honeymoon* (Gaumont-British); 1940: *Haunted Honeymoon* aka *Busman's Honeymoon* (MGM); 1941: *This England* (BN-Anglo-American-World); 1942: *The Foreman Went to France* aka *Somewhere in France* (Balcon-Ealing-UA); 1945: *Blithe Spirit* (Cineguild-Two Cities); 1951: *Into the Blue* aka *The Man in the Dinghy* (Imperadio-Snader-Wilcox); 1952: *Lady from Washington* (TV feature film); 1953: *Three's Company* (BC); *The Scream* (TV feature film); 1956: *With All My Heart* (British film); *Finger of Guilt* aka *The Intimate Stranger* (Anglo-Amalgamated-RKO); 1957: *John and Julie* (DCA); 1960: *The Battle of the Sexes* (Continental); 1962: *Sammy Going South* aka *A Boy Ten Feet Tall* (Seven Arts); 1963: *In the Cool of the Day* (MGM); 1971: *Jane Eyre* (Omnibus-Sagitarius-BL); 1983: *Wings* (PBS TV film); 1984: *Love Song* (TV feature film); 1986: *Dead Man's Folly* (TV feature film).

Evelyn Venable

1933: *Cradle Song* (Paramount); 1934: *Death Takes a Holiday* (Paramount); *David Harum* (Fox); *Double Door* (Paramount); *Mrs. Wiggs of the Cabbage Patch* (Paramount); 1935: *The County Chairman* (Fox); *The Little Colonel* (Fox); *Vagabond Lady* (Roach-MGM); *Alice Adams* (RKO); *Harmony Lane* (Republic); *Streamline Express* (Mascot-Republic); 1936: *Star for a Night* (20th Century–Fox); 1937: *North of Nome* (Columbia); *Racketeers in Exile* (Columbia); *Happy-Go-Lucky* (Republic); 1938: *The Hollywood Stadium Mystery* (Republic); *Female Fugitive* (Monogram); *The Frontiersman* (Paramount); *My Old Kentucky Home* (Monogram); *The Headleys at Home* (Standard); 1939: *Heritage of the Desert* (Paramount); 1940: *Pinocchio* (Disney-RKO); *Lucky Cisco Kid* (20th Century–Fox); 1943: *He Hired the Boss* (20th Century–Fox).

Jean Muir

1933: *The Bureau of Missing Persons* (Warner Brothers); *Female* (Warner Bros.); *The World Changes* (Warner Bros.); *Son of a Sailor* (Warner Bros.); 1934: *Bedside* (Warner Bros.); *As the Earth Turns* (Warner Bros.); *A Modern Hero* (Warner Bros.); *Dr. Monica* (Warner Bros.); *Desirable* (Warner Bros.); *Gentlemen Are Born* (Warner Bros.); 1935: *The White Cockatoo* (Warner Bros.); *Oil for the Lamps of China* (Warner Bros.); *Orchids to You* (Fox); *A Midsummer Night's Dream* (Warner Bros.); *Stars Over Broadway* (Warner Bros.); 1936: *Faithful* (Warner Bros.); *White Fang* (20th Century–Fox); 1937: *Fugitive in the Sky* (Warner Bros.); *Her Husband's Secretary* (Warner Bros.); *The Outcasts of Poker Flat*

(RKO); *White Bondage* (Warner Bros.); *Dance, Charlie, Dance* (Warner Bros.); *Draegerman Courage* (Warner Bros.); *Once a Doctor* (Warner Bros.); 1938: *Jane Steps Out* (Associated British Films); 1940: *And One Was Beautiful* (MGM); *The Lone Wolf Meets a Lady* (Columbia); 1943: *The Constant Nymph* (Warner Bros.).

Claire Trevor

1931: *The Imperfect Lover* (Short; Warner Bros.–Vitaphone); *The Meal Ticket* (Short; Warner Bros.–Vitaphone); *Angel Cake* (Short; Warner Bros.–Vitaphone); 1933: *Life in the Raw* (Fox); *The Last Trail* (Fox); *The Mad Game* (Fox); *Jimmy and Sally* (Fox); 1934: *Hold That Girl* (Fox); *Baby Take a Bow* (Fox); *Wild Gold* (Fox); 1935: *Black Sheep* (Fox); *Dante's Inferno* (Fox); *Elinor Norton* (Fox); *Spring Tonic* (Fox); *Navy Wife* (Fox); 1936: *My Marriage* (20th Century–Fox); *The Song-and-Dance Man* (20th Century–Fox); *Human Cargo* (20th Century–Fox); *To Mary—with Love* (20th Century–Fox); *Star for a Night* (20th Century–Fox); *Fifteen Maiden Lane* (20th Century–Fox); *Career Woman* (20th Century–Fox); 1937: *Time Out for Romance* (20th Century–Fox); *King of Gamblers* (Paramount); *One Mile from Heaven* (20th Century–Fox); *Dead End* (Goldwyn-United Artists); *Second Honeymoon* (20th Century–Fox); *Big Town Girl* (20th Century–Fox); 1938: *Walking Down Broadway* (20th Century–Fox); *The Amazing Dr. Clitterhouse* (Warner Bros.); *Valley of the Giants* (Warner Bros.); *Five of a Kind* (20th Century-Fox); 1939: *Stagecoach* (Wanger-United Artists); *I Stole a Million* (Universal); *Allegheny Uprising* (RKO); 1940: *Dark Command* (Republic); 1941: *Honky Tonk* (MGM); *Texas* (Columbia); 1942: *The Adventures of Martin Eden* (Columbia); *Crossroads* (MGM); *Street of Chance* (Paramount); 1943: *The Desperadoes* (Columbia); *Good Luck, Mr. Yates* (Columbia); *The Woman of the Town* (United Artists); 1945: *Murder, My Sweet* aka *Farewell, My Lovely* (RKO); *Johnny Angel* (RKO); 1946: *Crack-Up* (RKO); *The Bachelor's Daughters* (United Artists); 1947: *Born to Kill* (RKO); 1948: *Raw Deal* (Eagle Lion-Reliance); *Key Largo* (Warner Bros.); *The Babe Ruth Story* (Allied Artists); *The Velvet Touch* (RKO); 1949: *The Lucky Stiff* (United Artists); 1950: *Borderline* (Universal); 1951: *Hard, Fast and Beautiful* (RKO); *Best of the Badmen* (RKO); 1952: *Hoodlum Empire* (Republic); *My Man and I* (MGM); 1953: *Stop, You're Killing Me* (Warner Bros.); *The Stranger Wore a Gun* (Columbia); 1954: *The High and the Mighty* (Warner Bros.); 1955: *Man Without a Star* (Universal); *Lucy Gallant* (Paramount); 1956: *The Mountain* (Paramount); 1958: *Marjorie Morningstar* (Warner Bros.); 1962: *Two Weeks in Another Town* (MGM); 1963: *The Stripper* (20th Century–Fox); 1965: *How to Murder Your Wife* (United Artists); 1967: *Capetown Affair* (Killarney); 1982: *Kiss Me Goodbye* (20th Century–Fox); 1987: *Breaking Home Ties* (TV feature film).

Notes

Introduction

1. Terry Ramsaye, *A Million and One Nights,* reprint ed. (New York: Simon and Schuster, 1964), 118.
2. Kevin Brownlow, *The Parade's Gone By* (New York: Alfred A. Knopf, 1968), 6.

Part I: 1927—Silent Glory

1. Ally Acker, "Lois Weber," *Ms. Magazine,* (February 1988): 67.
2. Richard Koszarski, *The Man You Loved to Hate: Erich von Stroheim and Hollywood* (New York: Oxford University Press, 1983), 192–94.
3. Kevin Brownlow, *"Napoléon": Abel Gance's Classic Film* (New York: Alfred A. Knopf, 1983), 166–76.

Billie Dove

1. Letter from Douglas Fairbanks, Jr. to author, March 1996.
2. Ivan St. Johns, "The Dove Tries Her Wings," *Photoplay* (April 1927): 102.
3. Mordaunt Hall, review of *Sensation Seekers, New York Times,* 16 March 1927, 28 (N).
4. Myrtle Gebhart, "A Pot of Gold for Billie Dove," *Picture Play* (April 1927): 71.
5. Gebhart, "A Pot of Gold for Billie," 71.
6. Mordaunt Hall, review of *The Night Watch, New York Times,* 8 October 1928, 14 (N).
7. Hall, *New York Times,* 14 October 1928, Section 10, 7 (N).
8. Gebhart, "A Pot of Gold for Billie," 72.
9. Gebhart, "A Pot of Gold for Billie," 71.
10. Patricia King Hanson, ed., *The American Film Institute Catalog of Motion Pictures Produced in the United States: Feature Films, 1931–1940* (Berkeley: University of California Press, 1993), 366.
11. Mordaunt Hall, review of *Cock of the Air, New York Times,* 25 January 1932, 20 (N).
12. Leonard J. Leff and Jerold L. Simmons, *The Dame in the Kimono: Hollywood, Censorship and the Production Code from the 1920s to the 1960s* (New York: Grove Weidenfeld), 60.

Fay Wray

1. Thomas Quinn Curtis, *Von Stroheim* (New York: Farrar, Straus and Giroux, 1971), 229.
2. Harry Carr, "She's Beautiful and Sweet," *Motion Picture Magazine,* (February 1972): 37.
3. Mordaunt Hall, review of *The Texan, New York Times,* 17 May 1930, 21 (N).
4. Review of *Nikki, New York Times,* 30 September 1931, 23.
5. Fay Wray, *On the Other Hand: A Life Story* (New York: St. Martins Press, 1989).

Annabella

1. Caligarou, *Annabella* (Paris: La Nouvelle Librairie Française, 1932), 41.
2. Caligarou, *Annabella,* 22.
3. Roger Régent, review of *Quatorze Juillet* quoted in *Rediscovering French Film, 1930–1960* (New York: The Museum of Modern Art, 1981).
4. Catherine Ann Surowiec, *Rediscovering French Film.*

Part II: 1929—The Song-And-Dance Craze

1. Ethan Mordden, *The Hollywood Musical* (New York: St. Martin's Press, 1981), 13–16.
2. Mordaunt Hall, review of *The Broadway Melody, New York Times,* 17 February 1929, Section 9, 7 (N).
3. *Photoplay* review of *The Broadway Melody,* April, 1929, reprinted in Miles Kreuger, ed., *The Movie Musical from Vitaphone to "42nd Street"* (New York: Dover Publications, Inc., 1975), 20.
4. John Tibbetts, *The American Theatrical Film: Stages in Development* (Bowling Green, Ohio: Bowling Green State University Popular Press, 1985), 193.
5. Kreuger, *Movie Musical,* 11.
6. Tibbetts, *American Theatrical Film,* 202.
7. Mordden, *Hollywood Musical,* 29–30.

Anita Page

1. Joe Franklin, *Classics of the Silent Screen* (New York: The Citadel Press, 1959), 111.

Dorothy Lee

1. Brooks Atkinson, review of *Hello Yourself, New York Times,* 31 October 1928, 28 (N).
2. Quinn Martin, review of *Half Shot at Sunrise, New York World,* 11 October 1930 (N).
3. Review of *Half Shot at Sunrise, Theatre Magazine,* December 1930.
4. *New York Times,* 16 August 1936, Section 10, 3 (N).
5. Marcella Burke, "Hollywood's Pet Starlet," *Screen Play Secrets,* December 1930, 87.

Part III: 1931—From Stage To Screen

1. "Mr. Arliss Returns to Work," *New York Times,* 11 October 1931 Section 10, 6 (N).
2. Louis Weitzenkorn, *Five Star Final,* reprinted in Burns Mantle, ed., *The Best Plays of 1930–31* (New York: Dodd, Mead, and Company, 1931), 254–85.
3. Burns Mantle, ed., *The Best Plays of 1931–32* (New York: Dodd, Mead and Company, 1932), 408.
4. John Raeburn, "*American Madness* and American Values," in Richard Glatzer and Raeburn, ed., *Frank Capra: The Man and His Films* (Ann Arbor Paperbacks: The University of Michigan Press, 1975), 64–5.
5. *Photoplay* review of *Movie Crazy,* September, 1932, quoted in Frank N. Magill, ed., *Magill's Survey of Cinema, English-Language Films, Second Series* (Englewood Cliffs, NJ: Salem Press, 1982), 1663.

Marian Marsh

1. Hal Erickson, *All-Movie Guide* website.
2. Mordaunt Hall, review of *Beauty and the Boss, New York Times,* 10 April 1932, Section 8, 4 (N).
3. Erickson, *All-Movie Guide.*

Constance Cummings

1. Mordaunt Hall, review of *The Criminal Code, New York Times,* 5 January 1931, 21 (N).
2. Steven H. Scheuer, ed., *Movies on TV and Videocassette 1993–1994* (New York: Bantam Books, 1992), 708.
3. Brooks Atkinson, review of *Madame Bovary, New York Times,* 17 November 1937, 26 (N).
4. Letter from Roddy McDowall to author, January 1996.
5. Edward T. Jones, "The Tyrones as TV Family: O'Neill's *Long Day's Journey Into Night,* Primetime," *Literature/Film Quarterly,* Vol. 22, No. 2, 1994, 93, 94.
6. Richard Eder, review of *Wings, New York Times,* 29 January 1979, Section 3, 13 (N).
7. Eder, *New York Times,* 8 March 1978, Section 3, 16 (N).

Part IV: 1933—The Class Of '33

1. Ethan Mordden, *The American Theatre* (New York: Oxford University Press, 1981), 147.
2. Foster Hirsch, *A Method to Their Madness: The History of the Actors Studio* (New York: W. W. Norton and Company, 1984), 108.
3. Jeanine Basinger, *A Woman's View: How Hollywood Spoke to Women 1930–1960* (New York: Alfred A. Knopf, 1993), 266–72, 458–63.
4. Leonard J. Leff and Jerold L. Simmons, *The Dame in the Kimono: Hollywood, Censorship, and the Production Code from the 1920s to the 1960s* (New York: Grove Weidenfeld), 42–8.
5. Andre Sennwald, "A Word with Ernst Lubitsch,"

New York Times, 14 October 1934, Section 10, 5 (N).

6. Patricia King Hanson, ed., *The American Film Institute Catalog of Motion Pictures Produced in the United States: Feature Films, 1931–1940* (Berkeley: University of California Press, 1993), 518.

Evelyn Venable

1. David Chierichetti, article on *Death Takes a Holiday* in Frank N. Magill, ed., *Magill's Survey of Cinema: English Language Films* (Englewood Cliffs, NJ: Salem Press, 1980), vol. 1, 426.
2. Chierichetti, *Magill's Survey of Cinema,* vol. 1, 426.
3. André Sennwald, review of *Double Door, New York Times,* 5 May 1934, 22 (N).
4. Frank S. Nugent, review of *Vagabond Lady, New York Times,* 15 June 1935, 20 (N).
5. Edward Wagenknecht, *The Movies in the Age of Innocence* (Norman: University of Oklahoma Press, 1962), 243.

Jean Muir

1. André Sennwald, review of *Desirable, New York Times,* 15 September 1934, 20 (N).
2. Mordaunt Hall, review of *As the Earth Turns, New York Times,* 12 April 1934, 27 (N).
3. André Sennwald, review of *Oil for the Lamps of China, New York Times,* 6 June 1935, 25 (N).
4. *New York Times,* 28 August 1950, 1 (N).
5. *New York Times,* 6 September 1950, 31 (N).
6. *New York Times,* 29 August 1950, 1 (N).
7. *New York Times,* 12 September 1950, 15 (N).
8. "Freedom of Speech," *New York Times,* 30 August 1950, 30 (N).
9. Letter from Howard Lindsay, *New York Times,* 3 September 1950, Section 4, 8 (N).
10. "Jean Muir: Pro and Con" (letters from readers), *New York Times,* 10 September 1950, Section 2, 9 (N).
11. *New York Times,* 18 September 1950, 42 (N).
12. *New York Times,* 29 August 1950, 1 (N).

Claire Trevor

1. Letter from Robert Wise to author, May, 1996.
2. André Sennwald, review of *The Mad Game, New York Times,* 13 November 1933, 21 (N).
3. November 14, 1933 review of *The Mad Game* in *Variety,* quoted in Patricia King Hanson, ed., *The American Film Institute Catalog of Motion Pictures Produced in the United States: Feature Films, 1931–1940* (Berkeley: University of California Press, 1993), 1271.
4. Ronald Haver, *David O. Selznick's Hollywood* (New York: Alfred A. Knopf, 1980), 224, 226.

Part V: 1939—The Summer Of Dreams

1. F. Scott Fitzgerald, *The Last Tycoon* (New York: Charles Scribner's Sons, 1941), 141.
2. *Life Magazine,* Special Issue, "Hollywood 1939–1989," Spring 1989.
3. D. W. Griffith and James Hart, *The Man Who Invented Hollywood: The Autobiography of D. W. Griffith* (Louisville, KY: Touchstone Publishing Company, 1972), 163.
4. Frank Capra, *The Name Above the Title: An Autobiography* (New York: The Macmillan Company, 1971), 372.

Bibliography

Newspapers and Periodicals

L'Illustration, Life Magazine, Literature/Film Quarterly, The London Times, The Los Angeles Times, Motion Picture Classic, Motion Picture Magazine, The New York Times, The New York World, Photoplay Magazine, Picture Play, The San Francisco Chronicle, The Theatre Magazine

Books and Articles

Acker, Ally. "Lois Weber." *Ms. Magazine,* February, 1988.

———. *Reel Women: Pioneers of the Cinema, 1896 to the Present.* New York: Continuum, 1991.

Allgood, Jill. *Bebe and Ben.* London: Robert Hale and Co., 1975.

Anderegg, Michael A. *William Wyler.* Boston: Twayne, 1979.

Astor, Mary. *My Story: An Autobiography.* New York: Doubleday, 1959.

Basinger, Jeanine. *A Woman's View: How Hollywood Spoke to Women, 1930–1960.* New York: Alfred A. Knopf, 1993.

Black, Gregory D. *Hollywood Censored: Morality Codes, Catholics, and the Movies.* New York: Cambridge University Press, 1994.

Blesh, Rudi. *Keaton.* New York: The Macmillan Company, 1966.

Blum, Daniel. *A Pictorial History of the Silent Screen.* New York: G. P. Putnam's Sons, 1953.

———. *A Pictorial History of the Talkies.* New York: G. P. Putnam's Sons, 1958.

Brockman, Alfred. *The Movie Book: The 1930s.* New York: Crescent Books, 1986.

Brownlow, Kevin. *The Parade's Gone By.* New York: Alfred a. Knopf, 1968.

———. *"Napoléon": Abel Gance's Classic Film.* New York: Alfred A. Knopf, 1983.

Burke, Marcella. "Hollywood's Pet Starlet." *Screen Play Secrets,* December, 1930.

Caligarou. *Annabella.* Paris: La Nouvelle Librairie Française, 1932.

Capra, Frank. *The Name Above the Title: An Autobiography.* New York: The Macmillan Company, 1971.

Carney, Raymond. *American Vision: The Films of Frank Capra.* New York: Cambridge University Press, 1986.

Carr, Harry. "She's Beautiful and Sweet." *Motion Picture Magazine,* February, 1927.

Crowther, Bosley. *The Lion's Share: The Story of an Entertainment Empire.* New York: E. P. Dutton, 1957.

Curtis, Thomas Quinn. *Von Stroheim.* New York: Farrar, Straus and Giroux, 1971.

Dardis, Tom. *Harold Lloyd: The Man on the Clock.* New York: The Vikings Press, 1983.

Drew, William M. *Speaking of Silents: First Ladies of the Screen.* Vestal, NY: The Vestal Press, Ltd., 1989.

Fairbanks, Douglas, Jr. *The Salad Days.* New York: Doubleday, 1988.

Fitzgerald, F. Scott. *The Last Tycoon.* New York: Charles Scribner's Sons, 1941.

Franklin, Joe, with William K. Everson. *Classics of the Silent Screen.* New York: The Citadel Press, 1959.

Gallagher, Tag. *John Ford: The Man and His Films.* Berkeley: University of California Press, 1986.

Gebhart, Myrtle. "A Pot of Gold for Billie Dove." *Picture Play,* April, 1927.

Geduld, Harry M. *The Birth of the Talkies: From Edison to Jolson.* Bloomington: Indiana University Press, 1975.

Gish, Lillian, with Ann Pinchot. *The Movies, Mr. Griffith and Me.* Englewood Cliffs, NJ: Prentice-Hall, 1969.

Glatzer, Richard, and John Raeburn, ed. *Frank Capra: The Man and His Films.* Ann Arbor Paperbacks: The University of Michigan Press, 1975.

Griffith, D. W., and James Hart. *The Man Who Invented Hollywood: The Autobiography of D. W. Griffith.* Louisville, KY: Touchstone Publishing Company, 1972.

Hanson, Patricia King, ed. *The American Film Institute Catalog of Motion Pictures Produced in the United States: Feature Films, 1911–1920.* Berkeley: University of California Press, 1988.

———. *The American Film Institute Catalog of Motion Pictures Produced in the United States: Feature Films, 1931–1940.* Berkeley: University of California Press, 1993.

Haskell, Molly. *From Reverence to Rape: The Treatment of Women in the Movies.* New York: Holt, Rinehart and Winston, 1974.

Haver, Ronald. *David O. Selznick's Hollywood.* New York: Alfred A. Knopf, 1980.

Herndon, Booton. *Mary Pickford and Douglas Fairbanks.* New York: W. W. Norton and Company, Inc., 1977.

Hirsch, Foster. *A Method to Their Madness: The History of the Actors Studio.* New York: W. W. Norton and Company, 1984.

"Hollywood 1939–1989." *Life Magazine,* Special Issue, Spring, 1989.

Jones, Edward T. "The Tyrones as TV Family: O'Neill's *Long Day's Journey Into Night,* Primetime." *Literature/Film Quarterly,* Vol. 22, No. 2, 1994.

Katz, Ephraim. *The Film Encyclopedia.* New York: G. P. Putnam's Sons, 1979.

Koszarski, Richard. *The Man You Loved to Hate: Erich von Stroheim and Hollywood.* New York: Oxford University Press, 1983.

Kreuger, Miles, ed. *The Movie Musical from Vitaphone to "42nd Street".* New York: Dover Publications, Inc., 1975.

Leff, Leonard J., and Jerold L. Simmons. *The Dame in the Kimono: Hollywood, Censorship, and the Production Code from the 1920s to the 1960s.* New York: Grove Weidenfeld, 1990.

Love, Bessie. *From Hollywood with Love.* London: Elm Tree Books, 1977.

Loy, Myrna, and James Kotsilibas-Davis. *Myrna Loy: Being and Becoming.* New York: Alfred A. Knopf, 1987.

Magill, Frank N., ed. *Magill's Survey of Cinema: English-Language Films, First Series.* Englewood Cliffs, NJ: Salem Press, 1980.

———. *Magill's Survey of Cinema: English-Language Films, Second Series.* Englewood Cliffs, NJ: Salem Press, 1982.

———. *Magill's Survey of Cinema: Foreign Language Films.* Englewood Cliffs, NJ: Salem Press, 1983.

———. *Magill's Survey of Cinema: Silent Films.* Englewood Cliffs, NJ: Salem Press, 1984.

Mantle, Burns, ed. *The Best Plays of 1929–30.* New York: Dodd, Mead and Company, 1930.

———. *The Best Plays of 1930–31.* New York: Dodd, Mead and Company, 1931.

———. *The Best Plays of 1931–32.* New York: Dodd, Mead and Company, 1932.

———. *The Best Plays of 1932–33.* New York: Dodd, Mead and Company, 1933.

Mordden, Ethan. *The American Theatre.* New York: Oxford University Press, 1981.

———. *The Hollywood Musical.* New York: St. Martins Press, 1981.

Munden, Kenneth W., ed. *The American Film Institute Catalog of Motion Pictures Produced in the United States: Feature Films, 1921–30.* New York: R. R. Bowker, 1971.

Nash, Jay Robert, and Stanley Ralph Ross. *The Motion Picture Guide* (12 volumes). Des Moines, IA: Cinebooks, Inc., 1986.

Ramsaye, Terry. *A Million and One Nights: A History of the Motion Picture,* reprint ed. New York: Simon and Schuster, 1964.

Robinson, David. *Hollywood in the Twenties.* London: A. Zwemmer, 1968.

Sadoul, Georges. *Dictionary of Filmmakers.* Berkeley: University of California Press, 1972.

———. *Dictionary of Films.* Berkeley: University of California Press, 1972.

St. Johns, Ivan. "The Dove Tries Her Wings." *Photoplay,* April 1927.

Scheuer, Steven H., ed. *Movies on TV and Videocassette 1993–1994.* New York: Bantam Books, 1992.

Schickel, Richard. *The Men Who Made the Movies.* New York: Atheneum, 1975.

Sherman, William Thomas. *Mable Normand: A Source Book to Her Life and Films.* Seattle: Cinema Books, 1994.

Stenn, David. *Clara Bow: Runnin' Wild.* New York: Doubleday, 1988.

Strick, Philip. *Great Movie Actresses.* New York: Beech Tree Books—William Morrow and Co., Inc., 1985.

Surowiec, Catherine Ann. Program notes on *Quatorze Juillet* in *Rediscovering French Film, 1930–1960.* New York: The Museum of Modern Art, 1981.

Swanson, Gloria. *Swanson on Swanson.* New York: Random House, 1980.

Tibbetts, John. *The American Theatrical Film: Stages in Development.* Bowling Green, OH: Bowling Green State University Popular Press, 1985.

Tomlinson, Doug, ed. *Actors on Acting for the Screen: Roles and Collaborations.* New York: Garland Publishing, Inc., 1994.

Tyler, Parker. *Classics of the Foreign Film: A Pictorial Treasury.* Secaucus, NJ: The Citadel Press, 1962.

Wagenknecht, Edward. *The Movies in the Age of Innocence.* Norman, OK: University of Oklahoma Press, 1962.

Welsh, James, and Steven Kramer. *Abel Gance.* Boston: Twayne, 1978.

Wray, Fay. *On the Other Hand: A Life Story.* New York: St. Martins Press, 1989.

Index

Page numbers in italic indicate a photograph on that page.

About the Author

Film historian and researcher William M. Drew has been program director and lecturer for numerous college film series and reviewer for an entertainment monthly. His articles on film history have appeared in various journals including *Literature/Film Quarterly*, *Take One* and *American Classic Screen* as well as classic cinema websites like The Silents Majority. His books include *Speaking of Silents: First Ladies of the Screen* and *D. W. Griffith's "Intolerance": Its Genesis and Its Vision*. Mr. Drew holds a B.A. in English literature and an M.A. in history from Santa Clara University. He currently resides in California.